To Hackney

To Stratford

Stepney

THAMES

To Newin

To Deptford

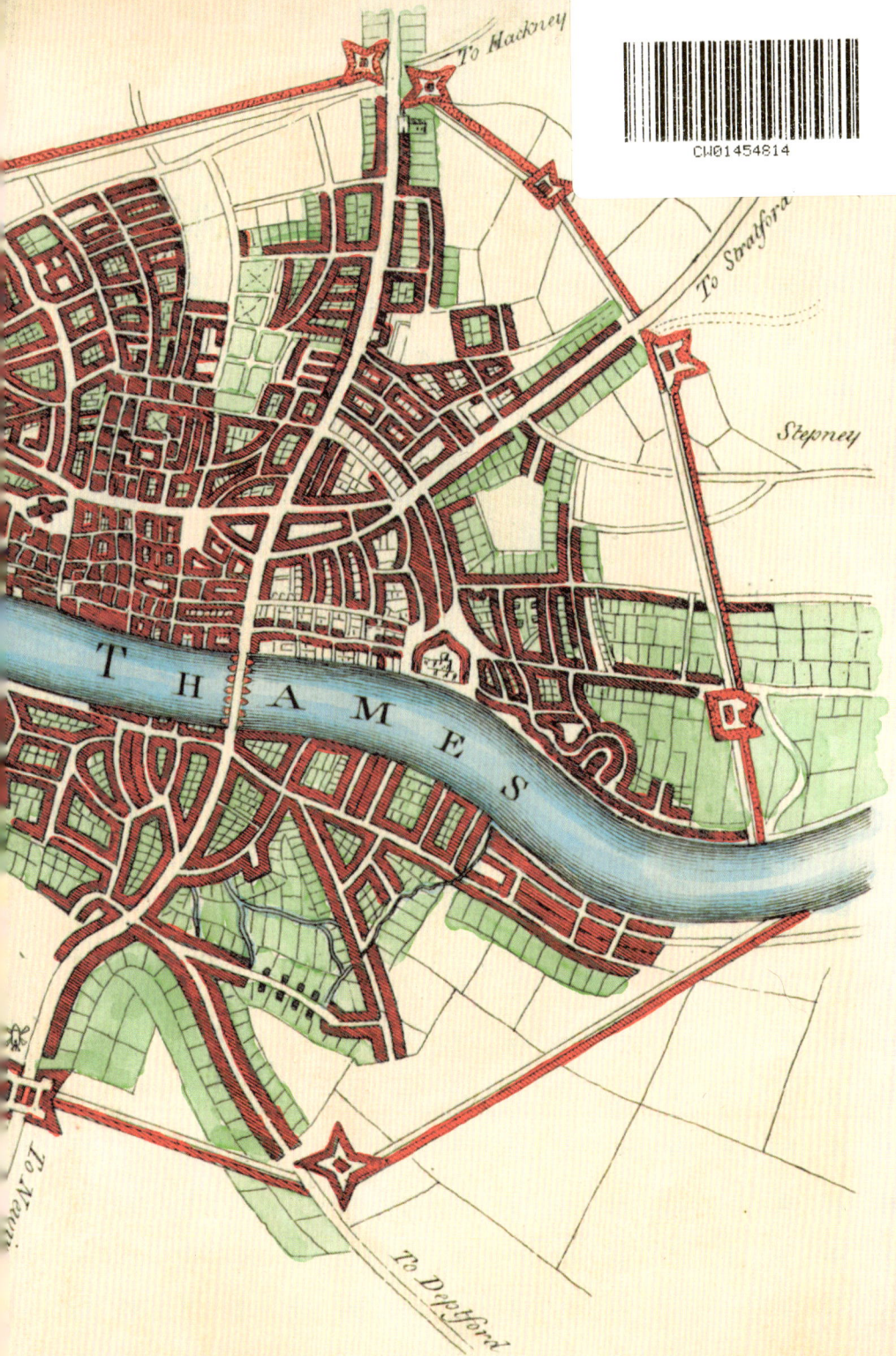

A PLAN of the City and Environs of LONDON as fortified by Order of PARLIAMENT in the Years 1642 & 1643.

THE BLOOD
IN WINTER

THE BLOOD IN WINTER

A Nation Descends, 1642

Jonathan Healey

BLOOMSBURY PUBLISHING
LONDON · OXFORD · NEW YORK · NEW DELHI · SYDNEY

BLOOMSBURY PUBLISHING
Bloomsbury Publishing Plc
50 Bedford Square, London, WC1B 3DP, UK
Bloomsbury Publishing Ireland Limited,
29 Earlsfort Terrace, Dublin 2, D02 AY28, Ireland

BLOOMSBURY, BLOOMSBURY PUBLISHING and the Diana logo are trademarks of
Bloomsbury Publishing Plc

First published in Great Britain 2025

Bloomsbury Publishing Plc does not have any control over, or responsibility for, any third-party
websites referred to in this book. All internet addresses given in this book were correct at the time
of going to press. The author and publisher regret any inconvenience caused if addresses have
changed or sites have ceased to exist, but can accept no responsibility for any such changes
A catalogue record for this book is available from the British Library

ISBN: HB: 9781526672292; EBOOK: 9781526672315; EPDF: 9781526672308

2 4 6 8 10 9 7 5 3 1

Typeset by Newgen KnowledgeWorks Pvt. Ltd., Chennai, India
Printed and bound in Great Britain by CPI Group (UK) Ltd, Croydon CR0 4YY

MIX
Paper | Supporting
responsible forestry
FSC
www.fsc.org   FSC® C013604

To find out more about our authors and books visit www.bloomsbury.com
and sign up for our newsletters

For product safety related questions contact productsafety@bloomsbury.com

For Sophie, with love and gratitude

Contents

Cast of Characters

THE LIVING

Ages on 1 May 1641

The Royal Family

Charles Stuart (40 years old): King of England, Scotland and Ireland

Henrietta Maria (31): Queen of England, Scotland and Ireland. A Frenchwoman and a Catholic

Prince Charles (10): young heir to the throne. Future Charles II

James, Duke of York (7): second son of the King and Queen

Elizabeth of Bohemia (45): the king's elder sister. Protestant heroine

Charles Louis, Prince-Elector Palatine (23): son of Elizabeth of Bohemia and potential pretender

Rupert (21): younger brother of the Prince-Elector

The Junto, the House of Commons

John Pym (56): leading dissident MP. Parliamentary wizard

John Hampden (45): Buckinghamshire MP, Ship Money martyr

Denzil Holles (42): angry politician from Dorset. Prosecuted in 1629 for political opposition

William Strode (45): 'fiery spirit' from Devon. Pronounced 'Stroud'

Arthur Haselrig (c. 40): Leicestershire knight

John Hotham, elder (50): MP, Yorkshireman
Oliver Cromwell (42): obscure

The Junto, the House of Lords

Earl of Warwick (53): Puritan
Earl of Northumberland (38): Admiral of the Fleet, member of Percy clan
Lord Mandeville (c. 39): likeable reformist, son of Manchester
Earl of Holland (50): slimy courtier. Suitor to Lady Carlisle
Earl of Pembroke (56): former friend to the King. Now rather forlorn
Earl of Essex (50): haughty aristocrat. Son of a traitor. Popular and Puritan
Lord Saye and Sele (58): wiry Oxfordshire noble. Cunning

The King's Party

Edward Nicholas (48): frustrated civil servant, pie-enjoyer
Lord Falkland (c. 31): likeable toff. Moderate
Earl of Bristol (61): former reformist, increasingly otherwise inclined
George Digby (28): Bristol's son. Clever, if unpredictable
John Culpeper (40): Kentishman, former reformist. Cynic
Edward Hyde (32): Wiltshireman, former reformist
John Strangways (55): Dorsetshire man, former reformist
Earl of Dorset (c. 51): fun-loving aristocrat and royal officer. Owner of Knole House
George Goring (32): soldier, rake, bed-enjoyer
John Suckling (32): poet, rake
Thomas Lunsford (c. 37): feared thug. Very tall
Earl of Manchester (c. 77): moderate, father to Mandeville
Richard Gurney (63): elected Lord Mayor of London in September 1641
Earl of Roxburgh (c. 71): Scottish courtier with violent past

William Morray (c. 40): former childhood servant of Charles, now trusted confidante

The Churchmen

William Laud (67): unpopular Archbishop of Canterbury, currently in the Tower. Pronounced 'Lord'
Matthew Wren (55): hardline Royalist, bishop of Ely. To his enemies, the 'Norwich Beast'
John Williams (59): former opposition bishop, now in royal favour. Promoted to Archbishop of York late in 1641

The Lawyers

John Bankes (52): Lord Chief Justice of the Common Pleas. Former Attorney-General. Cumbrian
Edward Littleton (51): Lord Keeper of the Great Seal, Speaker of the Lords. Often indisposed through sickness
Edward Herbert (c. 48): current Attorney-General. Loyal king's man
Oliver St John (c. 42): current Solicitor General, Junto supporter. (pronounced Sinjen)
William Lenthall (49): generally mild-mannered, venison-loving Oxfordshire man. Speaker of the House of Commons. Pronounced 'Lental'

The Writers

John Taylor (62): jolly water-poet. Puritan-hater
Henry Walker (29): ironmonger. John Taylor-hater
Katherine Chidley (unknown, perhaps nearly 50): religious writer. Proto-feminist
John Lilburne (c. 26): polemicist, future Leveller
John Thomas (unknown, possibly in 20s): printer and journalist

Others

Mary Bankes (née Hawtrey) (40): forceful character from Ruislip

Lucy Hay (née Percy), Countess of Carlisle (41): vivacious courtier and wit

Simonds D'Ewes (38): Puritan, diarist, note-taker, antiquarian, windbag

Richard Wiseman (about 40): fight-haver

Earl of Argyll (c. 35): Scottish Covenanter leader, ally to the Junto

Giovanni Giustinian (40): Venetian Ambassador

Johan van der Kerckhoven, Heer van Heenvliet (46): Dutch Ambassador

Jacques d'Etampes (c. 51): 1st Marquis de La Ferté-Imbault: French Ambassador

John Pennington (c. 56): Admiral, stationed at the Downs in Kent

THE DEAD

James VI of Scotland and I of England and Ireland (1566-1625): father to Charles. Politically astute if somewhat debauched in general carriage

Prince Henry (1594-1612): elder brother to Charles

George Abbot (1562-1633): Archbishop of Canterbury. Calvinist. Relatively popular. Terrible aim

George Villiers, Duke of Buckingham (1592-1628): favourite (likely lover) to King James. Beloved of Charles. Handsome. Stabbed to death

Edward Coke (1552-1634): ambitious lawyer. Irritant to the Crown. Former owner of Corfe Castle. Pronounced 'Cook'

John Eliot (1592-1632): dissident MP

Earl of Bedford (1587-1641): moderate reformist. Lost hope for peace, maybe?

IN-BETWEEN

Thomas Wentworth (from 1640, Earl of Strafford) (48): feared royal officer. Yorkshireman

Author's Note

One of Charles I's projects in the 1630s, enlisting the support of John Bankes and Edward Nicholas, was to change the start of the new calendar year from 25 March to 1 January. He was unsuccessful then but the alteration has subsequently come in, so I've followed his wishes. The attempted arrest of the Five Members therefore took place on 4 January 1642 (as we would see it), rather than 4 January 1641, as it was reported at the time. Dates, though, are Old Style, except in the endnotes relating to Giustinian's despatches to Venice. I've modernised spelling except in book titles.

The Latin epigraphs at the start of each section convey key themes. *Renovatio* represents the renewal that people expected after the fall of Charles's Personal Rule, and the idea that 1641 would be a miraculous year of reform. *Ovatio* comes from a published description of Charles's return to London on 25 November 1641: an ovation was a lesser form of Roman triumph. It reminds us of the very ambivalent nature of Charles's 'victory' over the Scots. The phrase *Qui Custodiet Ipsos Custodes* – 'who will guard us from the guards', appears in Juvenal's *Satires*, but it was Edward Hyde, later the Earl of Clarendon, who used it to characterise the fears of Parliament during the later months of 1641. A major part of the conflict with the king at this point related to exactly this question: who had control of the protective forces stood outside Westminster – who would they obey? Finally, *Hannibal ad Portas* 'Hannibal is at the gates' was another well-known phrase of the age. In the

English common law it could be used – as it was during the Ship Money trial – to denote a moment of such pressing emergency and crisis that the normal rules of law and procedure were no longer valid. It seems as an apt a summary as any of the slide to Civil War in 1642.

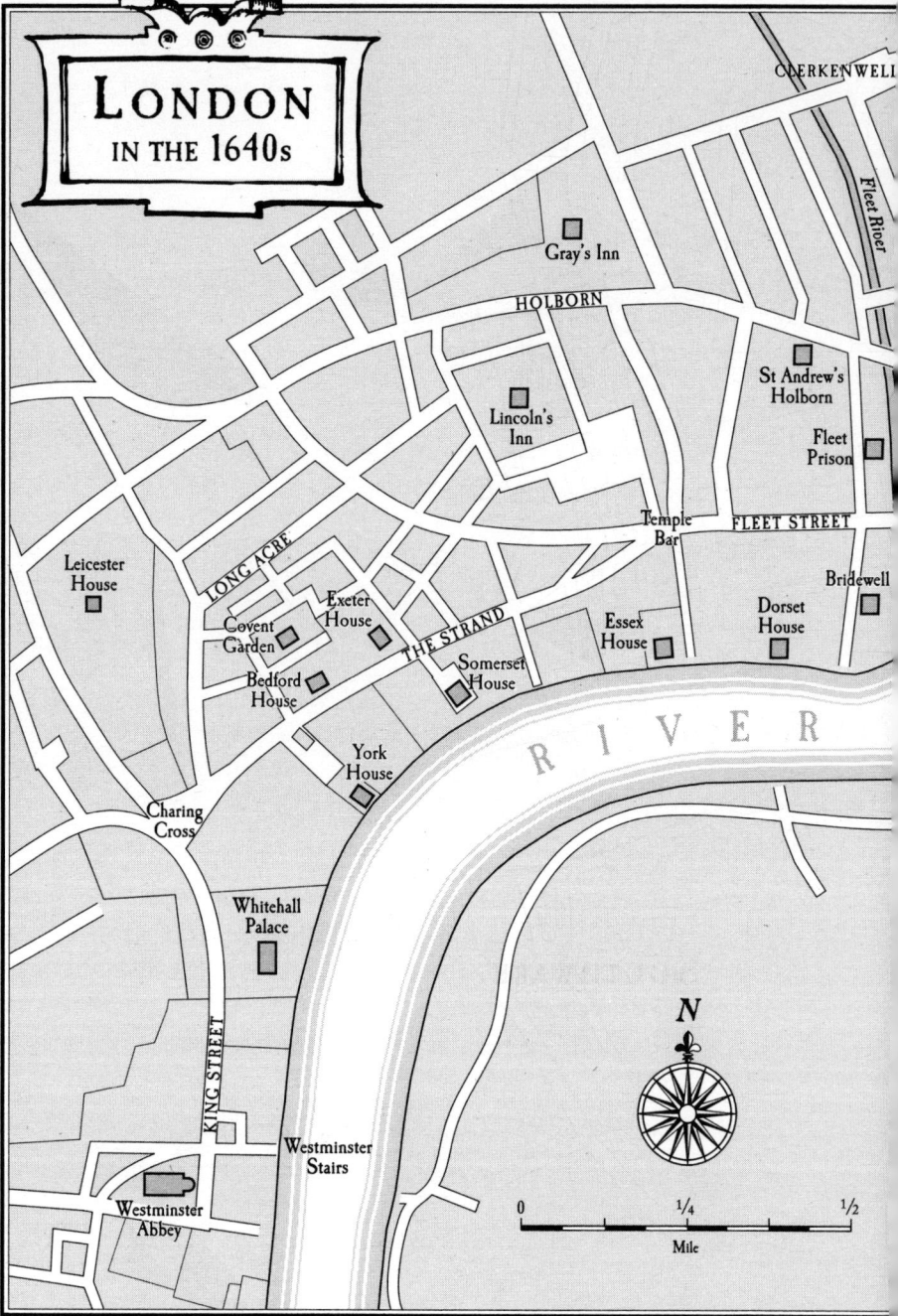

LONDON
IN THE 1640s

CLERKENWELL

Fleet River

Gray's Inn

HOLBORN

St Andrew's Holborn

Lincoln's Inn

Fleet Prison

Temple Bar

FLEET STREET

LONG ACRE

Leicester House

Bridewell

Exeter House

Covent Garden

Essex House

Dorset House

THE STRAND

Bedford House

Somerset House

RIVER

York House

Charing Cross

Whitehall Palace

KING STREET

N

Westminster Stairs

Westminster Abbey

0   1/4   1/2
Mile

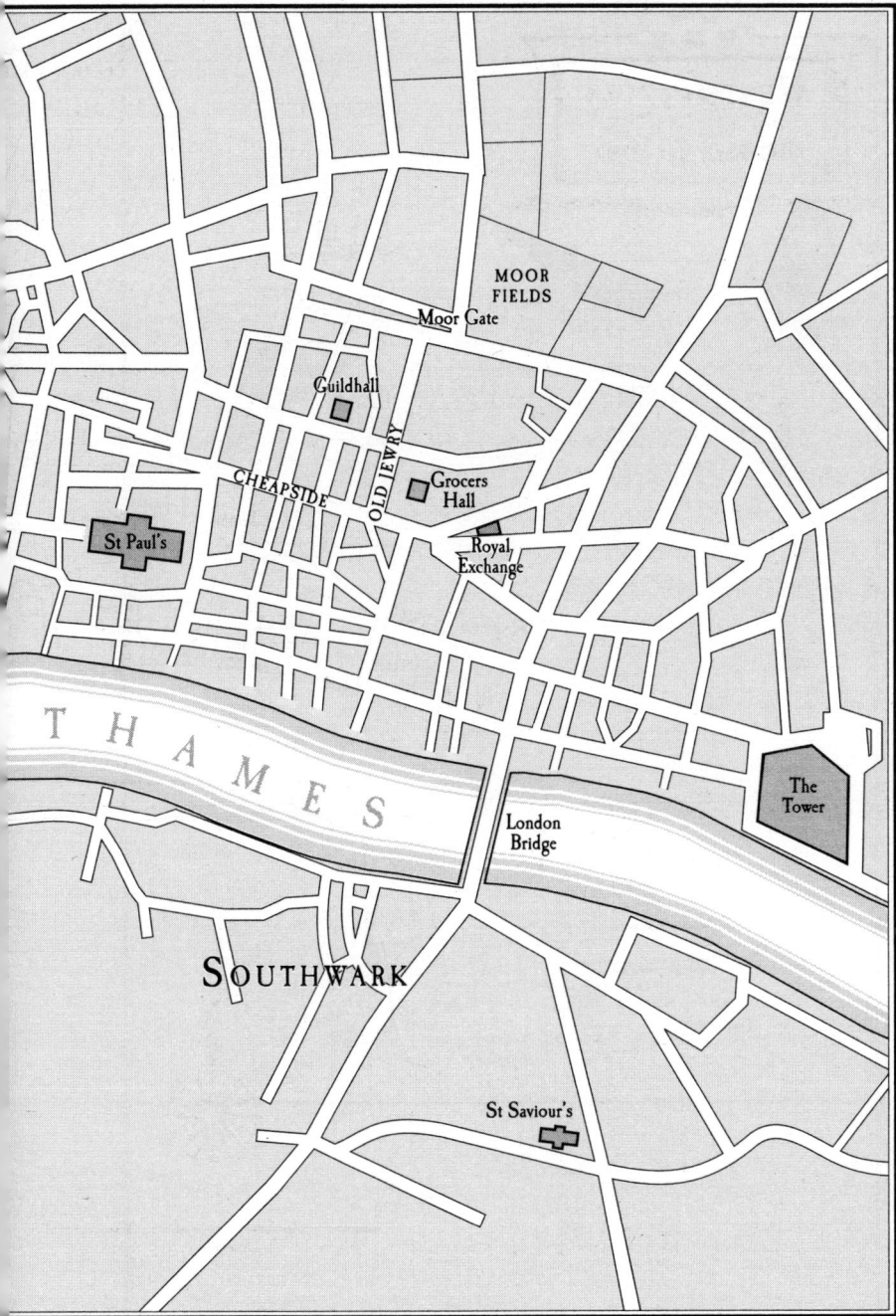

MOOR
FIELDS

Moor Gate

Guildhall

CHEAPSIDE

OLD JEWRY

Grocers
Hall

St Paul's

Royal
Exchange

THAMES

The
Tower

London
Bridge

SOUTHWARK

St Saviour's

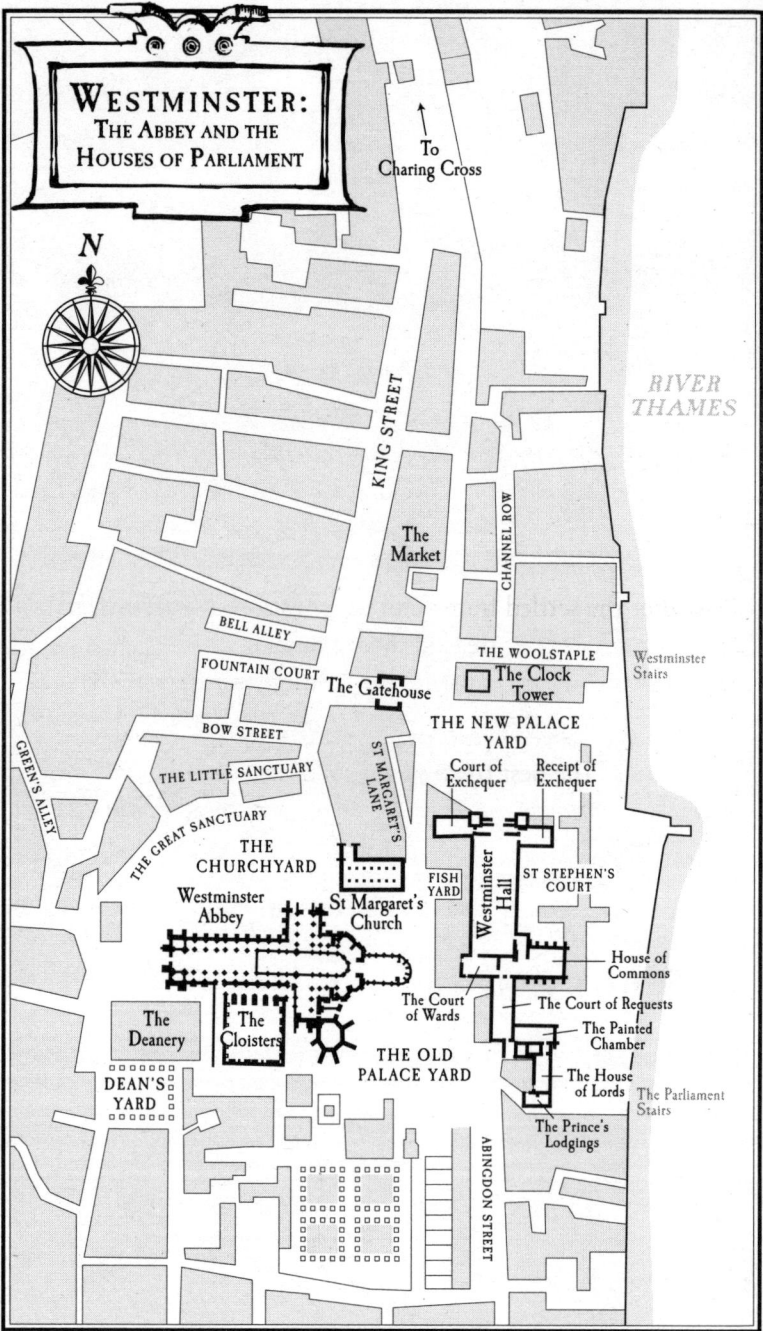

WESTMINSTER:
THE ABBEY AND THE
HOUSES OF PARLIAMENT

N

To
Charing Cross

RIVER
THAMES

KING STREET

CHANNEL ROW

The
Market

THE WOOLSTAPLE

BELL ALLEY

FOUNTAIN COURT

The Gatehouse

The Clock
Tower

Westminster
Stairs

BOW STREET

GREEN'S ALLEY

THE LITTLE SANCTUARY

THE NEW PALACE
YARD

ST MARGARET'S LANE

Court of
Exchequer

Receipt of
Exchequer

THE GREAT SANCTUARY

THE
CHURCHYARD

Westminster
Abbey

St Margaret's
Church

FISH
YARD

Westminster Hall

ST STEPHEN'S
COURT

House of
Commons

The Court of Requests

The Court
of Wards

The Painted
Chamber

The
Deanery

The
Cloisters

THE OLD
PALACE YARD

The House
of Lords

DEAN'S
YARD

The Prince's
Lodgings

The Parliament
Stairs

ABINGDON STREET

'To alter the settled frame and constitution of government is treason in any state.'

JOHN PYM, leading opposition MP, 1641

'The best treaty is with a drawn sword.'

KING CHARLES I

Introduction

In the beginning, there were no kings.

Where had they come from? Why had rule been left to these certain families, who looked and smelled no different to everyone else? By the seventeenth century there were two sets of theories.

One was that kings had been created by God. In some way or other, divine sanction had been handed down to certain favoured dynasties. This might have been through battle and conquest, or through the natural outgrowth of the patriarchal authority of fathers. But now they were anointed and now they could not be touched.[1]

There was another collection of ideas, though. These were different entirely. Kings, it was held, drew their power from those they reigned over. It came from the people. At some point, in the mists of a distant past, the people had gathered together and placed one family above them all. The repercussions of this original act remained, for though the authority monarchs had was strong and broad, ultimately there was always a chance that it might one day be rescinded.

These debates traversed borders and boundaries. They crossed the rivers and the snowy peaks that separated European states and nations. Each polity had its own nuances and England was no different. In this green and prosperous land on Europe's Atlantic edge, people wondered what it meant that, back in 1066, the country had been invaded and brutally subdued by the Normans.

Had William ruled by conquest? And did he, therefore, have a free hand to do as he wished? Or had he agreed to reign in keeping with old Saxon liberties? What about the rules and institutions that grew up afterwards as the Anglo-Norman monarchy matured? What came first, the Crown or the law? Were laws granted by kings, or were monarchs beholden to laws?

In medieval times, the English law had grown from royal seeds. Then there had been arguments and even wars about the powers of kings versus the rights of their nobles and people. Magna Carta (1215) had set out some limits to the Crown. Henry III had faced civil war and revolution; Richard II had been deposed. But the monarchy remained. Under the Tudor dynasty – which arrived after a century of dynastic disorder and the eventual deposition of another alleged tyrant – that monarchy grew stronger. However, even Henry VIII relied on his nobles, his laws, and his parliament. When England broke with Rome, the most epoch-defining event of that reign, the deed was done by parliamentary statute.

But what *was* Parliament? Where had *that* come from? What was the purpose of that body of representatives that now sat in the small riverside city of Westminster? Some said it enjoyed its role at the sufferance of the monarchy. That it was merely a tool for enacting the monarch's legislative programme and providing them with taxes. Others that it had a deeper presence, as a guarantor of English liberties. Maybe it was older than the monarchy itself? These were difficult, fundamental questions.

In 1642, England collapsed into a violent civil war. This is a book about why that happened, about the political crisis that brought the country to the brink. It is about how a functioning and sophisticated state, well-grounded in law, constitutionally mature, and with an educated political class, found itself descending into bloodshed.

The 'English Civil War' was really a broader set of conflicts. They crossed the archipelago and even spread over the great Atlantic Ocean to the new American colonies. These bitter wars would be at their bloodiest in Ireland, but even in England – for long a fairly settled state – the death toll would be huge. In proportional terms, more died then than during the industrial slaughter of the First World War.[2]

The religious significance of the seventeenth-century conflicts would be very great indeed. Many joined sides for reasons of faith – some historians even see this as not the 'first modern revolution' but the 'last of the wars of religion'.[3] The Parliamentarians were usually Puritans; the royalists, on the other hand, wanted a return to the old ways – the traditions and rhythms that had held the English Church together for generations – since the break with Rome at least, and sometimes beyond even that.

The royalists would lose. From the 1640s onwards, England became a strikingly pluralist society, with various small Protestant groups vying with a persistent Catholic minority and the Anglican mainstream. But in the longer run, it was the establishment's vision of Anglicanism – or Episcopalianism – that came to dominate. The reality is that the legacy of the civil war is diverse, and reflects the distinctive victories of *both* sides. In any English town, and in most English villages today, there is a bewildering variety of Christian sites of worship: churches, chapels, and meeting houses. As I write this, I'm staying in the glorious, honey-stoned Wiltshire town of Bradford-on-Avon. It has its grand parish church, for sure. But there are nonconformist sites too: a Presbyterian church and Baptist chapels. Tucked away, somewhat out of sight, is a Quaker meeting house. This diversity owes much of its origin to the seventeenth century, as of course – for very different reasons – does the survival of Catholicism.

The wars, which ran in England from 1642 to 1651, had long-term constitutional consequences, too, though not ones that could have been easily predicted. Under James I and then his son Charles I, the English monarchy pursued a roughly 'absolutist' path, arguing that its power came from God, and that it was ultimately above the law. It would lose that argument. In 1649, the monarchy would be abolished and the king found guilty of treason in circumstances that were either legally highly dubious, or politically revolutionary, depending on the reader's preference. Maybe they were both. And though the monarchy would return in 1660, the lessons of the 1640s were not forgotten. It would be a monarchy with limits, to a much greater degree than that of France, or Russia, Austria, or Prussia. The fact that the constitutional monarchy of the United Kingdom survives to this day is a product of this painful process of limitation.

It is a curious entity, that constitutional monarchy. Nowadays in the UK, we still try to avoid thinking too much about the precise powers of our sovereign, though I suspect that if it came down to it – if, say, Parliament tried to legislate and the king refused his assent – we would decide that it was the people, ultimately, who were the origins of power. That was the conclusion in 1649, and it was the basis of much of the Parliamentarian side in 1642 as well. Things are much clearer in other countries: in the United States of America, in particular, where these debates helped inform another constitutional revolution in 1776–83. In the US, there has also been a much clearer adoption of one the central elements to the Parliamentarian cause. As I write this, a new president has been elected, and he is picking his government officials. But they will be vetted by Congress, which is almost precisely the arrangement that the Parliamentarians tried to force on King Charles I in 1641–2, and which he so vehemently refused. After all, in his eyes, it would leave him no more than a figurehead in a republic. Time will tell how robust these constitutional safeguards will prove to the US.

England's story in those months before the war was, and is, a salutary lesson. It reminds us of an uncomfortable truth, that nations can collapse with alarming speed in the face of a constitutional crisis. In England this took five years at most – from the moment in 1637 when the Scots rebelled against King Charles to the opening salvoes of a shooting war in the summer of 1642. Yet really the breakdown happened even quicker. In the late summer of 1641, it had looked like Charles was in a position to win the political game. His support was growing, and his enemies were increasingly isolated and unpopular. With the right mix of political skill and determination, he might have been able to fight back and secure his authority.

Then came winter. With it, chaos, protests, political deadlock, and eventually a remarkable, dangerous, and now notorious attempt by Charles to destroy his opponents by arresting five of them in the very chamber of the House of Commons at the head of a small army. After this, compromise proved impossible: week followed week, escalation piled upon escalation.

The story of how England descended into war is a riveting and fascinating one, laced with intrigue and horror. It is also a very human story: a battle not just of ideas but of personalities. In telling this story, I hope to bring some of those people to life: not only the big hitters like King Charles I, or the opposition MP John Pym, but some of the lesser-known men and women – some of whom played a very significant role indeed, and all of whom eventually faced unpalatable choices.

We must get lost in their world. To understand this war, this catastrophe, this fracture, this great awakening – whatever it was – we must follow these characters, their foibles and failings, their moments of glory and bravery. It is not a story that provides easy heroes and villains: the seventeenth century never does. But it is a compelling one, nonetheless. Because to put ourselves in this world is to grapple with something momentous indeed. With a crisis and a revolution that broke, and made, a nation.

PART ONE

Renovatio

1

The Soldier, the Poet,
the King, and the Traitor

It was a Sunday morning, late in March 1641. London was starting to warm again after a deep winter. The trees in St James's Park were in bud and the flowers were dusting the grass verges with fresh little dots of colour. It was a beautiful time of year. Except that England was on the brink of civil war; and Colonel George Goring was in his bed, suffering a visit by a poet.

Colonel Goring was something of a drinker. A gamester, too, and in his thirty-three years he had become known as famously good company. He was a soldier: a brave one. It was now over three years since he had been shot in the ankle while fighting for the Protestant Dutch. But even lameness couldn't dampen his riotous ways. On one recent occasion he was in Newport on the Isle of Wight and utterly drunk. He hoisted himself up the ladder of the public gibbet, where criminals were hanged, and gave a slurring and raucous 'last dying speech', cautioning his audience about keeping bad company, like his own friends.[1]

Now, in London, he found himself being dragged out of his slumber by one of those friends. It was Sir John Suckling. Another gambler, but also a courtier, wit, and versifier, blessed with a dramatic blond mane of hair. Now Suckling was trying out a new endeavour. As a conspirator.

There were over five million people in England.[2] That spring, most of them were tending their fields and animals, weaving at their looms and spinning on the wheel; they were learning trades, hammering iron, looking after children and supporting their aged relatives. As the season warmed and the working day got longer, they looked forward to the summer. There were lambs and calves in the pastures now, and the meadow flowers were starting to bloom. The wheat and the barley that fed hungry workers, manual and otherwise, were getting higher, swaying more grandly in the swirling winds.

In London, though, the natural rhythms had been interrupted. Parliament had been sitting for nearly five months already, an almost unimaginable period of time. Yet its main business had just begun. In the House of Lords, the impeachment trial for treason had just commenced against the most hated politician in the land: the Earl of Strafford.

Charles I, King of England, Scotland and Ireland, lay at a perilously low ebb. He had suffered a catastrophic series of defeats. He had tried to rule without his English parliament, and he had tried to impose an unpopular religious settlement on Scotland. In the last four years both projects had come spiralling down. Strafford was one of Charles's best advisors. He trusted him. Strafford's treason was not against Charles, not directly at least. It was against the nation.

Now Charles was forced to risk everything. To plot and to gamble. Now he would need men like Goring, and the poet Suckling – long-standing courtiers and loyalists – to save Strafford, and to build his rule again.

———

Charles Stuart had never been born to rule England. When he came into the world in 1600, he was but a younger son of James VI, the King of Scotland. Childhood had not been especially kind to Charles, either.[3] He first arrived in England in 1604, after a long journey down the eastern side of the country. The previous year his father had succeeded Queen Elizabeth I, becoming James I of

England and Ireland, but it was initially hard to find Charles a noble family to host him. After all, he was so sickly that people worried he would die on their watch.[4]

Charles also had a much more outwardly impressive elder brother, Prince Henry. People who met the two royal siblings noted their differences in physique and temperament. Even for his age Henry was tall, athletic, and confident: 'full of gravity'; while Charles was short, delicate, and bookish.[5] Henry was charismatic, Charles diffident. Henry commanded respect, Charles suffered from a stammer. The younger brother was no warrior, even though he badly wished to be. On at least one occasion, Henry teased Charles to the point of tears, ribbing him by saying he would one day make him Archbishop of Canterbury. The long robes, he said, would cover up Charles's weakling legs.[6]

But then Henry died. In 1612, aged just eighteen, he got sick and didn't get better. His funeral was a sombre, grim affair. England, many thought, had been robbed of its next soldier-king. It was a hard shadow for Charles to step out from, not least when people sometimes accidentally called him 'Henry'. But he tried his best. Now he was Prince of Wales, Charles strove to improve his physique. He took up running and jousting. He proved an excellent shot and an increasingly skilled horseman.

He remained, too, an impressive scholar with a penetrating grasp of foreign policy.[7] It was a skill he needed in a perilous age. In 1613, his older sister, Elizabeth, married a German prince, Frederick of the Palatinate. Within a few years a Protestant revolution would place Frederick on the throne of Bohemia. He was attacked on all sides by the powerful Catholic Habsburgs, and quickly lost his lands, but in the process Frederick and Elizabeth became heroes of the reformed faith. It permanently embroiled the Stuart family in European geopolitics.

In the meantime, Charles himself had something of a religious awakening. In 1619, his mother had died and his father had fallen dangerously sick. In James's throes he was persuaded by Bishop Lancelot Andrewes to surround Charles with English instructors.[8] It came at a time of growing division in the English Church. Just over a hundred years after Martin Luther's first rebellion, the English Reformation was now complete. Or was it? Protestantism was fairly secure, but what *kind* of Protestantism should the country adopt? Did reform need to go further, or had it already done too much?[9]

Most clergymen were Calvinists, a rather austere faith which emphasised private prayer, sermons, equality before God, and the idea that people were 'predestined' to heaven or hell. Some Calvinists were particularly pious and thorough, known to their enemies as 'Puritans'. Those who came to instruct Charles took a different, opposing line. They were part of a new movement – partly inspired by developments in the Netherlands and partly inspired by a backlash against the more severe Calvinists. Its supporters held that the Church had become too plain and familiar, and instead should emphasise order and hierarchy. Their focus was on public ritual rather than private prayer; Holy Communion rather than sermons; and they even allowed a degree of free will on the path to salvation.

To some, these new 'Ceremonialists' were adopting views dangerously close to Catholicism. They seemed to be lurching England back towards Rome. What supporters called decorum and the 'beauty of holiness' – such as bowing at the name of Jesus, or holy tables placed at the east end of the church and railed off – could look to others like the trappings of 'popery'. It was a public image only reinforced when leading Ceremonialists like William Laud, a podgy, pompous little man from Reading, made the astonishing claim that the pope was merely misguided, and not the actual Antichrist (as Calvinists generally held).

Charles was attracted to this new churchmanship. He liked its order and dignity. He had grown up surrounded by Calvinists, but he had come to see them and the Puritans as dangerously populist, even anarchic.[10] Ceremonialist clergy recognised him as one of their own: Matthew Wren, among the most militant of their number, admitted that though Charles's 'learning is not equal to his father's, yet I know his judgement to be very right.'[11]

In 1625, Charles's father died and he succeeded the throne, aged twenty-four years. One of the first things he did was confirm the rise of the Ceremonialists in his church. William Laud was quickly promoted. Meanwhile, Charles married Henrietta Maria, a French Catholic princess. There was horror from many of Charles's subjects, though at least the new queen wasn't Spanish, which would have been even worse. Naturally, Charles warmed further to those like Laud who didn't consider his wife a follower of the Antichrist.

Now Charles was king, he was still his old thoughtful, bookish, and fussy self. He retained the hint of a Scottish accent, as well as his old stutter. He was physically petite, with delicate hands. Portraits show him with pale skin and shoulder-length, slightly mousy hair; his brown eyes alternate between soft and slightly stern – disapproving perhaps. He was refined and judgemental. One of his first acts as king was to clean up his father's court. It was an act of rebellion against James's riotous ways, but it also reflected the ordered temperament of a true aesthete. Not for Charles the rough carousing of old. He would surround himself with master painters, musicians, and architects. He wanted to live in a world of harmony and order, where everyone knew their place.

———

Charles's father had liked to compare himself to Solomon, the wise biblical king; but whatever his intellectual merits, he had left a tricky inheritance. There were three kingdoms, each with their own political, legal, and religious character. James had managed them by taking a step back; not ruffling too many feathers. It had worked, after a fashion. But by 1625, there were cracks.

In England, the most populous of the three kingdoms, a critical problem had related to finance. It was a wealthy place, yet the state was not good at raising taxes: it was, as Charles insisted, 'pressed beyond her strength'.[12] If a king wanted to fight a war – to join the fight currently engulfing the Continent, for example – they needed to ask Parliament for money. But Parliament could be a truculent partner.

Parliaments were called and dismissed by the king. This was the accepted way of things. They did not meet all the time, but were called when monarchs needed them to vote 'supply', or taxes, for the use of the government. When they were called, however, they played an important representative role. They brought 'grievances' to the attention of the monarch, and with the latter's assent, they passed statutes which were the accepted way of making binding new laws. Crown and Parliament worked best when they formed a partnership, and their aims were aligned. In 1625, though, there were visible disagreements.

For a time, those who sat in Parliament had had in their sights James's beloved favourite and leading politician, the Duke of Buckingham. He was handsome – and he and James had almost certainly been lovers – but he was also barely competent. By 1625, though, when James died, Buckingham had also developed a strong relationship with Charles, and it was said the two men 'never go asunder but arm in arm'.[13] So the duke continued in his role as chief minister, advisor, and confidant to the king (though, unlike with James, Buckingham and Charles never shared a bed).

Putting so much power in the hands of a man so widely seen as venal and corrupt did little to help with Parliament's misgivings about finance, and these would characterise the next few years. In 1625, Charles asked Parliament to grant a tax called 'tonnage and poundage' – essentially a fairly lucrative form of customs. For over two centuries, Parliament had always offered this at the beginning of a monarch's reign, and it had done so for each monarch's whole life. This time they weren't quite so sure: they desired a bit of extra scrutiny. So they granted tonnage and poundage for a year to give time to straighten things out. But then plague and politics intervened. Two parliaments were dissolved before a permanent grant could be settled, leaving Charles faced with a dilemma. He was out of money and he wanted to fight a war, but a critical source of revenue no longer had parliamentary approval.

The solution was blindingly simple. Charles collected tonnage and poundage anyway. He also issued a 'Forced Loan', whereby his subjects would lend money to the Crown, even though it was never likely to be repaid.[14] If they refused, they were sent to gaol. Sometimes they were threatened with even worse. In one particularly bitter case, five knights sued for habeas corpus, having been imprisoned for refusing to pay. The government was able to argue that in emergency situations it could imprison people without trial. After all, 'necessity hath no law', as one royal officer put it.[15]

It all looked dangerously authoritarian, though it chimed nicely with Charles's political ideology. Like his father, the young king believed in his own 'divine right', that he was only accountable to God, not to his people. 'Princes,' he would say in 1629, 'are not bound to give account of their actions but to God alone.'[16] His was a view of kingship in which power cascaded downwards from the Almighty onto him. It owed nothing to any contract with his people. They had no right to resist him.

In 1628, crisis came. England's military adventures, first against Spain and then against France, were disastrous. At Cadiz the English soldiers were butchered after getting drunk on local wine; at La Rochelle they were unable to scale the walls of a key fortress because the ladders were too short. Each time the king's favourite, Buckingham, bore the brunt of the blame. Meanwhile, both the Forced Loan and the rise of the Ceremonialists were stirring serious opposition at home.

Desperate for money, Charles called Parliament again, telling it that if it didn't do its duty, he would be forced, 'for the preservation of the public' to 'take some other courses'. This, he reassured them, wasn't the threat it looked like, 'for I scorn to threaten any but my equals'.[17] But Parliament wasn't likely to roll over. In the spring of 1628, they put forward a 'Petition of Right', which declared that taxation was illegal without the 'common consent in Parliament', and Charles was cajoled into accepting it.[18] Then, in August, the Duke of Buckingham was assassinated, cut down by the blade of an angry army officer. Come spring 1629, the rancour between Crown and some members of Parliament was even worse. In March, it descended into in astonishing scuffle in the House of Commons. Charles had decided to dissolve Parliament, but the Speaker, John Finch, was held down in his chair by three MPs: Benjamin Valentine, Sir John Eliot, and a Dorset man called Denzil Holles. A royal messenger was kept out of the chamber while a series of escalatory resolutions were passed. Members grabbed their swords and there was a remarkable melee. Some observers referred to the two sides as 'Patriots' and 'Royalists'.[19]

Order was restored, but after this, perhaps understandably, Charles decided to rule without Parliament. It was to be a period of 'Personal Rule', by the king, his principal officers, and his Privy Council. Some began to doubt whether Parliament would ever sit again. In 1632, the Clerk of the Commons died, and no replacement was appointed.[20] Charles saw Parliament as a 'hydra' – a many-headed monster – that was 'as well cunning as malicious'. Its meetings were 'of the nature of cats: they grow ever cursed with age'.[21]

The country was now at peace, and the government started finding ever more creative ways to finance itself without parliamentary taxes. Ideas included using fines for offences such as not presenting oneself for knighthood, encroaching on ancient forests, and for living in London without the king's permission. The government also pushed an old levy called 'Ship Money', where coastal counties were told to supply vessels for the Royal Navy. Meanwhile, the villains of 1629 – those behind the unseemly ruckus in the House of Commons – were punished. Some were left to rot. Sir John Eliot died of consumption in the Tower of London in 1632; Denzil Holles was fined heavily and remained on bail. Another dissident MP, William Strode, was left in prison until 1640.[22]

Charles desired order and the maintenance of hierarchy and stately gravitas. He committed to the restoration of St Paul's Cathedral and oversaw the addition of a grand Classical portico by Inigo Jones. He regulated everything from poor relief to London traffic. Ever the frustrated tinkerer, he tried to move the start of the new year from its traditional date of 25 March to 1 January, and ordered that hackney carriages shouldn't take customers on journeys shorter than three miles.[23] He demanded to be served on bended knee, and decided which members of the landed classes were allowed to stay in London for Christmas. He lionised the ancient nobility, seeing himself as an Arthurian leader of venerable warrior caste. The first thing Charles did every morning was to put on his Cross of St George, a symbol of the chivalric Order of the Garter. The Garter meant everything to Charles – about half of the books he owned were about it. Its annual feasts, around St George's Day, were some of the most sumptuous occasions in the calendar. At every turn, Charles tried to bolster the power of his nobility and protect them from upstarts. He banned fake jewellery – to stop people aping their betters – and declared that a noble could legitimately beat up a commoner who insulted them. In July 1637, Charles personally intervened in a case where two draymen had accidentally crashed into the coach of an earl in the streets of London. Although the draymen were acquitted by a local jury, Charles ordered that they be 'presently whipped publicly through the town' for their 'bold and insolent carriage towards the said earl'.[24] Hierarchy needed to be maintained.

———

Yet that very same month, Charles's rule was beginning to crumble. Since 1633, he had been trying to impose English-style worship in Scotland, but his northern kingdom had a very different tradition of churchmanship, with much less power given to bishops and much more focus on spontaneous prayer rather than common worship. In 1637, Charles's policy provoked a rebellion, beginning, that July, with riots in Edinburgh.[25] Within months the Scots had assented en masse to a 'National Covenant'. A rebel government in Edinburgh abolished Scottish bishops. Charles was furious, and inflexible. 'I will rather die than yield to their impertinent and damnable demands,' he fumed, underlining the key words for effect.[26] He began military preparations to invade and subdue his northern kingdom. To him, if he gave in to the rebel 'Covenanters', then he would have been no king worth the name: little better in Scotland, he said, than a duke of Venice – a figurehead in a republic, in other words. He scoffed at claims the Covenanters were motivated by their faith. No, he said, they were 'busy and traitorously affected men', who were using religion as a cover to destroy 'all monarchical government'.[27]

War was coming to Britain, and it reignited the constitutional conflicts in England. Ever since the fourteenth century, English kings had always summoned Parliament before going to war. After all, it was Parliament which could vote the necessary taxes. But in

1639, Charles decided to go it alone. Stirred by his chivalric ideals, he prepared, like Saint George, to slay the dragon. He started to have himself painted in armour and atop a warhorse. He decided to lead his army in person – the first English monarch to do so since Henry VIII in 1544.[28] At last, he would step out of his brother's shadow. A large force gathered at York. Colonel George Goring and Sir John Suckling were among those who marched with the king to the border.

But Charles's nerve failed him. At Kelso, he looked through a telescope at the Covenanter army, which deliberately arrayed itself to look bigger than it was. Rather than engage, Charles decided on a temporary retreat. There would be negotiations to buy more time. Reluctantly, he at last called Parliament.

It assembled in the spring of 1640: the two Houses, the Lords (the upper house) and the Commons (the lower), gathering for the first time in eleven years. But instead of immediately offering the king money, members railed against the 'grievances' that had grown up since the beginning of the reign. They carped at 'illegal' taxes and the rise of the Ceremonialists, like William Laud – now Archbishop of Canterbury. Leading the charge were men such as Oliver St John, a brooding virtuoso lawyer, and John Pym, a veteran of the 1620s conflicts. Alongside them was Francis Russell, the Earl of Bedford, a fabulously wealthy landowner who had built up Covent Garden in London. St John was his kinsman, and Pym his 'man of business'.

Between them they were able to grind the king's programme to a halt. Without reform, they made clear, there would be no money for the war against the Scots. Charles realised the most strident challenge was coming from the lower house, so he cultivated the Lords, encouraging them to avoid 'the preposterous course of the House of Commons'.[29] Even so the Parliament got nowhere, and within mere weeks of its meeting, Charles became frustrated and decided to use his ancient prerogative to dissolve it and send the members home. This would be known to posterity as the 'Short Parliament': an ignominious failure. Charles blamed the catastrophe on a small cabal of troublemakers who wished to 'render contemptible this glorious monarchy'.[30]

The dissolution of the Short Parliament was followed by a nasty burst of rioting. Lambeth Palace, the London mansion of Archbishop Laud, was attacked. In a flourish of cruelty, Charles had one of the rioters, John Archer, tortured on the rack, with the warrant written in the king's own hand; while another, a teenager called John Benstead, was hung, drawn, and quartered.[31] As the dust settled, and as Benstead's remains were left to rot on London Bridge, the country headed for conflict once more.

Charles still aimed to defeat the Scots in battle. Another army was raised. By the summer, it was gathered in the north of England, led in person by the king at York. Then, in August 1640, the Scots invaded. Charles's royal army was overcome at a sharp skirmish at Newburn Ford on the Tyne, near Newcastle. Among the king's humiliated commanders was Sir John Suckling. Reports said that his coach was captured, and with it £300 in cash and a pile of his clothes.[32]

As the Scots pushed south, a dissident group of English nobles, led by Bedford, initially twelve in number but growing by the day, gathered in London. They produced a petition demanding a new parliament to settle the nation's ills.[33] Their lawyer, St John, had discovered in the historical records a reference from 1258 to twelve peers having the right to call Parliament without the king's approval. One of their number – Edward Montagu, Lord Mandeville – was sent north to present the petition to Charles. Meanwhile some of the dissidents had been in contact with the Scottish rebels. Opposition was being coordinated.

Defeated, outmanoeuvred, and politically isolated, Charles agreed to call Parliament again. The only thing stopping the Scots from continuing their march south was regular payments from London. They were being bought off: paid not to penetrate any further into England. With Charles's financial resources stretched to their utter limit already, the only body who could provide this money was Parliament. It was guaranteed to sit for some time. It would become known, in contrast to its immediate predecessor, as the 'Long Parliament'. And it would be an engine of revolution.

2

Justice and Execution

The Long Parliament gathered on 3 November 1640. King Charles entered the Palace of Westminster quietly, almost incognito. Rather than process in triumph through the streets to the throne in the House of Lords, he alighted quietly from a listing boat in the autumn breezes, and passed up the stairs from the River Thames.

The elections had gone badly for the king. Voting was restricted to men: in the county seats, those who held freehold land worth £2 a year; in the towns, the franchise varied hugely – some urban electorates were reasonably large, others distinctly oligarchic.[1] Yet voting was wider now than at any time before. Coming after a century of inflation, more and more members of the 'middling sort' met the £2 threshold, and there were more urban voters. One of the key restrictions, though, was the lack of actual contests. In most places, the local community preselected their preferred candidate and simply put them before the electorate to be agreed to. Only around sixty elections were contested this time, or just over 12 per cent, though this was still an unusually large proportion.[2]

There was a broad consensus for reform. Government supporters only made up a few dozen of the nearly 500 MPs. Thus, when Parliament assembled, members would quickly attack the financial, legal, and religious policies of the Personal Rule. But the most pressing business was something – or some*one* – else. In the 1630s, a stern Yorkshireman called Thomas Wentworth had been sent over to govern Ireland, which he had done with firm efficiency. Wentworth's power in Ireland had been grounded on military force and sheer political willpower. He was a strongman, a colonialist who ruled with an iron fist and rarely ever bothered to cloak it with a velvet glove.[3] His aim was to make Charles, in Ireland at least, 'as absolute a monarch as Christendom can set forth'.[4] In the process, he had raised a competent army of 9,000 men – mostly Catholics. Many, including Wentworth himself, saw Ireland as a testing ground for a similar approach elsewhere. Thus, when Charles's rule had collapsed in Scotland and faltered in England, Wentworth was the obvious man to set things right. Late in 1639 he had been recalled to England and quickly promoted to the nobility as the Earl of Strafford. As Charles dissolved the Short Parliament in May 1640, Strafford had told the king to destroy the Scottish rebels by any means necessary. 'Go on with a vigorous war, as you first designed,' he urged chillingly, 'loose and absolved from all rules of government.'[5]

Strafford's iron methods were feared in England, for might he not use his Irish troops to crush dissent here? There were some deeply worrying signs about his intentions too. As the Long Parliament had assembled, Charles summoned Strafford to take his place in the House of Lords. At the same time, Charles's inner circle began making preparations to fortify the Tower of London. It was a sturdy old fortress, immediately overlooking the eastern reaches of the City, and was stocked with cannons and gunpowder. It was formidable and manned by well-armed soldiers: a looming reminder over London of the power the monarchy had to summon force and violence. Meanwhile, royal warships were heard testing their cannons in the Thames Estuary. The new parliament was but days old, and already there was a military threat to break it.[6]

The dissidents had to move quickly, and they did. On 11 November 1640, barely a week into the new parliament, Strafford was suddenly impeached. His crime had been 'subverting the fundamental laws' and 'erecting arbitrary and tyrannical government', and so alienating the people from the king.[7] Worse, he was accused of planning to use his Irish army against Parliament. Yet it was a strange kind of treason that Strafford stood accused of. He still had the king's support, after all. But such was Parliament's ascendancy in late 1640 that this didn't matter. Within weeks, Strafford had been moved to the Tower, for it was a prison as well as a fort.

The approaching trial would dominate the early months of 1641. Charles, meanwhile, had been forced into some crucial concessions. He abandoned his Ceremonialist friends in the Church. Laud was arrested, and in January 1641, Charles announced to a relieved audience that he would return the Church of England to the way it had been in the glory days of Queen Elizabeth.[8] The revenue-raising expedients of the previous decade were disavowed, leaving his government permanently dependent on Parliament for money. And, most critical of all, he gave his assent to a 'Triennial Act', which stipulated that – were a king to fail to call a Parliament for longer than three years – the Lord Keeper or any twelve peers could assemble in Westminster and send the writs out themselves. It was a remarkable reduction of the king's power, removing 'one of the supreme prerogatives of his crown, which was to call Parliaments', and it was met with great celebrations and bonfires, especially in London.[9]

To seal the deal, Charles agreed to appoint a number of refor-mists to government office. The idea was simple: offer places in the government to some of the men who had led the opposition, focusing on the more moderate figures. The key peer was the Earl of Bedford, who was held to be a potential bridge between king and Parliament. Prominent dissidents were given seats on the Privy Council. The lawyer Oliver St John was made Solicitor General, a junior but important legal office. Bedford himself was expected to be granted the position of Lord Treasurer – the leading, most lucrative government office. With him, so the rumours went, would come his longstanding associate John Pym, who would be appointed Chancellor of the Exchequer.

John Pym was the principal figure in the House of Commons, the larger but the lower of the two chambers of Parliament. He was a charismatic man, a pugnacious politician, and a seasoned and eloquent debater. From a Somerset family but London-born, he sported a fashionable moustache and goatee.[10] He had been four years old when the Spanish Armada had been defeated, so one of his earliest memories would have been the bells and bonfires that celebrated the victory over Catholic Spain. Now approaching his sixtieth year, he had a long career behind him as both a brilliant orator and a smart parliamentarian. In the 1620s, he had been an important figure in the opposition.[11] He was almost preternaturally astute, with a remarkable grasp of parliamentary procedure and – most critical of all – an impeccable sense of political timing. A Puritan, though generally a moderate one, he nonetheless possessed an almost fanatical fear of popish plots. These he saw, as many of his contemporaries did, in constitutional as much as religious terms, for 'papism' was a byword for authoritarianism.[12] It was a fear that led Pym to place his faith in parliaments to curtail kings and protect the people.

The dissidents who had challenged Charles in 1640 had coalesced into a parliamentary faction, a semi-organised interest group that contemporaries called a 'party', but which didn't yet have anything like the institutional capacity associated with the modern use of that word. Soon the group would come to be called the 'Junto', a word implying a joining: between men of similar interests and between ideological allies in the two houses: the Commons and the Lords.

As spring 1641 arrived, the Junto still incorporated a spread of views – notably on the future of the Church, and on what to do with the Earl of Strafford. Moderates in their ranks, including the effective leaders Bedford and – for now – Pym, could imagine a situation in which Strafford might be allowed to live. But there were hardliners, too, centred on two rich earls: Essex and Warwick. They wanted Strafford dead. To them he was simply too dangerous. Too talented, too driven. Too likely to push Charles himself towards desperate courses.

The forces within the Junto were balanced. Both houses of Parliament were divided. The agent of chaos was Charles I himself.

Since his defeat at the hands of the Scots, and his consequent prostration at the feet of Parliament, Charles had nursed a deep grievance against the men responsible. When the Scots had invaded the previous summer, he had been given intelligence by his spymaster and secretary of state, Francis Windebank, that certain nobles had been in contact with the Covenanter rebels. '*It shall not be forgotten*,' Charles had written.[13] He even still hoped, as late as spring 1641, to reanimate his war against the Scots and bring them down by force.[14]

Charles realised, too, that there was now considerable anger in his own army, still quartered in Yorkshire, aimed at his enemies: particularly at the politicians at Westminster who were sending money to the Scots while allowing English troops to go without wages. There was, then, a chance for Charles to win back the initiative. To restore his power, to save the Earl of Strafford, and to strike back at the Junto.

For this, he would need Colonel Goring, that Sunday morning in March.

—————

As Goring sat up in his bed, confronted by the courtier Suckling, he was brought into a conspiracy. There was – so Suckling informed the bleary-eyed colonel – a plot to bring the king's army south to London. Goring should know about it.

Suckling made himself scarce, but later in the day, Goring was travelling through the West End by coach. Stuck in traffic, he spied one Mr Henry Jermyn, another well-known courtier from the good times.

Before Goring could do anything, Jermyn had sent a footman to the colonel's coach and told him to follow. Goring obliged and the two coaches trundled for a while through the wide streets and the grand new buildings of the increasingly opulent district, Goring following until Jermyn's coach stopped beside a house. Out Jermyn clambered, entering by the door and ascending the stairs. Goring followed. At the top, Jermyn announced that he had something to say about the royal army, but this was no place to do it. Instead, Goring should come that evening to Whitehall, the great royal residence by the river, between London and Westminster. Here everything would be explained.

Goring kept his appointment. He met Jermyn that evening at the palace, and he was taken to the queen. The king was present too, in the background. The next day, Monday, Goring returned, and this time the queen brought him to Charles. Now Goring was introduced to a shadowy group of soldiers.

That evening, Goring met again with Jermyn and some more officers. An oath of secrecy was taken, and more plans discussed. Jermyn's idea was to mobilise the royal army, move it south, and take control of the Tower of London. Strafford would be released, the king's enemies in Parliament defeated, and the war against the rebel Scots would be resumed with vigour.[15]

Goring had a particular role. With Charles's approval, he would leak the plan. He made contact with the Earl of Newport – the Master of the Ordnance and brother-in-law to one of the most radical reformists, Warwick. Immediately, Newport brought Goring before three others: Bedford and two more Junto men – the young and affable Lord Mandeville, and the older, wiry, wily, Oxfordshire peer Lord Saye and Sele.[16]

It was a ploy. Goring knew Newport would bring the plot before members of the Junto.[17] Part of the plan was already being dropped. The idea to move the army south was just too risky. But Charles and the conspirators needed to maintain the threat. It was brinkmanship. If the Junto thought they were in imminent danger from the king's army, they might lay off Strafford. Goring, meanwhile, left for Portsmouth, now, thanks to his revelation of the plot, high in Parliament's trust. Since 1639, he had been governor of the town, and there he would wait.

Strafford's trial had begun. As an impeachment, the accusation was prepared by the House of Commons, and then tried by the House of Lords. It took place in Westminster Hall, a great medieval chamber with space for hundreds of spectators. Peers sat in the centre wearing their crimson and ermine-trimmed robes, marking the gravity of the occasion. Members of the Commons sat in grandstands (called 'scaffolds') to the side.[18]

The prosecution case was inherently weak as long as Strafford was visibly supported by the king. The evidence that he had planned to use the Irish army in England was thin, for a start. Indeed, the simplest way to prove treason was to use a parliamentary statute from 1352, in which the crime was defined as 'compassing or imagining' the king's death. Strafford hadn't done this. What he had done, so it was alleged, was to work to create a permanent change to the government. This, so it was alleged, constituted treason. 'To alter the settled frame and constitution of government,' said Pym, 'is treason in any state.'[19] In particular, they argued that Strafford's actions were making the king's rule arbitrary and tyrannical. This served to alienate the people from the king so severely that it risked civil war, and therefore (so they said) constituted treason.

The earl defended himself with skill and zeal, expertly probing weaknesses of both fact and law in the prosecution case.[20] So, in a move of quite fearsome cynicism, his enemies changed their approach. Now they launched an 'Act of Attainder', a piece of legislation whose logic and purpose was chillingly simple: it declared a person's acts to be treasonous, and forfeited their life. If it passed both houses of Parliament, and got the royal assent, its target could be dead within days.

For a time, the Attainder Bill struggled. Even if it passed the Commons, and this was by no means certain, it was likely to stick in the Lords. The peers were already the judges of the impeachment trial and they would correctly see the Attainder as a way of bypassing that. A compromise still seemed possible.

But then Charles made a disastrous error. On the weekend of 17–18 April, he told the army officers currently in London, including some sitting MPs, to return to their regiments in the north. Combined with Goring's revelations, it looked like a mobilisation. Charles seemed to be about to launch an imminent military attack. It was probably a deliberate threat by the king, just as Goring's leak was, but if he was aiming to terrify the Commons into compliance, then it quickly had the opposite effect. Within days, the Attainder passed in the lower house, by the clear margin of 204 votes to 59.[21] Then, on the 29th, the lawyer St John spoke to the trial, which was still carrying on in Westminster Hall, even as the Attainder gathered momentum. He savaged Strafford for three hours, playing on a novel understanding of treason, in which the king had two bodies – his body natural and his body politic. The latter, in part, resided with Parliament.[22] Strafford, by trying to use force to subvert Parliament, had thus committed treason. In any case, Strafford was like a dangerous predator. In such circumstances, sheer necessity demanded he be killed. The Lords were turned. Enough were convinced by the lawyer's arguments to make the Attainder a genuine possibility. Around this time also, John Pym, the most influential member of the Commons, came to the decision that Strafford had to die. The tide was turning anyway.

Still, though, the royalist plotters might be able to seize the Tower, release Strafford, and use the fort to overawe London. John Suckling was certainly not done yet. He was gathering a band of men in the capital, telling people he was raising troops to support the Portuguese in their independence struggle against Spain. Some, on hearing the news, had gone to visit the Portuguese ambassador, who more than once denied all knowledge. But it didn't matter.

On 1 May 1641, Charles received an audit from the Ordnance Office. It told him the amount of gunpowder available in the Tower; good information if you were planning to seize it.[23] Then, on Sunday 2nd May, Suckling's plot finally matured.

There was a grand royal wedding that day. It was the perfect screen for Suckling's plan.[24] The young Princess Mary, King Charles's eldest daughter, was to marry the fourteen-year-old William of Orange, a Dutch prince. The plotters knew that the capital would be alive with celebrations and the traffic positively stifling. If the Tower were seized, then the London militia, even if they stayed loyal to the Junto and Parliament, would struggle to respond in time. Charles would have control.

On the day, as expected, the streets were thoroughly clogged. With revels carrying on across town, few would have paid much attention to the gathering of men at the White Horse Tavern, a large hostelry near St Paul's. The plan was to collect a hundred men, loyal to the king, and to take them to the Tower. William Balfour, the Lieutenant of the Tower, had been given clear orders from Charles himself to admit them. Then they could overpower

Strafford's guards and take command. A hundred men would be plenty.

By the afternoon, only sixty or so had arrived. Suckling was starting to waver. Even the gambler in him no longer fancied the odds. News was spreading about the men at the tavern. John Pym and the Earl of Warwick were both made aware. Word was passed around the knotted old streets of the City, dispersed by runners under timbered eaves and past ancient stone churches. As dusk fell, a thousand people had assembled beside the Tower to protect it.[25] Suckling's plan, at last, was broken.

Strafford's outlook was getting darker indeed. The threat of the plot hadn't cowed the Junto. If anything, it had made them more determined to win. The conspirators, meanwhile, had given up and fled, with Suckling and Jermyn bolting for Goring's Portsmouth.

It was to be a crucial few days. On 3 May, Parliament drew up something they called the 'Protestation'. Every office-holder in England – down to the lowliest village constable – would affirm their support for 'the true reformed Protestant religion'. On the 5th, as the Lords were discussing the Attainder, a rumour bolted through London that the Commons had been set on fire and the 'papists' had surrounded Parliament with an armed force. People closed their shops and came out onto the streets, but it was a false alarm.[26] On the 6th, the Lords ordered the ports to be closed and the plotters, wherever they turned up, to be arrested.[27] Then, between the 6th and the 7th, both houses rushed through a bill against the dissolution of Parliament. If the king agreed to it, he would no longer be able to break the Long Parliament without its consent. His prerogative for calling and dismissing Parliaments was under further assault.

Around Westminster, and around the royal palace of Whitehall, angry crowds gathered. They chanted for 'Justice and Execution! Justice and Execution!' – aimed at Strafford. MPs who had voted against his conviction had their names posted up on walls and doorways. Peers were being pressurised into voting for the Attainder. Politics was spilling out onto the streets.[28]

The Earl of Bedford, meanwhile, was dying. The man on whom any moderate settlement depended, had developed smallpox, one of the deadliest, most feared of all diseases of the time. As Strafford's story reached its final act, Bedford was incapacitated.[29] Within days he would be dead.

On 7 May, both Suckling and Jermyn reached Portsmouth. Goring was later asked why he hadn't stopped them; after all, he was supposed to be loyal to Parliament. He replied that he had been asleep in his bed (again).[30] In the meantime the pair had slipped out to sea.

That same day, the Lords voted for Strafford's death. The Bill of Attainder and the Bill against Dissolution would be gathered together and brought, from Parliament, the short distance up the street to the Palace of Whitehall, here to be presented for the royal assent.[31] The grandstands in Westminster Hall were ordered to be taken down.[32] Strafford's trial was over. For Charles, it was a catastrophic defeat.

―――

The person who would lead the small delegation to take Charles the bad news was the acting Speaker of the House of Lords. He would take a coach from the Palace of Westminster, the home of Parliament, and make the journey to the Palace of Whitehall, the residence of the king. Briefly, fleetingly, he would stand as a representative of a determined political nation, before a reluctant monarch. It would be an electric moment, from which there might emerge multiple futures. For if the king could not be persuaded to assent to Strafford's death, then the country might descend into immediate bloodshed. It was the kind of task no public figure could wish for.

The man's name was Sir John Bankes.

3

The Sow's Ear and the Silken Purse

Sir John Bankes wasn't born rich, or famous, or near London. His rise to high office, and to that meeting with King Charles on 8 May 1641, had been quite remarkable.

Sir John's father, another John, had been a shopkeeper and a farmer. He had made his home at Keswick, in Cumberland, in the far north of England. It was a town of tumbling slate homes and cottages, aside the glistening ripples of Derwentwater and beneath the high, smooth mass of Skiddaw. Those who lived there worked with their hands. They came home swathed in mud and lashed by rain. Here the younger John was born, in the spring of 1589.[1]

His father grazed cattle and sheep on the great fellside of Helvellyn to the south, and he grew crops in the valley. More recently, he had invested in a great fish weir – a sound opportunity in a world where a person's livelihood banked upon the bounty of nature. He kept a shop, selling textiles. His house was in the centre of Keswick, next to the market square and beside the maypole: where the town celebrated and danced in good times. Here, on market day, stallholders displayed their wares on freshly cut and sweet-smelling bracken, and the streets hummed with shoppers.[2]

The elder John's life was local, but it was not devoid of politics. Little hillside towns and villages like Keswick effectively had to self-govern. The land was rough and poor, and people needed to sort out who could graze their animals when, and who could dig fuel where. Without rules, they might work their natural environment too hard. Land would be exhausted, fish and beasts overexploited. If man didn't find ways to control himself, nature might lash out.

Keswick knew natural hardship well. When the younger John was just eight years old, the region was hit by a famine in which poor folk had died in the streets.[3] To keep the delicate equilibrium, each village and town had to have its own miniature law courts.[4] Here people sorted out debt and brought prosecutions for offences like overgrazing, unruly dunghills, and the occasional minor brawl (known, in a marvellously evocative local dialect term, as a 'hubbleshow'). The law protected the community. It protected the fish and the fowl. It protected the very land itself.

By John's teenage years, his father had become quietly prosperous. When John senior died in 1616, an inventory of his goods was taken for probate, and it revealed a life of modest comfort.[5] He had a cellar with eight gallons of claret. In the house there were cushions, curtains, silver plate, 'pictures', and books. He also had a rapier, suggesting social status, and over £20 worth of clothes. The family had even married into a wealthy dynasty of German immigrants, who owned profitable mines and quarries in the nearby mountains. The Bankeses themselves had invested in the local graphite seams, which provided a soft substance that could be used for writing, initially on sheep but later in little implements called pencils.

For the younger John, though, his future was away from the fells. Like many talented northern lads, he decided to take his study south. He would go to Oxford, England's most ancient university, and he would matriculate as a member of Queen's College. He would begin his rise in the world: one that would bring him to that fateful meeting with King Charles I, in May 1641, with the Earl of Strafford's life in the balance.

Queen's would have been a jolt for young John Bankes. A haughty collection of golden buildings that overlooked Oxford's dusty High Street, the college had a long tradition of welcoming northerners. But it was nothing like the hard world of hill farming, where talk was of the price of wool and diets were leavened by freshwater trout. The Cumberland dialect was still laced with Viking words, and sheep were counted using a version of ancient British. Now, John was in a world of black-gowned churchmen, hurrying down fair side-streets into elegant quads, declaiming in Latin and Greek.

Like many Oxford students, young Bankes didn't take his degree, though this doesn't imply any lack of aptitude or application. We don't know why he left the university, but one thing we can say is that late in 1606, he will have heard some awful news from Keswick. On the night of 16 October, there had been a disturbance in which a group of local men, a 'riotous and tumultuous company' said to be over a hundred strong, had attacked and destroyed his father's fish weir.[6] It was too severe a business for the local courts, so it was sent up to London, where the elder John was able to prosecute his neighbours for riot in the feared court of Star Chamber. It was a salutary warning that business investment didn't always win friends. To the younger John, it will have reinforced a belief in the law as a thin skein, protecting society from the baser urges of man. Without the restraining force of the courts, humans might risk regression to a more natural, more violent state of being.

The law would be John Bankes's calling. Leaving Oxford, he went on to Gray's Inn, on the north-western outskirts of London. The Inns of Court, where lawyers trained, had chapels, dining halls, quads, for all the world like a third university, and arguably a much livelier one. Many sons of the gentry would get their education at the Inns, learning to navigate the bright lights of London as much as the arcane thickets of the law. It was legal scholars who provided many of London's playgoers, or the audiences for sermons. Or customers for alehouses, taverns, and brothels.

Whether he partook in all this, Bankes thrived. A later writer would describe him as 'born at Keswick, and bred at Gray's Inn'.[7] By the last years of the 1610s, he had begun to practise law. He had come into an inheritance now, but there was no chance he would leave his burgeoning career for a return to Keswick. That said, he kept a connection with home. His first clients were mostly fellow northerners. It was a fractious time in the region. The Crown was trying to raise people's rents and abolish their ancient tenures.[8] It did so by royal proclamation: a dubious move – for should this not be done by Parliament? What followed was a string of local legal disputes, particularly between private landlords and their tenant farmers. In Keswick, Bankes gave counsel to his old neighbours against the lord of the manor, and he secured them a half-decent compromise.[9]

He had married now, too. Mary Hawtrey was a fiercely intelligent sixteen-year-old, from a wealthy merchant's family of Ruislip in Middlesex. She wed John Bankes, who was twenty-nine, in 1618, in her home parish, and here they lived for now.[10] Just over three years later, by which time Mary was twenty and John thirty-two, their first child, Alice, was born.

As a man on the rise, meanwhile, John had decided to get himself elected to Parliament. In the fraught 1620s, he found himself gravitating towards the opposition, though he was very much a moderate. His view was that Parliament's privileges had come to it by long custom, not by a royal grant. It was a fine point, but an important one. It meant that there were areas the royal prerogative could not touch. In essence, Bankes advocated a balance. In 1628, he argued eloquently for this from the Commons chamber: 'I will not derogate from the power of kings. Subjects have their rights, and kings their prerogatives.' It was an equilibrium.[11]

By now, Bankes's skill and diligence were gaining notice, and whatever his flirtation with the opposition, he found himself cultivated by the government.[12] In May 1630, Queen Henrietta Maria gave birth to a healthy heir, Prince Charles, and, naturally, one of the first things the baby needed was a lawyer. So, within weeks of the happy royal birth, Bankes was appointed Attorney-General to the new Prince of Wales. It was quite the promotion.

With both favour and income secured, Bankes began to build up his estate. By now, he and Mary had six children of their own, and the family were flourishing. The couple's most spectacular investment came in 1631 when they began the purchase of a large Dorset estate. It centred on Corfe Castle, an ancient medieval fortress perched high on a steep knoll, overlooking miles of countryside. He bought it from the lawyer Edward Coke and his estranged wife, Lady Elizabeth Hatton. The full transaction wasn't completed until

1633, but from 1631 the Bankeses took over almost all of the Coke–Hatton lands in Dorset. Coke had been a thorn in the monarchy's side, the leading pen behind the Petition of Right of 1628.[13] But he was a representative of another age. It was lawyers like Bankes – who could reconcile themselves to Charles's new monarchy – who were the future. By the end of 1634, Coke was dead.

And Bankes had been promoted again. In 1631 he was knighted, but his great leap came in 1634, when the Attorney-General to the king, William Noy, had died. There were other candidates to fill that office, but Bankes got the nod. Part of his appeal was that he was not particularly attached to one court faction or other. He was in the middle. Thomas Wentworth, the future Earl of Strafford, took a rather lukewarm view of the new Attorney-General. He was convinced Bankes would have 'something of the indifferent of him'; after all he lay, Wentworth sniffed, 'betwixt the sow's ear and the silken purse'.[14]

The role of Attorney-General was stunningly lucrative, thanks to the many perks that came with it. All told it was probably worth a staggering £10,000 a year. When Bankes's father had died, his goods had been valued at nearly £250 in total, and he had been pretty prosperous for Keswick. Now Sir John had clambered into the world of the super-rich. 'God hath given a blessing upon my labours and studies,' he told his fellows at Gray's, 'and though my beginnings were but small, yet my latter end hath greatly increased.'[15] He divided his time between Holborn on the edge of London, where he had a pied-à-terre, and a house in Stanwell in Middlesex, to which he had moved with Mary. Occasionally he would visit his great castle and estate in Dorset, and he was a deputy lieutenant for the county from 1633.[16]

As Attorney-General, his job was to act as a legal factotum to the Crown, providing advice, making things happen, and ensuring that whatever the king wanted was legally watertight. It was Bankes, therefore, who collated precedents, and drafted royal proclamations: those regulating hackney cab journeys, or trying to change the date of the new year, were passed across Bankes's desk.[17] By now, Bankes was a well-known and respected figure. He found himself courted by those needing favour. He had books dedicated in his honour. He was one of the dedicatees to a tract written by the moderate Puritan preacher at Gray's Inn, Richard Sibbes. Another dedication was a little book attacking 'depopulation', the process by which enclosing landlords might throw tenants out of their houses.[18] It was an issue of social justice that Bankes had taken up in his role as Attorney-General.

Bankes's political views were fairly conservative and typical of the class to which he now belonged. No society could subsist, he thought, 'without order', and 'in order there must be a superior and an inferior'. For Bankes it was the certainties of the law that underpinned this natural and hierarchical social order. 'No laws are balanced upon weightier reasons than the laws of England,' he told Gray's patriotically.[19] He also, in another speech given at Gray's, had a word of warning for those who would challenge the status quo. There were three types of government, he argued: 'ecclesiastical', 'political', and 'domestical'. If any would shake up the first two, he cautioned, 'let him try first to take away the third & see how he likes it, let him give license to his children or servants in his family to do what they list'. Take away the hierarchies of Church and state, he was saying, and even those of the family might be under threat.[20]

His own family life, meanwhile, continue to blossom, with yet more children, all recorded in a little book with the times of their birth and the names of their godparents. John's focus on his legal work meant that – in common with many lawyer families – it was Mary who kept the family accounts. But the couple were never far away from each other.

By 1637, they had added a new tranche of Dorset lands to their estate – a dilapidated old manor near Wimborne Minster called Kingston Lacy. Nearby was a hunting chase called Holt, which John began to improve and enclose, causing a stir among the local peasants.[21] It was an ironic development for a man who had prosecuted enclosers, but of course he had the legal technical skill to make sure his plan would stick. He was looking too at the lands around Corfe. Here he was Lord of the Isle of Purbeck – not actually an island but a semi-isolated sweep of valleys, heaths, chalk and limestone hills, and rocky coast, plus various marshlands described by locals as 'oozy', 'slubby' and 'glibsey'.[22] He collected surveys of the local landholding customs of Purbeck, adding the occasional careful note in his distinctive spidery hand.[23] In him stirred the spirit of optimism. He had the chance to become an 'improving' landlord, making himself and his country richer.[24] Perhaps those soggy marshes could be transformed into flourishing farmland.

One of the things Bankes now also had in his possession was a great, elaborate map of the isle, made some fifty years before, with fields and cliffs and game depicted in elegant ink and colour.[25] Yet what the map didn't convey was the fragility of the landscape Bankes had bought into. As he looked out from the high towers of Corfe Castle, on one of his visits down from London, he saw a carpet of green pastures and lush deciduous woods. Below him was the village of Corfe, built from the elegant grey limestone hewn from the local quarries. But just beyond the horizon, out of view, the land suddenly cascaded away. Here, beneath, were fearsome jagged cliffs and treacherous rocks. Here the rapid tides could cut you off in minutes. In such a place, the distance between bucolic calm and mortal danger could be terrifyingly small.

———

At one point during Charles's Personal Rule, Attorney-General Bankes found himself dealing with one of the king's more comically disgruntled subjects. In 1635, Charles had been offended by the English people's all too frequent recourse to bad language, so he had issued a proclamation against 'profane swearing and cursing'.[26] Unfortunately, Thomas Paynell of Essex was having none of it. Paynell had been in conversation with two relatives, and evidently his potty-mouth had caused them some unease, so one of them, named James Flag, had told him off. What happened next is obscure, but whatever it was it ended with Paynell sitting in Bankes's office in London, denying that he ever said 'he cared not a fart for the King's proclamation for the suppressing profane swearing or cursing, nor a turd for the said James Flag's authority'.[27]*

As pleasingly burlesque as this was, there were others whose words were much more dangerous. 'King James was a wise and learned king,' allowed another subject, 'but King Charles wants a good head-piece.'[†28] 'Our kingdom never prospered since a Scot governed,' said one disgruntled gentleman. Charles himself was made aware, and sent off an order to Bankes, personally endorsed with his official signature, the 'sign manual', demanding prosecution.[29] Then there was Bankes's most notorious case of all. It was in 1637, and it related to three famous Puritans: William Prynne, Henry Burton, and John Bastwick.

Prynne was another lawyer, and a rather unlikeable, priggish fellow. He had caused a stir back in 1634 for writing a tract that contained the ungracious accusation that women who acted in plays were 'notorious whores'. Charles was offended – after all his queen liked to act in the great masques at court – and the wheels of prosecution were put into action, then led by Bankes's predecessor William Noy. Prynne was convicted by Star Chamber for seditious libel and sentenced to have his ears cut off. The unpleasant task was only partially done, with just the tops of Prynne's ears hacked away, though it must have been bloody enough.[30] He was then sent to prison, where he continued to write, and in 1637, he was arraigned again for yet more seditious Puritan polemic – this time with Burton and Bastwick too. All were brought by Bankes before Star Chamber, and all were convicted, imprisoned, and ordered to lose their ears. Bankes's prosecution claimed that the men's writings tended 'to the raising of faction and sedition' among the people, 'who otherwise would be obedient to your majesty's government'.[31] Charles was furious to learn that Prynne's ears had

---

*Fortunately for Paynell, his accuser, Flag, evidently had form. He was an innkeeper in Hedingham Castle, and – as his neighbours reported to Bankes – 'hath been of a very lewd and ill behaviour, a common swearer and blasphemer, one making a scoff at religion' and 'very contentious amongst his neighbours'. Paynell, they thought, was 'much wronged'.

†In the archaic sense, meaning skull or cranium; the implication being that he is stupid.

not been fully sliced off the first time.[32] Meanwhile Bankes, 'who hath ever been esteemed a religious and godly gentleman', was starting to be considered 'very violent against maintainers of the truth'.[33] His role was making him enemies.

Charles didn't really like lawyers either. To him, it was the one career he claimed he couldn't follow, for he could never 'defend a bad, nor yield a good cause'.[34] He needed them, though. The English constitution was a rather misty thing. There were different interpretations of what the arrangements actually were.[35] Most tended to see it as balanced in some way. Yet there was much less agreement as to where precisely lay the fulcrum.

On occasion the Crown allowed, or even encouraged, controversial policies to be tested in the courts. This the government could do because it was broadly confident that the judges would toe the line. After all, they had all been picked by the Crown. Those who did the king's bidding won promotion to the nobility and to high office. Those who didn't were met with disapproval, or possibly even dismissal. The pinnacle of this approach would be 'Ship Money', the most controversial of all of the Crown's financial policies, and something that would become the defining constitutional issue of the decade.

Traditionally, English coastal towns and counties had been obliged occasionally to furnish or finance ships for the Crown.[36] Charles, though, wanted to extend the logic of this to the whole country. Now inland counties were told they needed to pay, too – the money going to the growing Royal Navy. It all made perfect sense: after all, were not those inland counties also benefiting from peace and security? Europe was a dangerous place, and Charles recognised that even in a time of peace, military strength improved the country's diplomatic standing, for, as he put it in one of his maxims, 'The best treaty is with a drawn sword'.[37] A strong navy meant a strong England. But it was a novelty: effectively a new tax. Without Parliament it would be illegal, surely.

Or would it? What if a case could be made on grounds of precedent, or necessity? It would lay bare the foundations of the

English constitution. But perhaps, with the right lawyers, it could
be done.

By 1637, Ship Money was causing significant disquiet so Charles,
naturally, responded by turning to his judiciary. First, he asked
the twelve common law judges to give a ruling in his favour: that
Ship Money was legal. This they did, although privately three had
misgivings.[38] But it didn't end the debate or dissent. 'No honest
man had any hand in the shipping money,' grumbled one man to
a parish meeting in Watford, in a statement that inevitably landed
on Bankes's desk.[39]

Meanwhile, a Buckinghamshire gentleman called John Hampden
had defaulted on a tiny portion of his Ship Money bill. He was
making a point: disputing its legality. It was just the test case that
both Charles and his opponents needed. It would be no less than
a trial of the king's ability to rule effectively without Parliament.

Rex vs *Hampden* was heard before a special tribunal of the twelve
common law judges. On the king's side was John Bankes, joined
by the Solicitor General, Edward Littleton – himself a talented and
moderate lawyer. On Hampden's was Robert Holborne, and one of
the most brilliant dissidents of all Oliver St John.

Between them, Bankes and Littleton drew on a dizzying array of
historical precedents. Their argument was that it sometimes fell to
those in power to act out of necessity, to protect the common good.
Ship Money was one such moment. It was the king's role, as the
'fountain of justice', to protect the realm. Hampden's lawyers, on
the other hand, argued that the current problems in the Channel
did not constitute such a crisis that the usual rules be suspended. St
John accepted that the king was the 'fountain of justice', but claimed
that 'though all justice which is done within the realm flows from
this fountain, yet it must run in certain and known channels'.[40]
To them, it was only when the emergency became critical that the
normal flow could be suspended. As St John argued, this could be
taken to be a moment in which it became impossible to hold the
normal law courts. Self-evidently, in 1637, this was not the case.
After all, he was making his argument from a fully functioning
courtroom in the midst of Westminster Hall. But they also argued

that even in cases of emergency, the king should ideally summon Parliament before levying new taxes.

Bankes's arguments for the government were made over three separate days, in the late autumn and early winter of 1637. Recognising the significance of what was happening, crowds huddled in the airy hall to hear. Speeches were copied down by busy scribes, and sold for as much as 10 shillings on the streets of London.[41] 'The king is lord of the sea,' Bankes professed, but 'the seas are infested with pirates and Turks.' This was clearly an 'imminent danger', he said, after all the king's writ said it was, and this should be enough.[42] In cases of imminent danger, the king could command his subjects to pay for the defence of the realm. But he could also do so when there were 'opinions, rumours, relations, and informations of wars'. It was the anticipation of danger that mattered. As Bankes put it, the king should act 'not in case of *Hannibal ad portas* [Hannibal at the gates], or enemy discovered, or sudden invasion; but upon case of rumours, and in that a danger *might* happen'.[43] It was the king who decided when an emergency existed, not Parliament. This was because he had the special networks of diplomats and spies that gave him the extra information he needed; but it was also because power was innate in an absolute king: 'so inherent in the king's person,' as Bankes put it, that 'it is not any ways derived from the people, but reserved unto the king'.[44]

Here was the crux. The question was: Who had the power to decide when there was an emergency, and to choose what action was required? Was it the king, or was it Parliament? Bankes made the royalist case eloquently. 'This kingdom, it is a monarchy,' he said, 'it consists of head and members, the king is the head.' The head, he continued, 'is furnished with entire power and jurisdiction'.[45] It was an emergency because the king said it was, and it was in the monarch's power to anticipate danger and to act in the public interest.

Summing up, Bankes pushed a forceful argument. 'The king of England, he is an absolute monarch', therefore, he concluded, 'let us obey the king's command by his writ, and not dispute it. He is the first mover amongst these orbs of ours; and he is the circle of this circumference; and he is the centre of us all … he is the soul of this body, whose proper act is to command.'[46] And so Bankes rested.

———

As the twelve judgements were announced, it was clear that Bankes and Littleton had won the king a great victory, but only by the tightest of margins. The majority of the judges – seven – decided for the king. But there were five dissenting voices, of whom two were especially critical. One pointed out that if they, the judges, could declare a tax legal, then effectively this meant they could legislate. They could act in lieu of a Parliament.*

Bankes's triumph, therefore, came at a cost. The minority judgements were widely circulated. Even the pliant judiciary of the 1630s was split. At the same time, in order to win, Bankes and Littleton had argued from a point of absolutism. Ship Money was necessary because this was an emergency. Who decided when the country faced an emergency? The king. It mattered not whether the courts were sitting or not, or whether some latter-day Hannibal really was at the gates. If the king *deemed* that to be the case, then he could tax the English as far as he desired. What Bankes and Littleton had done was to convince the judges that England was, if one looked closely enough, a truly absolute monarchy. 'If we grant ship money,' one critic would write, 'we grant all besides.'[47] The king, when it came down to it, had an absolute right to take his subjects' property as and when he felt that he needed it. To those versed in Roman history, it implied that the English people were little better than slaves, for they had no secure control of their land and goods.[48] More to the point, it

---

*Bankes himself was admit to this within a year. A dissident peer Lord Saye still refused to pay Ship Money. He had his cattle taken away by local officers, so he sued for trespass. In the case that followed, Bankes as Attorney-General argued successfully that Saye's counsel couldn't claim the levy was illegal. It had already been determined by the judges. Parliament, he allowed, could overturn that judgement, but with Ship Money in place, Parliament was of course unlikely to sit.

underlined the viability of Charles's rule without Parliament for the foreseeable future.

Bankes was said to be 'much plauded' for the brilliance of his arguments against Hampden.[49] Charles now held him in great trust. Meanwhile, the money kept coming. Bankes's wife Mary had the cash to buy a necklace of a hundred pearls for one of their daughters, itemised at 24 shillings per pearl, plus a diamond ring, and later some French furniture for her brother. In 1639, the couple had yet another child, a boy named Charles. It was a fittingly loyal statement for a family whom the monarchy had made rich.[50]

But Sir John's day job was getting uglier. The sedition, in particular, was becoming especially nasty now the Scottish rebellion was in full flow. 'The king is deluded, and seduced, and made a baby,' said one dissident in London.[51] Ship Money was generating anger too. Many still considered it illegal, despite the outcome of *Rex* vs *Hampden*. Evidence was uncovered that suggested the Scots were circulating manuscripts against the tax, presumably hoping it would help destabilise the regime.[52] And their message was getting through. 'What the Scots did was for the good of this land,' said one man late in 1639, 'for they stood for a Parliament here.'[53]

––––––

At some point in 1640, Bankes found himself opposed to Oliver St John again, this time not in the courtroom but in the Tower archives. Just as St John was providing a brief, based on medieval precedents, telling the dissident petitioner peers that they could force a Parliament, Bankes was doing the same for the king, reassuring him that they could not. 'The king only may summon Parliaments, dissolve them, adjourn and prorogue them,' Bankes's report concluded.[54] It scarcely mattered, though, for by now the Short Parliament had come and gone, and Charles's army was careering towards defeat against the Scots. A Parliament was coming anyway.

When the Long Parliament first met, on 3 November 1640, Ship Money was one of the most immediate grievances. It 'strikes the *First-born* of every Family, I mean our Inheritance,' said Sir John Culpeper of Kent, for: 'If the Laws give the King Power in any danger of the Kingdom, whereof he is Judge, to impose *what* and *when* he pleases, we owe all that is left to the Goodness of the King, not to the Law.' The urbane and popular Lord Falkland, meanwhile, mocked the idea that England had been in imminent peril, 'in the most Serene, Quiet, and Halcyon Days that could possibly be imagined'. England's most formidable enemies, he noted, were nothing but 'a few contemptible Pirates'.[55]

Royal officers were in danger too. Strafford had been sent to the Tower; Archbishop Laud, the man who more than anything represented Charles's religious policy, had been arrested. Proceedings began against John Finch, the Lord Keeper, but he fled the country. So too did the unpopular secretary of state, Francis Windebank. The judges who had ruled in favour of Ship Money were also under threat. Some considered that they had undermined the law as much as Strafford had.[56] And the resurgent reformists were looking elsewhere.[57] Bankes was told that people were prying into his work. Many of those he had prosecuted, such as Prynne, Burton and Bastwick, were released and celebrated.[58]

Yet Bankes had friends on the other side. He had done legal work for one of the leading Junto peers, Algernon Percy, the Earl of Northumberland. It was also from Northumberland whom Bankes's father had leased his ill-fated fish weir. His most impressive patron, though, was the Earl of Bedford himself, the leading reformist peer. Ironically, when Bedford had been building Covent Garden, Bankes had prosecuted him for doing so without getting the necessary permission from the king. In the end, Bedford settled with a fine way below the economic value of the new piazza. Maybe this was when Bankes and Bedford first made a connection. Remarkably, Mary Bankes's merchant father also lent the rich earl money, quite possibly to help pay this building fine.[59] Bedford likely cultivated Bankes in the 1630s, for it was always sensible to have the ear of the Attorney-General.* Now the favours could be returned.

---

*In April or May 1635, Bedford paid a £2,000 fine to the Crown for building at Covent Garden, while in May, Ralph Hawtrey had £1,300 lent out to him. It seems possible that Bankes helped Bedford find the money he needed to pay the fine.

So it was that Bankes, far from facing ruin, found himself promoted. With the old one on the run, Charles needed a new Lord Keeper. He offered the role to Edward Littleton, who had recently leapfrogged his old senior, Bankes, to become Lord Chief Justice of the Common Pleas. That left the latter role vacant, and so it was given to Bankes. No doubt, after everything, Bankes was something of a compromise – a helpful link between the reformists and the king. As someone with friends on both sides, Bankes was exactly the kind of person who would be crucial in the coming months. He might even be a bridge, between royalists and reformers. He lay in the middle. Between the sow's ear and the silken purse, as someone perceptive had once said.

―――――

Before becoming Lord Chief Justice, Bankes was made a 'serjeant-at-law': a member of an ancient order of senior lawyers. As a serjeant, he could wear the 'coif', a tight skullcap. It was a prestigious garment: those who wore the coif were not expected to doff it to anyone, not even the king. His sponsors were Northumberland and Bedford, as well (slightly incongruously) as the ten-year-old Prince of Wales.[60] As Lord Chief Justice, Bankes took an oath, too, that he would 'serve our sovereign lord the king and his people', give equal justice to all, 'rich and poor', and that he would 'truly and justly counsel' the king.[61] When Bankes was Attorney-General, he was effectively a servant of the king and the government; now – as Lord Chief Justice – he was more of a trusted advisor. He was added to the Privy Council too, an honour not always given to those in his new role.[62]

Even so, Bankes's great masterpiece was in ruins, for Parliament was busy dismantling Ship Money and overturning the judgement in *Rex* vs *Hampden*. Then, on 23 January 1641, Charles himself spoke at Whitehall's Banqueting House, disavowing previous 'illegal' taxes.[63] The whole thing would eventually bring a moment of piquant irony for Bankes. One of his new tasks as Lord Chief Justice was to deputise for Lord Keeper Littleton as Speaker of the House of Lords when the latter was indisposed. Littleton was not always a healthy man, so when called, Bankes would preside from the famous 'woolsack', and it was he who sat there on 26 February, when the order was passed to 'vacate' the Ship Money judgement. The next morning, with Littleton still absent, various documents relating to Ship Money – writs, warrants, and judgements – were brought to the Lords by the Master of the Rolls, followed by other senior legal personages, including Bankes. This procession would bow three times before they came to the bar of the house and three times within the bar. They would then lay the records on the empty woolsack. After this, the documents would be passed to the Clerk of Parliament and placed on his table, while the Latin *vacat** was read, and the clerk took a pen and scored a great cross through all the records in question. It was a ritual that underlined Parliament's supremacy over the judges, reinforced by a declaration that the Ship Money proceedings had been 'against the Great Charter [Magna Carta] and therefore void in law'.[64]

Nor was this all. Parliament also ordered that the assize judges would announce the illegality of Ship Money on their winter circuits. The assizes were held twice a year, with central judges arriving in each county and presiding over the most serious criminal trials – often those charges which carried the penalty of death. They were also an avowedly political occasion: a moment in which the whims of the central government could be conveyed to ordinary people in the provinces. As Lord Chief Justice, Bankes was assigned to ride the 'Norfolk' circuit, covering much of the east of England. The first stop was Buckinghamshire: John Hampden's county.[65]

———

The pace of reform was now unstoppable. In February, Charles had reluctantly passed the Triennial Act, ordering regular parliaments. Next came the Strafford trial, and the Attainder Bill. Suckling's plot had blown. Bedford was dying. Now the radicals in the Junto,

*annulment.

joined at last by Bedford's former employees Oliver St John and John Pym, were pushing for Strafford's death.

Then, on 7 May, the Attainder finally passed the House of Lords, and the next day it was ready to take to the king.

It was one of many days that the Lord Keeper was ill, leaving John Bankes on the woolsack. So it was Bankes who would go to see the king. Now he would have to act as intermediary; between a revolutionary Parliament, and a defeated and humiliated king.

On the coach journey to Whitehall, Bankes and the other delegates from Parliament were accompanied by a huge crowd. Bankes carried two bills: one preventing Charles from dissolving Parliament without its consent, the other convicting Strafford of treason. Between them, they constituted a bruising defeat of Charles's monarchy.

As the men met with Charles at the great Italianate Banqueting House, chants could be heard outside for 'Justice! Justice!' Before the king, Bankes fell to his knees. He requested that Charles assent to the bills, 'in respect of the distractions and dangers of this present time'. Charles, it was said, looked at him 'very sadly'.[66]

All that remained was for the king to make his decision. He asked for time. When news filtered out that he had stalled, those gathered outside seethed with anger. For a moment it seemed like they might even try to storm the palace.

'Upon the Word of a King,' Charles had written to Strafford just two weeks earlier, 'you shall not suffer in Life, Honour, or Fortune.'[67] Now that king was under immense pressure to change his mind. Over the weekend, Charles consulted with his bishops. One of them, John Williams, a man Charles thoroughly disliked, told him to, 'submit in judgement to those learned in the law'.[68] On Sunday, he met his Privy Council, with Bankes in attendance, and they seem to have advised him to assent. Charles was reported to be in tears at the council table. The king's nephew Charles Louis, the Prince-Elector Palatine, was in favour of Strafford's death too.[69] With such counsel, and with the people still massing outside, Charles agreed, at last, to both bills.

Strafford was now approaching death. At one point he had called upon Balfour, the Lieutenant of the Tower, and offered him £20,000 to escape, plus to help arrange a good marriage for his daughter.[70] Balfour refused.

And so, on 12 May 1641, with vast crowds gathering in the streets and fields in and around London, the Earl of Strafford ascended a scaffold on Tower Hill, and was beheaded.

It was the dawn of a new England. Or so it was supposed to be.

4

These Preposterous Times

On the last day of May 1641, a stork flew along the Thames and perched on the top of St Stephen's Chapel, the old medieval building in which sat the House of Commons. It was an unusual occurrence, even at a time when Westminster was surrounded by fields, rough grasslands, and oozy marshes.

The spindly legged bird must, therefore, have been a sign, and the accepted reading was that it foretold peace and political calm. There had been a clash of ideas, and Charles I had lost. Now, as an English spring reached its warmest weeks, a programme of reforming legislation could be pursued with vigour. This had been an '*annus mirabilis*' – 'a wonderful year of God's mercies to England' – a year of 'renewal': *renovatio*.[1] The key now was to consolidate the gains and to finish things off. Now that Strafford was dead, and Parliament's position secured, members could continue on their cheery business of reforming the state, weeding out abuses in the Church, and finally putting King Charles's government on sound footing through grants of impeccably legal taxation.

But it wasn't just Parliamentarians who were optimistic. Both sides could now see a path to supremacy. On the afternoon of Strafford's execution, Charles had summoned the Scots negotiators – who were in London to discuss the treaty between king and Covenanters – to Whitehall. Here, to their great surprise, they found the king 'in a very good temper'.[2] The reason, it seems, was that he now had a plan. If he could finally make peace with the Scots, then he could drastically change the balance of power in England. Strafford had been a block to a final settlement in both countries, and now that was gone. Moreover, to achieve the earl's execution, the Junto had taken radical courses. As the summer progressed, the fear of this radicalism was beginning to reconcile people to the king's cause. For Charles, it meant he could hope for a restoration of his fortunes, maybe even revenge. He could see his own chance of renewal.

————

Charles had suffered many defeats. One of the most smarting was in the personnel of his government. The cluster of offices in the royal household, the government, the military, and the judiciary, all backed by the Privy Council, were central to the day-to-day running of the state. And they were always appointed by the monarch.

In the early seventeenth century, there had been some tentative moves by Parliament – whose role was traditionally centred on legislation and revenue-raising – to take on some oversight of the government. It had 'censured' minor Crown servants, and it also on occasion discussed removing them by acts of 'Attainder' – the same process that had once done for Thomas Cromwell and in 1641 would be used to kill Strafford.[3] Then, in the 1620s, Parliament revived the old medieval procedure of 'impeachment', whereby officers who committed offences were prosecuted by the House of Commons and tried by the Lords. The most celebrated target of that decade had been the king's favourite, Buckingham, but impeachments had also been pursued against, for example, a Lord Treasurer (arguably the leading government office) and a Lord Chancellor.[4]

The trouble was, the experience of the 1620s had shown that it was very hard to make impeachment work without the support of the king. Other means of getting the right people into government, and the wrong people out, were therefore necessary. In 1641, the Junto had attempted to encourage and cajole Charles into appointing fellow reformists to government office. In return for financial support, they managed to get key supporters put in positions of trust. Petitioner peers like Essex, Bedford, Saye and

Mandeville were added to the Privy Council, as – eventually – was the radical Warwick. Oliver St John, the leading Junto lawyer, was made Solicitor General. Other appointments – such as Pym's as Chancellor of the Exchequer – had been rumoured to follow.

Charles had long suspected that this was the ultimate aim of most of the Junto men. In his mind they were a group of would-be courtiers who were angry at being excluded in the 1630s, so when he dangled office before them, they would stop disrupting his government and fall into line. Indicative of this view is what would happen that summer when the position of Lord Chamberlain became vacant. Charles didn't pass the role to a royalist. Instead, he gave it to Essex, a radical Junto man. Charles's aim, no doubt, was to buy Essex off. But in trying to do so, he showed a fundamental misunderstanding of his enemies; for they were much less venal than he supposed, or was used to. They believed in their cause.

The Junto were linked by many ties: some were related, others joined by business interests. The earls of Essex and Warwick were cousins; the slippery Earl of Holland was Warwick's brother. Mandeville had married Warwick's daughter, Anne. Many, like Lord Saye, Lord Brooke, and John Pym, had been involved in a failed Puritan colonial venture in the 1630s. But it was ideology, more than anything, which held them together.

For the most part the Junto were Puritans. Warwick, for example, had sponsored a network of pious Puritan ministers. Saye had turned his local Oxfordshire town of Banbury into something approaching a 'Godly Commonwealth'. More to the point, during the 1630s, many had come close to leaving for America, such was the religious climate in England under Charles I and Archbishop Laud. A few of them actually *had* left the country, though not always across the Atlantic.

Essex's path to becoming a radical Junto peer was particularly remarkable. His father, Robert Devereux, 2nd Earl of Essex, had been Queen Elizabeth's dashing favourite, but had launched a quixotic rebellion in London, and ended his days on the block. The young Essex had remained close to the court, but his heritage had earned him repeated mocking by the late Prince Henry.

On one occasion, the two had fallen to blows when the prince reminded Essex of his father's treachery, so the earl hit him with a tennis racket. Then, aged twenty-two, Essex suffered an even greater humiliation. His glamorous wife, Frances Howard, who was also trying to poison him, got the law courts to declare him impotent thus annulling their marriage. From then on, Essex was a laughing stock, so he joined the army. As it happened, his ex-wife (and her new husband) would soon be convicted of the murder of a diplomat, Sir Thomas Overbury, whom she had also been poisoning. For Essex, meanwhile, fighting against the forces of Catholicism allowed him to steadily regain face. It also meant he spent much time in the Netherlands, living under a republican government, and he seems to have been impressed.[5]

It was often peers like Essex, Warwick, Northumberland and their more junior fellows, like Saye and Mandeville, who would be credited with leadership of the Junto. Such were the mores of the times: England was a hierarchical society, and people often looked to the aristocracy for direction. They were joined, though, by more modest allies; men who had risen to prominence through talent, more than titles. As the crisis developed, the Commons men would play an equally critical role. Such was their force that Pym, with savage irony, came to be mocked as a would-be monarch. 'King Pym', his enemies called him.

Like Pym, the Junto men in the Commons often had training in the law. Some were veterans of the struggles of the 1620s or the 1630s. There was John Hampden, for example, who had opposed Ship Money; and Oliver St John, his lawyer. And there was Denzil Holles, one of the three men who had held the Speaker down in his chair back in 1629. Many, again, were Puritans, though of varying levels of intensity. Some were content with Charles's recent jettisoning of Laud and the Ceremonialists. Some wanted to take things much further. Pym, for his part, was relatively moderate on church affairs, though he also carried a burning fear of 'papism'.

Anti-Catholicism was, of course, a general pathology of the English in the 1640s, but for some of the Junto it was more all-consuming than it was for most. The very nastiest bigotry was usually resisted. When Pym suggested to Parliament that Catholics be forced to wear badges, he was simply laughed at. On another occasion, the Ulsterman Sir John Clotworthy, joined by Yorkshire's Sir John Hotham, moved that captured Catholic priests and Jesuits be castrated, but Pym himself immediately opposed the idea, thinking it quite insane.[6] Nonetheless, it is impossible to understand the Junto without grasping their paranoid fears about Catholics, the pope, and the 'papist plot'. It was a thread that ran through their opposition to Ceremonialism in the Church and through their desire to curb royal power.

There were some Junto men for whom religion was rather less of a driving force. Henry Marten, the most radical constitutional reformist, appears to have been a conspicuous outlier. He was someone who, in the summer of 1641, would be prepared to present a petition to Parliament on behalf of lay Catholics. The fact was, he probably preferred horse-racing and cavorting to churchgoing, and no lesser figure than King Charles considered him nothing but a 'whoremonger' (Oliver Cromwell, some years later, would concur). Marten was about as close as the Junto came to outright republicanism, though there were other radical members – the so-called 'fiery spirits' like William Strode and his friend Walter Erle. Yet the main unifying factor, more than anything, was a really quite thorough reform of the constitution. And here it all came back to that initial question: Who controls the government?

———

It is a reassuringly modern idea: that representative institutions should control governments. One might even see it as a fundamental characteristic of democracy. Where a legislature today is able to vet presidential appointments, or if a government falls because it loses the confidence of lawmakers, it is a version of the ideas put forward in 1641 by the English parliamentary Junto. Some at the time saw the Junto's agenda as 'democratic', meaning that it placed power in the hands of the representatives of the people (few, as yet, pointed out how *un*representative Parliament really was). The Junto did not frame it in this way, however. Rather, they argued that they had precedent on their side. At some point in 1641, Pym would be found in the archives of the Tower of London, digging out medieval examples of Parliament making government appointments.[7] If he could prove this had happened in the past, then it could be resurrected in the present.

Another driving force was fear. The Junto realised that controlling the government was the best guarantee they could get against reprisals by the king. They also made a more obviously religious argument: one that was anything but modern or liberal. They claimed that such control was necessary, in the last analysis, to make sure power didn't fall to 'papists'.

It is a term we encounter with startling regularity in seventeenth-century politics: a byword for all that was bad. It is also one which we need to handle with extreme care, for all is not quite as it seems. For one thing, blaming 'papists' for bad government was not necessarily taken literally. Rather, it could be a politically correct way of criticising government policy without explicitly impugning the king. It was a linguistic sleight of hand, that avoided a charge of sedition. The term also had a much more complicated meaning than just adherence to the pope. It implied despotism, absolutism, and military tyranny. Thus Strafford could be widely considered a 'papist', even though he hated Catholics – because he was a tyrant. Yet the fact the English used this word as their shorthand for despotism was instructive in itself. There was always, however noble the constitutional principles were, more than a whiff of sectarianism too. One of the motivating factors behind the Junto, and one of the ways they justified their constitutional power grab, was always a fairly basic desire to save England from going back to Rome, and from the influence of the pope.

And there had, of course, been many signs of the growth of that influence of late. The rise of the Ceremonialists in the Church had been one – with their rituals and adornments, all reminiscent of pre-Reformation times. There had been adherents of the old faith at court, too, during the 1630s, who were seen as carrying a malign influence. But there was one person who caused particular worry. For, right at the centre of the state – near the pinnacle of the royal family itself – there was an avowed, open and unapologetic Catholic.

———

Queen Henrietta Maria, more than anyone, had always felt alien in England. Her hosts had made sure of this.[8] Physically smaller even than her diminutive husband, she made up for this with a forceful, even ferocious, personality. Being a woman in seventeenth-century England was tough; being a Frenchwoman and a Catholic, only made things worse. And though one might expect the fact of being queen brought some compensations, in reality it made life harder; for Henrietta Maria was constantly in the public glare. It wasn't something that sat especially well with a young royal whose father had been assassinated by one of his own subjects.

The queen had surrounded herself with Catholic courtiers and a Scots Catholic confessor. She had, by the terms of her marriage treaty, her own private chapels in which she was allowed to go to mass. She was attended by monks in full garb, who could be seen on the streets of London for the first time since the Reformation.[9] But the queen was proud of her faith and her heritage. She was a Bourbon princess, no less. She was a daughter of the great Henri IV, the man who had ended the French Wars of Religion. It gave her a very different set of priorities to many of the English political class. The niceties of the English common law were of little interest to someone nurtured in the French tradition. And why should they be? France was a European superpower; England, though a nation of great wealth, had a government mired in perpetual debt. While France was able to face up to the might of Spain, England these days could barely keep a navy together, and had only recently been humiliated in the field by rebels from Scotland, of all places. The queen was cosmopolitan and consciously continental. She looked to Paris and to Rome; to the great chateaus and monasteries and universities of Europe. Not to the petty squabbles of Oxford and Cambridge, and certainly not to the English law courts.

She and Charles had endured a difficult start to their marriage. When she first arrived in England, Henrietta Maria was a fifteen-year-old princess, while Charles was a haughty young king. He was nervous in the company of the opposite sex and in an obsessive friendship with the Duke of Buckingham. Neither had she been Charles's first choice of bride. In 1623, in a moment that combined high farce and political scandal, Charles and Buckingham had eloped to Madrid to woo the Spanish Infanta. The mission failed, and one consequence was a diplomatic realignment in which England sought to cosy up to Spain's enemy, France. Charles was duly expected to do his duty for the dynasty, and a marriage to the French princess was arranged.

Both of them were little more than diplomatic pawns, and to begin with the couple argued bitterly, Charles sometimes showing his wife a nasty and cruel streak. On one occasion, he petulantly cancelled a Christmas play that the queen and her ladies had been rehearsing for ages. On another, the French ambassador had to be summoned to settle a bitter row over whether or not it was raining. The worst argument saw Charles summon Henrietta to come and see him, and her refuse, pleading a toothache. Unsatisfied, the king stormed to her chambers, where he found her and her servants 'dancing and cavorting'. Furious, Charles informed her that the servants must be sent back to France. After a period of horrified silence, the diminutive queen went into a rage, breaking windows with her bare hands.[10]

But slowly things improved, and when Buckingham was assassinated in 1628, Charles's horror and despair helped consolidate something that canny observers had already seen. He and his wife were beginning, quite unexpectedly, to fall in love. Soon it was said that he was 'with the queen every night', and come the 1630s the two were thoroughly enjoying themselves.[11] After the tragic death of their first son, who was born and died the same day in 1629, there was a string of healthy children, starting with Prince Charles (born 1630) and Princess Mary (1631), and followed by James, Duke of York (1633), and then Elizabeth (1635). Two more then died young (Anne and Catherine), before Henry, Duke of Gloucester, was born healthy in 1640.

At court, there was art and music. There were the great masques, which brought together the words of Ben Jonson, the stage direction of William Davenant, and the set designs of Inigo Jones. There was painting – with Rubens and Van Dyck setting up in London – and courtly poetry. Architecture flourished too, with Inigo Jones emerging as the leading exponent of the new English Palladianism. The Banqueting House at Whitehall was the greatest example, but there were also delightfully proportioned constructions at Greenwich and at Kew, all in a new fashion that brought continental elegance to muddy old England.

Yet now it was all under mortal threat, from Parliamentarians and lawyers and Puritans, few of whom would know a quadrille from a sonatina. 'The voice of God,' said one placard placed outside Parliament that spring, 'is the cry of the people.'[12] In such times, with such people, one was never truly safe. More than once the queen found herself peering from the glass windows of Whitehall, out onto a mass of faces gathering in King Street below, protesting or petitioning. She remembered all too well what had happened to her father. No wonder she worried about the threat of the populace.

She wasn't the only observer who saw it this way, either. In London, one of the keenest political spectators was Giovanni Giustinian, the representative to Charles from the Most Serene Republic of Venice. To this rather irascible forty-year-old Italian, recent events in this strange little nation already suggested a constitutional earthquake. 'The wisest,' he reported back to his masters on the Adriatic, 'freely predict that this monarchy will soon be turned into a completely democratic government.' Charles's 'popularity with his people is clearly waning,' he wrote.[13] And Giustinian was not imagining it. There had been something intangible. A change to the mood, more than anything else. A subtle shift that you might see in a truculent gesture, or an irreverent phrase. It had been so for a while. A 'libel', a short, scandalous paper text, was being passed around that cast serious aspersions on the queen: 'the king was a Scot', it noted, 'the queen was French, and their children were Germans' – not referring to their nationality, but to the fact they were all sired by her Master of the Horse, Henry Jermyn, 'who was supposed to be too familiar with the queen'.[14] The courts were picking up cases of dangerous sedition from the people too, more menacing than those Bankes had found in the 1630s. There was Thomas Stafford, for example, who was indicted in January 1641, after he allegedly went to an alehouse one Sunday in the Yorkshire village of Youlthorpe and, 'high flown in drink', alleged that the king and queen attended mass together and that such a king was 'worthy to be hanged'.[15] Who could be sure that such violent talk wouldn't develop into physical attacks – even assassination attempts?

The new truculence had sprung, hydra-like, from the population itself, driven by a remarkable new thirst for discussion and debate. No longer were the people silent. No more did they self-censor. Now farm labourers opined about matters of state as they wiped the sweat from their brows and swigged on small beer in the cornfields. Servant girls chewed over the latest news as they wandered out of town to the fields and hung their washing out to dry on hedges and fences. Alehouses and taverns were sites of electric political discussion. People would bring printed pamphlets and manuscript newsletters and read them aloud and discuss them over pots of ale and pints of wine. Sometimes, discussion would end in hot disputes, even drunken brawls. Other times a solitary drinker would quietly rise from his table, pay his shot, and skulk off to bring news of radical talk to the authorities.

Just occasionally, perhaps in an upper room in an inn or tavern, small religious groups might meet, hear sermons, discuss the Bible, and pray. Every so often, people might clamber up onto a tub and preach, to a chorus of 'amens'. Occasionally, a window was cast open onto the busy street outside and the sermon became a more public affair. The most notorious such moment had been when Samuel How, a cobbler by trade, stood on a barrel in a room at the Nag's Head, near Coleman Street, and gave an extempore sermon while a crowd gathered outside. It was an event that passed into London folklore, replicated in a particularly famous woodcut image, even though How himself had died – excommunicated – in September 1640, and had been buried by the highway in Shoreditch.[16]

Since the last days of Queen Elizabeth, there had been those, like How, who had advocated a much more organic, grass-roots form of Church organisation. Some wanted the formation of semi-independent congregations within the official Church; others argued for complete separation, as did the *Mayflower* Pilgrims. Such ideas were amorphous and at times almost chaotic. Referring to the movement as 'Independency' obscures a lot. To many conservatives, who sometimes saw all this as a baleful and wholly predictable outgrowth of mainstream Puritanism, the radicals were simply referred to as 'sectaries' or – after the Elizabethan separatist Robert Browne, as 'Brownists'.

Whatever we call them, such groups suddenly bloomed from about 1640, and one of the most remarkable aspects of this was the appearance of a number of radical lay preachers. Those with no formal training, who may never even have set eyes on the hallowed quads of Oxford or Cambridge, might now feel a spirit that compelled them to share the Word. One lay preacher John Spencer argued in print that this was a thoroughly good thing, celebrating 'the lawfulness of every man's exercising his gift as God shall call him thereunto'.[17] God's spirit, he claimed, was not just vested in the educated and the ordained, but in anyone who heard the call, including women.

Preaching started to appear at some quite unexpected places too. There had always been public sermons in England, most famously at St Paul's Cross in London, where great crowds would gather in the old courtyards to hear stirring orators with billowing gowns. Now, though, 'mechanic' preachers – those who worked manual trades – started to appear in alehouses, taverns, barns, fields and wild heathlands. Every space was sacred, they said, not just those airy old stone buildings that some called churches. A London stationer in June, for example, said he would rather 'hear a sermon under a tree than out of a pulpit'.[18] John Rogers, a glover, reminded his audience in Goat Alley in London that: 'Our saviour chose a homely stable to be born in, and I dare avouch that his word is never the worse for being taught in a barn, a stable, or any such like place.'[19] There was even – so Parliament was sternly informed – a group that who claimed that churches were no more holy than toilets.[20]

By the summer and autumn of 1641, complaints of these 'pestilent sects couched in London' were common.[21] 'In these preposterous times,' one conservative would write, 'many vices are predominant, but amongst all the brood of vices, there is none so great, there is none grown to that height, there's none so leprous as this of Puritanism.'[22] Another writer attacked 'presumptuous tradesmen', including shoemakers, cobblers, tailors, button-makers, coachmen, and sellers of bottled ale, 'who dare to climb up into pulpits, and make themselves bold ambassadors of the great king of kings'.[23] Ambassador Giustinian was particularly disgusted. England, he thought, was paying the price for leaving religion 'to the ignorant comprehension of the common people'.[24]

Equally repulsive to conservatives was the role played by women. In Puritan circles, women had always been enthusiastic participants in religious piety, but the new environment provided opportunities to do so in a much more public way. A number of London sects appeared in which women debated, voted, and prophesised.[25] 'Quite recently,' reported a rather taken aback Giustinian, 'some women have held forth from the pulpits, bringing forth a new faith before a numerous concourse of people.'[26]

We usually, alas, have to rely on hostile male comments to learn about women preachers. One summer squib, for example, titillated readers with a 'Discoverie' of six women preachers, giving names, places of abode, and some information about their practises. There was Anne Hempstall of Holborn, who had an assembly of 'bibbing gossips' who were more interested 'upon the strong water bottle' than they were in Anne's religious instruction. One of her audience, though, was Mary Bilbrowe of St Giles in the Fields, wife of a bricklayer who did then hold her own meeting. Other examples were Joan Bauford of Faversham, who argued that wives might divorce their husbands, and Arabella Thomas, a Welsh woman living in Salisbury, who told ministers that only 'painful' (i.e. devout) people like herself went to heaven. Moreover, if they were not willing to preach twice on Sundays, then soon a black raven by day and a white owl by night would appear and scratch out their eyes.[27]

Naturally, to impugn these earnest religious enthusiasts, men reached for the most sexualised language they could find. Prayer meetings were really little more than mass orgies, critics implied. Or they simply said it outright. Gathering in the woods and remote places allowed Brownists to enjoy a spot of 'zealous lusting' or 'voluptuous wantonness'. Radicals, it was said, 'have drawn divers honest men's wives in the night time to frequent their assemblies', leading 'many chaste virgins to become harlots'. And such 'hot, private, lusty and promiscuous meetings', so the jokes went, led to the conception of monstrous children. It was all too much of a tempting opportunity for a grubby innuendo, too. One pamphlet told of the 'zealous brethren' who 'have stood stiffly for the cause, as the sisters can testify if they please'.[28] 'Now you must understand,' it was reported of an alleged gathering of radicals in Surrey, that the worshippers 'have certain days which are dedicated unto Saints as they call them, as to Ovid, who wrote the Art of Loving, to Priapus, the first bawdy Butcher that ever did stick pricks in flesh, and make it swell.'[29] The conclusion, ultimately, was that to cure women of the 'strange madness' of 'expounding scripture', they needed stronger discipline from their husbands.[30]

If the social order, even the patriarchy, was under threat, then a conservative backlash was always inevitable. The sense of crisis was heightened, too, by an ongoing debate, including in Parliament, about Church reform. In particular, a question mark was hanging over England's bishops.

The hierarchy of bishops and archbishops had been part of the English Church since its foundation: part of the country's fabric for a millennium, and an established pillar of the social order. Take them away and who knows what kind of radical agenda might be unleashed. 'No bishops, no king,' James I had famously claimed, and there were plenty now who repackaged his arguments with greater eloquence but rather less pith. Sir Thomas Aston, for example, thought the bishops to be the 'pillars of our state that prop up the regulated fabric of this glorious monarchy'.[31]

There were others, though, who thought they were pompous and dangerous, of very questionable biblical justification, and politically annoying. After all, they were direct royal appointees who had control of Church discipline, while twenty-six senior prelates (including the two archbishops) sat in the House of Lords. So the questions arose: How should their role be reformed? Should they be removed from their secular functions, for example, such as their seats in the House of Lords? Or maybe they should be abolished outright, as they had been in Scotland? It could have been an arcane debate about Church structure and government, but instead it became an argument about the very soul of England.

The issue had been dramatically pushed by two forces: the Scots Covenanters, who wanted the English to follow them in abolishing episcopacy; and a broader popular movement for reform. This latter had been displayed spectacularly in London in December 1640, when a petition calling for the removal of the bishops, 'Root and Branch', appeared. Many Junto MPs took a much more moderate line than this – calling for the reform of the bishops rather than their abolition – but they found themselves allied, temporarily at least, with those who had a considerably more radical agenda.

To those of moderate opinion, such talk of abolition was dangerous. It was yet more evidence that political reform had gone quite far enough already. The 'root and branchers' looked like they might be swinging the axe not just against bishops, but against the whole social order. It was a thin edge to a much bigger wedge. 'I look upon episcopacy,' said Edmund Waller, an MP and a poet, 'as a counterscarp or outwork, which if it be taken by this assault of the people ... we may in the next place have as hard a task to defend our property.' More to the point, if the claim was that poor people had suffered thanks to abuses by bishops, then 'you may be presented with a thousand instances of poor men that have received hard measure from their landlords'.[32] The same arguments used against bishops could make the case for a much broader social revolution. They were, in other words, extremely dangerous.

There was some remarkably aggressive language used against the bishops, too. These were not bumbling and donnish ecclesiastics; they were the footsoldiers of Satan. The poet John Milton was one of those making forceful calls for reform, for he saw a 'universal rottenness and gangrene in the whole function'.[33] The bishops, said a Puritan London woodturner, were 'ravening wolves and cunning foxes' threatening God's flock, and a 'stink in the nostrils of all good men that love God'. The popishness of the bishops, went one anti-episcopal jest, was: 'As plain as you can smell a turd from jelly.'[34] The Archbishop of Canterbury, William Laud, meanwhile, was called an 'orc'.[35]

———

It was a toxic debate, and it was part of something much bigger. Something rising from, and feeding into, the greater desire for information and ideas. For there had been a change in England, especially in London. It could be seen in the taverns and the alehouses, and in people's houses and workplaces. Most of all, it was seen in the little shops and stalls that had spread throughout the capital, all selling one thing: books.

The political turmoil of the last twelve months had been accompanied and fed by a sudden explosion in the availability of print. At the price of a pot of ale, you could now buy a pamphlet full of contested ideas and vigorous debate. It was exhilarating, though it wasn't a result of new technology. The basics of the print industry were the same in 1641 as they had been in the 1630s. And the growth in literacy had been going on for some time. Since at least the beginning of the sixteenth century the proportion of people – men and women – who could read had grown substantially, thanks to better education, greater wealth, and a heightened supply of, and demand for, printed matter. In the parishes, as the state became a more regular part of day-to-day life – telling people, for example, to record all baptisms, marriages, and deaths in a 'register', and enforcing a permanent local tax for the poor – people needed to learn to read and write to take part.[36]

These were long-term developments. What changed after 1640 was that the appetite for information and ideas suddenly grew, and the ability of the state to control print collapsed. In the 1630s, in theory at least, the censorship regime had been brutally restrictive, with the feared courts of Star Chamber and High Commission keeping an eagle eye on dissent. Bishops could veto publication, and those who printed illicit books were liable to prosecution, imprisonment, and savage bodily mutilation.*

In 1640 and 1641, though, as the king retreated against the onslaught of a reformist Parliament, the principal institutions charged with controlling print were hollowed out. The courts of High Commission and Star Chamber were abolished in the summer of 1641. Victims of the previous censorship regime, like Prynne, Burton, and Bastwick, had been released, reprieved, and, in some cases, garlanded through London. There was more to write about, too, for people wanted to grasp the current situation, while political actors wanted to get across their point of view. It wasn't just the sudden absence of censorship. It was more like a great conversation had opened up about the future of the country.

Or maybe that's too positive. For there was another way of thinking about it. Many saw this not as polite table talk, but as a jarring cacophony. 'Foul ink', wrote one commentator, was being 'besquittered and besquirted' in 'roguish pamphlets'.[37] Books were distracting and disruptive. At Isleworth in Middlesex, so the minister complained, there was an attorney, a Catholic who had been seen at the queen's chapel, who 'commonly brings pamphlets to the church and reads them in time of divine service'. Once he was seen passing a ballad to a gentlewoman in the next pew, and one Sunday in May, he interrupted the sermon by suddenly laughing and jeering, then went back to reading his latest pamphlet, refusing

---

*The most notorious case was that of Alexander Leighton, a short-statured Scotsman with a yellowish beard, who had published an anti-episcopal tract in 1628. He was pilloried for two hours in a snowstorm, had his left ear hacked off, his back whipped thirty-six times, and his skin branded. He was then hauled back to prison, where he quickly developed a fever, and he was still there in 1640. His case was then taken up in Parliament by a rather earnest backbencher called Oliver Cromwell, and he was released, though when he was it was said he could neither see, nor hear, nor walk.

to stop.[38] In July, an Oxfordshire minister recorded in his diary that 'infinite pasquils and base abusive ballads and trifling pamphlets came forth daily', not to mention 'very rude, uncivil and inhuman trifling babbles'.[39]

Yet whatever its drawbacks, print was politically useful, for all sides. Declarations by king and Parliament could be printed and distributed in ample quantities. Petitions were no longer just produced in manuscripts and left in the hands of the immediate target. Now they were also printed, often as cheap single-sheet texts, available to the most modest of budgets. Parliamentary speeches, too, were sent off to the printers' workshops to be typeset and rolled out for wider consumption: 'tuppenny speeches', they were sometimes called.[40] Certainly, for once, it was a great time to be a writer.

5

The Unquestionable Right of Kings in England

It was shaping up to be a warm spring and summer. The storms of May 1641 had been fierce but now the heat was dry and stale. The meadows were parched.[1] Plague, too, was taking hold in London and spreading outwards. 'God preserve us all,' hoped one in June.[2] The disease was creeping westwards. The same month, the outbreak reached King Street, the long passage that ran from the Charing Cross, past Whitehall Palace, and towards Parliament.

Some saw this deadly and miserable sickness as a scourge from God, others as something wholly avoidable.[3] Plague typically brought strong action from the authorities, and governors often used the royal prerogative to force through controversial quarantine measures and taxes. As recently as 1636 there had been a nasty outbreak which brought a suitably robust response. Then, when plague returned in 1640, it had been the king's Privy Council which had closed London's theatres, and they remained shuttered. So far the outbreak in 1641 hadn't been one of the worst, but no one could see the future, and the Privy Council – which had often taken the lead in plague relief – was a shadow of its former self. There were worries that royal proclamations, which had previously been used to tackle plague, were no longer valid. Parliament, meanwhile, was decidedly sluggish in its response. It would not be until September that the Houses took plague seriously, and then they simply printed out a set of orders based on those previously used by the royal government.[4]

If the capital was lucky, then the outbreak would pass. For now, though, the grip was tightening, and it was an increasingly unattractive place to stay. For the royal family especially, the reasons were mounting for them to simply leave.

Both king and queen were plotting escape: not just to one of their great country mansions, but further away still. To the queen, the health resorts of the Continent beckoned.[5] For Charles – his birthplace. Somewhere he'd left as a small child and to which he had barely ever returned: Scotland. In both cases they hoped not just to escape the diseased and truculent population of London, but to garner support and allies for the coming struggle.

The books, meanwhile, kept coming. Over a hundred texts were being published every month, and the writing of printed squibs was becoming a handy source of income for authors, of whom there suddenly seemed to be swarms. Many of these were fresh out of Oxford or Cambridge, and they had various levels of ethical commitment. Some were poets and playwrights in search of a quick shilling; others had genuine principles; plenty simply enjoyed the verbal sparring. The new literati had their particular hangouts, too, and the tobacco-filled alehouses around Fetter Lane, the Inns of Court, and Fleet Steet became the places you went to get news or secure the services of a hack.[6] Money was there to be made, and of all London's pens, none was more in demand than that of John Taylor, the famous 'Water Poet'.

———

Unlike some of his fellow writers, John Taylor had been around a while.[7] Born in Gloucester in 1578, he was nevertheless a Londoner through and through. He was now in his sixties and had enjoyed a flourishing career. He remembered the times of James I and William Shakespeare. His trade was as a waterman, ferrying people across the Thames. It was hard work and attracted men of physical strength and weather-beaten independence. Yet Taylor was also known for his wit and good manners – a cheery presence on the river, who rose to become one of the King's Watermen – a selective group tasked with carrying royal river-goers from bank to bank. He developed a taste for reading and books, and dabbled in poetry; and unlike so many others, he was good at it.

Taylor's life was amphibious, divided between water and land. So, in a way, was his writing. For he appealed to both the rich and well connected, and to the ordinary folk of London. He was sparky and fleet and – best of all – happy to get into the most vicious of literary spats. He had an entertaining taste for travel, sailing to Hamburg and returning to pen a jolly mocking of the Germans, and to Scotland, after which he was accused of lampooning Ben Jonson. He travelled to Prague, then Hull and on to York. He rowed all the way up the Avon to Salisbury, recounting his journey in jocular rhyme. He had a great eye for a title. One of his early boating tales was called *A Verry Merry Wherry-Ferry Voyage* (1622), while he also penned a verse tract entitled *Laugh, and Be Fat* (1612), a scathing satire on the famous Jacobean traveller Thomas Coryat. There was something of the impresario about Taylor, too. In 1630, he tried to bring a man called Nicholas Wood, 'the Greater Eater of Kent', to London so he could perform gourmandising feats at the Bear Garden before a paying audience. Then in 1639, he scored yet another publishing success with a tract about all different kinds of women: 'good and bad, from the modest to the maddest'.[8] Around the same time he published another misogynistic tract, and the two pamphlets then drew a riposte, *The Womens Sharp Revenge*, which may – in a possibility that says everything about the London print world – actually have been written by Taylor himself. It named its enemy as an author called 'Sir Seldom Sober' and claimed to have been penned by two women called 'Mary Tattle-well' and 'Joan Hit-him-home'.[9]

Alas, though, the political crisis threatened to upend Taylor's merry world. He lived in Southwark, one of the seamier outposts of the capital, where radical preaching and semi-illicit worship was taking hold. One day, Taylor's own church, St Saviour's, was assailed by a group who pulled down its altar rails. So the burly waterman began to fight back. On one occasion, a preacher at

Rotherhithe annoyed him so much that Taylor shouted out that the man should be hanged. He hadn't read the room, for the congregation quickly turned, and only a swift retreat allowed him to avoid a solid thumping.

Taylor was used to living by his oar and his quill, not by his fists, and as a man of his age he will have concluded there were better ways of getting his own back. So that same spring he penned a new, exquisitely virulent little book. Entitled *A Swarme of Sectaries, and Schismatiques*, it attacked 'the strange preaching (or prating) of such as are by their trades Cobblers, Tinkers, Peddlers, Weavers, Sow-gelders, and Chimney-Sweepers'. The title page, using an image which was to become iconic, showed the cobbler Samuel How preaching on a barrel at the Nag's Head tavern.[10]

Among the readers of the *Swarme* was a young ironmonger by the name of Henry Walker. He was horrified, but not in the way he was supposed to be. Walker was from Derbyshire and like so many, his introduction to London life had been as an apprentice, though he had also once been a student in Cambridge. In response to Taylor, he dashed out a squib entitled *An Answer to a Foolish Pamphlet entitled A Swarme of Sectaries*.[11] 'Seeing religion shot at by such a poisoned pistol,' Walker declared, 'I thought it meet to screw out the bullet of thy infamy before it grew rank.' Taylor, it was alleged, was a lascivious dissembler who was in cahoots with the disgraced Archbishop of Canterbury, and could be found dining with him in the Tower.

Taylor's response reached virtuosic depths of scurrility. He accused Walker of pawning his Bible for the price of a drink, and had his printers make up a woodcut image of his antagonist: holding an iron bar for good measure, being shat out of the devil's arse.[12] Whether Walker was offended or not, his response was of a piece. Taylor was ignorant and popish, and – in a remarkably similar woodcut image – this time it was the jolly waterman's time to be depicted with an incontinent devil.[13] Now Taylor was shown on the river in a boat, with the devil crouched over him, shitting in his mouth. Others joined in, too, with one George Richardson, an Irishman, leaping to Taylor's defence, in yet another pamphlet.

He mocked Walker for his lowly origins and included a subsection entitled 'His Religion', leaving it blank.[14]

For the time being this entertaining battle was left to fester. Yet Taylor's sudden burst of creativity was indicative of something of much wider importance. People were getting sick of the sectaries. The conservative backlash was picking up.

———

Taylor was a particular kind of royalist: implacably opposed to dowdy Puritans, and to disorderly freewheelers. If it is impossible to grasp the Junto ideology without anti-Catholicism, then it is equally hard to think about royalism without understanding the backlash against popular preaching. Royalism was a specifically conservative ideology, grounded in a desire to maintain the social order and to bolster it against popular disorder.

There had always been some who had opposed the actions of the Junto. One minister in Northamptonshire, for example, had even very publicly named ten of his pigs after leading reformists: 'parliaments in England never did good', he said, and his hogs were fit to be Parliament men, 'and their sty a fit place for them to sit in'.[15] By the summer of 1641, the implacable reactionaries were joined by others, of a much more moderate hue: those appalled by the political path of the Junto and by what one called 'general increase of open libertinism'.[16]

For many, the turning point had been the Strafford trial. Not only had the killing of the king's minister itself been pursued with a distasteful zeal, but the whole episode had been carried out against a background of mass protest and public anger. 'My Lord of Strafford had not died,' one Londoner had openly boasted, 'if the people had not pressed the Lords in a tumult as they did.'[17] This kind of outdoor politics was a perilous beast, many felt: an insult to the proper way of doing things. One high-profile MP who was now on a more conservative path was George Digby, son of the Earl of Bristol, son-in-law of the late Earl of Bedford, and a key supporter of the Triennial Act. Digby was nonetheless horrified by the populist drift of the Junto. 'I could not have flattered a king,' he had announced, rather grandly, 'And I do not intend now to flatter a multitude.'[18] His newfound royalism earned him rewards, too. In order to protect him from the Junto, who were furious at him turning coat, he was raised by Charles from his seat in the Commons to a place in the House of Lords.

Meanwhile, the new order was proving mightily expensive. To pay off the Scots and English armies, and to fix the hole in the state finances, Parliament had levied a poll tax. Together with their other direct taxes, they were trying to raise around £1 million, roughly four times the annual value of Ship Money, and twice that of any other parliamentary tax burden in English history.[19] Worse, the Junto seemed only partly committed to the only viable lasting solution. This was for Parliament to give Charles the right to collect tonnage and poundage, thus grounding the king's rule in impeccably legal taxation. Pym and his allies were reluctant to allow this, for if Charles got a permanent grant of tonnage and poundage – something he had craved since 1625 – then it might just free his hand to dissolve Parliament and even enact revenge on the Junto. So they blocked it, at least until they were able to put in effect the one, most sweeping constitutional change that they wanted. One that would protect them for good: to win control of the government.

This plan would become a key dividing line, arguably *the* key line. The Junto had successfully ensured perpetual parliaments; they had removed non-parliamentary taxation. All they needed to do now was to take over the king's right to pick his own government – namely the officers of state and the Privy Council. The principle, in Pym's words, would be that officers be appointed 'by those over whom their jurisdiction extended'.[20] In other words, the government would be accountable to the representatives of the people rather than the king. Once the Junto had achieved this, their constitutional revolution would be complete.

But it also fed another kind of royalism. This came from those who had likely opposed Charles's extra-parliamentary taxes as illegal, but now thought it was the Junto who threatened the ancient constitution. They were monarchists, but they were advocates of a balance.[21] They thought Charles had tried to move the fulcrum too far one way. They appreciated that Parliament had corrected that; and now they thought the Junto were lurching too far in the other direction. These 'constitutional' royalists were therefore more and more willing to stand up to the Junto, even on its home turf. Even in Parliament.

The queen's journey to the Continent had now been called off. In the end, Parliament had objected so loudly about the trip that it had to be cancelled. She would spend the summer and autumn stewing in her palace at Oatlands in Surrey, out of London and away from both plague and populace, at least. But there was nothing the Junto could do about the king's proposed trip to Scotland. By late June, his servants had already gone to Edinburgh, and his baggage had been carried down to ships on the East End docks and sent up along the grey North Sea coast.[22] By July, the king was nearly ready to leave.

What he needed was somebody to manage his affairs in the south. To resist the Junto, and maybe – just maybe – to harness that conservative backlash, and turn it into political capital.

The Scotland trip could be delayed no longer. And Charles had found just the man.

———

Edward Nicholas, clerk to the Privy Council, probably felt his best days were behind him. He had been born in Wiltshire in 1593, in a quiet village, the son of a lawyer.[23] His own calling would be administration rather than the law, however. His particular skill was not for the verbal virtuosity of legal arguments, but the intricacies of bureaucracy. He was smart, diligent, and knew how to make the right friends. One of his earliest mentors was Lord Zouche, Lord Warden of the Cinque Ports, who had given Nicholas some most useful advice: 'When a man dealeth with his betters, patience is a great virtue.'[24] Nicholas's secretarial aptitudes were very great: his handwriting was a fine italic, and he created his own form of shorthand. When writing for an audience, he was clear and legible. When writing only for his own consumption, his hand became hasty, spidery, opaque. Nicholas knew that transparency and legibility had their downsides. In service of the state, one had to dance between both worlds: the translucent and the obscure.

Nicholas had once been an MP, although not a very prominent one. He had seen the change in England's religious temper in the 1620s, albeit through a rather idiosyncratic – and dramatic – lens. During one parliamentary recess, in the summer of 1621, Nicholas found himself with Lord Zouche at the latter's estates at Bramshill, in the woody glades of northern Hampshire. One day in July, the Calvinist Archbishop of Canterbury, George Abbot, was visiting to hunt. At one point Abbot fired from his crossbow, aiming to fell one of the park's fat deer. By sheer misfortune, the hurtling bolt struck a park keeper, who died within an hour. It was Nicholas who found the man's bloodied body. After the tragedy Abbot was never the same again, nor did he command the respect of his bishops. It hastened Abbot's eclipse by the rising Ceremonialists, like William Laud.

Nor was this the last piece of bloodshed Nicholas saw. Promoted to the employment of the Duke of Buckingham, Nicholas was with the doomed favourite in August 1628, at Portsmouth, when a knife was plunged through his heart by the assassin, John Felton. Buckingham was able to cry out, 'Zounds! Villain!', but it wasn't clear who had actually struck the fatal blow. The only person who saw the assassin was Nicholas, who thought Felton was a Frenchman. Cries of 'French!' were yelled out by the horrified crowd, as the duke lay in a pool of blood on the floor and Felton skulked away. But the killer misheard them; he thought they were saying his name, so he immediately confessed.[25]

Buckingham was dead, but Nicholas had the talent to withstand such a potentially devastating career setback. The king's Personal Rule proved quietly kind to him, though his rise was less impressive than some others – like John Bankes for example, or Thomas Wentworth. Now he had been pulled towards the very political nerve centre of the nation, and given a role as a clerk to the Privy Council.* He worked from an overhanging timbered house, with

---

*He had been appointed 'Clerk Extraordinary' before Buckingham's death, and was promoted to Clerk-in-Ordinary in 1635.

a garden and coachhouse, off King Street. Ever the assiduous operator, he oversaw the organisation of the council registers into an alphabetic index, and sent his staff into the archives to arrange past records similarly.

His income was enough to maintain his family: he had married Jane Jaye, a wealthy Londoner, in 1622, and the couple had a brood of at least seven children. He invested, and gave a regular portion of his income to the church and poor. He took up a lease on a summer house out on the green in Richmond, which had an orchard and was free of the foul air of King Street. He bought olive-coloured Spanish cloth for the walls, and grazed animals in Richmond Park. Edward drew pleasure from books, pictures, dogs, and exotic birds. He bred pheasants, brewed wormwood beer, and puffed tobacco. He clearly adored Jane and sent her rather clumsy but earnest, even sensual, poems.[26] He also loved his food, like turkey, pullets, bacon, and pomegranate, and he kept a handwritten cookbook about pastries. It likely contributed to a chronic digestive problem that saw him pepper his notes and diaries with medical recipes.[27]

Nicholas never pushed too hard for preferment; indeed he spent these years trying to cultivate the impression of a 'drone'. But he was more than this. He was an administrator of remarkable capabilities. In a world where the business of government was getting ever more complex, he was like some secretarial magus. A man who, instead of turning base metals into gold, converted the thin strokes of ink on a piece of paper into action, into money, and ultimately into power.

The weather was changing now, though. In 1637, Nicholas had moved his country estate from Richmond to a somewhat grander pile at Thorpe in Surrey. Then came 1640. That year began with him taking stock of his growing estate, and buying new clothes of silk, camlet, and plush for Jane.[28] In the spring, though, his career had hit a jolt. When elections took place to the Short Parliament, Nicholas for the first time failed to win his seat.[29] Following quickly on from this was a devastating personal tragedy: the shattering death of his beloved thirteen-year-old daughter, Susan.

To Charles, Nicholas was still useful. But when the Long Parliament seized the political initiative, he found himself much less active. The Privy Council was no longer the force it once was: Parliament was taking over its job, and by the summer of 1641, Charles's government had been reformed, and Nicholas – with little to do – could only fear for what would happen next. The attack on bishops was a personal threat for, as he calculated, the abolition of their estates would knock £1,500 in value from his own.[30] He had also been eyeing up the now-vacant position of one of the two secretaries of state. But while there were some rumours saying he would get it, as yet it hadn't happened. 'I see nothing hereabout,' he worried, 'that may give a rational and moderate man any measure of content or hope for good.'[31] His race was run. The times had moved beyond him. Now he was planning at last to retire to his country estate at Thorpe.

But then the king came calling.

————

Charles's stated purpose in travelling to Scotland would be to finally settle peace terms with the Covenanters, in person. They wanted confirmation of the original aims of their rebellion: the independence of the Kirk (the Scottish Church), and the permanent abolition of Scottish bishops. Charles, for his part, wanted the Scots out of English affairs. At last, the two armies in England – royal and Covenanter – could disband.

Whatever Charles said, cynics worried that he planned to stir trouble either in his northern kingdom or on the way there. Scotland was facing an uncertain future once more. A hardline reformist faction held control for now, but their grasp on the government was looser than it once was. If Charles could overturn that dominance, and bring a royalist party to power in Edinburgh, then he might win the considerable military resources of Scotland to his side. For nearly twelve months now, the presence of the Scottish army around Newcastle had severely restricted Charles's options. If he could engineer a coup to win command of it for his supporters, then the scene would alter dramatically. And there were many, Ambassador Giustinian noted, who predicted that the Scots, having secured their aims, would happily assist the king 'to regain his original authority in England'.[32] It might allow Charles, the Venetian thought, to 'avenge himself'.[33]

The king was helped by a deep split in Scottish politics. It was partly ideological, between royalists who thought the Covenanter revolution had gone far enough on the one hand, and allies of the English Junto who wanted to push it further on the other. It was also about personalities and clan rivalries: the most important royalist was James Graham, 5th Earl of Montrose, who in turn hated – and was hated by – the leading hardliner: Archibald Campbell, 8th Earl of Argyll. Both were wealthy and ruthless. The royalist Edward Hyde, who later wrote a great history of the age, would remember how: 'The people looked upon them both as young men of unlimited ambition, and used to say that "they were like Caesar and Pompey, the one would endure no superior, and the other would have no equal".'[34]

The Earl of Montrose was an ebullient young aristocrat, the chief of Clan Graham but not yet thirty years old. He had once supported the Covenanters, but he had fallen away from them, and since March, had been in intrigues with the king himself.[35] In Montrose, Charles believed, there might lie the key to Scotland. And with that key, he might unlock the backdoor to England. Edward Nicholas, for one, thought it was a very smart plan.[36]

———

In London, the Junto was scrambling to get the English army disbanded. They knew that the Scots force was about to go home, and couldn't allow an unchecked royal host to stay in arms. The king's imminent departure, meanwhile, suddenly brought the question of government appointments to the forefront in England. Could Parliament be given effective control over Charles's advisors? It was a very touchy issue. To the Junto, this was one of the safest ways they could prevent a reversal of the gains they had already made, and protect their own lives and freedom. Their allies in Scotland were asking for the same, and seemed quite likely to get it. So why not the English Parliament? To Charles, however, his right to choose his own advisors and ministers was a deep and non-negotiable part of his power: he believed it to be, so said one observer, 'a special part of his prerogative, a great sinew of his government, the long possession of kings in Scotland, [and] the unquestionable right of kings in England'.[37]

There had already been moves to win some control of appointments in England, each following on from a leaked royal plot. In May, after Sir John Suckling's Tower Plot, Sir Arthur Haselrig had suggested petitioning the king and asking him to take parliamentary advice when making appointments. It was a fairly mild proposal, but it didn't progress. Then in June, Montrose's intriguing against Argyll came out into the open, and he was imprisoned in Edinburgh Castle. There was also another alleged royal scheme to raise disaffection in the English royal army.[38]

It all looked like yet more evidence of royalist conspiracy, and it led the Junto to bring a series of new constitutional provisions to the Commons. There were ten of these 'propositions', and they called for the delaying of the king's journey to Scotland until both armies had been disbanded and for close control of the Catholics around the queen.[39] Most direct of all, they demanded that evil counsellors be removed, and that from henceforth only those whom 'people and Parliament may have just cause to confide in' be entrusted with offices of state. The Ten Propositions suggested, then, a form of parliamentary control of the executive. They also demanded that all lords lieutenant be men who were 'faithful and trusty'.[40] These were critical local officers: almost always members of the titled aristocracy. They controlled the so-called 'Trained Bands' – the county militia. In normal times, these amateur troops made up the only land forces in England. The implication, therefore, was that the country's armed forces should be loyal to the people represented in Parliament, and that Westminster should have some control over them.

Then, with the king's journey imminent, Parliament suddenly floated a series of appointments to major offices: the Earl of Pembroke – a Junto lord recently dismissed as Lord Chamberlain at the behest of the queen – was suggested to the position of Lord Steward of the Household; while the key financial office of Lord Treasurer – currently in a commission that included Lord Keeper

Littleton, and Lord Chief Justice John Bankes – was slated for William Cecil, Earl of Salisbury, a rich if somewhat mediocre Junto man. The argument one MP made in the latter case was important: it was 'Parliament who give the money', so they have 'interest in him that is to keep and dispose it'.[41]

Even more crucially, Parliament pushed for the appointment of a *Custos regni* ('Guardian of the Kingdom') who would act as viceroy while the king was away. The most likely candidate was Northumberland, one of the leading Junto men.[42] None of these proposals got anywhere. Rather, when the king finally did leave for Scotland, on 10 August, he attended the Lords at 10 a.m. that morning, in an irascible mood after a notably bad night's sleep. A crowd of several hundred had gathered the previous day to pressurise Charles to stay, but he was resolved.[43] Parliament were told that the plan for a *Custos regni* was a non-starter and instead the absent king's role would be played by a 22-man committee, appointed by Charles and with a tightly limited remit. It would include figures from across the political spectrum, with Junto men, like Essex, Warwick, Mandeville and Northumberland, but places too for the lawyers Littleton and Bankes. Most notably, and in what may have been another calculated snub by the king, a seat on the committee was given to the Earl of Newcastle – a dyed-in-the-wool royalist, a friend of Strafford, and a man who had been implicated in Suckling's Tower Plot. All told, it did little to calm fears that Charles, now on the road north, might be planning a fightback.[44]

But Charles didn't try and raise his northern army against Parliament. He did not end his journey at York. Instead, he travelled on to Holyrood without delay, as he had said he would.

He reached Edinburgh on 14 August. The looming battle for parliamentary control of the government in London would have to wait until he returned. Far to the north of London, the royal army was finally starting to dissolve. The Junto had paid it off just in time. Soldiers were drifting back home. The Scottish army, too, began pulling out of its English quarters.

Charles's realms were finally demilitarising. With the Scots gone, the debate on the bishops subsided too. The parliamentary bill which would have abolished them, abruptly stopped being discussed.[45] At Westminster, there developed a state of uneasy calm, unheard of for months.

―――

When Charles left England, Edward Nicholas had been promised that he would soon earn a long-deserved promotion. He would get the vacant secretaryship of state. He would step into the role once held by such titanic figures as Thomas Cromwell, Francis Walsingham, and Lord Burghley. His fellow secretary, for now, would be Henry Vane the elder. But Vane was a Junto man, thoroughly distrusted by Charles and widely expected soon to be fired. All of this would have to wait, though, until the return of the king. For now, Nicholas would manage the king's business in England, while reporting to his master with regular letters.

John Bankes was out of London. He attended the Privy Council on 11 August, the day after Charles left for Scotland, then he rode out on the East Anglian assize circuit.[46] It dealt with the most serious criminal prosecutions, with Bankes and his fellow judge arriving in dry, timbered county towns on horseback, to some fanfare, and conducting grim trials, many of which ended in numerous hangings. It was nasty work, though it was considered necessary. The combination of brutality and majesty offered by the rituals of the law would keep the audacity of the people in check – and justice and punishment were duly accompanied by didactic sermons, reminding folk of their obligations to their fellows, and to the social order.[47]

Mary Bankes, and the couple's youngest children, were a long way from this. They passed their time at Stanwell in Middlesex. Alice, their eldest daughter, was married now, to a rather snooty-looking young Buckinghamshire gentleman called John Borlase, and there were grandchildren, as well as young baby Charles, now nearing his second birthday. On the family's new lands in Purbeck, meanwhile, the grass on the chalk and limestone downs grew paler, and the tapestry of wildflowers dried out, leaving just the arid yellow hue of the ragwort and the rattling hum of the grasshoppers. The great heathlands between Corfe Castle and the ancient little town of Wareham turned into tinder. Even something as small as a misplaced fire could spell disaster.

John Taylor, the Water Poet, left London that summer, too, for another of his expeditions. The plague outbreak was getting worse, and he was getting older. Who knew how long he would be able to do this kind of thing. He set off by wherry, up the Thames, and across to the Severn, taking in stretches of the Bristol Avon. He preferred the gentle, lapping waters of the rivers to the jarring stones and viscid mud of the main roads. In the baking summer sun and long basking evenings, he enjoyed peace and good cheer, with particularly jolly entertainment at Oxford, and his journey took him as far north as the old town of Shrewsbury.

But all was not quite well. For when *John Taylors Last Voyage* was published in London, its several pages of warm jollity and optimism descended into a lament at how common it was to encounter mechanic preachers. They included 'a blind old woman' who interpreted the Gospel; a strange baker who would 'sift, knead, and mould religion'; there was a brewer's clerk who 'preaches most wonderfully in a malthouse'; plus a zealous sowgelder 'that professeth most desperate doctrine'.

There are puns and elements of artistic licence here, but Taylor was describing something important and destabilising: a world in which tradesmen and women might take a break from kneading dough or even gelding pigs to expound upon Scripture. Liberating, perhaps, but not for Taylor: 'Good Lord in thy Mercy,' he asked, 'look upon us and give us true peace and unity, both in Church and Commonwealth.' It was an appeal that, given the political climate of 1641, was born of hope rather than expectation.[48]

But for those like Taylor there *was* hope. If Charles could play his hand right in Scotland, and if the conservative reaction at home could be galvanised, he could build a royalist party. Then the Junto could be outflanked, and the Long Parliament could finally be sent home.

6

Red Crimson Sins

Charles appeared in Edinburgh in August, after what was evidently a breakneck journey up the Great North Road.[1] A wealthy and densely populated city, the Scottish capital was a place of contrasts: none more so in 1641 than between the gleaming new French-Renaissance-style Parliament House and the increasingly tumbledown royal palace of Holyrood.[2] His stay got off to an inauspicious start. He missed the afternoon sermon on his first day in the city – after all, the Scottish style of worship was hardly to the king's taste. It earned him a brazen reprimand from Alexander Henderson, the leading Scots divine, so Charles quickly caved and from then on made sure he always attended.[3]

The ostensible purpose of the king's visit, of course, was to finalise the Anglo-Scots treaty. His basic aim was to get the Scots out of England and out of English politics. This could be achieved by the simple tactic of capitulation – granting concessions to the Covenanters so that they would go away. As yet, though, Charles was reluctant to go down this route, not least as there was another way in which Scottish affairs might realistically play out, much more in his favour. For there was a new royalist plot in train.

The leading figures in this conspiracy were various disaffected lairds, who found themselves at odds with the Covenanter ruling party and had aligned themselves with the imprisoned Earl of Montrose. There were royal agents involved too, though. The

lynchpin was 'little' William Morray, who had been a servant to the
king since Charles's childhood and was therefore a close confidant.
Among the others were the seventy-year-old Earl of Roxburgh, and
his volatile son William Ker. Roxburgh himself was a particularly
steadfast servant to Charles, though he had a violent past. Once,
many years before, he had arranged the murder of a rival kinsman
on a black Edinburgh night. Roxburgh's wife, Jane, a Catholic, was
another royal intimate. She had looked after Charles himself when
he was an infant in Scotland, and more recently, she had been made
governess to three of Charles's children: Mary, Elizabeth, and Henry.[4]

At some point, too, Morray made contact with one John
Cochrane, a disaffected colonel in the Covenanter army. On one
occasion, Cochrane was taken by Morray for a private meeting at
night, in the depths of Holyrood Palace, with the king himself.[5]
Aside from this strange appointment, Charles seems to have kept
at arm's length from the conspiracy, but there is little doubt that he
knew of it, and that he approved. Kings do not have clandestine
meetings with rebel soldiers in the dead of night without good
reason.

The plot suited Charles's purposes too. It didn't change his
ultimate aim – to get the Scots out of English affairs – but it held
the possibility of a much more positive situation in Edinburgh,
which can only have helped his cause further. More to the point,
it might deflect what was probably the greatest threat to his
power, represented by the Covenanters. They wanted the Scottish
Parliament to be given a veto on royal offices and membership of
the Scottish Privy Council. For Argyll and his allies were hoping to
win control of government appointments. If Charles gave this away,
then, as Giustinian wrote, it would be a 'remarkable diminution
of his despotic authority'. But not only this: it would also be a
template for a similar revolution in England.[6]

———

At Westminster, the plague was moving closer, as every dry summer
day passed. The Lords ordered the Water Gate to Parliament closed,
and decreed that members' coaches should stop in the New Palace

Yard to avoid contagion. Attendances in the two Houses were becoming very thin indeed. Fifteen to twenty peers were sitting in the Lords by the end of August, and only eight to ten peers by early September. By then the Commons was barely quorate, with fewer than sixty appearing on some days.[7]

And so the increasingly nervous members of Parliament decided to allow themselves a break. A six-week recess was set for the early autumn, to begin on 9 September. MPs would go back to their constituencies, where the country air might refresh their spirits and protect them from London's fetid peril. In the meantime, two 'recess committees' would be created – one for each house – which would continue to sit at Westminster. It was a telling innovation, for it implied a permanent role for Parliament, even when the chambers themselves were empty.

Edward Nicholas was watching carefully. He was also to keep Charles closely in contact with the queen. 'Advertise my wife upon every dispatch,' Nicholas had been told.[8] Henrietta Maria was sharp and politically savvy. On occasions, she gave Nicholas direct orders that went against those of the king. At the height of August 1641, Charles had sent two letters to Nicholas, one for the queen and the other for Lord Keeper Littleton. Nicholas went to the queen first, and she instructed him not to send the letter on to Littleton. It had, she said, been written on her behalf, and she no longer needed it. Nicholas obeyed her, and wrote to Charles to check that this had been the right thing to do. 'I hope I have done nothing but my duty in obeying Her Majesty's command touching that letter,' he asked. 'Ye ar verrie right,' allowed Charles.[9]

Letters would be sent by an individual rider up to Edinburgh and then returned with the king's annotated orders. The messengers would be trusted servants, and men who could ride fast. On one occasion a rider fell from his horse, was badly bruised, and had to use the ordinary postal service, but since this carried a much greater risk of the letters being intercepted and opened, it was a method generally avoided.[10]

Everyone was watching each other. In the middle of August, Nicholas had sent the troubling news that Parliament had despatched a commission to keep an eye on proceedings in Edinburgh.[11] Comprising a group of MPs, including John Hampden, in theory it was to involve itself in finalising the negotiations for disbandment and for the treaty, but its real purpose was to keep in contact with the Covenanters, and to watch the king. Charles, for his part, made sure the commission knew how displeased he was with their presence.[12]

In late August, as Parliament prepared for recess, Nicholas informed the king that his employment had drawn what he euphemistically called 'envy', and so (as he heard) some Junto men had been starting 'to pry into my actions past & present'. Was Nicholas being paranoid? Or was someone raking his career, looking to see what might be found? Nicholas assured Charles that he was not worried, 'since I enjoy the comfort of your Majesty's gracious opinion and acceptance of my poor and honest endeavours.' 'Indeed ye have it in a full measure,' Charles replied.[13]

Meanwhile, John Bankes, having returned from East Anglia and the bleak but necessary business of the assize circuit, found himself embroiled in a rather controversial royal policy. Before he left, he had been summoned to a meeting with Charles.[14] The king had promised a portion of Strafford's Irish army – still awaiting disbandment – to the Spanish ambassador, for service in the Netherlands. The king's rather optimistic understanding was that Parliament would be happy with this arrangement, and so Bankes was to make them aware of the royal will.

They were, it turned out, highly reluctant. The idea of handing over Irish troops to Spain, one of England's most ancient enemies, was anathema. But Charles was resolute. 'You must tell my Lord Chief Justice Bankes from me,' he wrote to Nicholas, 'that I am now so far engaged to the Spanish Ambassador for four regiments, that I cannot now go back.' So 'he must tell the Houses from me that these levies must not be stopped'.[15]

As September came, Nicholas was also involved in efforts to stamp out the growing social disorder. England was still seeing heightened levels of unrest, as the looming sense of crisis encouraged people to right longstanding wrongs. Drainage ditches in the eastern

Fens – long a source of peasant anger – were destroyed. There were riots in the Forest of Dean in Gloucestershire against enclosures, and near Colchester in Essex the fences laid out by the unpopular Lucas family were thrown down.[16] In the great flat fens around Soham in Cambridgeshire, it was reported how 'some rude people have in a tumultuous manner cast down & in great part destroyed' various ditches and enclosures.[17] Deer parks were attacked too, and on 31 August, Nicholas wrote to Charles to inform him that the royal forest of Windsor was suffering hunting raids from gangs of eighty to a hundred locals from the nearby town of Egham. Such was their brazenness that the attacks were taking place in broad daylight.

Charles ordered Nicholas to confer with Bankes and Littleton immediately, 'to see what course is best to be taken to stop these insolencies'.[18] Worst of all, at least for Parliament, was that it seemed that the riots had been inspired by a recent statute reforming forest law. The statute in question was supposed to be 'for settling the rights of the subject', but instead it had inspired 'divers riotous and tumultuous proceedings by the people'. Convinced that Parliament had made attacks on deer legal, local people were roving the countryside with hunting guns and carrying off the game. Yet again, the reformist Parliament looked like it was stoking social unrest.[19]

Parliament itself was spending the last days before recess in a rather combative mood. Charles's absence had persuaded members, on slightly questionable premises, that they might pass temporary 'ordinances', which would have legal force even without the royal assent, at least until the king returned. One such ordinance was passed near the end of August, for disarming Catholics: a response to various rumours about popish conspiracies that summer.[20]

But ordinance procedure was also the perfect vehicle for the furtherance of parish reform, something still very much outstanding even after ten months of Parliamentary business. If Laudian decorations and fittings could be torn down on the back of an ordinance, then the damage (or purification, depending on one's perspective) could be done before the king could stop it. There was a short window for further reformation while Charles was away and before recess, if those in favour of it moved with haste and focus.

Momentum already existed in some local communities, and in some places various elaborate church fittings had been pulled down. In Oxford, as early as April, things were already 'thoroughly reformed', and painted chapels 'quite defaced', and Communion tables 'fixed in the body of the Choir'.[21] Now, with recess approaching, minds were concentrated on achieving lasting change.

Soon the necessary ordinance was nearly ready. It sought to make it compulsory to return churches to their pre-Laudian state, banning crucifixes and 'scandalous' images. It passed the Commons. Yet on 9 September, the Junto were suddenly outmanoeuvred in the Lords.[22]

It was a busy day. Among the Lords' business was a bill against mixing wine, and a set of orders about the plague. The two houses also managed to pass an ordinance stopping the royal plan to give some of the Irish army to Spain. Instead, the troops would remain where they were. It was a powerful statement by both houses: using an ordinance specifically to undermine an important royal diplomatic policy.

Yet the religious ordinance got stuck. Missing key supporters, the Junto were defeated in the Lords by the astonishingly tight margin of 11 to 9. Instead, in what may have been a calculated insult, the peers decided to publish an old order of their own, from January, in defence of the Church as it was already established. This then touched off a snap debate in the Commons, after which the lower house voted to print their own order based on their draft ordinance, meaning that when Parliament finally rose for recess that afternoon, it had contrived to produce two separate declarations on Church reform, each espousing a rather different position. It was a mess.

The September orders were a watershed. Lords and Commons had been on divergent paths for some time, but now this was announced to the world. The Junto was strong in the Commons, but the forces of conservatism remained powerful in the Lords, partly of course because that house still had a complement of bishops. It left Edward Nicholas in the happy position of being able to write to Charles to tell him that the two houses had apparently fallen out. Or, as he put it with the knowing archness of a civil servant: 'There was not at parting a very perfect agreement (as I hear) between the 2 houses in all things.'[23] Charles responded to the news with some glee: 'I am not much sorry for it,' he wrote to Nicholas.[24] The political advantage was of greater interest to the king than any sense of loss at the destruction of Laudian church fittings.

Now, though, for those who wanted it, there was plausible justification from Westminster for a thorough reformation in the parishes. Parliament had gone into recess, but before doing so it had kindled a fire. Around a quarter of London parishes saw various offensive fittings removed.[25] In Old Jewry, a group 'in the time of divine service came into the church and did tear the Book of Common Prayer'.[26] One person gathering reports about this was the veteran admiral, Sir John Pennington. He was a man who had once accompanied Walter Ralegh up the Orinoco river, but was now approaching retirement. Stationed at the Downs in Kent, he received regular despatches from a number of correspondents in the capital, keeping him informed about political developments. Thomas Wiseman, City Remembrancer, was one of the admiral's best informants. 'The Brownists and other sectaries,' Wiseman wrote to Pennington, 'make such havoc in our churches by pulling down of ancient monuments, glass windows and rails, that their madness is intolerable.'[27] At Chelmsford, stained-glass windows depicting Christ and the Virgin Mary were removed and then smashed, with the 'escutcheons and arms of the ancient nobility and gentry who had contributed to the building' being destroyed in the process.[28] In their zeal, the Puritans were dragging down the icons not just of Rome but of the social order too.

Conservative parishioners fought back, resisting as best they could. They informed messengers that MPs 'were all asses', or that the House order itself was such that it could have 'come from a ballad monger'.[29] Some ministers refused to allow it to be read. Pym himself admitted that many parishes were now 'at blows and likely to come to blows', while Nicholas received a letter from a royalist ally in his native Wiltshire recounting how the contradictory orders 'breed no little distraction, at least very much disorder, for every man makes use of them according to their several pallets and humours'.[30]

Across England there was conflict and resistance. Confusion at Westminster only fed the discord in the country. At Kidderminster, a drunken crowd of poor workers and servants came to prevent the demolition of a churchyard crucifix.[31] In Cerne Abbas, an old monastic village in the Dorset downs, the churchwardens took down the communion rails but stored them away for the future, in case they got the chance to put them up again.[32] One rather elegiac response, meanwhile, came from the antiquarian Sir Christopher Hatton. He commissioned the herald William Dugdale to begin a great survey of cathedral monuments, so that 'by ink and paper the shadows of them, with their inscriptions, might be preserved for posterity'. Dugdale began with St Paul's in London.[33] Even that great cathedral was felt to be under threat.

Critically, the rather skilful ability of the Junto for avoiding truly controversial religious decisions was now dramatically undermined. Suddenly the reformists were seen to be behind a wave of disorderly parish vandalism.

For some the problem wasn't so much the cleansing of papist images itself as the demotic way in which it was done, with parishioners taking things into their own hands and smashing away with their mattocks and hammers. For others, it very much *was* the image-breaking. These were beauteous treasures, and they represented an exquisite and appropriate adornment to the worship of God. Either way, the Junto were starting to look thoroughly radical, and it threatened to cost them a significant swathe of support. As one anonymous correspondent put it, 'the confidence of the late prevailing party' had 'unmask'd them so fast that their deformity appeared, and their lovers fell off'.[34] As Ambassador Giustinian recognised, the consequence of all these disorders and divisions was 'that the royalist party may increase its numbers'. It played directly into the hands of Nicholas, the queen, and Charles.[35]

Meanwhile, dangerous words were being aimed at the Junto. One ominous squib, that began circulating in manuscript form, took merciless aim at them, threatening bloody vengeance. The leading reformist peers, it said, were 'a pack of half-witted Lords' who had no capacity for anything except betraying the nobility 'under the tutelage of the Lord Saye the Anabaptist'. They were joined in a litany of shame that included various leading Junto men in the Commons, 'bankrupt citizens', 'ten groat pettifoggers', and 'judases'. These men, said the paper, had 'beggared the nation, to enrich the Scotch'. They had endeavoured to destroy the Prayer Book while having 'protected the ignorant and licentious sectaries and schismatics to stir up sedition and bring in atheism'. The gentry, it declared, considered these men 'traitors to the king, church and state' who had brought 'disaffection betwixt the king and his people'. It was hoped they would either be banished, 'or else to be delivered up to be torn in pieces by the loyal subjects of our religious king'.[36]

––––––

By now, London was utterly rife with both the plague and smallpox. The red cross on doors was, said one author, a reminder of our 'red crimson sins'. God, they noted, 'has sent his angel of wrath, and nothing can appease him but prayers'.[37] It was time to get out and many, like the young gentleman John Evelyn, did everything they could to avoid coming to town.[38] According to Giustinian, some 200,000 people had left London, including all of the foreign ambassadors.[39]

Nicholas was worried, and asked permission to reside at his country estate at Thorpe or at Oatlands.[40] His would remain a busy, peripatetic lifestyle: splitting his time between his own and the queen's houses in Surrey, and regular trips into Westminster to keep an eye on the Junto and the Recess Committees.

It was from Thorpe, on 19 September, that Nicholas wrote to Charles with an intriguing idea of his own: 'some things', he humbly proposed, 'in my poor opinion worthy of your royal consideration'. The king must be aware, Nicholas wrote, that there had been insinuations of popery ('which is generally exceeding distasteful to your subjects of this kingdom') levelled against members of his court and clergy. Of course these were unjust, Nicholas assured the king. But might it not be helpful to the king's cause to 'give some public assurance to the contrary'? This could be done quite easily, Nicholas suggested. A handful of bishoprics had fallen vacant in the last few months. These, he thought, could be filled with 'persons, of whom there is not the least suspicion of favouring the Popish party'.[41] Nicholas was suggesting the king should court the middle ground.

It also matched the drift of Charles's religious politics since 1640. Whereas the king had fought hard to save Strafford, he had effectively, cynically, abandoned Laud to arrest, leaving him to languish in the Tower. Meanwhile, one of Laud's most implacable old enemies, Bishop John Williams of Lincoln, had been basking in royal favour, even though Charles didn't really like him. 'Swim with the tide,' Williams had once told the Duke of Buckingham 'and you will not be drowned.'[42] The irony is that Williams had been out in the cold during the 1630s, and for some time even imprisoned for his beliefs. Now it was Charles who was swimming with the tide, appointing Calvinist bishops in a direct repudiation of past policy and his own religious preference. 'I have somewhat altered from my former thoughts,' the king noted sardonically, 'to satisfy the times.'[43]

Before Charles's response arrived, Nicholas had written once more, this time rather more nervously.[44] News was that the king might concede to the Scots parliament the right of veto over royal officers. If this was the case, Nicholas urged, then Charles should also get a declaration from them to the effect that this would not be a precedent for England. The leadership of the English Junto were in regular contact with the Covenanter leaders in Scotland. Lord Mandeville, in particular, was corresponding with the Marquess of Hamilton, a kinsman of Charles and once very much in the royal favour, but now almost completely frozen out by the king.[45] Thus they were well aware of the concessions that Charles was preparing to grant in Edinburgh, and were ready to strike for the same bargain in England. Their plan, it appeared, would be to use Charles's financial weakness to their advantage. They would keep holding back on granting tonnage and poundage until sweeping constitutional reforms had been agreed.[46]

Nicholas could see what they were doing. He knew that the next act of the drama would take place in Parliament, at Westminster. Ideally, he thought the king's cause would be best served by the royal presence in the capital, not least because once Charles returned south, he could again use his royal veto on any legislation. Charles might even be able to break up the Parliament altogether, though it was not clear how – after all he would theoretically still need their consent for a dissolution.[47] In any case, on 27 September Nicholas wrote from Thorpe urging the king to leave Edinburgh as soon as was practically possible.[48]

Parliament was due to sit again on 20 October, and Nicholas had heard that there had been 'divers meetings' at Lord Mandeville's Chelsea residence, and other places, by the Junto men 'to consult what is best to be done'. Clearly, Nicholas was getting nervous about what the Junto were planning. He had a source in their camp who was feeding him compromising information about them. But he strongly suspected that the existing secretary of state, Henry Vane the elder, now in Scotland with the king, was also supplying information to the Junto. In Nicholas's letter sent to the king on 27 September, he all but accused Vane of being a spy.[49] He also enclosed a paper that implicated the Junto in something, which his own mole in their camp had sent him. Nicholas urged Charles, once he had read the paper, to burn it.

But Charles continued to hesitate.

―――――

If Nicholas had been paying close attention to the marginal notes that his master was adding to his letters by way of response, then he might have concluded that something big was about to happen in Scotland.

'When ye shall see little Will Morray,' Charles wrote on 5 October, 'ye shall know certainly not only of my return, but also how all will end here.' The Junto, Charles suggested, may be cheerful now, but 'I believe, before all be done, that they will not have such great cause of joy.'[50]

They will not have such great cause of joy.

Then, a week later, another reply came. 'Though I cannot return so soon as I could wish,' the king noted, 'yet I am confident that you will find there was necessity for it, and I hope that many will miss their ends.'[51]

Now what on earth, Nicholas should have paused to wonder, was the king planning up in Scotland?

If Charles were to be late back to Westminster, and if the Junto was preparing a major political offensive, then it was all the more imperative that Nicholas shore up the royal party in Parliament. With the appointment of new bishops proceeding but slowly, the most effective strategy was likely to be something else. In the longer term, the aim would be to gain enough support across the two houses to secure a dissolution (which, thanks to the act at the time of Strafford's trial, needed to be voted by Parliament now rather than simply ordered by the king). More immediately, he needed to ensure there were enough loyalist peers in the Lords to block any unseemly bills that came from the Commons. For this, Nicholas consulted with one of the most politically astute figures in the whole country: the queen.

Henrietta Maria had spent the last fifteen years immersed in court politics, so she knew the peerage as well as anyone. On 5 October, she wrote to Nicholas, in English but with spelling betraying a rather thick French accent, providing two pieces of very sensible advice: first, he must tell the existing group of bishops to attend the house for the next session. Secondly, he should send for a specific list of peers, which she now named. The queen's letter – direct and unburdened as it was by the usual conventions of epistolary flourish – shows a clear and realistic grasp of the political situation. The most useful element was the names: 'Cumberland, Huntintong, Bath, Northampton, Deevonchier, Bristol, Newcastle, Pawlett, Coventry, Seymer, Cotington.'[52] Eleven men, all available, all broadly loyalist.

Soon Nicholas would be told to use the queen's judge of character again. On 15 October, with the return of Parliament less than a week away, he wrote in a slightly despairing tone to the king, still in Edinburgh for reasons Nicholas did not quite understand. The king had told him to rally his 'best servants' to stall any bill in Parliament aimed at taking control of government appointments, and if Nicholas didn't know who these were – 'If your own observation do not sufficiently tell you,' Charles wrote rather tersely – then he should ask the queen: 'let my wife's direction guide you'.[53]

By the time this note reached Nicholas, though, Parliament had already returned. And the scale of the disaster that had unfolded in Scotland had now at last become clear.

————

The Scottish conspiracy developed as autumn grew deeper and darker. The targets would be the main Covenanter leaders, especially Argyll and the Marquess of Hamilton. Unlike so many of Charles's plots, this one was kept to the utmost secrecy. Presumably it wasn't just brinkmanship – a ploy to scare his enemies – but a genuine attempt to silence and even kill some of them.[54] At one point, however, a drunken meeting between conspirators threatened to blow the whole thing. Unexpectedly, one of Hamilton's relatives had turned up to the gathering, and things quickly descended into an ugly slanging match. Hamilton was loudly denounced and one plotter, quite drunk, went off to challenge him to a duel. Hearing of all this, Charles desperately tried to calm things down, with only limited success.[55]

It was on Monday 11 October, that the plan would finally be activated.[56] Argyll and Hamilton, both resident at Holyrood Palace, would be summoned for an audience with the king in the withdrawing chamber, deep in the building. When they got there they would not find King Charles but the Montrose ally Lord Almond and a file of soldiers, who would gain access via the stairs from the garden.[57] Almond would confront the two Covenanters and accuse them of treason, while another detachment of around 400 soldiers patrolled in the garden immediately beyond the chamber window. These would be needed if word got out and any attempt was made to bring a Covenanter force to Holyrood. Meanwhile, further reinforcements led by Roxburgh would arrive. Were any resistance to be offered from outside the palace, Argyll and Hamilton would be hurried through the gardens or Holyrood churchyard, in what would then be the encroaching dark, down to Leith where they would be bundled onto a royal ship. Once they were secure, they would either be sent for trial in the Scottish parliament or, if some of the plotters had their way, simply murdered there and then. Meanwhile, Lord Almond had written to his tenants in Linlithgowshire, ordering them to come to Edinburgh on the Monday of the intended plot, armed with muskets, 'a pound of powder, and a dozen of balls'.[58] He was preparing for serious violence.

But it never came. On the night of the 10th, one of the army officers involved had a change of heart. In the early hours he slipped away from his lodgings, went to see Lord General Alexander Leslie, the supreme commander of the Covenanter forces, and spilled everything. Leslie brought it straight to Argyll and Hamilton. The next morning, news of the plot was everywhere. It was over before it had even begun.

It took a few days for Edinburgh to wake up to the full scale of the conspiracy. 'At first', one letter recounted a week later, 'men only feared private quarrels', however 'it appears now, that the aim was not at particular persons, but at the cause'.[59] On the 12th, Charles appeared in the Scottish parliament himself, backed by a large armed force. Still at this point there was a potential for bloody violence on Edinburgh's streets, and Argyll and Hamilton, with the latter's brother, had quickly fled the city and bolted to Hamilton's fortified house at Kinneil, a few miles to the east.

Charles publicly disavowed what he called this 'Incident' (a euphemistic name which has stuck). He had nothing but affection for Hamilton, he lied. Over the coming days, Hamilton and Argyll rode the backlash against the plot, though it was more than a fortnight before they felt able to return to Edinburgh. Charles meanwhile was simply forced to give up any hope of opposing the Covenanter revolution. All he could do now was meekly grant enough concessions to the Scots, hoping to leave his hand free to win back control in England. Soon, a final agreement had been reached in the interminable negotiations. A new Scottish Privy Council was appointed with the 'advice and consent' of the Edinburgh parliament.[60] Just as galling, Charles felt compelled to give personal honours to his Covenanter enemies. Argyll became a marquess. As the royalist Edward Hyde later recalled, the Scots treated King Charles as a 'vanquished person'.[61] And so he was.

Within a week, word of the 'Incident' had reached London. It was not until the 14th that Hampden and his fellow commissioners finally wrote to their masters in the south, but the rider they sent managed to cover the six-day journey in four. News, therefore, arrived just in time for the final meeting of the Commons Recess Committee on Tuesday 19 October. The commissioners' letter was laconic almost to the point of negligence. Wisely, though, they seem to have fully briefed the rider himself, who was able to fill in Pym with much fuller details. Pym immediately jumped on a horse and rode to warn his ally Mandeville.[62]

Nicholas found out around the same time, and could see the fear that the Incident caused in London. The Commons Recess Committee, he noted, had been put 'in a great fright'.[63] Some of Charles's loyal supporters had rushed to his own house off King Street to ask if he had any more information.[64] The Junto men were even more fearful. Edward Hyde later remembered walking with the earls of Holland and Essex in Westminster Hall, and they were both thoroughly apprehensive 'that other men were in danger of the like assaults'.[65] Yet fear cut both ways. After news of the Incident, Giustinian noted the consternation among the king's officers. Those, most concerned for the king's welfare, he noted, 'are overcome by this event and are tortured by the greatest perplexity'. The queen at Oatlands, the Venetian was informed, was 'anxious beyond measure'.[66]

Now Nicholas wrote once more to Charles, and his advice was simple. 'With all possible diligence,' he said, the king should send a 'full and perfect relation of the present disturbance'. In other words, get your side of the story out, fast.[67] But the Junto were already there. Since they had been informed first, they were presented with the chance to control the narrative. Soon after the 19th, the contents of the commissioners' letter were printed and distributed, promising the 'Discovery' of a 'late and Bloody CONSPIRACIE at Edenburgh in SCOTLAND'.[68] Other print accounts followed, and soon everyone in London was talking about the Incident. Those connected with the court tried their best to talk the conspiracy down, but others considered it 'a treachery of most dreadful consequence'.[69]

———

The Water Poet John Taylor was back in London now. His summer jaunt was over, and no longer was his spat with Henry Walker dominating the bookstands. Rather, one of the most sensational publications was now a stirring argument for 'Independency' – the idea that churches should gather from the people rather than be imposed from above. It was an attack on a rather uninspired and reactionary Puritan named Thomas Edwards, and it was by a writer called Katherine Chidley. It carried her name clearly, right in the centre. No one could doubt that this was the work of a woman. Its arguments were strident, stirring, and dangerously democratic – feminist, even. Churches should separate themselves from 'idolators', she said, and even the lowliest members of England's hierarchical society, be they 'tailors, felt-makers, button-makers, tent-makers, shepherds or ploughmen' were in a better place to create Godly communities than 'ill-meaning priests'. A wife's conscience, meanwhile, was entirely independent of her husband's, whatever authority he might have 'in bodily and civil respects'.[70]

Chidley's text was bracing, a breath of fresh air in a world where the vast majority of publications were by men. But it fed into the conservative backlash, for if political reform was leading women to question their place in the world, then to some it had clearly gone far enough. Other texts that appeared around this time castigated the libertinism of the religious radicals. One tract promised the 'Discovery of 29 Sects here in London', including everyone from Puritans, papists and Brownists through to Adamites (who liked to walk about town naked), members of the Family of Love, Socinians, Heathens, Bacchanalians, Persians, 'Mahometans' (Muslims), and even Saturn-worshippers. Each was given a short paragraph of explanation. The Bacchanalians, for example, were 'more mad, ignorant, or impious than the rest, for they think, nay they certainly believe, that they shall gain Heaven by drinking healths, and he which can drink most is worshipped among them'. Most lurid of all was a short pamphlet exposing a *Nest of Serpents Discovered*, which described the origins and history of the Adamite movement and their 'ridiculous tenets'. It boasted a woodcut image featuring eight naked figures, with the 'serpents' of the title clearly having a rather crude double meaning. It ended with the dark suggestion that a sect of Adamites was active in London: 'Their meeting is sometime at Lambeth, at other times about Saint Katherine's, sometimes in the fields or in woods, at sometimes in cellars.'[71]

London was fracturing still, with radical sectaries like Katherine Chidley and Henry Walker vying with conservatives like John Taylor, and fears growing of Adamites gathering naked in cellars and woods. Yet there was a sense that the momentum firmly favoured the conservatives. Now, too, they had won a major victory.

The annual mayoral election had taken place in September, and success had gone to a man called Richard Gurney. He was of a venerable age, and remembered the London of Gloriana and of Shakespeare. As a rich silk merchant his interests were very much with the ruling class, and indeed Edward Nicholas had heard he was 'very well affected and stout', meaning he was a royalist.[72]

Charles had suffered a terrible defeat in Scotland. His attempts to overturn his enemies there before coming south had ended in disaster. But his prospects in England – even in London – were rapidly improving. Here the royalist backlash was gathering pace, just as Parliament prepared to return.

As autumn brought its fresher winds and heavier rains to London, a new temper was taking hold. What no one could quite see just yet was how much the political scene was about to change. How much, indeed, it had already done so.

PART TWO

Ovatio

7

A Vast Receptacle of a Disordered Multitude

There had been a lot of strange folk seen around London of late. Everyone had noticed. It wasn't just the usual beggars – unfortunate, ragged souls cast aside by a cruel world, though there were plenty still of those. This time it was something else. Different people. More menacing. Not pitiful and broken old women, or pleading mothers with tiny, crying, malnourished children, but young men. Sturdier types, sneering as they demanded coins from passers-by and gathering in dimly lit alehouses to spend their takings. Drinking strong beer and spirits, ready at the merest provocation to whip out a dagger and tussle and stab and scream in anger. Some bore scars. Some were silent and seething, others roaring and rowdy. All were veterans of the king's defeated army, now disbanded and disillusioned. They were underpaid, and underemployed.

At the beginning of October 1641, as the evenings got darker, the two parliamentary Recess Committees had tried to get these soldiers out. They had ordered a 'good and strong watch' on all the highways and villages within twenty miles of London. Magistrates across the south-east were told to take special care; inn and alehouse keepers were ordered not to harbour anyone they couldn't vouch for.[1] It wasn't just London. Soldiers were bringing fear across the country. One evening, as the sun was setting across the low, flat moors west of York, a local man was terrified to see 'a company

of resolute fellows' crossing the river by ferry. He supposed them
to be soldiers.[2] 'Troopers commit divers outrages by the highway,'
noted a letter.[3] A pamphlet published in October collated various
shocking incidents. 'Complaints fly abroad everywhere,' it reported,
and 'no man almost dares trust himself to the highways, for fear
lest he lose his purse, or his life.' There was group returning from
a wedding, robbed of clothes, jewels, and £120, while riding in
a coach at Islington; and a countess and some other ladies were
held up on their way between Watford and London. Attacks were
now taking place in Hyde Park and Cheapside. One Sunday, a
Londoner was mugged by three men in buff coats, while walking
along Whitecross Street. The following day a knight was attacked
in Kent Street, Southwark.[4]

Edward Nicholas knew well the kinds of thuggery associated
with this army. Back in the spring of 1640, when the English
force was gathering to face down the Covenanters, his father had
written to him describing the pitched battles between marauding
royal troops and local people in the country around Marlborough.
The soldiers, he wrote, 'beat many very sorely and at Idmiston cut
off the hand of one Nott, and hurt another very dangerously'.[5]
But there were those in the royal camp who were beginning to
see things differently. The disbanded officers in particular – the
so-called 'Reformadoes' – might be useful. A cut above the angry
common soldier, they were usually of gentry background and hated
the upstart Junto, whom they saw as prioritising the wages of their
Scots enemies over them. If the king needed muscle, these might
be the men who could provide it. Their anger could be channelled
into royalism.

On 20 October, John Bankes travelled from his lodgings in
Holborn, the wide street punctuated by aristocratic mansions that
curved west from the northern walls of the City, and made his way
to the great royal palace of Whitehall. On arrival, Bankes headed
into Whitehall's labyrinth of buildings, lodgings, and offices, to
one particular room. In that room members of the Privy Council
were gathering. The business that day was straightforward: what to
do with those strange men who had been appearing over London

and Westminster.[6] It was an urgent question, for that same day, Parliament had returned.

A few hundred yards away from Whitehall, deep in the tangle of chambers and lobbies that made up the Palace of Westminster was an old medieval chapel, dedicated to St Stephen. It was here, in what should have been a spacious room, with tall whitewashed walls, that the House of Commons met. The Speaker presided from the old altar steps, with MPs sitting in the choir stalls. These days it tended to be much more packed, for in the last century or so, the number of members of the Commons had grown significantly. Now there were around 500, with both knights of the shire elected for the county seats and the burgesses elected for the boroughs.

The Palace of Westminster was like a warren. Only after spending some time there did people start to instinctively know their way around. One slightly complex journey might be to come out of St Stephen's Chapel, through the lobby, down the stairs, and turn left into the long, high-ceilinged White Chamber. Were one to follow that through and turn left again, via a stone lobby, it would bring you to the Painted Chamber, so called for its colourful decorative murals. Turn right at the end of that, through another lobby, and you entered the House of Lords.[7]

Here met around 120 lay peers, joined by the 26 English and Welsh bishops, and attended also by members of the judiciary and the Attorney-General, now the loyalist Edward Herbert, who had replaced John Bankes in January.[8] The Lords Chamber was much more plush and spacious than St Stephen's, while the fine clothes of the peers stood in contrast to the rather sober, grey and white dress of the Commons MPs. No one who happened to stumble into the palace would have been under any illusion that this was the 'Upper' of the two houses.

Parliament represented the nation: the people assembled together as a body, but it also existed in a place. The Palace of Westminster itself was the pinnacle of the English legal system. Its centrepiece was Westminster Hall, an exceedingly grand medieval chamber which housed some of the principal courts of the realm and which had staged the Strafford trial that spring. But there was also a maze of other rooms and lobbies, plus various outbuildings including the old house of the antiquarian Robert Cotton – between the Commons and the Lords – and the annexe that had contained the Star Chamber, once the site of the feared law court. There was also, across the New Palace Yard, the old clock tower, next to the cistern.

Parliament's immediate surroundings were the town of Westminster. This was a growing city, though still dominated by the palaces of Whitehall and Westminster itself, and by its great medieval abbey. To the west lay the fields and villages of Chelsea and Kensington, and the hunting grounds of Hyde Park. The immediate outskirts of Westminster were dominated by the rough grasslands of Tothill Fields – a favoured spot for duels and illicit encounters – and the much better tended landscape of St James's Park.

To the north flowed the broad River Thames, coursing on its way to the vast, grey North Sea. On its left bank, it passed parts of Westminster that were building up rapidly. Brick mansions, new churches, and inns mingled with poorer dwellings. Two great thoroughfares dominated. One, King Street, was a slender carriageway running past Whitehall Palace (from which the road would eventually take its modern name). With the huge royal residence on one side, incorporating the Banqueting House, and with the great Holbein Gate in the middle, King Street had a narrow, enclosed feel to it, not least with the houses on the west side built several storeys high and overhanging somewhat. The road was in a poor state – 'ruinous' apparently – and was cluttered with the stalls of fishmongers, and herb and vegetable sellers.[9] Despite the adjacent palace, it was somewhere that could fall eerily dark when the sun set across St James's to the west, though the half dozen taverns on the street at least kept fires running late into the night.

At the top of King Street was an open space around the Charing Cross, an old medieval monument that was now attracting some controversy, for was it not a hangover from Romish times? Then, running north-east, along the curving river, was the Strand, the second great Westminster artery. Here were the grand townhouses of the aristocracy, backing onto the river: Essex House among others, as well as the queen's mansion at Somerset House. To the north of the Strand too, yet another new townscape was emerging, including the grand plaza of Covent Garden. It pointed towards a new future for the western end of London: elegant, classical, rich.

At the eastern limit of the Strand, it became Fleet Street, which took its name from an ancient river. Where the two roads joined, travellers would pass through the Temple Bar, marked by an ornate archway. Once beyond this, they were in the City of London itself.

London was a world away from the rest of the country. It was loud, smelly and dark. Heating was by acrid coal rather than sweet-smelling wood. Streets were busy, muddy, and packed with scurrying people. There were lumbering animals and jolting carts and coaches. Nowhere did rich and poor rub shoulders like they did in London, though even here there were increasing contrasts between each district. The West End and the City had particular concentrations of wealth, but in the east, London was a city of docklands, poverty and shoddy housing. South of the river in Southwark was another rapidly spreading settlement, famed for its recreational sites like theatres, and its relatively squalid dwellings, gradually stretching out into the fields of Surrey.

One of the first London buildings you would see if you were travelling, as many did, downriver from Westminster, was the huge Bridewell prison. Once a royal palace, this was now the centre of a complex policing operation, and was itself a combination of a workhouse, a gaol and a school for lost youths. Its officers, beadles in blue liveries, had summary powers to imprison, and were a frequent presence in the busy street scenes of the capital, especially as the sun went down of an evening and the forces of order struggled to keep their grip.[10] In true London fashion, though, Bridewell backed directly onto the mansion of a fabulously wealthy earl.

Bridewell's looming presence was a stark reminder to Londoners. It told them that stability was always fragile and that the prime concern of those in charge was somehow to maintain it. From stability, the City governors believed, came peace, and it was peace that allowed the quiet enjoyment of wealth. Instability, on the other hand, brought social disorder and political chaos. It was a lesson driven home in the last year or so. With the recent growth of religious radicalism, London now more than ever seemed to be teetering on the brink of something very dangerous indeed.

London was big, and growing rapidly. The city was like 'the great bee-hive of Christendom' wrote one commentator in 1632.[11] It had swollen hugely in the last hundred and fifty years or so, from around 50,000 people in 1500 to almost 400,000 by 1640.[12] By 1627, it was said quite simply to be 'exceeding full'; soon even the graveyards had no space.[13] Growth hardly helped the problem of order: while the number of inhabitants rose, the number of constables stayed the same. Worse, those in charge worried that much of the growth was driven by the wrong sorts of people. There were 'Unlimited' numbers of people 'of mean condition' living in grotty alleys, they moaned. The city was 'exceedingly pestered' by beggars, 'a vast receptacle of a disordered multitude of imperfect workmen and misgoverned people'. Never, complained Charles I's Privy Council in 1638, had so many vagrants 'pestered' London as now.[14]

Some griped that there were too many strangers and foreigners, but most of the growth was driven by the migration of young people from the English countryside. Something like three-quarters of London women had been born outside the capital.[15] It was a youthful place too. Many Londoners had come as apprentices or domestic servants to take up contracts of employment. Others simply arrived hoping to pick up work when they got there. Magdalen Lasley was seventeen in 1636 when she was called to give a witness statement in one of London's law courts: she said she had lived with a mistress in St Sepulchre for a year, before that in St Clement Danes also for a year, and before that Westminster, and before that she lived in Enfield, Middlesex, where she was born. She must have moved to London aged about twelve.[16] Others came from further afield. John Lilburne, a man whose radical politics would play a huge role in the next two decades, had left Newcastle Grammar School and, aged about fifteen, was apprenticed to a clothier in Candlewick Street in the City in 1630; Katherine Childley's printer, William Larner, hailed from the tiny Cotswold village of Little Rissington, before taking up an apprenticeship in London the same year as Lilburne.[17]

Service and apprenticeship were integral to the experience of most Londoners, but these institutions were not just work, they were also forms of education. They were training for the workplace, and a formative experience: training for life. One might leave an apprenticeship with skills, a small amount of money, and even a fiancée. It was about control too. The idea was that in that potentially turbulent period between leaving one's parents and eventually getting married, masters and mistresses provided a steady hand over the young. It was a solution, so the theory went, to the age-old problem of disorderly youngsters.

Control was reinforced with the potential for violence, though tempered by law and custom. Employers could legally beat their servants, though they were supposed to do it 'with such discretion, pity, and desire of their amendment, as loving parents use to deal with their dear children'.[18] Court records show the reality could be pretty brutal, but servants and apprentices still had rights, and they knew it. If, therefore, the whole experience was supposed to teach discipline, it also provided lessons in resistance to tyranny, and the degree to which patriarchs could be restrained by the law. In a world in which the household was supposed to be a microcosm of the state, it needn't take much for London's workforce to make the imaginative leap, and to apply the lessons they learned in their apprenticeships and service contracts to the world of kings and governments. There was something intrinsic to London. Something about the social institutions of the city that taught people to be critical of those in power.

If, that was, they could ever actually concentrate. For London was a cacophonous hubbub of clamour and filth. Animal dung clogged the streets, and there was always a risk of encountering human waste flung from one of the houses. One raucous dispute arose of a morning in Holborn in 1627 when Elizabeth Morton threw 'a pot of water or piss' out of a window onto the heads of two maids who were sitting in the doorway. This 'did much annoy' the girls, 'the same water or piss having long stood or been in the said pot' (they knew this by the 'filthy smell or strength thereof'). Irked, one of them responded by calling Elizabeth a 'filthy dirty slut and dirty sow'. She then retorted by accusing her adversary of having had 'a bastard by an old man in the country'.[19]

Here was a rancorous city in miniature. Gossip, insults, and bodily effluents were all tossed about. But there were cleaner smells and harmonious sounds to add to the mix, too. Perfumes, medicines, and herbs all added their sweet scents to the air. Clean clothes were hung out of windows, fresh from the washerwoman's basin. In busier thoroughfares, the wafting aromas of baked pies tempted customers. It was a port town, too, so the smell of fresh fish – sold at the roadside by women – added another bracing tang.

Then of course there was the noise: the constant hum, the auditory tumult of a busy capital city. Human voices were everywhere. Every daytime trip down a London street was accompanied by racket and bustle. Contemporaries reported the rumbling of carts, the wail of singers and jangle of musicians, as well as the bellowing of hawkers' cries. Everywhere there was street food, with vendors' stalls a keystone of the City's landscape, and its sounds: 'Their shop's but little, some two yards' compass, yet it holds all sorts of fish, or herbs, or roots, strawberries, apples, or plums, cowcumbers, and such like ware. Nay, it is not destitute some times of nuts, and oranges, and lemons.' The stalls 'change every day almost, for she that was this day for fish, may be tomorrow for fruit; next day for herbs, another for roots'. So, 'you must hear them cry' before you knew what they sold.[20]

Accents mingled. Women sat in doorways gossiping while washing at the basin and working the needle and thread. Shopkeepers exchanged tattle with customers: 'What news?' they asked. Speech could be rough and direct. Billingsgate, the main fish market, became a byword for bad language. Court records abound with the spiky, irreverent tongues of Londoners. In 1633, for example, Winifred Vulcombe called a neighbour 'an old rotten witch, an old jade and a queane'.[21] Others were told they were 'scurvy, fat-arsed queans', 'mangy carrion', or 'shitten whore[s]'.[22] In 1639, when Eleanor Wright attempted to collect money from an old goldsmith, she found herself attacked by one of his friends, Elizabeth Merrick, who demanded of her: 'What was the rogue or the fiddler that though wentst running up and down the country withal?' Pulling up her coats 'in a shameful manner', Elizabeth announced that 'the fiddler had fiddled her', shouting mockingly: 'Come buck me fiddler, come fuck me fiddler.'[23]

It was all part of the communal experience of living in London. There were the church bells, the public performances, and sermons. Hackney coaches were a relatively recent addition to the din – 'saucy intruder[s]', to John Taylor, who as a waterman had his own cause to resent such alternative forms of public transport.[24] One might hear the beat of a drum or a trumpet's fanfare to announce a royal proclamation, or to advertise a performance like a play or a bear-baiting.[25] The sounds of pain, punishment, and legal vengeance might be heard too: the clamour as a criminal resisted arrest, the crack of a whip against the bloodied back of a minor miscreant, even the thronging crowd on its way to a hanging at Tyburn, on the western outskirts of town. Public punishments were deliberately noisy, designed to draw attention, such as the clanging of basins that often accompanied the 'carting' of those convicted of 'whoredom', symbolically expelling them from the City to the rough music of pounded pots and pans. These were sounds that had embedded themselves in the popular idiom: 'Away, away, thou filthy queane!' one woman yelled at another in 1611, clapping her hands: 'The cart and the basin is more fit for thee than thine own house! Ting, ting, ting!'[26]

———

As night fell, the clamour would recede. The city changed.

The twilight hours, as the sun set over the great parks of the west, were particularly strange: a liminal time when darkness encroached but the working day hadn't yet ended. It was a time of 'many mischiefs and assaults'. A moment when 'idle, lewd, and vagrant persons' emerged from their daytime haunts if 'lantern and candle-light is not hung out'.[27]

So, on dark nights, and especially from November onwards, beadles would do the rounds at about 6 p.m., clattering on people's doors, ordering householders to hang out their lanterns and candles.

As darkness enveloped the city, its human inhabitants tried to hold back the night with an array of flickering and fiery lights. Lanterns were set on street corners; certain key buildings, like the Guildhall, burned lights to ease passers-by. Young lads, 'link boys', carried flaming torches and offered to ferry people around for a few coins.[28]

At 9 p.m., curfew began: an age-old defence by the authorities against the dangerous dark. Now this was 'the dead time of the night when all good subjects should be at quiet taking their natural rest in their beds'.[29] Gradually, many of the lights were extinguished, leaving just a few to guide the small number of shuffling nocturnal travellers. For several hours, especially in wintertime, London was almost entirely black and deathly quiet, save the occasional shrill of an animal, or a domestic flare-up heard through the walls, or drunken scuffle between the nightwatch and some late returner from the tavern. It was said that the only respectable women who were out after sunset were 'honest matrons', rushing to attend a birth (something especially critical in the capital, where the fatality rate for pregnant women was double that of the countryside).[30]

'Nightwalking', the crime of being out at night without a good reason, kept the authorities busy. After the Long Parliament met in November 1640, and as the political crisis unfolded, the night-time arrests continued as normal: Margaret Huddleston of Oxfordshire, taken by the watch in St Martin's Lane, drunk.[31] Frances Wootton, alias Johnson – 'a common nightwalker and a rude person', 'very unruly' – arrested in June, and ordered to be 'put in a turret till will be quiet and work'.[32] Or Rowland Roberts, 'taken roaring in the street in the night in Fleet Street tumbling in the dirt he saith he was drunk he is miserable poor and naked'. He was given a shirt and a canvas doublet, 'admonished', and released.[33]

Certainly, Londoners liked a drink. The playwright Thomas Dekker was no doubt enjoying a degree of artistic licence when he wrote in 1632 that 'all trades, all professions sit tippling all day, all night, singing, dancing (when they can stand), laughing, cursing, swearing, fighting. A whole street is in some places but a continued alehouse.'[34] But there were numerous spots to buy a bottle of beer or a pint of wine. One count in 1620 found some 400 taverns in London, and these were just the classier establishments. In England as a whole there was more than one alehouse per hundred inhabitants, which would equate to nearly 4,000 in London by the 1630s.[35] Small wonder that Londoners might occasionally find themselves having to be carried home drunk in a chair.[36] Even genteel Covent Garden was found to have 24 alehouses in 1639.

Covent Garden was opulent and ordered, despite its drinking holes. But other parts of London were downright seedy. In Whitechapel there was a street known as 'Codpiece Row', while the whole ward of Farringdon Without, which included Holborn and Bridewell itself, was among London's seamiest locales.[37] 'Very spacious and full of dangerous persons,' someone said of it in 1619.[38] It was also the home to John Bankes, who must have found it rather different to Keswick.

Another dodgy area was Turnmill Street, said to be the domicile of 'many lewd and loose persons'. These were folk who would 'keep common and notorious brothel houses and harbour and entertain divers impudent and infamous queanes and whores', women whose trade was described as the 'alluring and enticing of such as pass by to commit the detestable sin of whoredom and fornication'. Among the street's inhabitants in the 1630s was a notorious character known as 'Pocky Faced Dall'.[39]

In 1602, Bridewell prison itself had briefly been run by a thoroughly disreputable master, Thomas Stanley, as a high-end bordello, complete with meals of 'crabs, lobsters, artichoke pies and gallons of wine'.[40] For there was always a thin line in London between respectability and disrepute. This was a city of margins, of twilight, a place where many people never really settled. The rich had their places in the country; the poor would move from house to house. Even the streets themselves ran with a kind of muddy slime that was neither quite solid nor liquid. Criminals appeared in places people gathered, like marketplaces and the sites of public sermons, and then they vanished into the shadows. Some had come from afar, like a thief brought in for stealing from his master, who was identified as a northerner who 'speaketh very broad and northernly'.[41] Some wore disguises or cross-dressed, like Margaret

Porter (alias Smith), arrested in 1633, who 'often went abroad in man's apparel' and was 'the overthrow of divers persons by her lewd course of life'.[42] If the authorities picked them up, they were sent away. In 1635, one Christopher Lusher was arrested as a 'daily pickpocket in the markets' and sent to Virginia.[43] Anthony Grimes was found in Cripplegate begging, and on examination it was recorded that he 'saith he is a Yorkshireman and would gladly return'.[44]

It was difficult, even, to see where London ended and the countryside began. Fields outside the city would flutter with washing left out to dry and textiles on tenterhooks. You would never be more than twenty minutes' walk from open country, so Londoners might head out there for air, for exercise, or just to escape. Or they might go for sex. Londoners could suffer insults like being called a 'pocky lousy hedge whore', or told 'thou hast been occupied under every hedge over thy milk pail': testament to the practise of retiring to the fields for sexual encounters.[45]

Small wonder, for there was never much scope for privacy in the metropolis. Sounds travelled through walls and floorboards. Anyone engaging in illicit behaviour, especially of the noisy kind, ran the risk of discovery. The records of Bridewell prison abound with lovers 'taken in bed' with each other, or the like. In June 1641, one Alice Parker was 'taken in bed with two men at one time on a bed', while Ann Doewell was arrested 'for keeping company with Edward Haynes in a wild & uncivil manner' (meaning they were engaged in either drunkenness or very loud sex), much to the annoyance of Edward's wife.[46] Front doors could never quite block out the disorder of the street: such as when, in 1641, a man from Cambridge was arrested 'for running into mens houses with a prong and truncheon to their great terror'.[47] The bestselling Puritan minister William Gouge, who was a sometime governor of the Bridewell and who regularly enjoyed the prison's wine-fuelled annual dinners, was in 1640 shocked to see three 'nightwalkers' clambering into his yard, one carrying a knife.[48] Burglary, too, was a fact of life. In the 1630s, houses near that of Edward Nicholas in King Street – right next to Whitehall Palace – had been rustled in the night.[49]

Beggars came to doors: in 1632, one 'John Dumb', who 'either cannot or will not speak', made the mistake of seeking alms at the door of Robert Heath, then Lord Chief Justice of the Common Pleas, and was arrested for his pains.[50] The rich travelled around in coaches so as to avoid the throng, although they didn't always succeed. Beggars sometimes tried to pull wealthy folk out of their carriages and rifle them for money then and there. On one occasion in 1635, John Bankes, when Attorney-General, had a woman spit into his coach. It must have been an unpleasant experience.[51]

———

King Charles did not love London. He was a man who sought order; London was a city of complexity and clamour. In the 1630s, he had wished to bring regularity to the streets, putting in pavements and banning short cab journeys, but his relationship with the English capital was always complicated, never smooth.[52] The City had invested heavily in an Irish plantation, centred on Derry. They even tried to rename the place 'Londonderry'. But there were allegations of mismanagement and Charles had the City prosecuted in Star Chamber and handed a ruinous fine. The issue was a major cause of anger in the City, and Londoners anyway were proud of their independence and irreverence. One jesting ballad, published in 1635, imagined the Devil coming to the Earth and deciding – naturally – to set himself up as a London property magnate, only to be driven out by 'fishwives'.[53] If Londoners felt they could parry the attention of the Devil, then a mere King of England was nothing.

They had, indeed, been regularly confronted with the operation of the royal prerogative. In the 1630s, Charles had adopted a policy of forcing the gentry and nobility out of London during the winter season, so that they weren't gadding about town when they should be on their estates being good charitable landowners and relieving the poor. It was a noble policy, but it had very shaky constitutional foundations.[54] Essentially it was grounded in royal proclamations, backed by prosecution for 'contempt' in Star Chamber. To many, this was a bright red flag. Legislating by proclamation rather than

Parliament was the kind of behaviour to be expected of an absolutist, not a respecter of the English common law. So when Charles had his attorneys-general draw up lists of those who sojourned around London when they should have gone home to the provinces, as a prelude to a potential prosecution, it raised many hackles.

Then there were the building regulations. As unglamorous as these might seem to us today, they sometimes created major constitutional flashpoints. London was growing, and it needed more buildings. But the royal government worried that it was growing too fast. In addition, it realised that there was money to be made fining people for illegal construction. The trouble, again, was that there wasn't effective statute law to do so. Here once more, therefore, the government relied on the prerogative. Technically, there was a relevant common law offence – which was to commit nuisance by taking away someone's light, air, or prospect (their view). But the courts didn't always convict. A particular cause célèbre was that of one Ralph Macro – possibly an Italian émigré. He had constructed a new building, but had been prosecuted for nuisance on the grounds that he (allegedly) blocked a neighbour's sunlight. The courts found in his favour, so the case was passed to Attorney-General Bankes, who brought it to Star Chamber, at which Macro was fined and made to pay significant damages. Then, when Parliament returned, Macro petitioned the House of Lords. His appeal was on the grounds that Bankes's Star Chamber case was illegal – we might say unconstitutional – as it was based on the royal prerogative rather than statute or common law.[55]

Such cases might look like mere local squabbles, but the language Macro used in his petition showed they were given a much broader resonance. If this particular Londoner was prosecuted by Bankes in this way, then it opened the door to the king – once more – creating enforceable laws, not through Parliament but by proclamation. It was of deep significance, and it gave London a vested interest in the big constitutional debates.

And yet, there was another side to London's view. The king's power, after all, could be useful. For those who wanted to see the potential value of the royal prerogative, they might look no further than Bridewell itself. For it was never grounded in any statute, yet it had wide powers to arrest and imprison. And with the growing disorders associated with the religious sects – not to mention the street protests and the disbanded soldiers still prowling the streets – maybe the brute force of order and discipline was more helpful to those in charge than the niceties of the law. It was food for thought, at least.

8

What is Begun with the Tongue
and the Pen

One of those returning to the capital as Parliament reassembled on 20 October was the Speaker of the House of Commons, William Lenthall.

A successful lawyer, now entering his fifties, Lenthall had spent the recess at his home in north Oxfordshire, enjoying the long, warm evenings in the sleepy town of Woodstock. The place was built in sturdy Cotswold stone with slated roofs and chimneys. It had a market, a cross, a guildhall, an almshouse for the poor with a garden, and a grammar school. It was a calm, even idyllic place – at least compared to London. Lenthall was the town's Recorder, responsible for managing its legal business. It brought generally happy relations with the inhabitants: they not only paid him a small wage but they also sent him gifts, like a cake at Christmas, worth 18 shillings and despatched to his lodgings in London.[1]

Lenthall evidently enjoyed his work at Woodstock, and not just for the cakes. On 17 September 1641, just over a week into the parliamentary recess, the town accounts recorded him gifting venison for feasting. He had stayed there with his wife, the two of them giving 8s. 11d. worth of wine to the town.[2] But soon he would be dragged back to Westminster, making the journey down through the Chilterns – resplendent in their autumn coat of colourful deciduous woods. By 20 October, he had returned to his lodgings at Charing Cross, the fresh country air left behind him.

It had been a tense week. More and more disbanded royal soldiers were skulking into the capital, and placards had been appearing around the city denouncing the Junto. Ambassador Giustinian had seen these earlier in the month, noting the public posters accusing the Junto 'of being the authors of seditious deliberations, traitors to the king, the kingdom and the nobility and of having conspired with the Scots to the hurt of the people here'.[3]

Sometime after eight in the morning of the 20th, Lenthall left his lodgings and proceeded to the Palace of Westminster. Though it was the day of return from summer recess, the Commons was virtually empty. St Stephen's Chapel was hauntingly quiet: the murmurs of fewer than forty men echoed through the high-walled chamber. It was not yet quorate, so after prayers, Lenthall and those MPs present had to wait until, one by one, enough of their colleagues arrived for them to begin business. It took a quarter of an hour or so. An utter embarrassment.[4]

One of those who waited, looking up towards Lenthall's raised seat, was a Suffolk MP with a busy little face. His name was Sir Simonds D'Ewes.

———

For Simonds D'Ewes, if there was one moment in which he decided to pursue the path of politics, it was when, as a youngster, he fell headlong into a pit of horseshit.

D'Ewes was born at Coaxden Hall by the River Axe, in a lush, rainswept river valley in the far west of Dorset.[5] Later, he remembered his kindly grandfather, with his cellar full of 'cider, strong beer, and several wines', which the seven-year-old D'Ewes once raided and drank, and from which he got mortally sick.[6] The same year, though, the family suddenly moved to Suffolk, and it was on the journey there that Simonds, who would dearly miss his old home and his grandparents, had his misadventure with the horse manure. He had been trying to catch birds in a barn, attached to the Red Lion in Blandford, and the lesson he took was that God had preserved his life – if not the clean smell of his clothes – for a future of 'good service both to Church and Commonwealth'.[7]

He was earnest and hardworking. Already, aged thirteen, Simonds was collecting sermons and writing letters about the latest political news, and it was his schoolmaster who taught Simonds what may have been his greatest lesson. It was not enough, he said, to merely attend sermons and listen. You had to take notes – to become what D'Ewes would later call 'a rational hearer'. Notetaking was to dominate Simonds's life. At church, he scribbled down a record of what he heard, collating and editing it into manageable memoirs in the evening. Later in life, when he embarked on a career in law, D'Ewes would sit in Westminster Hall and record cases, arguments, and judgements. He also, from a very specific date – 27 February 1620 – while a student at Cambridge University, decided to record 'each particular day's passages', relating to his life, 'which were most memorable'. The diaries he wrote from then have been lost, but they would be distilled into an autobiography written in the late 1630s which survives: a remarkable record of a tumultuous age.

D'Ewes was a voracious scholar. He sometimes skipped meals so he could continue reading.[8] He flourished at Cambridge, referring to the university later as his 'dear mother', from whose 'full breasts' he had 'sucked so much variety of learning'.[9] In religion, he was a Calvinist and a Puritan, though contrary to the modern stereotype he lived life to the full: eating, drinking, and gossiping. As a student he had also enjoyed sports like bowling, tennis, running, angling, and even an occasionally rather rough game of football. He just also made sure he attended church when necessary and that he engaged with sermons and the Word of God. Not for him any dumb rituals: his was an active piety. He read, thought, discussed, and prayed.

Away from his faith, his most profound love would be for history. More than just a buff, he was an archive nut. He had reached the conclusion that 'records, and other exotic monuments of antiquity, were the most ravishing and satisfying part of human knowledge'.[10] Helpfully he had married an heiress, the significantly younger Anne, thus removing the need for such irritations as a career. And so he ensconced himself in the archives of the Tower of London, hoping one day to write a great history of Britain. By the 1630s he lived in some comfort at Islington, surrounded by his burgeoning library – a life devoted to study.

Then things went wrong. The 1630s were not kind to D'Ewes. His father died, shortly after an unpleasant row with the lawyer Nicholas Hyde. Although Simonds's marriage was mostly happy, several of his and Anne's children died young. He had also seen his great antiquarian mentor Robert Cotton ruined. Cotton had allowed his glorious library to be used by those opposing Charles's policies, so the king had it closed and filleted by government agents. Cotton was even briefly imprisoned, and soon died – so D'Ewes believed – of a broken heart. Charles's government seemed to be striking at everything D'Ewes held so dear.

D'Ewes was also, to his horror, forced out of Islington to the country, away from his beloved archives, when Charles tried to use his prerogative powers to compel wealthy landowners to leave the capital. To a cosmopolitan man like D'Ewes, it was deeply annoying and legally questionable. In Suffolk he then ended up clashing with his local minister, a busy Ceremonialist. And more humiliations were to come. D'Ewes would be chosen as a sheriff, and his job would include collecting Ship Money, a levy he considered entirely illegal. No surprise that he followed John Hampden's case carefully and wrote up copious notes – though he was forced to keep them to himself for fear of prosecution. D'Ewes also wrote a tract arguing in favour of religious liberty, but again kept that quiet and in manuscript form. The government was forcing him to suppress his conscience. It was not something that came easily to D'Ewes. He could be pompous and vain, but he wasn't venal.

Come late 1640 and D'Ewes was finally ready to put into effect his calling from God, as revealed to him three decades ago in the pile of Dorset horseshit. He stood for Parliament, and was duly elected as MP for Sudbury. Taking his seat, he put two of his greatest passions to use. The first was for antiquarian scholarship: he regularly spoke in debates and was often sent to his lodgings near Parliament – in Goat Alley – to recover notes on historical records.[11]

The second was for notetaking, for he wrote down extensive records of every day's proceedings, taking time most evenings to collate them into a parliamentary diary. It wasn't the only such diary at this time: there are several that survive. But D'Ewes's account is stunning in its detail. Motions, speeches, even reactions, are captured. It isn't an objective record: D'Ewes was utterly self-important, so his own speeches – however obscure – are reported at length. He also, of course, had to be there to take notes. He often arrived late, or left early. Like anyone, his stamina for endless debates was not unlimited, and he suffered from colds, sickness, and tiredness that led him occasionally to slip out of the house, either back to Goat Alley or to his new lodgings at Covent Garden. And in early August 1641, his wife, Anne, died – tragically young, from smallpox. For a time, he stayed away from Parliament, and even when he returned his diary entries were terse and laconic. It was like his purpose had simply gone, though in time it would come back.

D'Ewes also had his own views of his fellow members and on the issues of the day, which coloured his record. He had fairly little time for Speaker Lenthall, whom he saw as not much more than a rustic ingenu. D'Ewes favoured a reformed episcopacy, but he evidently greatly disliked the tub-preachers and sects. At one point he proposed an act for the 'severe punishing of tradesmen and other ignorant persons who shall presume to preach'.[12] And he was a constitutionalist: he had been appalled by Ship Money, was fiercely protective of the privileges of Parliament, and had an entirely honourable repeated willingness to defend the voting rights of the poor. Now though, he worried about the hardliners in the Junto – the 'fiery spirits' as he called them. Men like William Strode, the radical Devonian who had spent most of the 1630s in prison without trial for his allegedly seditious behaviour as an MP in 1629. Such people, D'Ewes thought, were a threat to the 'ancient constitution' because they wanted to reform it so far away from the king.

Sir Simonds would be a nearly constant presence in Parliament over the coming months. But as he sat on the benches, near the front, both his ability to stand up for the 'ancient constitution', and his patience for Speaker Lenthall would be severely tested.

———

It was to be a testing time. That much was already apparent, for as members gradually made their way to the palace on the 20th, they were unnerved to notice that Parliament now had a guard of soldiers. These had been placed there, under the command of the Earl of Essex, by the Junto-dominated recess committee the previous day, a response to the threat posed by the Scottish 'Incident'.[13] It was a harbinger for what would become a critical question: Who controlled England's armed forces? The Junto's first target, however, was the bishops in the House of Lords.

It was a political manoeuvre – a tactical gambit. The fallout between Lords and Commons before recess had concentrated the Junto's minds on their weakness in the upper house. They knew, though, that if they could remove the bishops, then they could change the balance. A bill to exclude the bishops from secular offices, critically including their seats in the House of Lords, was pushed onward with some speed. On the 21st, it was read twice, then sent immediately to committee, and then passed on the 23rd, and sent up to the Lords.[14] Pym's idea was to have it in force within three weeks.[15] The tempo had changed dramatically, and the Junto was back on the attack.

The Commons remained pretty thin. Many MPs were still commuting in from outside London because of lingering fears of the plague – so most days they didn't arrive until around 10 a.m. Others stayed away altogether. A division on the 22nd saw just 70 ayes and 59 noes, implying that three-quarters of MPs were absent.[16] On Saturday 23rd, there were just 41 present after prayers, and at one point the serjeant had to be sent with the mace into Westminster Hall to round up MPs who were strolling there.[17]

Then, on 25 October, MPs were given a terrifying reminder of the threats of both plague and conspiracy.

Speaker Lenthall had taken his seat between nine and ten in the morning and the day had carried on as normal. At some point D'Ewes, who was feeling ill, withdrew from the house and returned to his lodgings. Then, shortly after he left, a porter – one of those men who carried things across London – approached the Serjeant of the House at the door. He had, he said, a letter for Pym himself. Unaware of what he was carrying, the serjeant brought the letter to Pym in his seat. Pym opened it, and out fell 'an abominable rag', covered in filth and blood.

In what was no doubt a developing commotion on the benches, Pym pulled out the letter that accompanied the rag. It was a 'scandalous libel', and was passed to the assistant clerk, John Rushworth, who read it out. In the text, Pym was called a bribetaker and a traitor, 'and other opprobrious names'. But the greatest horror came in the description of the rag itself, for the letter claimed it was 'a clout drawn through a plague sore', which he, the author, 'had running upon him hoping that the same should kill him [Pym] by infection'. If this didn't work, the author wrote, then he also had a dagger.

Recoiling in shock, Rushworth immediately threw down the infected letter, and it was carried out of the house in haste. The porter, who was evidently still milling around, was called in and demanded where he had got the letter from. All he could say was that it had been given to him that morning by a man on horseback on Fishstreet Hill in the City, who had paid him a shilling to deliver it 'with great care and speed'.[18]

It was a sure sign that there were those out there who wished the Junto harm, and a sensational pamphlet was soon ready to recount the incident – complete with a woodcut image of Pym – to a horrified public.[19] But the house continued to sit.

––––––

The day after this alarm, Lord Keeper Littleton read a letter from Charles to the upper house. It promised the king's return as soon as possible.[20] All this made the Junto's next move the more urgent. On Thursday 28th, Robert Goodwin, MP for East Grinstead and another backbench Junto man, brought a motion to remove 'ill counsellors' around the king, and to prevent new ones being appointed. It was a direct attack on the king's power to choose his government.[21]

The debate was electric, though it started slowly. A speech by Mr Smith of the Middle Temple rambled – D'Ewes thought it had been recycled from one intended to oppose Ship Money. It was followed, though, by a tour de force by William Strode. D'Ewes, who didn't care for the Devonian, said it was a speech of 'great violence'. Strode's core argument was simple: Parliament must have a veto over government officers, otherwise all the previous gains would be lost.

The speech then drew a remarkable response from Edward Hyde. A well-connected Wiltshire MP, Hyde was talented, opinionated, and eloquent. He was one of those who had moved from being a moderate reformer to a stance of ever more defiant royalism. He rose to speak. Strode was mistaken, he argued. The Parliament had done plenty of good for the country. But the king's right to appoint his own great officers was 'an hereditary flower of the crown'.[22] Removing this would be a constitutional leap into the unknown.

The next day, Edward Nicholas wrote once more to Charles, who was finally winding up his affairs in Scotland. Nicholas was an incisive witness to events in Parliament. When he himself had been an MP back in the 1620s, his notes were often more detailed than the official record, and he had brought this careful vigilance to his new role as Charles's eyes. Nicholas clearly felt the debate on 28 October was a critical moment, reporting in detail the Junto's arguments in favour of Parliament taking control of royal appointments. But he was also optimistic; in fact rather more so than he had been for some time. 'There appeared,' he wrote, 'so many in the Commons House against this business, that some conceive that there will be no further proceeding in it.' He doubted this was so, alas, but he did note the prominence of a group of moderate MPs: Lord Falkland, Sir John Strangways, Mr Waller, Mr Holborne, and Edward Hyde.[23]

Tellingly, many of the men identified by Nicholas had once been reformists. Lord Falkland, for example, was an urbane aristocrat, of remarkable intellect and widely beloved, who had also vehemently opposed Ship Money. Holborne had even been one of John Hampden's lawyers during the great Ship Money case of 1637, arguing against Bankes and Littleton. Now these men were beginning to think that reform had gone too far, and that the Junto was treading into dangerous constitutional territory.

The appearance of what looked like a co-ordinated royalist party in the Commons was very bad news for the Junto. Already struggling to get their way in the Lords, now they had to beware of losing their core power-base in the lower house too. But they had a plan. Back in November 1640, a suggestion had been made that Parliament collect its grievances and present them to the king.[24] It picked up on a suggestion that Pym had made back in the spring of 1640, during the Short Parliament: that the complaints of the kingdom should be collected into a grand 'Remonstrance'. Now the idea was revived. A committee, created some months ago to discuss it, had now been reanimated. On the 29th, it was ordered to report to the Commons on its progress. The date set for this was Monday 1 November.[25]

The Remonstrance, when it came, was likely to be explosive – a broadside aimed as much at the Lords, who were blocking necessary reform, as at the royal government. And it would be made public. It would, so the idea went, render the Junto's programme so popular as to be irresistible.

As October passed, London grew darker, and the nights got longer. The Bridewell was still sweeping the streets of people it considered dangerous. On the 22nd, two men calling themselves Miles Burrows and Henry Cragge were nabbed, 'for absenting themselves from their masters' service & lying out in the night a week together, selling their clothes and were taken drinking in the night late'. It was ordered that 'their hair to be cut' and they were to be 'set to labour & none to come to them to give them strong drink or tobacco'.[26] Everywhere there was suspicion. That same day there was an altercation in which a company of disbanded troopers from the king's army confronted and threatened the men guarding Parliament. It ended with five of the soldiers being apprehended and thrown in the Gatehouse prison.[27] One Westminster inhabitant told a friend who worked in the Exchequer that the town was starting to feel like a garrison, 'continually guarded night and day by some of the Trained Bands'.[28] Ambassador Giustinian could see the jeopardy that England was in: 'There is a danger,' he wrote to the Senate, 'that what is begun with the tongue and the pen, may end at length with the sword.'[29]

Edward Nicholas, meanwhile, was convinced he was being watched and that his letters were being opened and told the king as much.[30] When Charles responded, he agreed it was wise to be as discreet as possible. He had a specific instruction, too. In his reply, he enclosed a letter to the queen. And he was especially clear about one thing: Nicholas was to take the letter to Oatlands himself – but 'when ye deliver this inclosed to my wife, desire her not to open it but when she was alone'.[31]

Even the royal household might be filled with spies.

9

The Wizard's Daughter

The walls of the Stuart court were permeable. People moved in and out. Several of those with access to the king and queen were allied with the Junto. The Lord Chamberlain, one of the officers managing the royal household, was the Earl of Essex, a radical Junto man. There is, therefore, little surprise that information passed across political thresholds. There were those, like cats in the night, who prowled between the two camps. It was to be expected in this porous age.

One of those connected to both court and Junto was Lucy Hay, Lady Carlisle. She had quite the background. Born Lucy Percy in 1599, her father had been a sorcerer, and her brother was Admiral of the Fleet. Yet she was still the most remarkable member of her family.[1]

Young Lucy had endured a troubled early life. When she was just six, her father, Henry Percy, 9th Earl of Northumberland, was sent to the Tower for involvement in the Gunpowder Plot. Here he would spend over fifteen years, during which time Lucy grew up and married a Scot. His name was James Hay, and he was a man so physically unprepossessing that Charles's waspish sister, Elizabeth, christened him 'Camel-face'. Lucy's incarcerated father – the sorcerer – cordially despised the young James Hay, and offered her £20,000 to call off the marriage. Such a sum would normally break the deepest enchantment, but Lucy – who was anything but attracted to the man – had a better sense of her own interests, and rather impolitely refused.

James Hay's attraction was simple enough, for he had excellent connections. At the Hays' wedding feast in 1617, King James, Prince Charles, and the future Duke of Buckingham had all been present. Maybe it was then that Lucy first caught Buckingham's roving eye, for within a few years the two were lovers. With James Hay away on a diplomatic mission in 1619, Buckingham (allegedly) made sure any return was delayed long enough so he could sleep with Lucy. Neither did Buckingham's own wedding, in 1620, lead to any pause to the relationship.

By the early years of Charles's reign, not only the duke's wife but also his sister and mother were all said to hate Lucy 'to death'.[2] The greatest of Lucy Hay's crimes, in their eyes, was not that she was Buckingham's lover, but that she was more popular than they were with the queen. In many ways, this was surprising. Not only were Lucy Hay and Queen Henrietta Maria strikingly different; they were also rivals for the affections of the one man who mattered most, even more than the Duke of Buckingham: the king. With the royal marriage sailing through rocky waters, Buckingham had sensed an opportunity. To secure his own interests, he would share his lover. Lucy Hay, Lady Carlisle after her husband had taken an earldom, would be paraded before Charles as tempting sexual bait. In 1626, she was brought into the royal bedchamber, decidedly – and tellingly – against the wishes of the queen. The trap was set.

Charles, though, was so undersexed in his early adulthood that some suspected he suffered the 'green sickness' – the infamous ailment of the erotically frustrated.[3] * The reality was that he was way too shy a match for the vivacious Lucy. More to the point, he was gradually falling in love with the one woman no one expected him to – his wife. The irony, then, was that Buckingham's failure to tempt the king into a spot of traditional monarchical infidelity probably ensured Lucy's rise at court. For now, she was attached to the queen.

---

*The green sickness, in which sexual inactivity led to an unusually pale complexion, was generally seen as a disease in girls, but sometimes boys got it too.

In 1627, a rearrangement at court saw the Queen's Bedchamber formally separated from the King's Privy Chamber, leaving the queen's ladies-in-waiting to enjoy greater autonomy from the men. As the queen rose in influence, and with Buckingham dead, the ladies-in-waiting blossomed. Now, in the halcyon days of the 1630s, when everything depended on the politics of the royal court, they could act as brokers between members of the aristocracy and the queen, and by extension the king himself. Lucy was in her element.

It was one of Lady Carlisle's misfortunes that she quickly attracted the attention of the poets. Over a dozen court versifiers found the time to comment upon her, some praising her beauty and wit, others critiquing her immorality, ego, ambition, and penchant for intrigue. Sir John Suckling, for his part, fantasised about undressing her in the gardens at Hampton Court. She was a key figure. Sometimes, in collections of ciphers used for secret diplomatic correspondence, Lady Carlisle was considered important enough to have her own code number. The English agent in Turin, for example, had her as '380'.[4] She attended the queen's masques and occasionally danced in them. In one stunning production, she performed in Ben Jonson's masque *Chloridia*, in which the queen played the Goddess of Spring, and Lucy and the ladies-in-waiting were her nymphs. The story saw the goddess bringing harmony after the violence of winter, with the scene eventually transforming into a peaceful garden.

Charles's court played on this image of melodious concord, grounded by a neat social hierarchy. Yet the reality of court politics was that it was a contest in which some rose and some fell, and where the orderly façade concealed backbiting and ambition. There were moments when Lucy looked like losing. The forthright Lady Denbigh, sister to the recently assassinated Duke of Buckingham, remained an utterly fearsome rival, and in 1629 Lucy was briefly banished from court for offending the French ambassador. Tongues wagged later, too, when it seemed Lucy was promoting Catholics at court, though one of those she was alleged to be in league with was unimpressed: 'Lady Carlisle has no religion but her own complexion,' he sniffed.[5]

To some, Lady Carlisle was almost a rival to the queen. Yet her character always offered a marked contrast to that of Henrietta Maria. The queen was lively in her own way; courtiers commented on her sense of fun and charm – a welcome contrast to her rather austere husband. And she brought a French style of courtly demureness, based on the Platonic love of her admirers. Devotion and modesty, so the idea went, would ultimately promote social harmony and order. Lady Carlisle was different. Her image – and, we must suppose, her real personality – was grounded in wit and sensuality. While those male courtiers devoted to the queen were drawn by her elegant politesse, those drawn to Lucy Hay wanted to make jokes with her and ultimately to sleep with her. She was what one smitten courtier – a direct descendent of Thomas Cromwell no less – called 'the killing beauty of the world'.[6]

Courtly relationships were always symbiotic. Ladies would form alliances with men who had something to offer the king – often such unglamorous fruits as administrative skill and diligence. Lucy, for example, had maintained regular contact with Thomas Wentworth, the future Earl of Strafford, and she may have helped oil the wheels of promotion for him. Her husband, it seems, helped gain Wentworth his position as Lord Deputy of Ireland. It was a useful contact to have, because James Hay had bought extensive lands there, and the interests of these needed protecting.

Lucy's relationship with Wentworth only deepened when her husband, James, died in 1636, heavily in debt.[7] Partly, it seems, she was intrigued by – even attracted to – the earnest Yorkshireman. On the other hand, she now possessed her husband's Irish lands, so there was an element of self-preservation too. Wentworth himself was rather taken by Lucy, and there are moments his Platonic desire for her threatened to be overcome by something else. The two exchanged stunning Van Dyck portraits of each other. His was slightly awkward, hers suggestive.

There is an interesting contrast to be made to the same painter's portrait of the queen around the same time. Henrietta Maria appears formal and almost stiff, but Lucy Carlisle is inviting, enticing, even seductive – her hand playfully pulling back a curtain. What

Wentworth read into this we can only imagine. A 'nobler nor more intelligent friendship did I never meet with in all my life', he gushed. 'You might tell her,' he wrote in an uncharacteristic moment of candour, that 'sometimes when she looks at herself at night in the glass that I have the ambition to be one of those servants she will suffer to honour her.'[8] Wentworth was happily married and infamously stern, yet Lady Carlisle made him forget himself.

Her main interests, though, always remained with her own family, and if there is one thing people needed to remember about Lucy Hay, Lady Carlisle, it is that she remained at heart a Percy. She was a representative of, and an agent for, one of the greatest noble households of England. When not at court, she spent much time with her sister, Dorothy – a very different woman, with whom Lucy had a complex relationship. Dorothy had married another great aristocrat, Robert Sidney, later the Earl of Leicester, and had moved to his great mansion at Penshurst in the wooded Kent countryside.

Lucy Carlisle's biggest coup of all came in 1638, when she was able to help her beloved brother Algernon, now the Earl of Northumberland, gain the position of Lord High Admiral.* Meanwhile her brother-in-law, now the Earl of Leicester, presented another such project. His star was rising, matched by a grand new mansion in the capital. In 1631, the king had allowed the licensing of a newbuild at Swan Close in St Martin-in-the-Fields. It took five years for work to begin, but by 1637, an upper storey was on the way to completion.[9] Lucy would be a regular visitor when in town, enjoying the earl's fine Burgundy. By now, too, she had attracted yet another admirer: this time the slippery Earl of Holland, who was said to be her 'dog'. A Puritan of some considerable wealth, Holland had taken to writing poems in Lucy's honour. According to Dorothy, they were 'the worst that was ever seen'.[10]

––––––

*A move that had the additional consequence of removing Edward Nicholas from lucrative office.

As Charles's rule faltered, Lucy watched. In 1639, she and her great rival Lady Denbigh were appointed to collect money for the war effort against the Scots, from England's women. The two court ladies may have been able to patch over their differences, temporarily at least, but their contribution to the royal cause failed to be decisive. By 1640, indeed, Lucy had become enmeshed in the world of the Junto peers, with her brother Northumberland and her admirer Holland. She also had kin links to the Bedfords, while Essex was a maternal cousin, and among the family friends of the Leicesters was Lord Mandeville.

Lucy Carlisle and Lord Mandeville occupied a similar world, their most obvious point of contact being the Leicesters. Mandeville was something of a trusted uncle to Dorothy's daughter Doll, to whom – in a family running joke – he would act as a playful suitor. Like Mandeville, Lucy was an astute observer of contemporary politics. When the Short Parliament sat, she noted a general sense of foreboding: 'The Parliament has begun this day so strangely as I find everybody despairs of any good that can come from it.'[11] On 3 November 1640, she'd attended the opening of the Long Parliament, writing to Dorothy with a scathing review of Lord Keeper Finch's oration: 'The worst speech, to my thinking, that was ever made.'[12]

She kept her ear to the ground for the comings and goings within the royal government.[13] She visited Strafford at least twice during the cold winter months when he was imprisoned in the Tower, on Christmas Eve and New Year's Eve 1640.[14] Yet however bitterly she took the public beheading of her friend in May, the following month did bring a major promotion for one of her kin. For Leicester, her brother-in-law, now became Lord Lieutenant of Ireland. Meanwhile Lucy was making herself a rather surprising new personal alliance. Having spent the 1620s and 1630s in the celestial realm of the king's court, surrounded by the rich and the flamboyant, she now found herself connecting with someone from a very different world altogether: John Pym.

No one knew exactly the nature of Lady Carlisle's relationship with Pym. The gossips put it about that they were lovers, but that is singularly unlikely. Extramarital dalliances were even less in John

Pym's character than they were in King Charles's. And in any case, for Lucy, the Puritan's power was attractive enough without ever needing to be an aphrodisiac. It was later recalled that Lucy had become a Puritan, and though this is apparently far-fetched, it is less improbable than she and Pym ever sharing a bed. The royalist Philip Warwick was scathingly sarcastic in his memoirs. 'That busy stateswoman, the Countess of Carlisle,' he recalled, at this time 'changed her gallant from Strafford to Mr Pym, and was become such a she-saint, that she frequented their sermons and took notes.'[15]

Yet whatever we make of Lucy's new connection, she remained close to the queen. If this again seems remarkable at first glance, there is another possibility, a very likely one indeed, which is that all sides knew Lucy had feet in both camps. She was a go-between, but also potentially a spy – a double agent, even. Neither the queen nor Pym can have been naïve enough not to understand that Lucy was primarily out for herself and her family. But both probably saw her as a potentially useful tool: passing on bits of gossip, feeding information each way.

One intriguing – indeed tantalising – moment in the early autumn of 1641 gives a sense of one of the roles she played. On 26 September, Edward Nicholas had been attending on the queen at Oatlands. Here, the queen gave him a paper, which she said had been brought to her by Lady Carlisle, who in turn said she had it from Mandeville.[16] The contents are not mentioned, but they seem to have involved some information that would have been embarrassing to the Junto. Nicholas thought it worth making public, though not by the king or queen themselves. It was too grubby a business for them. Rather, the king should wait for a couple of days before doing anything, by which time the contents of the paper would have been made available anyway.

But what was it? Had Lucy taken something from Mandeville's possession – perhaps at Chelsea or Leicester's grand new London house? Or was Mandeville feeding information to the queen for his own purposes? The paper, for what it is worth, was seemingly never published, though Nicholas alluded to its contents later in his own letter. Reading between his careful lines, it seems to have involved some leak around the king's person in Scotland.[17] The only individual with the means to be at the centre of that was the secretary of state, the elder Henry Vane. Useful information for Nicholas, but not something he didn't already suspect. It was low-grade intelligence, therefore, but it helped reinforce Lucy's position in the queen's household. Maybe Mandeville was feeding her expendable information, which would then help Lucy keep the trust of the queen, and maybe even win that of Edward Nicholas?

For his part, Nicholas was also interested in what was going on at Mandeville's Chelsea residence. He knew this, and other places, had hosted a series of gatherings during the recess, in which Pym and others had sat to discuss tactics. Edward Hyde later named the Earl of Holland's house in Kensington as another meeting place, and noted how there were 'some men' at the Junto meetings who still saw the queen as their best path to advancement, so leaked information to her. Their aim, after all, was personal promotion more so than the cause. Hyde also thought Lucy was passing intelligence about the queen to Holland.[18] It was an increasingly murky world.

But did the queen really trust her old friend any more? On 10 November, Nicholas received a letter from Henrietta Maria, noting how difficult it was to find people to carry letters to Scotland to her husband. 'I am so ill provided with persons that I dare trust,' she wrote, 'that at this instant I have no living creature that I dare send.'[19] It was unlikely the queen was considering sending Lady Carlisle to Scotland. But the language is wider-reaching than this. It is almost as if the queen was trying, in words of the utmost care and discretion, to warn Nicholas that her own household was not to be trusted. Or members of it.

───────

It's possible Lucy Carlisle was with sister and brother-in-law, Leicester, at their great house in the West End on the afternoon of 31 October. That was the day when everything changed.

Wherever Lucy was, the man who arrived there in the dead of night would bring devastating news. He had ridden hard across England, through the wet lanes clogged with newly fallen leaves.

His name was Owen O'Connelly, and it was a matter of the most pressing urgency. It related to Ireland. Something had happened. Something terrible. He must speak to Leicester, the rider urged. Only the earl would do.

Ushered into the great mansion with its ornate fittings and plush new carpets, the rider removed his muddy spurs and was given a seat, and Leicester was summoned. O'Connelly's news was fearsome indeed. Ireland, suddenly, had risen in revolt.

————

Ireland's history had been intertwined with England's for centuries, mostly for ill. In the twelfth century, the Anglo-Normans had landed with their wooden boats and brought large areas of the island under England's dominion, but it was the Tudors who really introduced colonial control. Henry VIII had declared himself King of Ireland, and began imposing the English language and religion, against the wishes of the Catholic Gaelic population. Resistance followed, and that brought brutal repression under Henry's daughter, Elizabeth I. After a series of violent conflicts, the old Gaelic aristocracy was shattered; a situation confirmed when, in 1607, two leading Irish earls, plus dozens of their followers, fled and went into exile. This then provided the opportunity for the new Anglo-Scottish monarchy of James VI and I to begin a more rigorous policy of plantation, particularly in Ulster. Thousands of Protestant settlers came from James's other realms, and the landscape and religion of Ireland was changed permanently. Now there were three broad groups: the native Gaelic population, the descendants of the old Norman conquerors, and the new Protestant settlers. It was a tough society for anyone to govern.[20]

Strafford had just about managed it, through his own brand of stern efficiency – military tyranny, some said. But even under him the British administration was weak. Edward Nicholas thought that the main mistake of successive Irish governments was their over-tolerance of Catholics: they had, he thought, been 'imprudently connived at or rather tolerated there a long time, and especially by the Earl of Strafford'.[21] But what choice had the earl had? Now, anyway, he was dead. In the immediate months before his demise, he had left Ireland in an even more dangerous state. To aid his royal master, Strafford had raised a largely Catholic army. Now he was gone, they were left there.

After Strafford's execution, there had been the plan to move parts of that army to Flanders, where it would serve under the Spanish flag.[22] Parliament had bristled at this and blocked the scheme. This in itself would have dangerous consequences, for it left angry disbanded soldiers – mostly Catholic – with nothing to do. But what Parliament didn't know at the time was that the recruitment had always been part of a plot by Irish dissidents, with Spanish support. It was a cover. Most of the troops were always planned to be used in Ireland, to rise against Westminster rule. That conspiracy centred on an Irish courtier called Daniel O'Neill, who was popular with the king and close to the queen. As ever, there is no definitive evidence that either knew of the plot, but it is interesting the force with which Charles had pushed John Bankes to get the scheme moving that summer.

Meanwhile in Ireland itself, a mouldering discord against English rule and the Anglo-Scottish plantations threatened to turn into something much more dangerous. Moreover, for those with an eye on the politics of the whole archipelago, one of the biggest lessons of the past four years had come from the Scots, and it was that major religious gains could be made by the simple tactic of rising in rebellion. The Scots had defeated Charles in the name of Presbyterianism. Perhaps the Irish could defeat England in the cause of Catholicism.

On 23 October 1641, parts of Ireland rose. The initial plan had been to surprise Dublin Castle, but this had been betrayed by the same Owen O'Connelly, a Protestant convert, who would ride to Leicester House with news of the insurgency. Yet despite the failure of the Dublin conspiracy, within days the whole of Ulster was in arms. The rebellion was spreading fast.

Once Leicester had read the letter he acted quickly. He managed to get the Privy Council urgently summoned, and it met at Whitehall at 4 p.m. that afternoon.²³ Immediately, the councillors decided the matter needed to come to Parliament, but the House of Lords had been adjourned until Wednesday, so instead, as a second-best option, they brought it en masse to the Commons.

The next morning, 1 November, MPs had settled in their seats, ready to discuss the Remonstrance. But they were soon startled at the unexpected appearance of seventeen privy councillors at the bar. Chairs were provided, and St Stephen's fell to a hush. Lord Keeper Littleton spoke. There was a 'deep silence'.²⁴

Ireland changed everything. It wasn't just a rebellion. Soon, reports began to filter in of something worse: a massacre. They were exaggerated, of course, but the escalating violence and bloodshed was real. The numbers of deaths rose quickly into the thousands: in one particularly horrifying incident at Portadown, around a hundred settlers were murdered after they were herded onto a bridge, cast into the river, and shot as they tried to swim.²⁵

With a kingdom in flames, someone had to do something. In the first place, it was Leicester who would have to head the government response. But the issue was much deeper than this. Armed rebellion required an armed reaction. In England, and perhaps also in Scotland, a force of men sufficient to restore control and order to Ireland would have to be raised. The recruiter's drum would be heard again in England's market towns and cathedral cities. Once more, young men would leave their farms and cottages, pull on the thick leather and woollen clothes of the soldier, sharpen pikes and polish muskets.

―――――

Since the Scottish 'Incident', the Junto had felt an urgent need to take control of the royal government. Now they needed more. Now they needed control of the military. Through November, news continued to come in of atrocities in Ireland committed by the rebels. Within a few weeks, boats full of ragged and traumatised refugees were landing on England's shores, especially in the north-west.²⁶ In some cases, the arrival of displaced Irish Protestants in the more backwoods corners of the English countryside caused alarm: could these strange folk not be gangs of papists seeking to bring the bloodshed over here? An Irish invasion of England was widely expected. 'All these plots in Ireland are but one plot against England,' thought the Londoner Nehemiah Wallington. For 'it is England that is that fine sweet bit which they so long for', he noted, 'and their cruel teeth so much water at'.[27]

Worse, the Irish news was joined by rumours of plotting and arms-gathering by English Catholics. The Marquess of Winchester's mansion at Basing House in Hampshire, it was reported, had gathered enough weapons for a sizeable little army of 300 horse and 1,200 foot. Meanwhile, a Catholic soldier of fortune had lodged in the parish of St Martin-le-Grand in the City and was overheard to say that the Scots were 'Puritan rogues' and 'rebels and dogs', and that the Irish rebellion was just the beginning.[28]

Suddenly, as autumn's chiller winds began to cool England's browning trees, the latent tension of that hot, radical summer was giving way to nothing short of a national panic.

10

To Speak Plain English

When England panicked, Catholics were usually the first to suffer. Although they were only around 1 per cent of the population, those who stayed in the old faith were a perpetual source of fear and concern for the majority.[1] In the good times, neighbours tended to downplay this, but in times of crisis the uneasy tolerance could quickly strain.

The tension had been evident from the first days of the Long Parliament the previous year. Early speeches by Pym and others blamed England's political woes on 'papists'. Meanwhile, the violence began. Within days of Parliament meeting, a crowd attacked and hurled stones at Catholics attending the queen's chapel. Then, on 21 November 1640, a respected old magistrate Peter Heywood was to be found in a busy Westminster Hall carrying a list of 'suspected and notorious papists' living nearby. Heywood had been one of those who, in 1605, had apprehended Guy Fawkes in the cellars under Parliament: it had been him who had seized the Gunpowder plotter's lamp. This time, Heywood was approached by a man called John James, who stabbed him. James was unhinged – angry that Heywood had put him in the stocks a month ago. Yet most people just assumed that he was a Catholic terrorist. Heywood survived the stabbing, but the House of Commons – on Pym's motion – ordered James's hand to be cut off (though it was never actually done).[2]

By the summer of 1641, with tension mounting after Charles's journey to Scotland, Peter Heywood – now happily recovered – was once again called upon to search the cellars under the Lords for barrels of powder.[3] Whether there was a credible threat, or whether this was just theatre, is not quite clear. Either way, the persecution of Catholics had already taken a bloodier turn. After years of relative disuse, the savage laws against priests and Jesuits were suddenly put into play. On 26 July, an 81-year-old called William Ward, after being convicted at the Old Bailey, was hung, drawn, and quartered at Tyburn – his body parts left to rot around the City. By September, in which month another priest was executed, an Irish Catholic living at Covent Garden felt unable to leave his lodgings, 'the persecution is so fearfully cruel and hot'.[4]

Queen Henrietta Maria saw this too. 'I feel worse about the suffering of Catholics and others who serve the king than I do about myself,' she wrote to her sister.[5] In the Commons, the paranoia and repression was becoming frenzied even before news came of the Irish rebellion. But that made things much worse. Some dared call it the 'Queen's Rebellion', and there were, said Pym, 'secret forces' that were 'ready in some places'. There had been 'secret meetings' in Hampshire, he said, with various Catholics hatching some 'wicked design' or other. Most worrying of all, young Prince Charles was spending a lot of time at the queen's residence at Oatlands, where it was believed the heir to the throne would 'receive no good there for soul nor body'.[6]

With the king absent in Scotland, his heir coming under the direct instruction of the Catholic queen was concerning indeed. An order was quickly forthcoming that Prince Charles be removed from the custody of his mother and returned to Richmond. It was an issue that united both sides in Parliament. A committee of four peers, comprising three king's party men and one Junto supporter, was tasked with drafting a message. Then the Earl of Holland, once a friend to the queen but now a Junto man, and an associate of Lucy Carlisle, was despatched with it to Oatlands.

It was a nervous few weeks for the queen. Around the same time she was visited by a local gentleman who said he had been told to rendezvous with an armed band, on Parliament's instruction. She took this as a direct threat and quickly got weapons to as many people in the palace as possible, including the kitchen servants, and waited. Showing what was to become a characteristic fortitude, she took the air in the great park while reports came in of around twenty mounted men in the area. Word was sent to Colonel Goring at Portsmouth, in case she needed to bolt. But, for now, the alarm passed.[7]

In such jittery times, the raising of military force became the single defining issue. The king had written to Parliament from Scotland, telling them he thought the Irish rebellion was of the utmost seriousness, and that it required a 'sharp war'.[8] He and Parliament were in close agreement about this. The question was how to do it, and under what authority. Here the prospects for concord were not good at all. Neither side, in essence, could trust the other with an armed force. It was a thoroughly tricky issue.

The king's northern army had been disbanded that summer, so that couldn't be used. The most obvious solution was therefore simply to raise a new force of volunteers. As D'Ewes himself told the Commons with characteristic antiquarian pomposity, Henry II had once conquered Ireland without conscripting a man.[9] But, to the Junto, a volunteer force like this ran a considerable risk. Many who signed up were likely to be disgruntled veterans of the old royal army: men who broadly despised Parliament and who were therefore dangerous people to give weapons to. Recent reports from around London suggested the searches ordered in late October were having some effect, and the disbanded soldiers had been dispersed.[10] There was little appetite for gathering them together again, for it might provide Charles with yet another opportunity to pursue military force against his political opponents.

The other option, preferred by the Junto, was to create a new 'pressed' army, that is: one of conscripts. These could be recruited afresh, creating a rookie force, but a less angry one. Yet, as D'Ewes pointed out, this would require the passing of a bill. Englishmen could not be forced to serve in an army, any more than they could be compelled to pay taxes, without first giving their consent to it via their representatives in Parliament. A bill, though, would need to get the royal assent, and the king was in Scotland. The only way around this would be to pass an ordinance without the king, but this was another radical precedent. To raise an army without the king's assent would be a major step into the unknown.*

There was an obvious third possibility, which was to call again on the Scots. In the eyes of the Westminster Parliament, Ireland was a dominion of England, so it was the southern kingdom's responsibility. Yet Scotland was geographically closer and had a more reliable track record of armed mobilisation in recent years. More to the point, as D'Ewes argued in one of his fastidiously self-reported speeches, much of Ireland was now 'planted' by Scots.[11] And, as the parliamentary commissioners in Edinburgh suggested, the Scottish 'redshanks' (Highlanders) were particularly suited to the coming campaign, they being the 'fittest soldiers to be sent against the Irish being able to grapple with them in their bogs'.[12]

Charles wouldn't like it, though. Frankly, he'd had his fill of his northern kingdom, and he wasn't likely to concede them the creation of yet another Scottish armed host. Thus, with all military options unacceptable to one side or the other, England was firmly stuck in political deadlock.

———

As November progressed, MPs were attending Parliament in a state of ever more feverish paranoia, and the sense of fear fed into a new, radical drive by the Junto to gain control of the state. On 5 November, the anniversary of the Gunpowder Plot, Pym made a remarkable proposal. In a so-called 'Additional Instruction', he

---

*It even threatened to split the Junto on the left, too. For when the bill was introduced on 4 November, it was immediately opposed by the radical Henry Marten as being against the 'liberty of the subject', seconded by Sir John Hotham. This itself was an intriguing argument, implying as it did that there were certain areas that parliamentary power could not touch, not because they were the preserve of the king, but because they were fundamental common rights. But it immediately ran into the common lawyer's argument – given this time by the royalist Edmund Waller, that 'what was done by act of Parliament is done by consent of the subject': D'Ewes, *Journal*, p. 83; Bodleian MS, Rawlinson D 932, f. 3a.

demanded that the king remove his 'evil counsellors' and only appoint those acceptable to Parliament. If the king didn't accept, Pym added what amounted to a threat. Parliament would feel absolved from any responsibility towards Ireland.[13]

Next came a motion from the MP for Cambridge, Oliver Cromwell. On 6 November, he proposed that the Earl of Essex be given power to call out the militia south of the River Trent, 'upon all occasions'.[14] Essex had been appointed as Lord General of the South when the king went to Scotland, but Cromwell's suggestion would have granted him similar authority *from Parliament*. It was another assault on the royal prerogative.

The Commons was now at last much better attended than it had been. MPs were drifting back as the plague continued to lift. Around a half or more were there.[15] By the second week of the month, the Commons was finally starting to debate the great Remonstrance: the projected grand statement on what had been achieved and what was still to be done. It was tricky business, but it was now the centrepiece of the Junto's political strategy. The text itself was long, and took considerable time to read out loud. As soon as the house fell to debate, members rose to add their own 'oppressions and grievances', which the clerk dutifully noted.[16] Over the next two weeks, the Remonstrance would be discussed and edited, and to an extent, watered down. An attack on the Book of Common Prayer was dropped and replaced with an affirmation not to cast 'aspersions or scandal' on it. A move to take away bishops' lands was abandoned, as was an attempt to defend the September Commons order about 'popish' church fittings.[17]

And yet, the greater purpose of the Remonstrance was still remarkably strident. It held a torch to government mismanagement. There had been, the text alleged, 'a malignant and pernicious design of subverting the fundamental laws and principles of government, upon which the religion and justice of this kingdom are firmly established'.[18] Religion and laws had been undermined by bad government and bad counsellors to the king. And if ill counsels were the major issue, then the implied solution was to remove control of appointments from the king and to give it to Parliament.

Edward Nicholas could see this plainly. He also noted a key feature: the date at which these alleged ill counsels had begun was the third year of the king's reign, that is around 1627. The critical event at this point was the Forced Loan, of course, as well as a notorious official prayer campaign in favour of divine right kingship.[19] But as Nicholas pointed out, this also meant the Remonstrance couldn't simply be a piece of puff for the current Parliament. Rather, it was trying to say something deeper – more structural. It wouldn't be enough to simply remove the current crop of officers (who after all included many Junto supporters). Only a constitutional revolution could solve the problems highlighted. 'You must needs speak with such of my servants that you may best trust, in my name,' Charles wrote to Nicholas, 'that by all means possible this may be stopped.'[20]

––––––

Parliament was fighting the encroaching winter as well as the sheer weight of the business. By 5 p.m. each day, it was starting to get dark. One evening in mid-November, it had become so gloomy by 4.30 that D'Ewes could hardly see to write his notes, so he made a rather facetious motion that 'we may sit according to the ancient use of Parliaments having the use of as well of our eyes as well as our ears', and that candles be brought in.[21] In the end, the house simply waited for a break in the debate and rose, before the clock tower across the yard had even struck five.

Nicholas's royal party were steadily becoming more organised. Particularly notable was the father-and-son team of the Earl of Bristol and Lord Digby in the upper house. 'Your majesty,' wrote Nicholas on 12 November, after a particularly heroic stonewalling in the Lords, 'may be pleased to take notice of the singular good service that was in that business done by those 2 noblemen, and especially by the son, who (I hear) did beyond admiration.' Both had been reformists, but now their transition to king's party men seemed well-nigh complete. 'Thank them from me,' replied Charles.[22]

Meanwhile, Nicholas and the queen were working together to rally those moderate and royalist members who remained absent. One, in the Lords, was the Earl of Carnarvon, who was sitting things out in his house just twenty miles outside London. The queen took notice, and told Nicholas to tell Carnarvon to get back to Westminster with rather more haste.[23] Alas, he was not at home when the letter arrived, so it was returned to the queen, who promptly burned it. Her enquiries had, though, unearthed that Lords Cottington and Dunsmore, plus the Earl of Southampton, were all available to come to Parliament – or, for the time being to send proxies. So they were duly summoned.[24]

While the queen tried to establish the whereabouts of various loyal peers, Nicholas focused on absent members of the Commons. He realised, as did the king, that these men constituted a vast untapped resource, who – if they could be cajoled into returning – were likely to provide a decisive boost to the new royalist party. By November, both Nicholas and Charles were writing to each other, toying with the idea of a royal proclamation to order these men back to Westminster.[25]

For now, though, the royal firewall in Parliament was strong enough. And although Nicholas himself was rather ill from around the 11th to the 18th, and therefore not quite his usual busy self, there was enough momentum in the party to keep it active and effective. Whatever radical measures the Junto proposed were going nowhere. Any legislation Pym and his allies succeeded in getting through the Commons was increasingly likely to stick in the Lords, and would continue to do so – as Northumberland grumbled – 'without some alteration'.[26]

There seemed little immediate prospect of any such alteration. Moreover, the military panic was having an even more urgent effect. In the country, towns and castles were now being hastily armed and fortified, as the horrifying news from Ireland was spreading from port to market town to village. Hilltop beacons were being repaired and readied. Near the south coast, in Dorchester, the windows of the shire hall were fortified with bars and covers. Townspeople were told to prepare their weapons, while a watchman was put on the top of a church tower to survey the surrounding hills. Other towns repaired firearms and procured gunpowder. In Exeter, residents were asked to lay their hands on clubs to use as weapons in case of an invasion. In Herefordshire, the Puritan gentlewoman Brilliana Harley bought extra cannonballs for her castle at Brampton Bryan. In Lancashire, the militia was put on high alert. Not for two generations – not since 1588 and the great Spanish Armada crisis under Queen Elizabeth I – had there been such a widespread invasion scare.[27]

There was seditious talk in the King's Bench prison, too, deep in the dark of the night, where someone was heard hoping 'that wars and blood might never cease in England till all the judges were hanged and all the prisoners set at liberty'.[28] Investigations were launched into the activities of Catholics and Irish. The Lords ordered a survey to be made of Irishmen around London. Local magistrates worked with vigour, and the lists were ready within five days. The names went into the hundreds, and included servants to the Lord Keeper and the Junto-supporting Earl of Northumberland.[29] John Bankes also had a role to play, for on 15 November, he and another judge were sent to the Gatehouse prison to examine one John Browne, a doctor of divinity.[30] Browne gave them a list of various monks and priests who were in English prisons, claiming that he didn't know of any at the house of any lords. He also told Bankes of how Catholics, to avoid detection, would change their names: 'He saith that the Jesuits and Priests are called by sundry names, and one called Brown hath been called by 18 several names.' Bankes wrote this all down in his own hand, and reported immediately to the Lords.[31]

Meanwhile, that very day, the Junto sprung what looked suspiciously like a co-ordinated ploy. Midway through a debate about the Remonstrance, Pym announced that someone was ready to attend the house with information pertinent to the safety of some of the members. Pym's source was one Thomas Beale, a tailor of London, who – after examination by a committee – was brought before the house. To a combination of horror and utter cynicism from MPs, he recounted his story.[32]

He had been in the fields around London, Beale said, near the Pesthouse (apparently 'amending the notes he had taken of a sermon'[33]). Here he managed to spy a gang of Catholics, on the other side of a hedge, who were plotting to bring 108 conspirators to Parliament, on 18 November, to kill an MP or a peer each. This would be joined by mass uprisings in Lancashire, Warwickshire, Buckinghamshire, and Staffordshire. Once the plan had been successful, the plotters would then each take possession of the goods of the man they had slain.

Unfortunately for the eavesdropping Beale, the conspiratorial pack of papists heard him rustling about in the hedge. So they pulled him out by the ears and – according to his testimony – ran him through with a sword before scarpering. Rather than sit about nursing his allegedly sharp injuries, Beale ran straight to Parliament.[34]

The story of the plot was promptly distilled into a handy pamphlet, though it quickly proved to be rather exaggerated. It implicated the Earl of Worcester, a Catholic convert, and when his house on the Strand was searched, nothing was found. To Edward Nicholas, these conspiracies were nothing but the 'tales and fictions of brain-sick Brownists', though they are also open to a more cynical explanation than genuinely held paranoia. Keeping up the flow of conspiracies and plots helped the Junto focus minds on their critical aim: taking control of the government.[35]

———

Charles, now, was finally bidding a rather bitter farewell to Edinburgh. Here in Scotland he had capitulated to a revolutionary government while nearly getting his fingers covered in blood. It was not a successful trip by any means. And yet, the fact was he had now placated the Covenanters. Their aims had been met. No longer were they likely to offer military support to the Junto. Charles had admitted his own weakness in Scotland, but this had given him renewed possibilities in England. And this, for Charles, was where it mattered.

On the 18th, he had passed through Berwick-upon-Tweed. His journey would take him down the eastern side of the country. Charles was serenaded by 'well-tuned' church bells and lauded by great speeches.[36] As he travelled south, he was heartened by the crowds who came out to see him. The air was cooling still, the sun getting lower and hazier, and the late autumn winds were scattering the golden leaves of the trees. At York, though, he was told that 'the woods do seem to contemn a falling autumn or a nipping winter and assume unto themselves their spring liveries'.[37] His aura was enough to overturn the seasons themselves.

At Huntingdon, the mayor told Charles that though 'sects and schisms do daily increase', there was now much hope that religion would be returned to the days of Queen Elizabeth and King James, and 'loyal and well affected subjects will be perpetually your humble slaves'.[38] From Ware in Hertfordshire, 'divers principal gentlemen' wrote to Nicholas asking to be able to come out in force to welcome Charles. Nicholas, recovering slowly from his illness, thought it an excellent plan. It would not, he wrote to Charles, 'be amiss for your Majesty in these times to accept graciously the affections of your subjects', and of course 'you will have opportunity to shew yourself gracious to your people as your Majesty passeth, and to speak a few good words to them'. It was something that 'will gain the affections (especially of the vulgar) more than any thing that hath been done for them this Parliament'.[39] Crucially, Nicholas thought it would be a 'good encouragement and comfort to your well affected people here [in London], to understand, that they have neighbours that have the like dutiful affections to your Majesty's person and government'.[40] The ever-more confident royalist factions in both London and Westminster would be duly heartened.

These were wonderfully cheering signs for the king as he pressed on south, for it seemed that loyalism was taking root. A conservative backlash was in flow and the royal party in Parliament was strengthening. What better time, then, to make an appeal to the one place Charles had struggled most to connect with: London.

Here, the City government was settling down under the dependable Lord Mayor Richard Gurney, and whatever dis-agreements London previously had with the king were now fading into the past. Moreover, to moderate voices in town, the Junto were beginning to appear much the greater threat to the stability that the

City needed to ensure their main goal, which was to make money. Indeed, they were becoming an annoyance in themselves, and the fact that MPs were protected from creditors while Parliament sat was a particularly direct irritant to the City. Some members had taken on debts, and now they could not be chased for payment until Parliament was dissolved.[41]

In short, London was increasingly tired of the representative body which seemed to have permanently stuck itself to the capital's western reaches like a limpet. For Charles, it was a grand opportunity.

———

The idea for a formal royal entry into London seems to have come from Henrietta Maria. Nicholas thought it made good sense too, as – crucially – did Mayor Gurney. Indeed, it was a plan to correct something that frankly did need addressing. For Charles had never formally undertaken a state entry into the City of London, and now, surely, was the perfect time to do it.

Both sides were trying to appeal to the people. The Junto through their ongoing plan for a Remonstrance, Charles through a public procession into London. It was a sign of the times. More than ever before, politics was taking place in the glare of publicity. Trust meanwhile was as rare as ever. Parliamentary committees were now spying on foreign ambassadors. Giustinian in particular was incensed that his letters were being intercepted and opened. It was not an insult he laid aside lightly, and the Venetian's despatches home were increasingly characterised by a festering hatred of the Junto.[42] The queen, for her part, insisted Nicholas did not tell Essex that the king was now on his way south – a remarkable piece of information to withhold from the Lord Chamberlain, who was supposed to manage the royal household.[43] People were keeping their deepest thoughts out of written letters, for the post was no longer secure. Reformadoes, highwaymen, royal agents, and Junto spies all threatened the security of those who communicated in writing. A few weeks previously, the post between the queen and Council in England and the king in Scotland had been robbed by 'fellows with vizards on their faces'. The perpetrators were suspected to be disbanded soldiers: 'such an insolency,' suggested the City Remembrancer Thomas Wiseman, in a despatch to Admiral Pennington at the Downs, 'has not been known before'.[44]

On 20 November, the queen wrote to Nicholas one more time. He could now, she said, inform the Earl of Essex that the king's arrival was imminent. She wouldn't do it herself, she added sarcastically, because Essex was too great a prince 'to receive any instruction from me'. On 'vendnesday' Charles would be at Theobalds, the grand royal mansion in the muddy Hertfordshire countryside, where he would stay the night. Then, on Thursday, he would enter the City and dine with the Lord Mayor, before sleeping at Whitehall 'only for one night'. Finally, on Friday, he would retire to Hampton Court, 'where he means to stay this vinter'.[45] It would be a flying visit to the capital, but it would be made to count.

The Junto were meanwhile pushing ahead with the Remonstrance. Come Saturday 20th and the full text was ready, properly engrossed on parchment and brought in by the clerk.[46] Briefly, almost speculatively, the Junto tried to rush it through. But it was decided instead that the text must receive full consideration on Monday. Oliver Cromwell was among those who thought this was unnecessary. Turning at one point to Lord Falkland, Cromwell asked why some wanted the Remonstrance put off. 'There would not have been time enough,' said Falkland, 'for sure it would take some debate.' It would be 'a very sorry one,' replied a sceptical Cromwell.[47]

On Monday, the 22nd, the moment had at last come to vote. The day began as normal, with prayers just before 10 a.m. By midday, the morning's business had passed. It was time.

Almost immediately, Edward Hyde sought to rally the royalist party. After a not insignificant debate of its own, it was ordered that the serjeant be sent to Westminster Hall to gather in any MPs who were walking there. With these men duly rounded up, the mace was placed upon the table, meaning the house was in session. Next to it was the engrossed copy of the Remonstrance, the text of which had been read on Saturday.[48]

The royalists had a good debate. Hyde, Falkland and Edward Dering all spoke with force. Dering, a rather vain and ambitious man, and one who had formerly been allied with the Junto, was on this occasion very eloquent, at least if the published version of his speech is reliable. 'I did not dream,' he told the house, 'that we should remonstrate downward, tell tales to the people, and talk of the king as a third person.'[49] Yet the best lines were delivered by Sir John Culpeper. He skewered the Remonstrance as a dangerously radical precedent. Never mind the text itself, he was against the very form of it. This was not being sent to the Lords, like a bill. 'This is a Remonstrance to the people. Remonstrances ought to be to the king for redress.'[50] D'Ewes's diary is disappointing here – he was struggling with a cold, and left the house at 4 p.m. But taking notes on Culpeper and others' speeches was the MP Sir John Holland, in a record preserved in Oxford's Bodleian Library. Holland's notes are laconic and bulleted, but no less revealing for that. 'This may exasperate,' Culpeper was saying. 'This unseasonable' … 'The Humours much stirred; and that this kingdom much distracted; and this may increase the division of the kingdom.'

Pym argued the other side. It was the appeal to the people that was the point. 'The honour of the King,' Pym told the house, 'is the safety of his people.'[51] 'It's time to speak plain English,' Holland has him saying, 'lest posterity say that England was lost and no man durst speak truth.'[52] This declaration, Pym said, 'will bind the peoples' hearts to us'.[53] Denzil Holles, too, spoke in praise of the Remonstrance: 'The kingdom consists of three sorts of men, the bad, the good, and the indifferent.' It was the last they needed to persuade, for 'they can turn the scales'.[54]

Evening encroached. Candles were called for and brought. Some MPs 'withdrew themselves out of pure faintness'.[55] Debate continued as the Trained Bands stood nervous guard outside.

Late at night, Nicholas was still working at his Whitehall desk, writing to Charles. The house was debating their Remonstrance, he said. They had started at midday 'and are at it still, it being now near 12 at midnight'. Nicholas had hoped to be able to write to the king with news of the vote, 'but it is so late, as I dare not (after my sickness) adventure to watch it any longer to see the issue of it'.[56] He thought the royal party was putting up a good fight. 'I assure your Majesty,' he wrote, 'there are divers in the Commons House, that are resolved to stand very stiff for rejecting that Declaration, and if they prevail not then to protest against it.'[57]

As he was writing this, the debate was finally edging towards a conclusion. Just after twelve, it was time to vote. The ayes would stand and leave, the noes remain. The question was put: 'Whether this Declaration, thus amended shall pass', and at last the house divided. For the yeas, leaving their seats, 159 votes. For the noes, staying seated, not quite as much: 148. The Remonstrance had passed, with over 300 MPs still present for the division.

But it was not yet over. George Peard, a Junto supporter, moved that the Remonstrance be printed. It was a critical gambit, for this was the whole point. Immediately, the royalists, rallied by Hyde and Culpeper, staged a rear-guard. First, the two king's party men tried to enter a formal protest, but this was not allowed; so – with the clock now at 1 a.m. – people started to drift away, assuming the matter would now rest. But there was more to come. Geoffrey Palmer, MP for Stamford in Lincolnshire and a Middle Temple lawyer, rose and demanded that a protest be recorded 'in the name of himself and all the rest'. Suddenly, the tired house broke into pandemonium. Royalists cried 'All! All!', while some took off their hats and waved them over their heads. Others took their scabbarded swords out of their belts and banged them on the floor.[58] According to a later history written by Edward Nicholas (who wasn't in the house), some royalists rose to denounce the 'rabble of inconsiderable persons, set on by a juggling Junto', who were pushing the Remonstrance.[59]

As the noise subsided and order slowly returned, from somewhere a vote was passed by acclamation that the Remonstrance should not be 'printed or published' without the order of the house.[60] This may have been something of a temporary truce, which would allow both sides to regroup; but the Junto had one more surprise. Pushing a final division, they asked that the word 'published' be removed. The question was then put as to whether the word 'published' should be retained. With a thin house, the yeas were able to muster 101 votes for the royalist side. But the vote for the

Junto was larger: 124 noes. So it was resolved that the Remonstrance 'shall not be printed, without the particular Order of this House'.[61] It could not be printed. But it could still be published.

It was now about 2 a.m. MPs could finally vanish into the Westminster night. As they were leaving the building, Oliver Cromwell crossed paths once more with Lord Falkland. Well, Falkland asked, recalling their conversation on Saturday: Had there been a debate after all? Cromwell agreed that he had been too hasty. Then, speaking softly in Falkland's ear, he admitted 'that if the Remonstrance had been rejected he would have sold all he had the next morning, and never seen England more'.[62] All that was left at the palace were the Trained Bands keeping guard until about 3 a.m., when they, too, at last were stood down.[63]

––––––

The following day, quite understandably, the house didn't meet first thing. Or even before lunch. It was not until around 2 p.m. that bleary-eyed MPs finally gathered in their seats at St Stephen's. The fallout from the Remonstrance debate the previous night was likely to be huge. Enterprising scriveners were already busy scratching the text by pen. But as much as manuscript circulation remained part of the political culture, it belonged to the media technology of an earlier age. In 1641, print was everything, and printing had been blocked.

In the house, one of the most unsettling aspects of the whole thing was the protest lodged by Geoffrey Palmer. This threatened to expose the unpleasant truth that the lower house – the representative body for the English people – was deeply, thoroughly, perhaps irretrievably, divided. Thus Palmer's actions, and his potential censure, led to yet another rancorous debate the following day, the 24th, in a relatively full house, lasting for six hours. By the time it finished at around 4 p.m., it was so dark that Speaker Lenthall could no longer tell who had stood up to contribute.[64]

At some point that day, as successive MPs at St Stephen's rose to make their arguments, the London MP John Venn started to fear that the Junto would lose the debate. He sent a messenger to his wife. She then despatched a servant to a grocer's shop in Bread

Street to look for one Mr Lavender and tell him 'that in the House of Commons they were together by the ears' and 'the worser party was like to get the better of the good party'. So they should get their arms, assemble, and come to Parliament 'to help the good party'. Mr Lavender wasn't there, but the servant was able to find him at a house in Wood Street, where he was taking tobacco with some friends. The servant urgently informed him that there was an 'uproar' in the house, 'and swords drawn'. So Lavender grabbed a sword of his own and his pistol, and ran to find Mrs Venn. When he arrived she was 'crying and wringing her hands', fearing that her husband might have been killed. By now the message was being passed around, and some 300 Londoners and apprentices were on their way down to Westminster to protest.[65]

Here, though, they found it was a false alarm – all was quiet –and they dispersed back into the evening. Later, an apprentice called Cole – said to be a 'lusty young man' – had gone to the room of John Michaelson at the Spreadeagle in Gracechurch Street, deep in the City of London. He announced, 'in a boasting manner', that he had come from the Palace Yard where 'a thousand more armed with swords' had gathered 'to put fear upon the Parliament'. The lesson was clear: the London crowd had the potential to enter dramatically into politics once more, as it had during the Strafford trial. Who had called them? Cole was asked. 'They were sent for by some Parliament men,' he replied. More to the point, his master was a constable, 'who gave him a sword, & bade him go'. An alliance was forming again between the Junto and the radical voices of the City and the street.[66]

For now, though, the focus was about to shift dramatically away from Parliament. For that same day, King Charles had reached Theobalds, just north of London. Tomorrow he would enter the capital itself. The king, who had rarely been seen in public for six months, was about to make his presence felt in the most spectacular way possible.

11

London's Joy

Royal entries into capital cities were grand, memorable occasions. They were events in which monarchs could show their liberality and patronage, and where their citizens could reciprocate with conspicuous displays of wealth and loyalty. Printed accounts, meanwhile, could be produced that conveyed the grandeur of the event to the country and beyond. The hope on 25 November was that Charles's return would end 'England's various distempers, and distractions'.[1] He would bring the country together and restore order. He would revive the strength of his monarchy too. His position since the spring, since the death of Strafford, had improved dramatically. Once faltering, now the monarchy's power was resplendent. Or, at least, that was what the planned festivities were supposed to show.

London was preparing for winter. Wool-coated workmen were offloading coal from coastal ships at the port. It was essential fuel and now, at last, it was coming much more freely from Newcastle with the Scots army gone. The capital offered two great assets to Charles: its money and its militia. He knew – or at least his cleverest advisors did – that the coming weeks would see two struggles, both equally vital. One would take place in Westminster, the small satellite city to the south-west, in the two houses of Parliament. It would be a battle of votes and political organisation, where the ammunition was procedure and oratory. The other was in London itself, in the chambers of the City government, but more especially in the streets, and here the weapons would be of a much more physical kind.

Charles's return to London, from the royal journey south to the entry itself, was an attempt to win the support of the 'vulgar' (as Edward Nicholas put it).[2] It was a counterblast, specifically, to the Remonstrance. Small wonder the whole idea caused jitters among the Junto men. One of the City MPs wanted the whole thing pared back, since it was 'displeasing to the Parliament', though he was overruled.[3] And there were dissident voices among the London population, too. Worries about disorder were such that a treble watch was prepared, and two companies of the Trained Bands told to stand by.[4]

The day began with a gathering at Mayor Gurney's house in Old Jewry. Here were the twenty-six aldermen, the Recorder, and some 500 members of the livery companies.[5] From there, dressed in their finest clothes they processed out to Moorfields. Some were on horseback, each accompanied by a footman wearing jackets and breeches, trimmed with the colours of their livery companies, plus a gilded truncheon.[6] The liverymen wore swords, too. One pamphlet reported that the mayor and City men were prepared 'in all their warlike habiliments, as if Mars himself the God of Battle had been their conductor'.[7] And so, once at Moorfields to the north of the City, with a great tent pitched on the cold ground, they waited.

The king, having left Theobalds by coach, had already met a party from the City at Stamford Hill: the two sheriffs, seventy-two men in scarlet liveries with feathers in their hats, and fourteen trumpeters.[8] Soon they were on their way south. In the king's party was the queen, the three eldest royal children, Charles, James, and Mary, and the Elector Palatine: Charles Louis. They were joined, too, by 'Dukes, Marquesses, Earls, Viscounts, Barons, Lords, Knights, Gentlemen-Pensioners', and 'Ladies of Honour', all in fine clothes and horses, plus twenty Scottish lords 'and others'. The symbolism was important: this was a unified monarchy and nobility, and a unified Britain. It showed both the fecundity of the royal couple and the unity of the Stuart clan: four men were there who had plausible if distant claims to the throne – the Elector Palatine, the Marquess of Hamilton, the Marquess of Hertford, and the Duke of Richmond. All of these could have been alternate monarchs had Charles been deposed. All were here touting their loyalty.[9]

At Kingsland, the party traversed a special bridge of planks to convey them in comfort over the soggy ground to Moorfields, where the main City delegation was waiting for them.[10] At the meeting of the two parties, there was the customary welcome by the Recorder, Thomas Gardiner, and the requisite speech of thanks from the king. In this, Charles promised favour to the City, and that he would govern England 'according to the laws of this kingdom, and in maintaining you in your full liberties, but chiefly in maintaining and protecting the true Protestant religion'. Particularly telling was his denunciation of the popular protests and politics with which London was becoming associated. 'For now I see,' he said, 'that all these former Tumults and disorders, have only risen from the meaner sort of people: and that the affections of the better and main part of the City, have ever been loyal and affectionate to my person, and government.'[11] More to the point, he was heartened to see – from the enthusiastic reception he was getting – that Londoners clearly hadn't believed those 'misreports that have made of me in my absence', a clear reference to fallout from the Scottish 'Incident'.[12]

Charles was then presented with a 'rich and costly gift'. It was £20,000, given in a great cup of gold, while Henrietta Maria received £5,000 in a golden basin.[13] The total value of the offerings ran to £30,000 – which was about the same as it cost to run the Irish government for more than a year.[14] Charles responded by knighting the mayor and Recorder, and both he and the queen presented their hands to be kissed by the two City men.[15]

At this point Charles mounted his horse, as did the eleven-year-old Prince of Wales. Then the main procession began, setting off through the Moorgate to a fanfare, and into the dense streets of the City. It was a huge affair, with citizens, aldermen, both king's and prince's trumpeters, the knight marshal, and the pursuivants at arms. Then, prominently on his own on horseback, came Sir John Bankes, Lord Chief Justice of the Common Pleas, 'being a Knight of the Privy Council'. He was followed by more nobles and heralds, plus Lord Keeper Littleton, and Lord Privy Seal Manchester – Mandeville's loyalist father.

Still the procession continued, with officers, city men, and nobles. The king himself was on horseback, trailed by the queen's coach, 'richly embroidered', out of which peered Princess Mary, James Duke of York, the Elector Palatine, and Henrietta Maria herself. Following the core royals were Hamilton with the Horse of State, and the Earl of Salisbury leading the gentlemen-pensioners – all carrying their gilt poleaxes and each mounted on a horse 'with pistols at their saddles'. At the rear were 'many other principal commanders in late Northern Expedition', plus 'divers ladies', 'other great personages of note', and finally the Yeomen of the Guard.[16]

As the cavalcade made its way through the streets, there were – at least as far as a colourful printed account had it – 'loud and joyful acclamations', to which both king and queen responded by 'heartily blessing and thanking the people, with as great expressions of joy'. The poet John Milton was in the crowds that day, and would later recall how Charles, as he rode through the City streets, regularly took off his hat to salute the people, 'a favour which till then neither himself or his Father before him had never bestowed upon the vulgar'.[17] Houses were decorated and the conduits at Cornhill and Cheapside flowed with wine. People shouted: 'God Bless and Long Live King Charles and Queen Mary.'[18] At the Exchange, there was another trumpet fanfare, before the party carried on to the Guildhall, where a feast was prepared.

Here, the City leadership bowed out to allow more space for royalty and nobility. 'No cost was spared,' said an excitable pamphlet, though what it didn't quite admit was that everything was paid for by the City – after all the Crown couldn't afford it.[19] The dinner itself was lavish, with course after course of flesh and fish, all accompanied by music.[20] It was an occasion that wouldn't have disgraced Henry VIII, the warmth of the thundering Guildhall fire a respite, for the guests at least, from the chilly streets outside. It was also, specifically, a pointed marriage between king and nobility. The establishment had returned.

The strong military element to the procession can have escaped no one. There was plenty of legitimising symbolism: the attendance of the Lord Keeper and the prominent role of Lord Chief Justice Bankes sought to emphasise the king's dedication to the law. But the sight of the gentlemen-pensioners with their poleaxes and pistols, the liverymen with their swords, the footmen with their gilt truncheons, and the Yeomen of the Guards, was enough to underline the salient point: that the robe of justice might be lifted to reveal the rusty menace of state violence. 'Drums beat, Trumpets sound, Muskets rattle, Cannons roar, Flags display'd,' trilled one account.[21] Possibly the most notable presence of all were the northern commanders. This was a statement: a show of force. A threat, even. All told, something like a thousand armed men were accompanying the triumphant royal return to London.[22]

And what of the Junto? Essex was in the procession, in his role as Lord Chamberlain, as was the Earl of Holland.* Room was made for some of the more loyal reformists, like Hertford and Salisbury. There was Hamilton, too, one of the intended victims of the Incident.[23] Yet there was also an especially conspicuous absence – for there were no representatives of the House of Commons. Some senior Junto men were sidelined too, like Warwick, Mandeville, and Northumberland. Even Essex was not given the place his role would normally command. He was told to process with the earls rather than the office-holders. His disloyalty had earned him a very visible demotion.[24]

After the banquet, as the skies darkened, came the final act. At 4 p.m., the king left the Guildhall and rose once more to his horse.[25] The mayor rejoined the procession, the dimming streets still lined with tapestries and cheering crowds. There was music and trumpets, plus – when the party passed St Paul's – a glorious anthem sung by

*Holland was Groom of the Stool, theoretically one of the most intimate of court office-holders.

the choir, wearing their surplices and accompanied by sackbuts and cornets. The crowds cheered and shouted: 'The Lord Preserve King Charles!'[26] The bells of over a hundred City churches rang out in the dusky light.[27] The City footmen now carried torches, creating a remarkable spectacle. For those who cared to remember, it was similar to the royal parade for the great masque of 1634, when James Shirley's *The Triumph of Peace* had been staged by members of the Inns of Court.[28] That had been both a challenge to the Puritans and a reminder, by the lawyers, that monarchy should be grounded in law. This time, Charles was appealing not just to legality, but to popular acclaim and the force of arms. But this was very definitely a 'Triumph'. This was a word used repeatedly in the published accounts. It brought to mind conquering Roman generals, and played on Charles's own desire to be seen as a military leader. It was a victory parade – for a victory that lay in the future.

Passing through Temple Bar, the ancient gate to the City, Charles processed down the Strand, past the Charing Cross, and into Whitehall Palace. Here he broke with tradition by physically embracing the Lord Mayor.[29] Then the royal party disappeared into the great palace.

———

While the City celebrated, the House of Lords did not meet. The majority of peers were clearly involved in – or at least present at – the celebrations. But the Commons did sit, almost like it was a normal day.

The stern business of the lower house, with MPs in their usual austere dark suits, seemed like a different world to the royal parades taking place in London at the same time. The first matter on the 25th was a report from Oliver St John about a new 'book of rates'. It was unglamorous stuff, relating to the short-term grant of tonnage and poundage that was about to expire. The explicit reaction to the procession that was going on just a mile or so away was muted, meanwhile.[30]

The Commons did react in one crucial way. For they decided to give the Remonstrance a further push. If the king could appeal to the people, then so could they. Thus, that morning, Denzil Holles had proposed the production of a petition to the king, 'with reasons to show what did necessitate the house to make the late Declaration', that is: the Remonstrance. A committee was appointed, and – almost as an afterthought – Sir Gilbert Gerrard, a minor Junto figure, succeeded with a motion that the same committee 'might draw a form also of congratulation for his Majesty's return'.[31]

———

The royal entry immediately drew a slew of publications celebrating Charles's return from Scotland. They were short and therefore cheap; the aim was for mass appeal. One writer who naturally jumped on the chance to parade his loyalty and make a tidy shilling was John Taylor, the Water Poet. His *Englands Comfort and Londons Joy* was resplendent with memorable woodcut images: Charles on horseback; mounted City men carrying banners and swords; Charles meeting Gurney and Recorder Gardiner; and the procession carrying on with trumpets, and with a poleaxe-wielding gentleman-pensioner, plus various other halberds lining the streets. Strikingly, Taylor's last two images showed a line of faces – men and women – watching from behind the barriers. Taylor had got the message that this Triumph was supposed to be glorious, sumptuous, militaristic, and popular. He recounted how the 'banks, hedges, highways, streets, stalls and windows, were all embroidered with millions of people, of all sorts and fashions', while 'all the way the boys did climb up trees/ And clung close to the boughs like swarms of bees'. The return of 'God's Great Lieutenant', sang Taylor, would 'salve this Kingdoms discontents', cure the dislocations, 'wrenches, fractures, sprains and rents', and cast the various mischiefs 'to Hell's black vault'.[32] The poet of popular royalism was enjoying himself.

Another busy publisher was a man named John Thomas. He was a printer whose business included producing many official or semi-official pamphlets, for both king and Parliament, though mostly for the latter. He had published lurid and violent reports from Ireland, and at least one fairly bawdy pamphlet about London prostitutes, featuring a woodcut image of a couple kissing on a bed.[33] In recent months he had found himself working with Pym, including the accounts of the recent 'Beale Plot' – the phantom conspiracy that had briefly panicked the Commons less than a fortnight earlier. Now Thomas also received a new commission. Something altogether quite novel.

It was common during this time for people to read regular news, but they usually did so in manuscript. Print periodicals had existed in England, and dated back to the 1620s, but they were only allowed to deal with foreign news: after all allowing them to write about home affairs was far too dangerous.[34] Come 1641, though, with the old forms of censorship now toothless, there was little stopping printers making the obvious next step: regular domestic news. But they didn't, yet.

Filling the gap were manuscript reports, usually called *Diurnal Occurrences*, that recounted business in Parliament. The word 'diurnal' meant 'daily', though it was pronounced with a soft first syllable: *jou*rnal. A large number of these survive in various manuscript collections, and have a roughly standard format. The process of production must have been laborious and expensive, as each copy had to be written out by a professional scribe by hand.

At the beginning of the summer, a large compendium of speeches and reports from Parliament had been printed from the shop of William Cooke, another of London's shadowy booksellers, based at Furnival's Inn, off Holborn. This had drawn consternation in the Commons. There were still plenty who took the old view that matters of state were not for public consumption. A committee was formed – which included Simonds D'Ewes – to 'advise of some means to restrain this licentious printing', while at the same time enquiring into the circulation of manuscript news. Then, in early November, a sequel was produced from the same workshop. Running to some 429 pages plus front matter, the *Diurnal Occurrences, or Dayly Proceedings of Both Houses* offered a digest of business in the Long Parliament since it first met. This once again drew censure from MPs, who on 18 November reanimated the 'Committee for Printing', which was to meet (rather symbolically) in the Star Chamber.

How ironic, then, that less than two weeks later the printer John Thomas would receive a visitor from within the Junto, asking him to do something new. It may well have been Pym himself, for the Parliament man was not averse to doing his own shady business. The publishing world was a murky place, with shops in dark alleys and hushed meetings in the backrooms of smoky taverns. But Pym and Thomas clearly had a connection. It was Thomas, for example, who had printed the first account of the Incident, complete with 'the Names of those Lords that should have been slain', and also featuring a woodcut image of Pym.

Thomas had also, in the days following the reassembly of Parliament, printed another pamphlet that reproduced a letter sent from the Lords and Commons to the king, and appended: 'The Heads of Several Proceedings in Parliament now Assembled, from October 20 to the 26'. It was a heavily abridged version – less than two pages – of a manuscript *Diurnal Occurrences*. Now, at the end of November, Thomas decided to do this once more, but in a more sustained and self-contained way. At some point he decided that this would become a regular publication. Every week, he would digest the business of Parliament and print it for the reading public, presenting them with a brief summary of each day's political news. On the 29th, the first edition of Thomas's *Heads of Several Proceedings* was ready. It was published, as would be the pattern, on a Monday so as to make the post that left London for the north of England on Tuesday.[35] It was the first ever printed English periodical to cover home news. It was, therefore, the earliest English political newspaper.

The first day Thomas chronicled was the previous Monday: 22 November. This was the day of the final debate and vote on the Remonstrance. The paper's tone was restrained, sticking largely to the matters of fact, but it admitted there was conflict and disagreement. It hinted that there was a threat to Parliament, noting the presence of the Trained Bands until the debate had finished in the small hours. Its aim was to concentrate sympathetic minds, for there was still much to be done. And it emphasised to the reading public that there was opposition to reform. It also, happily for

Pym, ensured maximum publicity for the Remonstrance, which of course was now circulating in manuscript. Readers of the *Heads of Several Proceedings* were given notice of the existence of the Remonstrance – and surely, therefore, an encouragement to seek out a copy.

This, with the forthcoming petition to the king, were not the same as the ability to print the Remonstrance itself; but they were probably the next best thing. In some ways they might even be better, because both the petition and the newspaper were shorter than the almost comically prolix Remonstrance. That petition, too, was now in production, ready to be presented to Charles. Naturally it was also sent to a printer so that it could be readied for mass consumption. The printer chosen for this important piece of Junto propaganda was John Thomas.

––––––

In the last days of November, as Thomas's *Heads* was going into production, Westminster tensed even further. On the 26th, Charles conspicuously failed to address Parliament, claiming he had a cold and was hoarse from the previous day. Instead, he made straight for Hampton Court, from which he sent a message ordering the dismissal of the guard who had been stationed outside Parliament to protect it from plotters. Charles's claim was that his own royal presence near the capital meant such a guard was no longer necessary.[36] It was a remark that drew the rather acid comment from one observer, referencing the Incident, that 'if his Majesty could not protect the Marquis [of Hamilton] in his own bedchamber, he could scarce protect them in the Parliament chamber'.[37] The Commons immediately sought out support from the Lords to petition the king, and the upper house was content to send two of their number – Warwick and Bristol – to move the king to allow them a guard until the affairs of the kingdom were better settled.[38]

There was more. Charles also removed the Earl of Essex from his role as Lord General of the South – a military position he had held since the summer. Parliament was being patently stripped of any military protection it had. Meanwhile at Whitehall, Charles was promoting loyal servants. Edward Nicholas was the first beneficiary – he was knighted on the 26th, and on the 27th was finally given the much-coveted role of secretary of state. More to the point, the other secretary, Henry Vane the elder, was soon to be fired, leaving Nicholas effectively the nerve centre of government.[39]

Charles's new determination was noticed by Ambassador Giustinian. Not so long ago, the representative of the Most Serene Republic had been decidedly agitated by his discovery that agents of Parliament were opening his letters. Now Charles, 'almost immediately' on his return, took the matter in hand, expressing his personal disgust to the Earl of Holland, and ordering Lord Feilding, a minor courtier, 'without further delay' to present himself at the embassy and to apologise. Giustinian was noting, too, that members of the House of Commons were now having to adopt a much more reticent posture towards their sovereign. The ambassador linked this directly to their tactical military defeat. The removal of the Scottish army, followed now by the dismissal of Essex's guard, had given Charles the whip hand. It held out the prospect that 'his Majesty may be able to resume the just possession of the authority enjoyed by his predecessors'.[40] It was an interesting comment. Was a total counter-revolution in the offing? Were the reforms of earlier that year in danger? More than anything, maybe, there was also now the possibility for revenge: for all the humiliations Charles had suffered going back to the Scottish rebellion; for the defeat of his military response and the petition of the twelve peers. For the Triennial Act; and for the execution of Strafford.

There had, indeed, been moments of late in which the desire for retribution had slipped, almost accidentally, from the pens of those close to the king. Nicholas, for one, had written to Henry Vane in October, to say: 'I wish that those who have been the cause of these miserable distractions in his Majesty's dominions may feel the weight of punishment which they deserve,' and that he expected they would, 'in due time'.[41] There were more general statements of intent, too, particularly as Charles made his way back to London. The mayor of the quiet Lincolnshire town of Stamford, for example, is recorded as hoping that 'all ill effected traitors may be destroyed, your Majesty may be eternally blessed, your spouse and offspring perpetually flourish'.[42] Charles's enemies, wrote the author of another celebration, would feel his wrath: 'those that were inclin'd/ To practice mischief, of this Judge shall have/ A Regal judgement, and a legal grave'.[43]

John Taylor got in the spirit too. He told his readers how, on the day of Charles's return, he had approached the king and placed a poem in his hand. After making a suitably merry joke about Ovid's *Metamorphoses* and how 'a greater wonder is perform'd by me/ I have transform'd a boat from off the Thames/ Unto a horse, to come to welcome thee', Taylor's verse took a much darker turn. 'And all whom thy return doth not delight,' he rhymed. 'Let them be hang'd, and then they have their right.'[44]

Charles's opportunities for a final victory were broadening. His outlook was looking most promising; that of the Junto very fragile. As winter began to tighten its grip on the city, the decisive struggle was about to begin.

PART THREE

Qui Custodiet Ipsos Custodes

12

Indiscreet Rashness

Just over ten years earlier, a rather troubling scandal had broken. It suggested, to some at least, that Charles simply could not be trusted. That the king might try to use military force against those who dared question his regime.

It was known as the 'Machavillian Plot', and it centred on a strange document that was found to be circulating among critics of Charles's government.[1] The manuscript purported to be a description of how Charles could dramatically curb the power of Parliament. He would take control of the country's fortresses, and he would exact new taxes. Garrisons of troops, ideally foreign, would be established and guards would patrol the highways. The reason was simple: 'In policy it is a greater tie of the people by force and necessity than merely by love and affection.' It was a plot, as one observer put it, to make Charles an 'absolute tyrant' – to turn England into a 'Turkish State'.[2] It owed its political theory, and hence name, to the notorious Italian philosopher Niccolò Machiavelli, and to one his maxims: 'It is better to be feared than to be loved, if you cannot be both.'

In the summer of 1629, just after the fractious dissolution of Parliament, copies of the 'Machavillian Plot' could be bought at certain London manuscript dealers. The author, it seems, had been Sir Robert Dudley. He was the illegitimate Catholic son of Queen Elizabeth's leading favourite, and had left England to carve a career as – among other things – an explorer, engineer and warship designer. He had also taken up writing, and in 1614 had put down a set of propositions aimed at King James I, who was then having his own problems with Parliament.

There's no strong evidence that the plan was ever considered by members of Charles's government, yet they did react very tetchily when they found the document being passed around. In the late autumn of 1629, the Privy Council was sitting until midnight, trying to get to the bottom of it, prioritising the document over other business, and eventually beginning prosecutions of the men found to be sharing it. Offices and studies were searched, and the men were accused of spreading a 'damnable project' intended to 'draw upon his Majesty the hatred of his subjects who might imagine, though unjustly, that his Majesty intended to put the same into execution'. Among those arrested were the Earl of Bedford, Oliver St John, and Denzil Holles's father.

Such memories remained fresh in the minds of the Junto in 1641.* For if Charles could gain military control of London, all their reforms might be rendered meaningless. Rather than the reformed, Parliamentarian 'commonwealth' they had strived for – and to some extent, already achieved – England might career down a 'Machavillian' path.

In truth, Charles probably wasn't thinking along these lines at this point, though he was starting to build up military power in the capital, and the potential use of this against Parliament would be a constant threat in the coming weeks. Now that he was back near London, the jockeying for position over the previous months would be suddenly heightened. It would become a battle for supremacy in Westminster and in London. Charles had tried to win over Scotland, he had tried – with Nicholas – to build up a royalist party in Parliament, and he was now trying to appeal to a broader, popular constituency, as a force for stability and traditional

---

*And Dudley's plan would be brought into print the following year, albeit in heavily edited form: *A Machavillian Plot, or a Caution for England* (1642).

religion. He was also, though, looking to consolidate something else: his control of the armed forces in and around Parliament.

The Irish rebellion, meanwhile, had concentrated the critical issues at stake. The Junto had already begun its attempt to take control of the royal government; now their plan was given added urgency, because they needed to complete a similar grab for the means of raising and commanding the new army too. In response, Charles would aim to dissolve Parliament, hopefully while also gaining a lasting financial settlement. On his agenda too, no doubt, was revenge for the humiliations he had suffered since the Scottish wars.

Thus, after seeing the militarism on display during Charles's royal entry on the 25th, the Junto could be forgiven for feeling increasingly vulnerable. Especially when, on 29 November, Westminster narrowly avoided a massacre.

———

Edward Sackville, 4th Earl of Dorset, was an experienced royal servant. Not a firebrand, by any means, but rather a fairly sturdy loyalist.[3] No wonder, for the Sackvilles had risen through Crown service. Dorset's grandfather had been a famously rich Lord Treasurer. His great-grandfather was a Chancellor of the Exchequer so grasping that he was known to wits not as Sackville but 'Fill Sack'. The family had settled themselves at Knole in Kent, a grand brick mansion with a vast deer park. Once an archbishop's palace and a favoured hunting haunt of King Henry VIII, its great hall was now one of the glories of the Elizabethan age. As too were its oak-panelled galleries, and the house boasted a remarkable array of paintings featuring the stern faces of sovereigns, prelates, and the Tudor queens.

When the young Edward inherited the family estate from his wastrel brother in 1624, he took up local office and used this to his, and the Crown's advantage. The two interests were intertwined: central government and local magnate performing their roles in perfectly tuned harmony, for the greater good. When Charles wanted a Forced Loan, Dorset (as he now was) set aside any personal misgivings and threatened to quarter his militiamen anywhere that tried to avoid paying.[4]

But Dorset was not some gruff soldier. His friends considered him fun-loving and witty, pleasant and learned: 'sparkling', was one assessment.[5] He was of the Order of the Garter, making him one of Charles's most trusted nobles.[6] Like any good courtier, Dorset divided his life between country and town. Knole kept tight a hold on his heart, but much of his time was spent in London, where the pleasures were rather less rustic. Here Dorset occupied a great mansion on the Strand: a statement of political prominence and wealth, though the undoubted grandeur was tainted somewhat by the fact it backed against Bridewell prison. Indeed, Dorset found himself constantly offended by the prisoners, who peered and pissed out of the windows; and by the all too frequent escape of the Bridewell chickens and dogs into his adjoining gardens.[7] In London, the boundaries between wealth and poverty, order and disorder, stately beauty and grotesque disharmony, were ever permeable.

Yet, whatever the foulness of the capital, indeed partly because of it, this was a place where a capable man like Dorset was useful. In the 1630s – with the Earl of Holland – he acted as Lord Lieutenant of Middlesex, an office which carried jurisdiction over Westminster. When turbulent times hit, it was Dorset who was ordered by the Privy Council to call out the militia and keep order. He was, therefore, an obvious choice to lead the guard placed around Parliament.

So, having removed Essex, the king had placed Dorset in charge. It was something to secure Parliament 'not only from real, but even imaginary dangers', as Charles sarcastically remarked.[8] The Junto men were incensed. The protective cordon had been replaced, they thought, with a royal noose. Who will guard the guards, they worried: *Quis custodiet ipsos custodes*?[9]

On Monday 29 November, Dorset's men faced their first test. In the Commons that day, much of the debate had been given over to the urgent renewal of tonnage and poundage, which was due to expire on Wednesday.[10] The Commons were prepared to offer a new bill, renewing the tax for another three months, but wanted to tack on a petition in favour of Salisbury's promotion to the lord treasurership, plus that of Pembroke to the position of Lord Steward of the Household.[11] It was a fairly classic Junto ploy: if the king wanted his taxes, he would need to concede certain government appointments. If this particular move was successful, it would have given the Junto control of both the royal finances and the king's household. Then Pym read a letter from Ireland, recounting how the rebels had 'burnt and spoiled all the British plantations they could come at' and were rapidly gaining ground. It was all linked.[12] Ireland had made the need to sort out English governance a matter of immediate and grave necessity.

As the afternoon turned to evening, a large crowd began to grow around Parliament. It was the biggest protest for some weeks – at least since the king had left for Scotland in August. Possibly since the Strafford trial. It is likely that both the Remonstrance and the new printed matter, like John Thomas's newspaper, were starting to pay off and to galvanise public opinion. The people of London had a new slogan, too, and a new aim. According to reports, 'many hundred citizens', with swords at their sides, came down the thread-like thoroughfare of King Street to Westminster, massing around the old buildings 'yawling and crying', it was said, 'NO BISHOPS! NO BISHOPS!'[13]

This was not a general attack on the episcopacy. Rather, the slogan referenced the key procedural battle in the House of Lords. With the king's party getting stronger, the removal of bishops from their seats in the Upper House had became a pressing priority for both the Junto and the London crowd. This in turn was an apparently remarkable shift from the king's return just four days earlier. The streets had gone from broadly loyalist to Charles to pressing the Junto's agenda. London was a complex city, of course, with a diversity of opinions; yet there must be more than a suspicion that the loyalty shown towards the king on the 25th was only ever skin-deep. Over the coming weeks, the London crowd would present its true face, and they would prove a mighty ally to the Junto. It was something that became abundantly clear on Monday 29 November.

Gradually, as the day progressed, some of the protestors seeped into Westminster Hall, where one MP found himself corralled into the long chamber that housed the Court of Requests. The protesters demanded he vote against the bishops.[14] He chided that they should 'desire in a legal way what they would have legally done', and hastily pushed himself away. As he left, he heard one of the protestors turn to another: 'Do you know who you spoke to,' he asked? 'No,' was the reply. 'Why, it was Sir John Strangways,' said the first voice, 'one of the greatest enemies we have.'[15] Strangways was a king's party man.

Word passed to the House of Lords that 'a great company of men' was waiting, 'crying down with the papist lords and bishops' and carrying clubs and swords.[16] In response, the Lords sent an order telling them to leave, but this didn't work, so instead some of the protestors were called for. The Lords were especially concerned to investigate the allegation that someone had said that 'if they could not be heard, they would have far greater number the next day to back them'.[17] By now, the crowd had spilled from the Court of Requests into the small stone-walled lobbies beyond, and some protestors were now outside the House of Lords itself – pressing at the door 'with great rudeness'.

This could not stand. The Earl of Dorset was told to call in his guardsmen, to clear the area. As the militiamen poured in, they found themselves confronted by an increasingly angry and assertive crowd. Dorset tried to calm things down. Removing his hat in a gesture of conciliation, he entreated the protestors to leave. Yet, said a witness, 'the scoundrels would not move'.[18] Now things were getting very heated, and the guards were beginning to push the citizens back, to which the protestors responded with bluster. But then Dorset snapped. 'Give fire upon them!' he barked. Immediately, the protestors panicked. 'The rabble,' went one recollection, 'frightened, left the place, and hasted away.'[19] The guardsmen didn't obey the order to fire. This time they didn't have to. Their muskets were only charged with powder anyway. They would have produced noise and smoke, but shot no bullets. Instead, the flats of their cuirasses were enough.[20] Even so, it was lucky that the crush wasn't deadly. The Palace of Westminster had come much too close to bloodshed: 'the indiscreet rashness' of the Earl of Dorset, wrote the diarist D'Ewes, 'might have occasioned the shedding of much blood'.[21]

It was an ill portent. To the king's supporters, it showed that the London crowd – those outside the political elite: 'multitudes of mean people', said Hyde[22] – was rearing its head once more. Worse, John Strangways alleged to the house that certain members had actively encouraged the crowds, indeed that some of their actions 'did amount to high treason'.[23] To the Junto, though, the events of 29 November had a different lesson. A massacre had only narrowly been avoided. Would they be so lucky next time? And what did this say about those serving the king? To what lengths were they prepared to go to restore order and control?

The next morning the Commons heard of some worrying talk by one William Chillingworth, an academic theologian who had been hanging about in London. He had said, during a meeting with an attorney at Clement's Inn, that within a couple of days some members of the Commons would be accused of treason.[24] This was potentially nerve-shredding information for the Junto, so Chillingworth was sent for.[25] He was certainly a man with interesting connections.

Chillingworth hailed from Oxford, where his father had risen to become mayor. His godfather was none other than William Laud, the future Archbishop of Canterbury, then an academic at St John's. When the young student matriculated to Trinity College in 1618, he made a name for himself for two things in particular. One was as a subtle, nimble, and even mischievous thinker who liked to accost unsuspecting fellow students in the quad and challenge them to debate. The other was as a snitch. Apparently, he made it his habit to take notes on his fellow students' views, and then betray them to Laud, who at that point was rapidly rising in Church, university, and royal favour.

Having briefly emigrated to Douai – the location of the English Catholic seminary – and converted to Rome, Chillingworth found that the Jesuits there were all rather tiresome and condescending.

So, in a pique, he returned home, and back to the Church of England, where in the later 1630s, he was able to carve out a career as a theological writer of some distinction. Late in the decade, he was part of the circle of intellects who met at Lord Falkland's Cotswold mansion at Great Tew. Falkland's house, it was later written, 'was like a College, full of learned men', including Edward Hyde, the poet Edmund Waller, and Sir John Suckling. It was an interesting network for Chillingworth to be part of; indeed, he had been a leading, possibly *the* leading figure in Falkland's circle. Of his fellows, Suckling of course was now in exile after the Tower Plot and may well have already been dead. But Hyde, Falkland and Waller were different: by November, these were leading members of the king's party.[26] So *was* Chillingworth merely reporting rumours? Or did he have more specific intelligence from one or more of his old friends from Great Tew?

Or was it all just talk? After all, the atmosphere around Westminster and London was febrile. There was plenty of unsubstantiated conversation about plots to go around. In a world in which anyone could print just about anything, in which gossip could be treated as fact before the houses of Parliament, it was hard to know what to trust.

On 30 November, the day Chillingworth's outbursts were brought to the Commons, the buildings had been surrounded again by 'many hundred of Citizens flocking to the houses of Parliament', crying out against bishops.[27] The near bloodbath under Dorset, meanwhile, had put the focus on a crucial issue. The Junto were genuinely convinced that Parliament needed an armed guard, but they also needed it to be led by someone they could trust. Dorset was not that man; Essex was. It was heartening, of course, that Dorset's men hadn't obeyed the order to fire. But such insubordination could hardly be taken for granted. Who guards the guards?

In the house, the MP Edward Hyde was prepared to offer some mitigation for Dorset and his guards, namely that the citizens had been fairly heavily armed 'with swords and staves', and had surrounded, harangued and harassed Sir John Strangways – who had just told the house as much. Strangways pushed the issue too, arguing 'that the privilege of Parliament was utterly broken if men might not come in safety to give their votes freely'.[28] It was an argument gaining traction among the king's men. If Parliament was beset with protestors, was it strictly *free*? Was it really a true Parliament any more?

As the daylight faded on the evening of the 30th, a conference took place between the two houses, to discuss the popular protests of the previous day. The Lords considered the protests a 'great scandal', which should be stopped as soon as possible 'lest they should make all the acts void'.[29] It was a pertinent point. If Parliament's enemies were able to make a case that the legislature was at the mercy of a mob, then they might also be able to claim it was unfree, or invalid. The king could use it to meet one of his principal aims: for it might even be a pretext for a dissolution of Parliament, an outcome that would be catastrophic for the Junto.

There was now quite feverish speculation about changes to the government. Everyone could see that Charles was suddenly more confident, and the word was that he was about to pack his administration with loyalists. News of Edward Nicholas's appointment as secretary had got out quickly, and it was no surprise to anyone. That Sir Henry Vane was on his way out, too, was an open secret. Among the most persistent rumours, though, was one that Sir John Bankes would gain promotion from the judiciary to the government. His, it was widely supposed, would be the position of Lord Treasurer – although some thought the Earl of Bristol might get that post, for Bristol and his son Digby were said to be in high favour.[30] And the Junto's preference was still that the Earl of Salisbury be given the role.[31]

For now, Bankes remained in limbo. Meanwhile a piquant humiliation was meted out to the Earl of Pembroke, the Wiltshire grandee who was being pushed by the Commons as a suitable Lord Steward. He was approaching later middle age and his life had taken a rather melancholy path. He had been dismissed as Lord Chamberlain in the summer, at the instigation of the queen, after having allied with the Junto and the London crowd against Strafford. With Charles now back in England, Pembroke had begged for a return to royal favour. But Nicholas could only report a disdainful dismissal from his royal master. Then, in a move of calculated spite, the king announced that he was giving the stewardship to the Duke of Richmond, who at twenty-nine years old, was half Pembroke's age.[32]

Rumour had it that Northumberland would be the next victim of the royal frown. He was a Junto man, if one who might potentially have reconciled himself to the court. He had earned the special ire of the queen, for reasons unknown, and she was seriously influential on her husband. As one despatch had it, rather coyly, Northumberland was on his way out, 'if the feminine gender might have their will'.[33] Watching all this, naturally, was the earl's sister, Lucy Carlisle. If Charles was about to turn out key Junto men from his administration, then several of her associates and family members might be at risk.

———

On Wednesday 1 December, Charles was enjoying himself at Hampton Court, a few miles out of London among the bare trees and mud of the Middlesex countryside. The king's cold from the previous days was now abating, and he spent much of the daylight hours hunting in the palace's glorious parks, before retiring to the warmth of the great house's bellowing hearths as dusk set in.[34] Until, that was, he was disturbed by a delegation of twelve MPs from Parliament, led by a Somersetshire MP, Sir Ralph Hopton, and including Simonds D'Ewes, bringing the petition and the text of the Remonstrance.

The delegation was not especially Junto-dominated, and Hopton himself was a steadfast loyalist, but they still found the king in a cantankerous humour. As Hopton read out the petition, Charles interjected repeatedly. He scoffed at the idea that anyone had ever told him to turn Catholic, pronouncing, 'with a hearty fervency', 'the Devil take him whosoever he be that has a design to change religion.' When Hopton came to plans to use confiscated Irish lands to support the state, the king joked that it was surely a bad idea to

sell a bear's skin before the bear was even dead. Charles then tried
to persuade the MPs never to print their accursed Remonstrance,
which was not something a mere delegation could ever agree to.
So, in the end Charles told them, with more than just a hint of
regal disdain, that he would consider their petition in good time,
and – having had them all kiss his hand – sent them trudging back
to Westminster in their rickety coaches, scuffing their way through
the Middlesex mud with little to show for their efforts.[35]

The following morning, Charles made his own journey from
Hampton Court to Westminster. Here he attended the Lords,
where, sitting on the throne in the middle of the house, he gave
his assent to a bill extending tonnage and poundage for a further
three months and took the opportunity to cast scorn on various
recent alarms and fears. In a short address, Charles claimed to have
had a 'good success' in settling Scotland, leaving 'that Nation a
most peaceable and contented People'. He boasted that before
going there he had settled the laws and liberties of England, and
remarked that he had rather hoped, on his return, to find his
people reaping the benefits. Yet instead, 'I find them disturbed
with jealousies, frights, and alarms of dangerous designs and plots;
in consequence of which, Guards have been set to defend both
Houses.' Happily, his joyous reception in London showed that he
himself could allay the fears. He assured his audience that he didn't
repent any act done this session. He was happy to grant anything
else that 'can be justly desired for satisfaction in point of Liberties,
or in maintenance of the true Religion that is here established', so
he said. 'I must conclude in telling you,' he finished, 'that I seek
my peoples happiness, for their flourishing is my greatest glory.'
Naturally the speech was soon printed and available for the public
to read.[36] It all felt a bit like a royal dressing-down.

For D'Ewes, meanwhile, the appearance of the king had
offered a precious opportunity to engage in one of his favourite
sports: baiting Speaker Lenthall.

The diarist had arrived slightly late and found the house already
considering where they might find lodgings for the new Scottish
commissioners in London, here to settle terms for a new army

for Ireland.[37] Discussion then wandered through military matters, before being interrupted by the appearance of the Gentleman Usher of the Black Rod, who informed the house that the king had come before the Lords and expected attendance from the Commons. Black Rod then withdrew into the back corridors of the building from whence he came, and at this point, according to D'Ewes at least, the Speaker stumbled. Unsure whether Black Rod needed to be called back to hear the house's answer, Lenthall had to be informed by a rather smug D'Ewes, who was in his normal seat looking straight at him, that in fact the usher did not.

Once the king had given his speech, and the Commons delegation – led by Lenthall – returned, the house was ready to settle back to debate the Earl of Dorset's bungled attempt at crowd control. Things got off to a bad start when Lenthall once again clashed with D'Ewes, this time over whether a recap was needed of a key report the previous night, when the diarist had been at Hampton Court. Once more a frustrated Lenthall was overruled. After this, the arguments flowed. Leading for the king's party was Waller the poet, who spoke sharply against the citizens, justifying Dorset 'saying that he had done nothing but what he was necessitated to do'. D'Ewes himself made a characteristically grandiose oration, laced with superfluous historical analogies, which excused the wearing of swords because the citizens had come in the evening (and wasn't Westminster *dangerous* in the evening?). On Dorset, D'Ewes claimed to honour his person as much as any man, but he simply could not justify the orders to shoot: 'I cannot allow this his late act of violence,' he pontificated, 'and for him [Dorset] to bid the musketeers discharge upon so many citizens and the pikemen to run them through', it was something that could have caused 'much slaughter between the guard and the citizens' and 'danger to the members of both houses also'.[38]

At this point, D'Ewes had – not for the first time in his career – gone on for a while. So Lenthall began shuffling about and more than once made to rise from his seat to interrupt. Eventually, D'Ewes noticed, and challenged Lenthall to say his piece, at which the Speaker stood up fully and told D'Ewes that he had been talking for too long and had strayed from the point. D'Ewes then retorted that Lenthall had allowed the previous contributor – Waller – to do so, and he was only following him, to which Lenthall, with yet more embarrassment, backed down. If D'Ewes is to be believed, then this created mirth from the benches. It seemed quite possible at this point that the Speaker had simply had enough.[39]

And so he had. The next day, Friday 3 December, Lenthall was in the house for 10 a.m. After a discussion about pirates, there was an alarming report that Sir Phelim O'Neill, who had recently taken Armagh for the Irish insurgents, had exhibited 'a commission under the Broad Seal of England by which he said that he was authorised by the King to restore the Roman religion to Ireland'.[40] It was hearsay about a document that would ultimately turn out to be a fake – but this wasn't at all clear yet. For now, it was potentially blood-curdling evidence that King Charles might have given his support to the Irish rebels. Once again, no one quite knew what to believe, but if even part of this was true, then the implications were unthinkable. A king of England might be fostering a Catholic rising in Ireland, and complicit in the massacre of Protestants.

The revelations brought an immediate reaction from Pym. The issue, he said, was that the Commons was putting forward good bills for the defence of the kingdom, but they were being stopped in the Lords. The answer, in true Pym fashion, was to appoint a committee. This would be charged with impressing on the Lords the reason and the necessity behind these good bills. But the plan would have to go further than this. For if the Lords as a whole still refused, Pym's suggestion was that the committee would 'acquaint them that we [meaning the Commons] being *the representative body of the kingdom* shall join with those Lords who are more careful of the safety of the kingdom, they being but private persons, and having a liberty of protestation, shall join with them to represent the same to his majesty'.[41]

It was a clever point. Members of the Lords did have the right to record 'protests' against majority votes. The idea was that a Junto bloc might join with the Commons en masse to represent their views to the king. It would have little constitutional force, but there was a radical implication nonetheless: namely that the Lords as a body was not necessary for legislation. It was also buttressed by the threat that the Commons and sympathetic Lords would 'make a declaration to the people, to let them see where the obstructions lie'.[42] The underlying idea was smart, but this element was pure populism.

Remarkably Pym got his committee: a testament, perhaps, to the belligerent temper of the Commons. It was full, too, of Junto men. The sole representative of the king's party was John Culpeper. The committee was also given another responsibility: 'to take into Consideration, some course for the guarding of the towns of Hull and Newcastle'.[43] This was a significant moment: Pym had managed to secure the appointment of a committee overwhelmingly dominated by Junto men – even radical Junto men – whose remit was not only to pressurise the Lords but also to begin making military preparations. Hull and Newcastle were crucial north-eastern port towns, but it was also the principle. Parliament was starting to take control of military assets.

Now, yet again, the house fell to debating the Monday protests. Clearly these had emerged as the key dividing line: the king's party were against the citizens and with Dorset; the Junto vice versa. William Strode, sat opposite the chamber from D'Ewes, was offended that the Lords had declared the protests to be tumultuous; Culpeper rose to say that this was a perfectly accurate characterisation. Strangways, who clearly felt he had personal experience of the matter, having been briefly assailed by the crowd, suggested that in his opinion there really had been 'a very great tumult'.[44] D'Ewes spoke in favour of the citizens, even likening Dorset at one point to the late Earl of Strafford. Culpeper then accused D'Ewes of referring to the citizens' loyalty 'to *us*' (i.e. to the Junto rather than the king), which D'Ewes denied, though conceded that if he had indeed spoken these words, then Culpeper might be do well to read the medieval lawyer Lyttleton's words on 'Homage', which showed one could be loyal to one's fellow subjects as well as the king.[45]

Others spoke, and the afternoon wore on. By 4 p.m., the sky was beginning to darken, so it was decided to lay aside the debate until the following morning. At 5 p.m., the house rose. It had been a rancorous day, and a thoroughly dispiriting one for Speaker Lenthall.

What no one quite realised, as yet, was that at that very moment a fateful decision was being taken, at Hampton Court, by the king.

That day, a delegation had attended on the king and queen at the great Tudor palace, set out in the meadows and pastures by the winding Thames.[46] It comprised men not from Parliament, but the City of London. The group was led by the Recorder, and included six aldermen, the two sheriffs, and eight common councilmen. The reception was provided by a band of courtiers, headed by the Earl of Dorset, who was clearly being rather pointedly embraced by the king. The City men were kept waiting for a while. Then the king and queen came to the latter's presence chamber, and the citizens were called in. After a humble address, the City men presented two petitions. One of these related to the Monday disorders. These had not, the citizens assured his majesty, been sanctioned by the City government. More to the point, the delegation hoped that the king would not impute blame on the better folk of the City. It was the poorer, ruffianly sort who were to blame, they said. It was language which deliberately recalled the king's speech on the 25th, just over a week ago, and it hinted at a potential alliance between Crown and City to control the unruly streets.

The other petition, though, was to be the most consequential. It noted the deadness of trade in the City as a result of the political impasse. And it suggested a potential remedy, one the citizens hoped would be acceptable to Charles. It asked that he move his court to Whitehall for the Christmas season, an act which – if Charles decided in favour – would place him right at the heart of the coming political storm.

The king responded immediately. He had, he said, been planning to winter at Hampton Court, but having received the two petitions, he'd changed his mind. Now he would come to Whitehall. He was ready, he said, 'to do any thing else, that might promote the Trade of the City'. Charles would forego the crisp winter afternoons in the deer parks around the Tudor palace. Instead, he would place

himself in the jumble of Whitehall, next to the icy path of King
Street, and in close proximity both to the sooty mass of London
and the Palace of Westminster.

Drawing a sword, the king then surprised the City delegation
by knighting some of them. He then commanded that they should
dine, and Dorset and others ushered the citizens into a room, where
a table had been prepared. Dinner followed, with Dorset acting as
host. He no doubt found dining at Hampton Court considerably
more congenial than crowd control at Westminster. The whole
thing had been a meeting of minds, between City elite, king, and
his loyal servants like Dorset. It was all perfectly captured in a print
account that was on the stands within days.[47]

———

That evening, Speaker Lenthall left Parliament at some time after
about 5 p.m., and made the short, cold journey up King Street to
his lodgings near Charing Cross. He had plenty on his mind.

As a freezing winter's evening enveloped the city, Lenthall sat at
his desk by candlelight, picked up his pen, and dipped the nib in a
pot of ink. The pen scratched across the paper, and he thought of
where the tide of politics had pushed him. Parliament had now sat
for over a year, it had seen impeachments, the trial of the century,
and thorough reform of the body politic. But if Parliament was a
doctor, providing physic to heal a hurting nation, then it was getting
to the stage when the foul taste of the medicine was becoming
worse than the disease. Hot tempers and fiery spirits were giving
the Commons a dangerous edge. Mass protests and strange public
sermons by mechanic people were creating a nervous dynamic in
the wintery streets of London.

Lenthall wanted out. He'd had enough. He was exhausted.
On one occasion late in October, he had not been able to leave
his Speaker's chair between ten in the morning and three in the
afternoon.[48] On another recent day, in a fit of exasperation, he
had told the house that 'he could not hold out to sit daily seven
or eight hours'.[49] He wished to be back in the calmer world of
the Oxfordshire countryside. If he could get out soon, he might

be able to travel back up the coach tracks to spend Christmas in the warmth of the grey stone houses of Woodstock, or the honey-coloured streets of Burford in the Cotswolds, where he had recently bought a mansion. His pen continued to score across the paper, until his letter was finished. He addressed it to Edward Nicholas.

'I have now in this employment spent almost 14 months,' he wrote, 'which has so exhausted the labours of 25 years that I am enforced to fly to the sanctuary of his [Majesty's] sacred mercy.' He was willing, he pleaded, 'to offer my self & fortune a sacrifice for his royal service'. Nonetheless, he begged Nicholas to intercede for him: 'I must humbly desire you on my behalf in the lowest posture of obedience, to crave his royal leave that I may use my best endeavour to the House of Commons to be quit of this employment, and to retire back to my former private life.'[50] Please let me quit, he was asking.

Lenthall put down his pen. Then, some point later, he picked it up again, and etched out another letter. 'If this other way do not take, if you may find opportunity let me entreat you to incline his Majesty to recommend me to the consideration of the House, by which means I may hope for some satisfaction, but this is totally left to your honour's consideration as opportunity offers.'[51] The force of the first letter was replaced by something much more tepid. If Nicholas saw fit, then he could ask Charles to put the matter before the Commons. It was a characteristically weak, equivocal, request from the Speaker.

Both letters were folded up, sealed, and passed to a servant. Get these to Nicholas, as soon as you can, Lenthall ordered. Only to Nicholas.

The night was now late, and temperatures were freezing. Charing Cross had fallen quiet. The only sounds left were the cries of the dogs, and the occasional stumbling drunk, slipping and cursing on the ice outside.

13

Dangerous Expectation

Nicholas received the two letters from Lenthall the next day, Saturday 4 December. If the new secretary of state briefed the king – at this point preparing to move himself and most of his household from Hampton Court to Whitehall – then the advice was likely that this was not the time for a new Speaker. In any case, Lenthall's promise of service might be read as an offer of support. It was therefore probably best to keep him in place for now; and so the letters were filed away among Secretary Nicholas's papers. If Nicholas ever replied, it was to tell Lenthall that his Christmas would be spent not in the country but in the smoky streets of the capital.

Then, on Sunday 5th, there was a serious altercation in the City. It was the Sabbath and a group of apprentices were found trying to gather signatures for a petition at St Michael Cornhill during divine service. The petition was about the militia, probably calling for parliamentary control – something that was about to dramatically appear on the Commons agenda.[1] Immediately, the matter was brought to Mayor Gurney, who admonished the apprentices with sharp words and imprisoned some of them in his house. But this only raised the heat. Word quickly got out that the mayor had detained the young lads, and a crowd of nearly 200 gathered outside, pressing against Gurney's gate to the point that it eventually snapped.[2] The optimism Charles felt at his return from

Scotland – just over a week earlier – was already starting to look distinctly premature.

Most dangerous of all, London was just over fortnight away from a critical moment in its annual calendar. The City was governed by a Lord Mayor, a 'Court of Aldermen', and a 'Common Council'. The last of these was increasingly assertive in the government of the capital and each year it held elections on 21 December. Usually these local contests were relatively bland affairs, with few significant alterations. But in December 1641, who could say what might happen? If Junto supporters won, then a challenge could be made to Gurney and the upper chamber, the Court of Aldermen: one that might even bring a change in control of the London militia.

On the other hand, Charles's sweep of his government was gaining momentum. Henry Vane the elder was now, finally, removed from his ministerial posts, and Charles even created a new Earl of Strafford – the son of the last one – which caused quite a stir. It was a symbolic move, rather than one with much immediate practical significance, but was important nonetheless.[3] A trial of strength was coming. Everywhere, the king was replacing Junto men with more loyal ministers. Essex was thought likely to be sent to Ireland.[4] Bristol was on the up; his son, Digby, possibly in line to join Nicholas as secretary of state.[5] Pym's party, so the rumours said, was 'tottering'.[6] The king's Privy Council at Whitehall seemed busy again.

On Monday 6 December, Charles arrived at Whitehall with the rump of his household, ready to settle in for the Christmas season. His government, too, was showing some determination.[7] There had been a flurry of activity since the king had come back from Scotland. At a Privy Council meeting the day after Charles's return, John Bankes had been tasked with examining the state of the royal finances.[8] Bankes had to work diligently and fast, meeting with Treasury and Exchequer officials and with Secretary Nicholas.

Then a report had been produced on 1 December, which had a distinctly sinister implication. It itemised the amount of gunpowder stored at the key royal arsenals, one at Portsmouth on the south coast, one at Hull in Yorkshire, and the last – by some margin the most heavily provisioned – the Tower of London. Some of this powder was already earmarked for Ireland, so the report went, but there was plenty left. Most indeed was slated to remain at home, and such was the stock at the Tower that even if every barrel of powder for Ireland was sourced from there, it would still have the largest arsenal of explosives in England.[9] The last time Charles had taken such an interest in the Tower was in May, when he and his courtiers had planned to seize it. For now, the paper was kept between a tight group of advisors.

And there was more. The disbanded soldiers that had been converging on London had not gone away. Some may have left after the October sweeps, but the royal return had brought several hundred 'northern commanders' – i.e. Reformado officers – back to the capital. Parliament, meanwhile, had been busy adding to the soldiers' miseries, coming up with a series of frankly insulting offers of pay.[10] Here, then, lay the roots of a thoroughly belligerent royal strategy. If the king could capture some of the anger of these disbanded soldiers, then he might be able to gather a military following in the capital. These men were likely to be more reliable than the Trained Bands, whose loyalty might be to the City or even to Parliament, especially if the Common Council elections on the 21st went against the king. If Charles could gain control of the Tower of London, with its vast array of munitions, then he would have a formidably strong force in the capital. Parliament could then be overawed, dissolved, and any resistance simply quelled by brute strength. For those who remembered, it could even end up something like the notorious 'Machavillian Plot' of 1629. Seize military power, disband the Parliament, rule by force.

There were more and more voices in the king's court now in favour of this path of military aggression. Among the loudest were some of the Scottish courtiers who had come from Edinburgh with Charles. One was the Earl of Roxburgh, who had been deeply engorged in the plotting around the Incident.[11] But it seems highly likely that another voice was now added to the supporters of force, one which stood well above the blood and steel of Scottish politics. One that Charles trusted and would listen to over any other.

Queen Henrietta Maria had been scared for months now of
what the Junto might do – not just to the small but thriving
Catholic community she had fostered, but to her and her family.
She had tried leaving the country, and she had tried working with
Edward Nicholas to build a royalist party. This second strategy was
very much still active. Now, though, she could see another set of
options. Where arguments and political intrigue might fail, the
king could use the Scottish faction and the Reformadoes. They
could place their trust in musket, sword, and powder.

———

Watching developments with the utmost diligence were the foreign
ambassadors. Two of the most important were those from France
and the Dutch Republic. Each presented nuanced – even counter-
intuitive – views of the English situation.

Ironically it was the Protestant Dutch who were the closest to
the allegedly 'papist' royal court, while Catholic France was more
closely aligned to the Junto. In the 1630s, Charles had heartily
disliked both: the Dutch because they were Calvinist, the
French because they were untrustworthy – the 'false, inconstant
Monsieurs' as he had put it.[12] Now though, relations with the
United Provinces of the Netherlands – the Dutch Republic –
had changed significantly. Represented by Ambassador Johan
van der Kerckhoven – Heer van Heenvliet, the Republic was
going through one of its more 'monarchical' phases. The
current stadtholder, Frederick Henry of Orange, was connected
to Charles I by marriage, for his son, William, had married
Princess Mary in the spring: the backdrop, of course, to Sir John
Suckling's ill-fated attempt on the Tower. Heenvliet's agenda
was to try and push for a full restoration of Charles's power, for
in 1641 the interests of the House of Orange were those of the
House of Stuart.

France was different. Their ambassador, Jacques d'Étampes –
1st Marquis de La Ferté-Imbault – realised that the interests of
France were not necessarily those of King Charles, or even Queen
Henrietta Maria. Thus La Ferté cultivated Pym and the Junto. So

when he reported back that there was likely to be a major clear-out of Junto supporters on the Privy Council, this would not be considered a positive development for the interests of the Louvre. It was something the French ambassador would have to watch.[13]

The same day as La Ferté's despatch, Tuesday the 7th, the Commons took another radical step. Speaking from the gallery, Sir Arthur Haselrig – the man who brought the Attainder against Strafford – introduced a new bill for control of the militia. It would have put all the Trained Bands of the country under the command of a 'Lord General' (left blank – but everyone assumed Essex), giving him power to raise and command troops, to levy money to pay for them, and to impose martial law. A similar plan was included for the admiralship of the navy, although again the name of the new appointee was left blank (everyone assumed either Warwick or Northumberland). It was, in short, a bill to put military power – defensive military power – in the hands of people appointed by Parliament, and to take it from the king.[14]

The horror from the king's party was immediately apparent. Sir John Culpeper cried that Haselrig's bill should be cast out: it was something that 'took away that power from the King which the law had left in him, and placed an unlimited arbitrary power in another'.[15] One MP even suggested the bill be burned in the Palace Yard.[16] Eventually the house was forced to divide as to whether the bill should simply be rejected out of hand. It voted against: 158 to 125. Haselrig's Militia Bill would remain, though in the coming days no one would try to get it read, let alone passed.

Next day, a letter arrived from Ireland revealing that the insurgency was still spreading fast. The south of the island was catching fire much more rapidly than the tiny loyalist force could contain it. Wicklow and Wexford were in full rebellion, and the gentry in Louth and Meath had now joined the uprising. Sir Henry Tichborne, a veteran soldier from the Hampshire gentry, was holed up in the small walled town of Drogheda. As Ireland burned, the arguments in England over who controlled the military would only get more urgent.

———

The 10th of December was a Friday. It was three days since the discussion of Haselrig's Militia Bill and today there was a greater sense of apprehension among those who watched Westminster and Whitehall. The previous day, Sidney Bere, a Whitehall clerk, had written to the veteran Admiral Pennington, still monitoring events from his base at the Downs in Kent. Bere's tone was thoroughly pessimistic. 'The fears of distractions here increase daily,' he wrote, 'truly not without cause, for this division in the House, & on points of so high nature cannot cause less than confusion & combustion in the end, if God do not prevent it.'[17]

In the Commons, there came two interventions from William Strode and Walter Erle. The two men were friends, so observers could have been forgiven for suspecting that their speeches had been planned beforehand.

Strode noted that there were currently five priests condemned and awaiting execution in Newgate prison.* He thought these men might have some information about recent plots, so his suggestion was that they be offered pardons if they were forthcoming with it. Then Erle spoke more of plots. There was a Catholic, he said, one 'of good rank and quality and one familiar at Court' who, on Saturday 4 December, had claimed 'that there should shortly be a great change in this kingdom'. This change would show whether there was a king or not. Charles, the courtier had said, 'had now the stronger party in the city of London'. More to the point, there would be a great change of officers.[18]

Who was this Catholic courtier, talking of an imminent royal coup? Erle declined to say, and the debate moved on – until Philip Stapleton suddenly stood. He had been given alarming and urgent news. Without warning, 200 soldiers had appeared outside Parliament, all armed with halberds.

The unease was immediate. Where had the men come from? What was their purpose? Who had sent them? Someone went out

---

*There were actually seven, so either D'Ewes got his numbers wrong, or Strode did, or the latter felt that two of the condemned men were a lost cause (see p. 201).

to question the men. They said they had been summoned 'by the Sheriffs of London by the Command of the King'.[19]

It soon transpired that the men were mostly householders from the western skirts of London. They had been called out by order of the sheriff and JPs of Middlesex, and when one of their leaders was rushed to the bar of the Commons for a hasty interview before nervous MPs, he announced that the purpose was to suppress riots and routs in the City of Westminster.

The original order, though, had come not from the sheriff and JPs, but from higher up: from Lord Keeper Littleton. When this became clear, it didn't calm the MPs' fears one bit. D'Ewes worried that the pretence of danger was being used for military preparations against Parliament itself, threatening 'not only our privileges but the liberty also of the whole commons of England whom we represent'.[20] Gradually, the full story came out.

————

The immediate context was the awareness that something big was coming from the City that weekend. Charles himself seems to have had some foreknowledge, and on the 9th, had issued an order to the Lord Mayor to keep the apprentices under control and to ensure they weren't 'going abroad to make any tumults or unlawful meetings'.[21] The same day, the 9th, Littleton issued writs to magistrates in Surrey, Middlesex, and Westminster, telling them they must act to stop assemblies and riots. One of the magistrates had then been brought a petition in support of the Junto, which he indignantly took to be nothing less than an incitement to illegal assembly. So, early next morning, he organised the raising of men to be sent to the Palace of Westminster, to block any 'tumults and assemblies of people'.[22]

The petition itself called for the removal of the bishops and the Catholic lords from the upper house, since they were stopping necessary action by the Commons.[23] It was clearly a major operation, and everywhere across the City, people were mobilising to gather signatures. We get glimpses of this from a collection of witness statements taken by the Lord Mayor. One says that on the morning of Thursday 9th, John Greensmith, a tobacconist, had come to the shop of the drugster Edward Curle in Bucklersbury and asked him if he had signed. He said there were some then at the White Lion tavern in Canning Street who had the document, and desired him to go there and put his name to it. Curle answered that he was busy, and anyway he was not prepared to sign a petition against bishops – at which Greensmith replied: 'then you are like to have your throat cut'.[24] The menace here was real: not a specific threat to slash Curle's throat then and there, but a belief that the petition itself was a way of preventing an outbreak of bloodshed on the streets of London.

Leading the petition was a rich City merchant called John Fowke.[25] Initially, the plan was to deliver it to Parliament on the 13th, but this was urgently brought forward when it became clear that a large crowd would likely accompany it. The petitioners wanted to avoid the taint of the 'meaner sort' which both Charles and the London oligarchs had put on popular politics. The new plan, therefore, was to take the petition to Parliament on Saturday 11th, but this was kept 'so secret as few had notice of it'.[26]

There was still room for some dramatic theatre in the presentation, though. On the day, Saturday, the citizens selected 400 of their wealthiest supporters, and had them dress in their finest clothes. From the City, they paraded in some fifty coaches to Westminster, navigating the tight passage of King Street. At Parliament, the arrival of these 'able and grave citizens' was announced with due solemnity, and around a dozen of them, led by Fowke, came to the Commons to deliver the petition, 'with a speech civil and discreet' in which he accused the Lord Mayor of trying to stop it.[27] The text itself was short, but it had so many signatures – 15,000, it was said – that the document was three-quarters of a yard wide and 24 yards in length. Fowke's petition was a stunning show of unity by the Junto-supporting faction in the City.

Charles, though, was trying again to galvanise the religious centre ground. On the 10th, he had a proclamation issued across the country telling people to obey the church laws as they stood. It was a direct attempt to cosy up to those who may have opposed the high ceremonialism associated with Archbishop Laud, but were now equally horrified by London's radical religious awakening. And among that constituency there was at least some positive reaction: when the proclamation reached Dover on the Kent coast, there were public cries of 'God bless his Majesty! We shall have our old religion settled again!'[28]

On Saturday 11th, the day of Fowkes's petition, Charles attended the Privy Council in person. It was the first time he had done so since returning from Scotland. It was to be a busy meeting.[29] Seventeen councillors attended the gathering at Whitehall, including Junto lords like Essex and Saye. Footing the list, because they remained without noble titles, were Mr Secretary Nicholas and Lord Chief Justice Bankes. As a hush descended on the meeting, Charles announced a new plan. The proposal was recorded in the council register in unusually expressive terms. One of those rare moments when the dry ink of a formal record actually does convey the palpable anger that must have been on the king's tongue.

Charles was resolved, the register said, no longer to 'live from hand to mouth'. Since tonnage and poundage had not been granted in perpetuity, 'but only for a few months or weeks', the king had decided he must do without it. So, in order to not 'infringe the liberty and property of his subjects', or 'suffer himself to be starved or bought out of any more flowers of his crown', he would now live off his own income. A group of privy councillors was immediately ordered to investigate the royal finances, and find a way. Bankes's own work was about to have significant political resonance. Charles wanted to rule without parliamentary taxes, as a way to rule without Parliament.

But could he? There is no way of knowing what the reaction was to Charles's announcement at that packed meeting. These things are not recorded in the laconic notes in the surviving register. Did those councillors who already had some sense of the royal finances warn him of the scale of the task? Did Nicholas sound a note of caution? Or maybe Bankes, with Cumbrian directness, gently but firmly pushed back at the king. It was his role, as a wearer of the coif, to give advice, even when it might have fallen on unwilling ears. Money was something he knew about. His father back in Keswick had managed a shop, keeping an eye on income and outgoings, and while Bankes's own accounts had been entrusted to Mary, he had once overseen the finances of Gray's Inn.[30] More to the point, he himself had been looking after the government coffers for some months now as part of the Treasury commission. If anyone knew the scale of the task, it was Bankes.

It is just possible that it was out of these discussions that another royal stratagem arose. The new finance commission would go about its business. But in the meantime, Charles would try something else. Something bolder yet arguably more realistic. He would try and win control back where he had lost it in the first place. He would try to win back Parliament itself.

———

Since well before the recess, both houses had remained unusually thin, and it was normally the more royalist MPs who had been staying away: men who were much more likely to adhere to the king's party than the Junto.[31] The plan would be to issue a proclamation ordering absent MPs to come back. If it worked, the impact would be striking. Given how tight the vote on the Remonstrance had been, it would not take many royalist returnees to change the political shape of the house decisively. The Junto – already struggling in the Lords – would lose the Commons too. Charles would have a majority in both houses. He could vote the taxes he needed, and he could vote the dissolution he wanted. If the precedent of the 1630s was a guide, he could might even be able to spend the next few years prosecuting his enemies.

Charles's proclamation was quickly ready, and by the 12th, it was at the printers. It ordered members of both houses of Parliament to return to Westminster, by 12 January at the latest – exactly a month's time. The print run was small, but this was to be a targeted order, sent, in the words of Ambassador Giustinian, to 210 peers and members, who 'most abhor the changes and who disliked being involved in such troublesome disorders'.[32] By Tuesday the 14th, the news was out, and MPs were aware.[33] It was a very dangerous moment for the Junto.

Proclamations were exercises in image-making. The fanfare of their public reading began with a solemn call of '*Oyez, Oyez, Oyez*'. It was a performance that announced the authority of the monarch and their state. This one was not however intended to be read out. Instead, it was sent to a specific audience. Yet the text itself was an opportunity for spin. The font, the layout, the associated image, were all chosen to maximise impact and authority. And this one bore a very striking imagery.

The first letter of the proclamation had an elaborate design: an image of Hercules fighting a six-headed hydra. In the iconography of age, the multiple-headed monster or hydra was a potent symbol. It denoted rebellion, and – more than this – represented the dangerous populace. Long before Charles came to the throne, one of his tutors had described the people as a 'many-headed monster, which hath neither head for brains, nor brains for government'.[34] It was a reminder of what the king's party were fighting against: not just a parliamentary rebellion but a *popular* uprising: tumultuous crowds, tub preachers, and she-zealots.

There was just a hint here, too, of retribution. The text of the proclamation itself was all about ensuring Charles's legislators were in place to do their constitutional duties, but the image of a Classical demigod, swinging his blade to cut off six ugly protruding heads, would have carried a specific resonance. A few days later, Ambassador La Ferté penned another despatch to Paris. A decision had been taken, he reported, on the 12th: the same day as the proclamation was issued. His sources had told him that very soon there would be formal accusations of treason. The aim of these would be, quite literally, the 'cutting off the heads of several of the Parliament men'.[35] Giustinian picked up on this too. There was a 'well founded apprehension', he told Venice, 'that if his Majesty recovers his authority the blow will fall upon them for what they have done'.[36]

Privy Council meetings were not public. They were not reported in the same way as sittings of the houses of Parliament, let alone itemised in the new weekly newsbooks. But the presence of various Junto lords that weekend means that we can be sure the king's strategy will have been widely known. It was soon understood that

Charles was actively trying to live within his means, and would cancel all tables at court except those for the queen, the Prince of Wales, and for himself.[37] Meanwhile the Hercules Proclamation immediately brought consternation to the Junto. Within days the MP William Strode even tried to lock in their support in the Commons by proposing that any member who left town was either to be fined £50 or expelled. It was immediately shouted down; after all, even Junto supporters wanted the freedom to leave Westminster if they needed to.[38]

The Junto did have one ally, at least, for at some point that weekend the weather took a significant turn.[39] On the coasts it was especially bad. At the Downs on Monday night, a royal pinnace called the *Roebuck* sank after colliding with a flyboat which had lost its cables and anchors in the tempest.[40] In London it was wet, cold, and the winds whipped through the tight streets and up the river. The nights drew in earlier and waxed ever darker. And, as the town's hearths guzzled ever more coal to warm people's freezing homes, the skies were clogged with yet more smoke. Such an urban hellscape was not an attractive prospect for an MP who had left Westminster for the shires: the kind of person targeted by the proclamation.

Nor was the approach of Christmas in the City much of a draw – for this was often a time of disorder, where the world could be turned upside down in festival misrule which skirted the boundaries of riot and rebellion. For all the holly boughs that would be put up on some of the City churches, the festive period might be one of danger. A carnivalesque time in which servants became masters, and in which the forces of order had only the thinnest veil of control. Add to the mix the protests which had only narrowly avoided bloodshed at the hands of the Earl of Dorset's men, and it would have been a brave MP who obeyed the king's summons.

And even if the targeted MPs had wanted to return to the capital, the heavy rains that started around the weekend were causing floods and mudslides, as the roads – poor at the best of times – became nigh impassable. It was as if God was locking down the City.

———

Disorder was growing across London and its suburbs. On the day of the proclamation, Sunday 12 December, there was a great assembly of religious Separatists at St George's, the grand parish church of Southwark.[41] At the front of the crowd was a cobbler, who ascended the pulpit and began a sermon, while concerned parishioners ran to raise the alarm. The constables were called out, but facing the prospect of dispersing a large crowd of radicals, they decided they needed more muscle. Gathering this took time, so the preacher held forth in the pulpit for an hour before the constables and their posse returned and were able to shut him down. But instead of going quietly away, the cobbler simply led his congregation around the corner to the small riverside church of St Olave's near London Bridge, where he planned to give another sermon to his dedicated followers. He found the door to the church bolted, so he spoke in the porch, while a crowd grew outside in the cold.

Then, on Monday 13th, something quite terrifying took place in the full glare of the City.

Newgate prison was a grim gaol on the western skirts of London. According to legend, it was haunted by a devilish hound that howled through the dark corridors and cells in the night. Here, seven Catholic priests stood condemned to death, under the brutal laws against priests in England. The king and queen had both been lobbying for their reprieve, but the trouble was there were also another eighteen prisoners in Newgate scheduled to be hanged. Thus, when these unfortunates realised that their Catholic fellow-inmates were about to earn a stay of execution, they rioted.

Seizing the keys from the gaoler, they barricaded themselves in. With the utmost haste, the Trained Bands were called upon, and as they mustered in the streets outside the prison, the sheriffs drew up their plan. The prisoners would be smothered. A batch of damp hay was found – an easy task in a city that crawled with horses – and brought into the gaol and set alight. The door was forced open and the smouldering bale was pushed into the dungeon controlled by the rebellious inmates. As the dark smoke billowed within the walls and prisoners started to choke, the militiamen drew their weapons and poured in. The rebels were secured and the following day all eighteen were hanged. It caused a 'great murmuring of the common people'.[42]

The same day the fearsome ritual of eighteen hangings was taking place at Newgate, the Commons heard a despatch from Ireland of horrifying atrocities committed by the rebels. It reported that a detachment of 500 men had been sent to relieve Sir Henry Tichbourne at Drogheda. On their way they had been drawn into a narrow lane in the nearby countryside. Suddenly surrounded, they had been cut off, and slain to a man.[43]

As MPs were discussing this, they were interrupted by Black Rod, who made the surprising announcement that Charles had come to the Lords and had sent for the Commons to attend on him. The king gave what the newspapers described as a 'short speech', calling for the speedy despatch of forces to Ireland. It was, said Charles, a time for 'deeds and not declarations'.[44] He understood that there was a bill in the Lords about pressing men for the forces, and he wished it known that he was content to accept it. There had been debate, he noted, about the implications for the royal prerogatives and the people's liberty, and a clause had been inserted in detriment to the former. His view, so he wanted to make clear, was that the Irish rebellion was such an urgent matter that the bill should be passed, though with a *salvo jure* clause, 'without prejudice', so as to reserve debates about the finer constitutional implications until later.[45]

Charles probably saw this as a concession: after all it would allow the Impressment Bill – a key Junto policy – to pass. But there is no getting away from what was happening. This was the king, coming down to the Parliament, telling members (the Lords in this case) how they should vote on a bill, and even suggesting that they make amendments. At the very least, it was an unfortunate constitutional faux pas.[46]

The following day, Wednesday 15th – while Edward Nicholas was moving into Henry Vane's old offices in Whitehall – there was a curious moment in the Commons.[47] One of the knights of the shire for Nottinghamshire stood up, several times, and tried to present a petition from his county, which he said had been subscribed by some 5,000 inhabitants. It was an appeal in support of the bishops and the Prayer Book: a notable expression of popular conservatism. It was not, so it seems, the only such text circulating. Similar ones were being gathered in Huntingdonshire, Somerset, Dorset, and Gloucestershire. After a long debate, the petition was set aside, with no date agreed for a reading.[48] It was being stonewalled.

The Junto, anyway, had another plan in train, a thoroughly cynical one. They kept the debate going until the light started to fade. By early evening, many royalists had started to drift back to their lodgings. Then, midway through a discussion about the armed forces, an MP for Warwick William Purefoy, rose and declared that while Parliament stood in need of money, the best way to get it was to have the recent declaration printed, 'so that we might satisfy the whole kingdom'. Immediately there had been cries of 'Order it! Order it!', which D'Ewes considered rather strange, and a clear sign that 'many members' were already privy to Purefoy's intended motion. Speaker Lenthall then asked Purefoy to clarify: Did he mean the great Remonstrance? This, too, seemed strange. Normally, the Speaker would have been warned about a new motion like this. To Lenthall's question, Purefoy rose again, and said he meant the declaration that had gone to the king on the 2nd, in other words, the Remonstrance. This, then, was an attempt to overthrow the vote against printing it. Again, the cries came of 'Order It! Order It!'[49]

The poet Waller responded. *Surely*, he said, with almost audible exhaustion, this was not the time for debating this *again*. It was already getting dark and the last time the question had proved so difficult that the arguments had run well into the night. Outside, the clock tower in the yard struck four. The light was now so low that D'Ewes could no longer make notes, so he withdrew. The clerk by now 'could not see to write', so an acrimonious scrap commenced about whether to bring in candles to alleviate the gloom. First, it was put to acclamation, and the ayes were clearly the loudest, but the noes demanded a division, so the ayes rose and the noes stayed seated. At the count, the ayes were 152 and the noes 53. Candles were sent for.

The debate continued by flickering light. Again it was rancorous. Eventually, a division was called. The ayes rose and the noes sat. This time the vote was closer: 135 ayes to 83 noes.

It was a devious and deliberate coup, entirely left out of the daily reports in John Thomas's newspaper. But now, at last, the Remonstrance could be printed. Outmanoeuvred, the royalist party in the house was enraged. Immediately around sixty of them demanded the right to register a protest against the majority vote. For now, this issue was simply postponed until Monday. And so the house rose. It was 7 p.m.

———

Relations between the two palaces were reaching new lows as the winter winds continued to rattle the wooden residences of King Street between them. The Junto were increasingly nervous about their hold on Parliament itself. The Hercules Proclamation had opened up a distinct possibility that the king's party would be able to take control of both houses. Ambassador Giustinian thought the Junto men were 'fearful for their own safety', and therefore contemplating 'the most desperate expedients'.[50] But there was also a more general sense of a country on the edge of a precipice. Thomas Wiseman wrote again to Admiral Pennington. Parliament, he said, were every day at great heats. Few days passed, he quipped sourly, without someone or other being sent to the Tower.[51] On Friday 17 December, another of Pennington's correspondents informed him that there was 'much discourse in Court, Parliament & City, nay in Country too, & much discontent in all of them'. Factions were now a fact of life, and men were 'governing themselves rather by passion than judgement'.[52] The outlook was bleak. The country was 'not far from ruin', thought Wiseman.[53] 'All things grow daily into a more dangerous expectation,' warned yet another of Pennington's London intelligencers.[54] 'Poor England,' wailed a pamphlet, 'in what a miserable estate art thou, groaning under the burden of so many divisions.'[55]

Tempers could flare at any minute. There was a row in the Lords between John Williams, recently promoted as Archbishop of York, and the radical Earl of Warwick. Williams called Warwick 'Sir', but Warwick misheard, and thought he had been addressed by the disrespectful 'Sirrah'.[56] Then there was a slightly farcical kerfuffle in the same house on Friday 17th, when one Andrew Windsor, a rather dissolute army captain, made a far-fetched claim to a seat in the house as a baron, and 'thrust himself into the Lords house rudely', landing a punch on one of the officers. The peers knew him to be a 'distracted man', so they simply put him out of their doors with a rebuke, but the burlesque took a rather dark turn later that evening when Windsor murdered his own servant.[57]

Another Sunday was approaching, and there was clearly nervousness about a repeat of the previous week's disorderly street sermons. The Common Council elections were just days away, and that Friday, the Lords gave order that the only form of worship to be allowed was that prescribed by law.[58] But when the Sabbath came, the fears were fully realised.

At St Sepulchre's, the enterprising and self-proclaimed prophet James Hunt, a Kentishman who was becoming a regular feature on the London preaching scene, gave one of his radical sermons. Then, that afternoon, a rather gaunt-looking Puritan called Praisegod Barebone, a leather-seller by trade, preached loudly to a group of Separatists in a house on Fleet Street. It was reported of the crowd that 'there were as many women as men', and that Barebone brought the hellfire: 'crying divers times, as was audibly heard, Hell and Damnation, telling them they were all damned'. Soon more people were outside, attracted by the fact that Barebone 'yelped so loud with an horrid exclamation'. This time an angry mob gathered, 'impatient of the aforesaid Leather-seller's sermons, which was full of heretical opinions',[59] and smashed the glass windows.

Fortunately, the constables arrived just in time to disperse the assailants, but it was nearly a lynching, and the whole episode was a sure sign that London was more divided than might immediately appear. Religious radicals didn't quite have the run of the streets, and the anonymous pamphlet that described the escapade was entirely sympathetic to the angry crowd. Recounting how one of the audience was cornered, and how the apprentices 'kicked him so

vehemently, as if they meant to beat him into a jelly', the author –
possibly John Taylor – noted: 'I confess it had been no matter, if
they had beaten their whole tribe in the like manner.'[60]

The City was looking dangerously split. Then, on 21 December
came the council elections.[61] The outcome would determine
who held the balance of power in the capital. Throughout the
day, male Londoners of the middling sort and above attended
meetings within their ward and voted on candidates.[62] The results
of these open and public elections will have become clear as the
day progressed, and they were, against a background of economic
crisis, a dramatic success for supporters of the Junto. One of those
elected, for example, was John Fowke, the man who had led the
controversial City petition two weekends ago.[63] It would take a
while for these newly elected Common Council men to take their
seats – traditionally the handover took place well into January – but
when they did, it would represent a remarkable shift in London.

Earlier that day, too, another menacing tactic had been activated.
For that morning, a new Militia Bill had appeared, and had
proceeded to a first reading.[64] At a moment of heightened urgency,
the Junto had reanimated their plan to take control of the military.

Charles could no longer wait for 12 January, the date set down in
the Hercules Proclamation. He needed to act now.

14

The Jaws of Destruction

As Christmas approached, John Bankes began a series of backchannel meetings with key members of the Junto, specifically Lords Saye and Mandeville. It was a hushed mission, kept entirely off the books. The aim was to find the beginnings of the basis for a settlement, born of the belief that the situation was escalating too far. But agreement was hard to come by. Saye and Mandeville were pushing for a thorough revision of the liturgy, while Bankes knew there were places the king would not be prepared to go. Charles had reluctantly abandoned Laud and his high Ceremonialism, but that was far enough. The bishops and the Prayer Book were non-negotiable. The prospects for concord were small, and the meetings evidently ceased. It is far from clear that the king even knew about them.[1]

At the same time, three names reappeared from Bankes's past. All of them had been men he'd prosecuted when Attorney-General. All of them would play a dramatic role in the following days.

The first was Sir Richard Wiseman, one of Bankes's nastiest cases. Wiseman was of a relatively wealthy background, hailing from a decent-sized manor house at Thundersley in Essex. In the 1630s, he was heavily in debt and in the midst of a serious feud with one of his neighbours, a man called John Stones.[2] At one point, Stones had told Sir Richard that his wife, Susan Wiseman, was a whore and their daughter a bastard, and that 'he would maintain it with his sword (or life)'.[3] Wiseman brought a lawsuit in the Star Chamber in 1638, but it stalled, which led him to utter some ill-chosen words in which he accused the then Lord Keeper, Thomas Coventry, of taking a bribe. Thus Attorney-General Bankes had been called upon. What had started as a party-on-party defamation suit, became a state prosecution for sedition, against Wiseman.

Bankes collected evidence meticulously and had a good case.[4] The privy councillors who sat in judgement agreed, and Wiseman was duly convicted. It was decided he must be made an example of. Impugning a holder of a high office of state was a serious business. In the political theory of the time, in which the king had 'two bodies', a natural body and a political body, the latter was partly occupied by those he chose for high office, including his judges and his Lord Keeper. Slandering the officers chosen by the king was akin to slandering the king. So Wiseman suffered a savage sentence: he was to lose his baronetcy, pay fines and damages totalling £18,000, and be put in the pillory with papers declaring his offence, have his ears cut off, and be sent to prison for life. He was despatched to the Fleet, where he was kept in dismal conditions (though his ears, at least, seem to have been spared). It could have been even worse – had the Earl of Dorset had his way, then Wiseman would have had to stand in the pillory with a whetstone hung around his neck.[5]

Come 1640 and Susan Wiseman was desperate to get her husband out of prison, even though relations between the two had evidently broken down, with an increasingly paranoid Sir Richard blaming his wife for some of his misfortune.[6] She was successful, and in January 1641, Wiseman was released and compensated by Parliament.[7] He wasn't exactly happy though: he wanted more. That summer, he was in the Lords where he accused someone else of taking bribes – this time a parliamentary clerk named Throckmorton, whom Wiseman ended up thumping with a cudgel. A few days later, he got into a brawl with Viscount Andover, a minor peer, which saw Wiseman himself getting hit and being called an 'insolent lying fellow', to which he retorted that he 'would strike any subject in England' (even a peer).[8] It's possible that by this point Wiseman was simply unhinged. Come winter, he was still seething with discontent, angry at his treatment, and ready to throw himself into any fight he could find.

———

The second name that came up from Bankes's past was that of John Lilburne. Here the connection was even more explicit.

Lilburne had been another victim of Star Chamber, also in 1638, for importing 'scandalous' and 'factious' books. He was whipped and placed in the pillory, from which he somehow managed to scatter among the crowd three pamphlets by the Puritan polemicist John Bastwick. They included one entitled *An Answer to Sir John Bancks*, which criticised Bastwick's prosecution. Lilburne was then hauled before Bankes and Solicitor General Littleton to confess to this latest outrage. He signed off with what would become a rather characteristically dramatic flourish: 'This I will seal with my dearest blood, per me, John Lilburne.' Bankes still kept the confession in his papers.[9]

By coincidence, both Lilburne and Wiseman had found themselves in Star Chamber on the very same day, 9 February 1638.[10] Indeed, by 1641, the two men very likely knew each other quite well. They had been sent to the same prison, had been released (Lilburne at the instigation of Oliver Cromwell), and were hanging around Parliament around the same time. The biggest difference was that Lilburne had been able to put his side of the story in print. After his conviction, he'd penned a pamphlet describing his ordeal. It had been printed in the Netherlands and smuggled into England, although it was likely a very small run as no copy now survives.[11] Not so the second edition, which – taking advantage of the much freer environment – was brought out in December 1641. By now Lilburne was becoming rather better known in London. His Star Chamber sentence had been denounced in Parliament as 'bloody, wicked, cruel, barbarous, and tyrannical', and had even been obliquely referenced in the final text of the Junto's great Remonstrance.

He was ready to become genuinely famous. The second edition of *The Christian Mans Triall* (as it was called) was a slick, enticing volume. On the facing title-page it boasted an image of its author.[12]

Now, he would be a recognisable face in London. And one of the lead characters in Lilburne's sorry tale was John Bankes. It was a rather unhappy and inconvenient reminder of the latter's role as the legal enforcer of Personal Rule. Given the rumours that he was in line to be appointed Lord Treasurer, in opposition to the Junto's favoured candidate Salisbury, it seems just possible that the timing of publication was not entirely coincidental.

It was the third name, though, that was the most dramatic, and it was another man whom Bankes had once prosecuted. Someone who had once been described even by the royalist Dorset as a 'swaggering ruffian', a 'young outlaw ... who neither fears God nor man, and who, having given himself over unto all lewdness and dissoluteness, only studies to affront justice'.[13]

His name was Thomas Lunsford, and he was about to be given the most dangerous post in the royal government. He would be made Lieutenant of the Tower of London.

The Tower remained the most heavily fortified bastion in the City – in fact in the whole country. One of London's tallest buildings, it was virtually impregnable. More than this, it possessed a colossal arsenal of cannons, which could quite easily be turned against the eastern reaches of the City.

Now Charles's plan would be to secure it, and the weapons within. The only problem, for Charles at least, was the command structure. The Tower had a constable – a nobleman in nominal charge – and a lieutenant, who actually ran it. At the start of December 1641, both positions were held by Junto men. The constable was the Earl of Newport, who was the Earl of Warwick's half-brother and Essex's cousin. The lieutenant was William Balfour, a Scot who had shown ample loyalty to the Junto. If Charles were to take control of the Tower, and thus tip the military balance in the capital his way, he would need to remove and replace both these men.[14]

The priority was Balfour. His was the more pressing role. Plus he was not of the nobility, and he was Scottish, so he was a soft target. As Edward Hyde later recalled, the fact he had even been appointed at all had been 'to the great and general scandal and offence of the English nation'.[15] By Tuesday 21st, the day of the Common Council elections, Parliament knew that Balfour was being asked to resign.[16] He had been given little choice, though apparently he was offered a sweetener of £3,000, to be paid from the queen's account. Concerned, the Commons sent the serjeant to look into Westminster Hall to see if Balfour was walking there. He wasn't, but by the end of the lunch break he had been tracked down and was able to confirm that he had indeed surrendered his position.[17]

The next day, the king, in his own hand, made out a warrant to four trusted privy councillors, including Manchester and Dorset, to put the Tower in new hands. The document itself shows the king was central to this initiative.[18] It must have been a critical part of Charles's strategy. It named Sir Thomas Lunsford as the new Lieutenant of the Tower.

Immediately, rumours of Lunsford's promotion spread in Westminster and the City. To many, it was a horrifying appointment. For Lunsford's past was chequered, to say the least. Born in Kent in 1604, he had grown up in East Hoathly, Sussex, as a member of the landed gentry. A man of strikingly large physical bulk, he'd entered into a feud with another local family, the Pelhams. In the course of these hostilities Lunsford had not only (allegedly) poached deer from his enemies' park, but also announced that he 'cared not a fart' for Sir Thomas Pelham. Things escalated to the point that Lunsford fired off a pistol – more than once – at Pelham as the latter left church in a coach. Lunsford was arrested and sent to Newgate, with a prosecution planned by the then Attorney-General William Noy. Soon afterwards, Noy died, but before his replacement Bankes could pick up the case, the gaoler at Newgate had made the questionable decision to accept Lunsford's parole and allow him to move to more genial lodgings in town, from which he promptly disappeared. Lunsford's next few years were spent as a blade for hire in the Continental wars, though he was also tried *in absentia* by Star Chamber, with Bankes managing to secure a swingeing, if meaningless, £5,000 fine (plus £3,000 damages to Pelham), for the 'foul conspiracy and assault'.[19]

Lunsford, though, did return. In 1639, with plans afoot for the first Scottish war, he was welcomed into the royal army and received the necessary pardon. In 1640, with a second Scottish war looming, he was commissioned as an infantry colonel and told to raise a force in Somerset. Lunsford's Star Chamber fine, 'for a barbarous attempt to have murdered Sir Thomas Pelham' was set aside.[20] His regiment found its way to the front line, and fought bravely at the defeat at Newburn, near Newcastle. Lunsford himself was especially vigorous and valiant. His loyalty was proven, to his fellow soldiers as much as to the king.

The Reformado officers were continuing to congregate around London. They had, so it was reported, 'offered their majesties to untie the knot'. To offer king and queen a way out the impasse. A violent one.[21] They were taking on a new name, too. It was a name that had been used before, when Charles had again gathered a force of loyal troopers around him at York. But now it gained a much deeper resonance. It was a foreign-sounding word, drawn from the Italian: *cavaliere*, meaning one who rode a horse, but rendered into English: 'Cavaliers'.

In the past the word had referred both to brave soldiers, especially cavalrymen, and to gallant, fashionable gentlemen. There had also been a whiff of the roaring dissolute about it, too. Way back in 1612, none other than John Taylor, then a young waterman, caricatured such a man, a 'Cavalero Hot-shott'. He was one who would be rowed across the Thames shouting at the oarsmen: 'Zounds! Row, ye Rogues! Ye lazy knaves, make haste! A noise of Fiddlers and a brace of whores at Lambeth!'[22] Since the spring, the term had found increasing use, especially associated with the poet, gambler, and royalist Sir John Suckling, who had been forced into exile after the Tower Plot. With him in mind, the word 'Cavalier' was taking on a new sense that combined all of these and added a layer of party loyalty. Now it was being applied to the Reformadoes, and to their new hero: Thomas Lunsford.

There were two views on Lunsford in 1641. One was that he was a steadfast gallant, if maybe a bit rough around the edges; undiplomatic, but loyal. To the Reformadoes, indeed, he was infinitely preferable to the slimy politicians like Pym, who had been notably recalcitrant about such things as paying soldiers' wages. The other view was that he was nasty and thoroughly brutish. Heavily in debt, rarely seen at church. Some even said he was a cannibal. Yet the reality was that the two views are not wholly incompatible. What Charles needed in December 1641 was not a thinker, a questioning man, or anyone with a hint of the timid or the hesitant. What he needed was a loyal thug. This is exactly what Lunsford was.

The possibility of a violent denouement was to be an ever present one. Yet at the same time Charles, or at least those around him, were clearly still also pursuing a more conciliatory approach. Courtiers like Bristol and Digby, now very staunchly of the king's party, had once been allies of the moderate Bedford, who had died back in May 1641. In them, perhaps, there still lay some hope of building bridges between royalists and reformers.[23]

The appointment of Lunsford is hard to square with this 'moderate' strategy, but it was apparently Digby who suggested taking control of the Tower. His preference had been his own half-brother, Lewis Dyve, but he was out of town, so Digby proposed Lunsford.[24] It is a role that immediately throws up questions about Digby's own priorities. In the coming days, he would pursue a disruptive path, but one that tried at least to maintain a skein of constitutionalism. It seems clear that even he, though, was thinking partly in terms of force and violence.

———

Parliament had decided 22 December would see 'a great fast', a celebration led by sermons and prayers. The same day, Balfour yielded the keys to the Tower. It was now in Lunsford's possession. Charles, meanwhile, put out an official riposte to the Remonstrance.[25] Its tone was firm, but moderate and legalistic, grounded in the constitutionalism that was coming to characterise a particular group of royalists. It appealed to people like Falkland, or Culpeper, or Strangways, or even to Bristol and maybe still Digby.

Yet for those on the streets of London, conscious that Sir Thomas Lunsford was now glaring down at them from his cannon-studded fortress on the Thames, the claims of moderation will have seemed decidedly hollow.

Christmas was approaching. It was a time for righting wrongs, given an extra edge this year by stalling trade. The City's youthful apprentices were giving off that they were ready, 'if need be to over-match a Royal coup'.[26] The day after Lunsford's appointment, the 23rd, two more petitions were presented to Parliament. One, predictably, protested against Lunsford's appointment to the Tower, claiming that he was 'most notorious for outrages'.[27]

The other was a forceful appeal from young London men, who had served their apprenticeships and just become journeymen, but were now concerned that the trade depression would stop them finding work. They were worried that the slump would 'nip us in the bud, when we are first entering into the world'. Despite the respectful tone, this was a remarkable petition from below, presented with a great roll of paper purporting to have 30,000 signatures. It had to be put together against the fierce opposition of Mayor Gurney and Recorder Gardiner – who had ensured that some of the petitioners were simply thrown in gaol.[28] When it was read in the Commons, the initial reaction was silence, though D'Ewes found himself able to commend the fact that 'the meanest of the people were sensible both of the danger and safety of the kingdom'.[29]

The immediate issue, though, was still Lunsford. It was this on which the fate of London hung. An urgent conference was sought with the Lords. Lunsford, the Commons delegates argued, was unacceptable. Highly so. No one would take coin to the Tower because he couldn't be trusted. Trade would decay. More than this, look at the way Lunsford had dealt with Thomas Pelham and others. Had he not, as they alleged, refused to attend church when he had been with the royal forces at York?[30] But all this was just special pleading. The real reason was that Lunsford was a royalist ultra, and the Commons knew it.

That day, a panicked newsletter from the capital told its readers that it was time to arm. 'I say still, provide weapons, get muskets, powder and shot. Let not the Popish party surprise us with a riding rod only in our hands.'[31] In London the reports were that: 'There is a great ado made for arms ... there is not any muskets or other guns to be bought, not iron to make them of, so great is the fears of the people here, especially about the Tower.'[32]

The next day was Christmas Eve. Lunsford was busily being sworn in by the earls of Dorset and Manchester.[33] In the afternoon, the Militia Bill – which would give Parliament control of the county forces – received a second reading, though there was as yet no move towards final committal.[34] The Commons were trying to persuade the Lords to declare against Lunsford. But they wouldn't. They would postpone the discussion until Monday, possibly to give Charles the opportunity to back down of his own accord.[35] Even in the Lords this vacillation created immediate rancour, with twenty-two peers entering protests, citing fears for the 'instant good and safety of the King and kingdom', but it stood.[36] Faced with a clear and present threat from Lunsford, the two houses still couldn't unite.

All the Commons could do for now, as the freezing winter evening drew on, was order Newport, the Constable of the Tower, to take up personal command himself.[37] D'Ewes was despondent. 'All things hastened apace to confusion and calamity,' he wrote in his diary. He saw no reason that Church or kingdom would escape. His only hope was that God, who had already several times saved Parliament, would do so again, delivering England 'from the jaws of destruction'.[38]

He would have been even more terrified if he had known that as soon as Newport was told to reside in the Tower, Charles had simply dismissed him. It was still in the king's power to do so – for now. Charles's control of the Tower was secure.

———

On Christmas Day, London was calm and quiet, but unbearably tense. Shops were shut. Some people went to church, although the strictest Puritan view was that they should work and that church services were neither necessary nor desirable. Most of London's younger folk were happy to avoid church, but it was rather harder to keep them at work or out of the alehouses.

Late that day, the temporary quiet began to look worryingly fragile as a crowd of hundreds, likely bolstered by drink, gathered around the Tower to oppose any attempt to reinforce it with more soldiers.[39] For now, though, things just about held.

It was the following day, St Stephen's Day, that London began to slide into anarchy.

————

The 26th fell on a Sunday, so the brief calm of Christmas was suddenly, as the sun rose, shattered by a morning chorus of church bells clanging and chiming. Inside the churches, ministers opened frozen wooden doors to welcome congregants, and ascended pulpits. From these, declarations against Lunsford came thundering down to horrified audiences.[40] Rumours of his appointment had already spread, but the church services of the 26th will have confirmed the news for everyone. The woodturner Nehemiah Wallington wrote down his own reaction. 'That wicked, bloody colonel, was sworn Lieutenant of the Tower,' he recorded. 'I did hear that he was an outlawed man, and that he had killed two, and was put into Newgate, and that he broke forth of Newgate, and fled beyond the sea. And now he was come again to have the charge of the strength of our City, that upon the least occasion he might batter down our houses on our heads.'[41]

With sermons in the churches over, people began milling in the streets. Apprentices gathered in crowds. Some talked of storming the Tower if Lunsford's appointment was not immediately rescinded. Twice, Mayor Gurney left his house in Old Jewry and hurried to Whitehall to inform the king that order was about to collapse.[42]

In response, the king called an emergency meeting of the Privy Council: of the attendees most were loyal men. The new Scottish courtiers like Roxburgh were there, as were Lord Keeper Littleton and Chief Justice Bankes. Edward Nicholas, of course, was present in his new role as secretary of state. The council acted quickly. An urgent proclamation was ordered, to be issued the following day, against any tumultuous gatherings. But the main business was Lunsford who, it was noted, had tendered his 'voluntary resignment'. The lieutenancy would instead go to Sir John Byron, another steadfast loyalist, but one with a rather less violent reputation.[43]

In all, it was a considerably smarter move on the king's part.[44] From the brink, Charles had conceded a climbdown, though only a partial one, and not one of much good to the Junto. It would have two unexpected consequences as well. Firstly, once word passed around, it would give the crowds extra confidence. They had destroyed Strafford in the spring, and got Lunsford removed in the winter. What else might they achieve? Secondly, it meant that Lunsford himself – rather than being in the Tower – now found himself free-roaming around Whitehall, looking for trouble.

Time passed before news of Lunsford's 'voluntary resignment' got out. The next day – Monday 27 December – most still hadn't heard. Even more people were out in the streets than had been previously, and now, added to the mix, was the return of Parliament after the short Christmas break.

Large companies of Londoners gathered and left the City and marched towards Westminster, demanding to know what had become of their petition against the colonel, chanting: 'No bishops, No popish lords!' They were joined by ranks of sailors and watermen, who'd both been suffering significant underemployment thanks to stagnation of trade. The great City of London was angry, and crowds of its inhabitants were braving the snow and the bitter winds, to vent their frustrations.

In the midst of this, the royal proclamation ordered yesterday by the Privy Council was announced. It told the protestors to go home, but all it seems to have done is incensed them further.[45] Gradually, news was passed around that Lunsford had been removed, but still the protestors didn't disperse. The numbers were now so great that it was proving very difficult for anyone to push through the crowds around Parliament. According to one hostile observer, the crowd made a passageway 'in both the Palace Yards, and no man could pass but whom the rabble gave leave to, crying "A Good Lord!" or "A Good Man! Let him pass!" ' Soon, chants of 'NO BISHOPS!' 'NO BISHOPS!' were filling the icy courtyards.[46]

In the Commons, debate had been meandering since 10 a.m. Then, suddenly, news came that there was a 'tumult' in Westminster Hall.[47] The protests had spilled in from the streets and into the palace itself, and were threatening to break into a full-blown riot. Five hundred persons had pushed in and 'divers swords were drawn'.[48] The crowd had been gathering for some time, but the added ingredient now came from the surprise appearance of Lunsford himself and about thirty other men. As they passed through into Westminster Hall, they found themselves confronted with the huge body of protestors. Quickly, Lunsford and the other Cavaliers drew their swords, and the citizens and apprentices did the same, picking up loose bits of brick to use as weapons.[49]

One of the men they ran into was Sir Richard Wiseman, who had been there pursuing his seemingly interminable case for compensation. Seeing Lunsford and his gang setting upon the crowd, Wiseman drew his own sword and joined the protestors, declaring he would 'spend my dearest and best blood in defence of the House of Commons'. He called out, 'Come! Fall on!' John Lilburne was also there; he would later recount how the Cavaliers had drawn their swords and slashed at the protestors, forcing some of them to retreat up the Parliament stairs, others into the rooms that housed the Court of Requests and the Court of Wards.[50] The protestors, though, were rallied by Wiseman, who fought three Cavaliers at once, breaking one of their swords. Lilburne and a group of club-carrying sailors joined in, and eventually the Cavaliers were forced to retreat.

The protestors, Lilburne later recalled, fought like 'enraged lions'. Lunsford himself had to leave the building by the back stairs, wading into the slubby Thames until the water seeped over the top of his boots. He clambered into a boat and hastily disappeared.[51]

News of the fight in the Palace of Westminster spread rapidly through London, where it caused what one observer described as a 'great uproar'.[52] People poured out of houses and shops and gathered outside. In the developing chaos, the City authorities battled to keep control. Some apprentices were arrested and corralled in the Mermaid Tavern on Cheapside, a hostelry beloved of the capital's poets and playwrights. This only aggravated matters, and the forces of order were anyway divided against themselves. One constable, Peter Scott of St Martin-in-the-Fields, told an angry gathering that he would try to use his authority to get the lads in the Mermaid released.[53] When he tried to get in to speak to those in charge, an ugly scene developed. A sword was swung and Scott was cut in the leg. Suddenly the crowd outside the Mermaid boiled over. With shouting and cries, a huge surge of apprentices pushed into the tavern and pulled their fellows out.[54]

———

The Lords were finely divided that day. The Junto had just raised the temperature by launching an attack on the Earl of Bristol. They named him as an 'evil counsellor' and alleged that when he had accompanied Charles and Buckingham to Madrid, in 1623, Bristol had tried to persuade the then Prince of Wales to convert to Catholicism. There was an incriminating letter from Charles, but it was a far-fetched charge even so. The purpose was broader, though. It was the first salvo in an attempt by Parliament to clear out Charles's Privy Council.[55]

Still sitting – now rather defiantly – were twelve of the bishops, the focus of so much of the anger in the streets.[56] Those who attended could hear the crowd outside, chanting against them as the evening darkened. As one of them later recalled: 'It grew to torch-light', and one of the lords, the Marquess of Hertford, approached the sitting bishops. Informing them that they were in 'great danger', he advised they take some course for their own safety.[57] When the anxious bishops asked him what he suggested, his proposal was that they stay in Parliament that night, for the crowds outside 'vow they will watch you at your going out, and will search every coach for you with torches, so as you cannot escape'.[58] Whether this was a viable plan or not, the bishops decided not to spend the night in the palace. Instead, some managed to leave the labyrinthine building by 'secret and far-fetched passages', while others were escorted by the Earl of Manchester.[59]

As members left Parliament that evening, the scene outside was overwhelming. Filing down the stairs and into the public spaces outside they were confronted with a sea of 'links', flaming torches, lighting the dark streets, overlooked by Westminster Abbey and the Palace of Whitehall. The Earl of Huntingdon left a vivid description, with Lords clambering into coaches outside Parliament and then trying to pass along King Street, through the masses of people, towards London. '10,000 'prentices,' he recalled, 'were betwixt York House [Whitehall Palace] and Charing Cross with halberds, staves and some swords. They stood so thick that we had much ado to pass with our coaches, and though it were a dark night their innumerable number of links made it as light as day.' The crowd, he wrote, 'cried, "No bishops, no papist lords", [and] looked in our coaches whether any bishops were therein'.[60]

Matthew Wren, the unpopular Bishop of Ely, left another account of the evening. Referring to himself in the third person, as was his style, he described how the peers rose at 7 p.m., at which time: 'The Bishop of Ely not without difficulty and danger was forced to pass home into Holborn, there standing a great rout of disordered people at Charing Cross, and searching who passed by in every coach.'[61] It was with some relief that he reached the gate of Ely Palace, his grand Holborn residence.

John Williams, Archbishop of York, was another who'd had a rough day. Once a reformist hero, now a king's party man, he seems to have attracted particular anger. Making his way to the Lords that morning, members of the crowd had grabbed and pulled at him. On his way from the stairs to the House of Peers, someone had yanked so hard at his gown that it had torn. Reports varied as to exactly what happened. Some said that he had been threatened so badly with physical violence that he was nearly 'pulled in pieces'.[62] Others thought he only had himself to blame, for in anger he had grabbed a young lad who had shouted, 'No bishops!' at him, and only backed off when part of the crowd surrounded him and chanted loudly, 'NO BISHOPS! NO BISHOPS!' Either way, at one point he found himself backed by one Captain David Hyde, another rather dissolute Cavalier – apparently clad in scarlet breeches and boots,

King Charles I (by Anthony van Dyck, 1638), monarch of England, Scotland and Ireland from 1625, painted in armour in the lead-up to the war against the Scots Covenanters.

Henrietta Maria (by Anthony van Dyck), Queen of England, Scotland and Ireland from 1625. Henrietta Maria was French and Catholic, and a forceful and resolute personality.

Seventeenth-century London. England's only metropolis had grown quickly over the last century and a half, and was now increasingly difficult to govern.

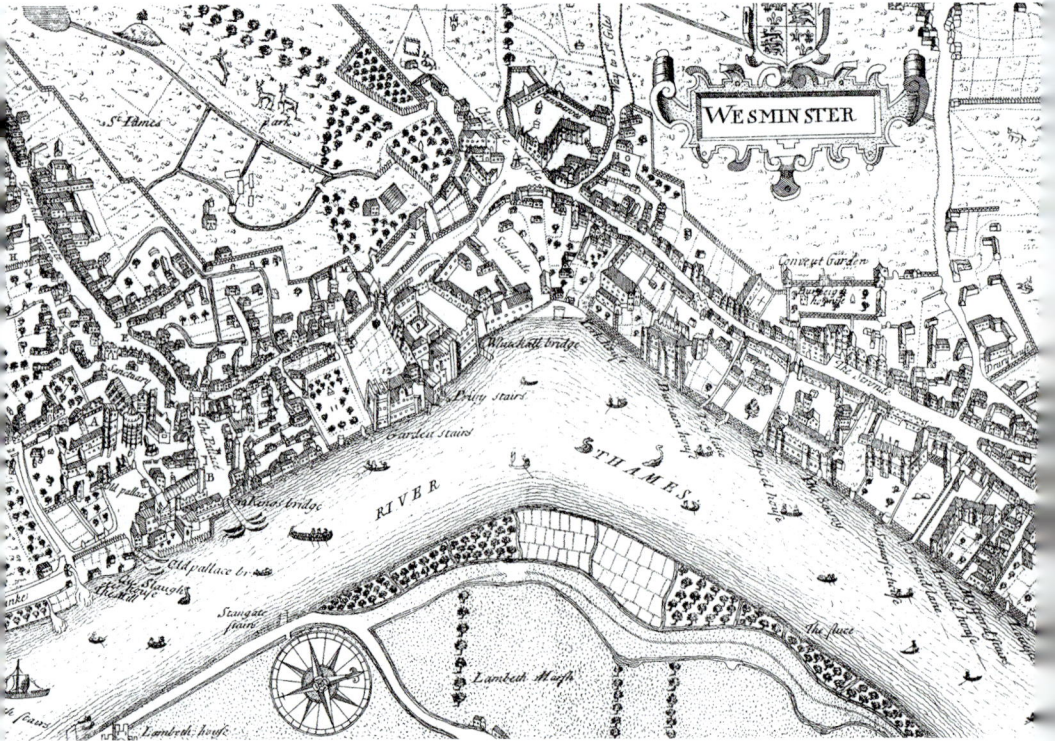

The main political institutions of England were centred not in London, but in the nearby town of Westminster. Here sat Parliament, and here too was Whitehall Palace, one of the principal residences of the king.

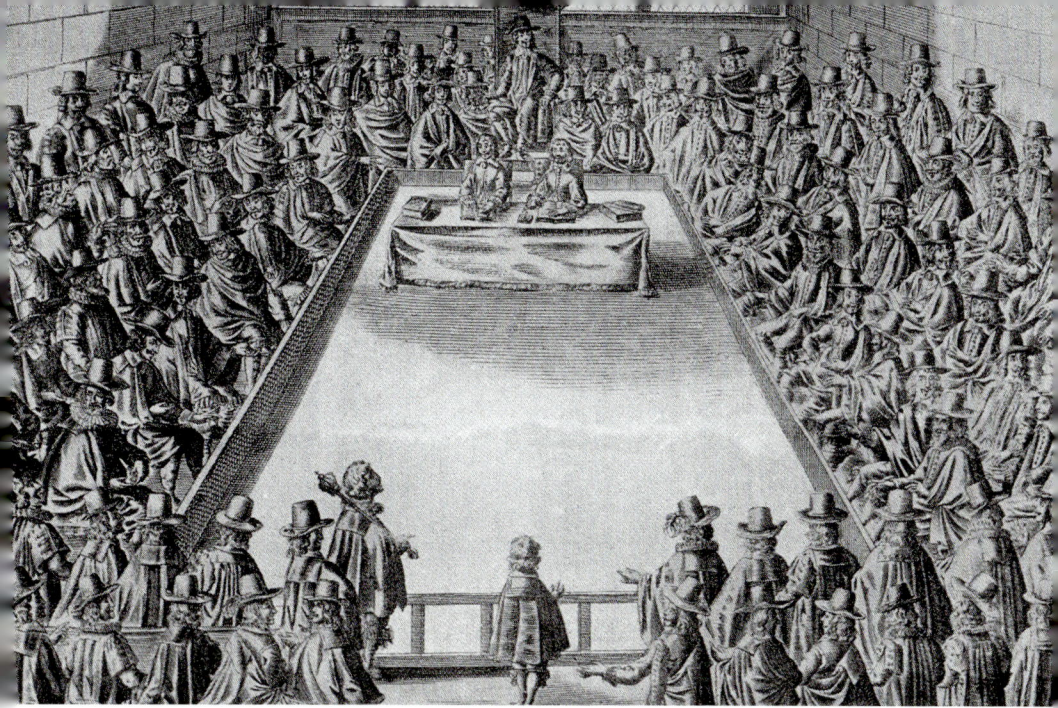

House of Commons. The lower house of Parliament crammed around 500 MPs into an old medieval chapel, although it was rare indeed that such a number were ever in attendance.

Whitehall Palace. The royal residence in the capital was a complex array of buildings adjacent to the River Thames. Prominent among them was Inigo Jones's new Banqueting House, the gleaming white building at the back.

Sir John Bankes (by Gilbert Jackson), painted here towards the end of his career, in the red robes of a Lord Chief Justice of the Common Pleas, and wearing the serjeant's coif.

Keswick, John Bankes's birthplace in 1589. A mountainous land a world away from London.

CORFE CASTLE IN 1643.

CORFE CASTLE IN 1843.

Corfe Castle. An ancient royal castle, it was bought by John and Mary Bankes in 1631, the fruits of his successful legal career.

John Pym (by Edward Bower), the Junto's political magus in the Commons.

Denzil Holles (by Edward Bower), Junto leader, and one of the key dissidents in 1629. Painted later in military clothes.

Edward Montagu, Lord Mandeville (by Peter Lely). Painted much later in life. Mandeville was a popular aristocrat, and one of the leading Junto figures.

Edward Nicholas (by Peter Lely). Charles I's secretary of state, and bureaucratic wizard.

William Lenthall, Speaker of the House of Commons. A native of Oxfordshire, to which in 1641 he badly wanted to return.

John Hampden, a much later statue of the Parliamentarian hero and opponent of Ship Money.

Thomas Wentworth, later Earl of Strafford, painted by Anthony van Dyck in 1636. The painting was sent as a gift to his friend, Lucy Hay, the Countess of Carlisle.

Lucy Hay, the Countess of Carlisle, painted by Anthony van Dyck in 1636. This painting was gifted to Wentworth.

John Taylor, depicted on the water in his younger years.

VII.
ARTICLES
DRAWEN VP AGAINST

Lord Kimelton.
M. Iohn Pimme.
M. Densil Hollis.
S. Arthur Haslerick.
M. Hamden.
M. Stroud.

CHARGING THEM OF
High *TREASON* VVith his Maiestie
his Speech in the House of Commons *Janu.* 4.
1641,

And a Petition to the Kings MAJESTY.

LONDON:
Printed for *W.R.* 1642.

(6)
*His Majestie having herein exp-
rest himself, departed again from there
House and returned to Whitehall: And
imediately the hovse Rejorned until the
morrow being Wednesday, at Noone.*

TO THE KINGS MOST
EXCELLENT MAJESTIE

HVmbly beseecheth that your most Excellent
Majestie, would be, Gratiously pleased to
meditate on that place of Scripture written,
1. Kings. 12. 15, 16. Wherefore the King harkened
not unto his people: for the cause was from the
Lord, that he might performe his saying, which
the Lord spake by *Abija* the *Shulonite* vnto Ierobo-
om the sonne of *Nebat.*
So when *Israel* saw that the King harkned not vnto
them, the people answered the King, saying, what
Portion have we in *David?* neither have we Portion in the sonne of *Iesse:* to yovr tents, O *Israel:* now
see to thine owne, &c.

*The Lord protect, guide, and direct
Yovr Gratiovs* MAJESTIE.
*And increase the number of your faithfull
Loyall Subiects*
AMEN
FINIS.

To Your Tents, O Israel – the first and last pages. This radical squib was thrown into Charles's coach by its author.

A Reply as true as Steele,
To a Rusty, Rayling, Ridiculous, Lying
Libell; which was lately written by an impudent
unsoder'd *Ironmonger* and called by the name
of *An Answer to a foolish Pamphlet Entt-
tuled, A Swarme of Sectaries
and Schismatiques.*

By IOHN TAYLOVR.

*The Divell is hard bovnd and did hardly straine,
To shit a Libeller a knave in graine.*

Printed anno Dom. 1641.

John Taylor's scabrous attack on Henry
Walker, 1641.

TAYLORS
Physicke has purged the DIVEL.
OR,
The Divell has got a squirt, and the simple, seame-rent, thredbare *Taylor* translates
it into railing Poetry, and is now
soundly cudgelled for it.

By *Voluntas Ambulatoria.*

Such is the lan-
guage of a beast-
ly railor,
The Divels privi-
house most fit
for *Taylor.*

Printed in the yeere 1641.

Henry Walker's equally scurrilous riposte, 1641.

Oh S.ʳ Ime ready, tid you never heare,
How forward I haue byn tis many a yeare,
T'oppose the practiçe dat is now on foote
Which plucks my Brethren vp poth pranch and roote;
My posture and my hart toth well agree
To fight, now pludis vp: come follow mee

I'le helpe to kill, to pillage and destroy
All the Opposers of the Prelacy.
My Fortunes are growne small, my Freinds are le
I'le venter therefore life to have redresś
By picking, stealing, or by cutting throates
Although my practiçe crosse the Kingdoms vote

By William

Col L undfford

Bishop Williams and Thomas Lunsford mocked in a 1642 pamphlet. Williams is shown
carrying a musket and a band of powder cartridges, Lunsford with burning houses behind him.

Katherine Chidley's *Justification of the Independent Churches of Christ*, a radical tour-de-force in 1641.

The order in the name of Charles I on 28 December 1641, that the Trained Bands be called out to suppress protests. Edward Nicholas's amendments, including that the troopers 'slay and kill' those who refused to disperse, are to the left and the bottom.

Two modern and highly stylized depictions of the 'Five Members' Crisis. Charles in the House of Commons, and the Members' escape to the river.

The King and Gentlemen of Yorkshire demand Entrance at Hull, but is from the Wall Refused it by Sr John Hotham, who is thereupon Proclaim'd a Traitor.

Hulett Sculp

King Charles summoning Hull, and being denied entry by Sir John Hotham.

A pamphlet showing the raising of the Royal Standard at Nottingham, 1642

A true and exact Relation of the manner of his Maiesties setting up of His Standard at *Nottingham*, on Munday the 22. of August 1642.

First, The forme of the Standard, as it is here figured, and who were present at the advancing of it

Secondly, The danger of setting up of former Standards, and the damage which ensued thereon.

Thirdly, A relation of all the Standards that ever were set up by any King.

Fourthly, the names of those Knights who are appointed to be the Kings Standard-bearers. With the forces that are appoynted to guard it.

Fifthly, The manner of the Kings comming fist to Coventry.

Sixtly, The *Cavaliers* resolution and dangerous threats which they have uttered, if the King concludes a peace without them, or hearkens unto his great Cuuncell the Parliament : Moreover how they have shared and divided *London* amongst themselves already.

Nottingham.

A nineteenth century bronze statue of Mary Bankes, holding the keys to Corfe Castle, at Kingston Lacy.

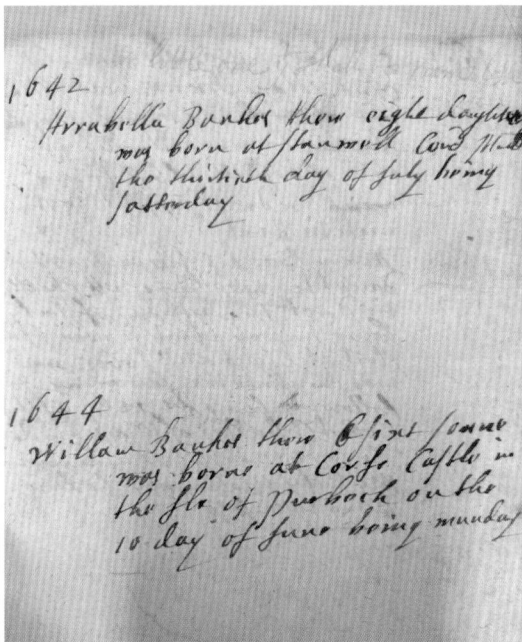

The Bankes family book, showing the births of Arabella at Stanwell (1642) and William at Corfe (1644). The faint note at the top reads: 'little one that be name lesse'.

and puffing tobacco.[63] Hyde was on his way to Westminster Hall, but seeing Williams assailed, he drew his sword and gave off that he would cut the throats of the 'round-headed dogs that bawled against bishops'. The 'round-head' epithet was one that would soon catch on, a reference to the close-cropped hair of London's apprentices: a mark of youth, and subservience. In any case, the archbishop was in no mood to suffer any further humiliations.

With evening now set in, the authorities tried their utmost to keep order through the dark hours. The king had commanded that the Trained Bands of Middlesex and Westminster be called out 'to guard his own person and the Queen at Whitehall'.[64] In the City, a triple watch was set, with one-third armed with muskets, powder and bullets. Mayor Gurney and the sheriffs spent the night riding around trying to stop any trouble before it caught on. The City gates were locked.[65]

Early the next morning, the 28th, the crowds began to gather again in the streets. Some of them carried halberds, others swords, and their numbers were even greater than the previous day. Their particular target was once more the bishops trying to make their way to the Lords. 'The rout,' said one observer, 'did not stick openly to profess that they would pull the bishops in pieces.' When boats arrived on the churning river, the apprentices on the shore would watch carefully to spy out the passengers. If it was a bishop bound for the Lords, they would shout: 'A bishop! A bishop!' and prevent the boat from landing, forcing it to cross the river and lay down its passengers by Lambeth Palace.[66] When the Bishop of Durham found his coach surrounded by protestors chanting 'Down with him!', he made the decision to turn around and not attend the house that day. The Bishop of Coventry and Lichfield was simply advised 'to keep in and not stir abroad because of the people'.[67] Matthew Wren, wisely, 'abstained from going to Parliament, hearing that the rout was greater than before'.[68] Only two bishops managed to attend, and even they drew threats from the crowd to slice their corner caps. Having made a show of attendance, they sensibly decided to beat a retreat, leaving by the river almost as soon as they arrived.

The crowds apparently remained through the day as the Commons debated what to do. Then, there was a sudden 'buzz' among the apprentices, as the evening began to draw in.[69] By now they knew that they had successfully toppled Lunsford, and their confidence was swelling with their numbers. They began moving towards Westminster Abbey. Here – so it was alleged – they planned to pull down the organs, monuments, 'and other relics of popery'. But John Williams got word. When he became Archbishop of York, he'd retained one of his former positions, that of Dean of Westminster. This gave him access to the building, and to muscle. With his own servants, those of the abbey canons, and with the officers of the church who happened to be on site, he had the doors barred. Some of his followers looked down from an adjacent roof. The crowd pushed against the wooden doors, hard. Soon they had gained entry, but Williams's men drew their swords and chased the first wave of rioters out 'like fearful hares'.[70] Stones rained down from the roof.

Earlier, a group of apprentices had been apprehended by Williams's men, and were now being detained in the abbey.[71] Hearing of this, at around 5 p.m., another group of protestors led by John Lilburne and Richard Wiseman, gathered and made their way there. Outside the abbey there were about forty gentlemen stationed, commanded by one Mr Pemberton. As the evening drew in, Pemberton snapped and shouted: 'God damn me! Kill them!', at which his men fell upon the protestors pell-mell with swords and pistols.[72] Those on the roof continued to pelt down stones. Many beneath them, it seems, were hurt, including Lilburne: one news report from the day has a 'Master John Lilbourn' being 'very sore wounded'.[73] At some point, a heavy stone was hurled from the roof, which landed in the midst of the melee. As the crowd began to disperse, one person remained still on the ground: Sir Richard Wiseman had been hit. Members of the crowd attended him, picking up his body – gaunt from years of imprisonment – from the freezing ground. Grievously hurt, Wiseman was taken to a house in King Street.[74]

With the crowds massed in the streets, and with reports now of serious violence outside the abbey, Charles realised that he might be losing control. Courtiers were ordered to wear swords when at Whitehall. The royal palace was swelling with outraged gentlemen offering their support to the king. Many, indeed, were getting thoroughly angry at the audacity of the people. There had been dangerous talk from the 'mechanic citizens and apprentices' as they passed by the windows of Whitehall itself.[75] The soldiers and officers around the king were furious, and Charles was now openly feasting his Cavaliers at Whitehall. Soon too, carpenters were called in to construct, as hastily as they could, a Court of Guard – a small, fortified military post – at the entrance to the palace.[76] It was manned by the Cavaliers and members of the local Trained Bands.[77] Beside Whitehall, the crowds were still strong; inside, the royal court was arming itself.

————

In Parliament, debate continued, and messengers scurried between the two houses. Outside, the crowds ebbed and flowed with the daylight. At Whitehall, the Cavaliers were stockpiling weapons. The king's main London residence increasingly felt like a barracks. Thomas Lunsford, the bête noire of the citizens, was this very day knighted by Charles for his loyal service and – so the reports went – given a pension of £500 a year.[78]

That evening some 300 copies of the king's proclamation were posted up around London, Westminster, and the suburbs.[79] It was a short text, using the official Gothic black letter and once again deploying the image of Hercules and the six-headed hydra.[80] It ordered that no persons 'without his majesties authority' assemble themselves in a riotous or tumultuous manner. Anyone who was presently assembled must go home to their dwellings, otherwise they would be punished to the full severity of the law. It was an insult to the crowd, and the proclamation seems to have brought little but contempt. One Stepney man was accosted and later prosecuted for giving off 'scandalous words' against it.[81]

At some point that day, Charles also decided to bolster the proclamation by sending an order to the Lord Mayor. To Gurney he noted that 'great numbers of people, have of late, and as we understand are likely again to assemble together in a tumultuary and disorderly way within our City of London and the liberties thereof'. Charles continued: 'Our will and pleasure is that if any such occasions offer', then Gurney was to call out the Trained Bands, 'well armed and provided for to suppress all such tumults and disorders'. The order was passed to Edward Nicholas.

Would it be enough? Nicholas was not sure. The king's order could be strengthened, he thought. Taking his pen, he etched around the text, adding his own words, before showing it to the king.*

What Nicholas passed back to Charles was an order of blunt ferocity. 'If there shall be again at any time any such tumultuary or disorderly assemblies of people,' Nicholas had added, 'that you give order to the captains and officers of such our trained bands to suppress all such tumults and disorders.' And if they continued or met resistance, then 'for the better keeping of the peace and preventing of further mischiefs', the captains and officers of the Trained Bands, 'by shooting with bullets or otherwise' were 'to slay and kill such of them as shall persist in their tumultuary and seditious ways and disorders'. The king was 'unwilling and sorry to use such extremity against any our subjects', but the times justified the means. If the protests didn't stop, then the London Trained Bands knew what they must do.[82] They must shoot to kill.

---

*Nicholas and Charles had developed a close working relationship in recent weeks. Key documents were passed to the new secretary of state to write up and amend, before they were shown again to Charles, who would often make his own alterations. On this occasion, there is no record of any subsequent amendments by the king. The last version that survives is the one that Nicholas kept. This must be the text that was sent to Gurney.

15

The Maddest One That I Ever Saw

Since 26 December, the London crowds had changed the scene, but they were balanced by a strong royal response. Charles and Nicholas's bloodthirsty order to Mayor Gurney was an attempt, while it was still possible, to get the City Trained Bands out to quell the protests. If these proved sluggish, then Charles would have to rely on the Cavaliers.

Different options now presented themselves to Charles. One, still, was to take a concessionary path: to build bridges between the two sides. There is a hint of this in the private meetings between Bankes, Saye, and Mandeville before Christmas. On the other hand, Charles might try a strategy of disruption: he could prorogue Parliament – possibly using the pretext that the crowds had rendered it under duress. After a period of cooling-off, it could then return after 12 January, when more loyalist members would be sitting: Pym and his allies in the Commons, and the Junto peers in the Lords, could be outvoted.

Or he could break it completely, again using the pretext of duress, and dissolve it against its will. This would likely go against the May statute that prevented a dissolution without Parliament's consent. Here, though, he could use the military strength he was gathering at Whitehall and beyond, deploy the Cavaliers, and strike. He could dissolve the Parliament by force and presumably follow it up – as he had done after Parliament had been dissolved in angry disorder back in 1629 – with a series of targeted arrests.

The three potential strategies of concession, disruption, and blunt confrontation were all on the table. One critical factor now was the financial position. If Charles could balance his accounts without tonnage and poundage, then the confrontation strategy was inherently more viable. In this case, Parliament might realistically be dissolved. But by the 28th, this was already unravelling. At some point that day, Nicholas, and very likely also Bankes, was presented with a paper about the king's finances. It showed plainly enough that, without tonnage and poundage, the king's government would collapse.[1]

This might not entirely rule out a hardline military strategy. Charles might choose, goaded by his more uncompromising advisors, to dissolve Parliament and take taxes by force anyway. After all, he had collected tonnage and poundage without a parliamentary grant for many years before. But it is likely now that Charles would have to focus his energies on a more nuanced approach. He would attempt the disruption of Parliament until his loyalists returned on 12 January.

In the afternoon of the 28th, something approaching the prorogation plan was seriously proposed by a leading courtier. That courtier was George Digby. Once a Bedfordian, on the surface Digby might have offered the prospect of a bridge between court and Junto. But by late December, things had likely gone way beyond there.[2] The Junto already despised him for his change of heart over Strafford. Now, too, his father had been attacked as an 'evil counsellor' in the Lords. There was little love lost, and the fact that – behind the scenes – Digby had been a prime mover behind the Lunsford debacle shows he was thinking about deploying force in the king's aid. Now he would play the role of disruptor.

As the peers discussed the 'tumults', and the projected expedition to Ireland, Digby stood up. He moved that thanks to the protests outside, the Parliament was no longer a free one, and thus it was invalid.[3] He was drawing upon arguments that had been made repeatedly over the past weeks. The implication was that Parliament should – at least temporarily – be prorogued.

There was immediate rancour in the Lords. Even the minute-book has a rare unfinished sentence: 'Upon the rabble's coming and pressing about the Parliament, there was much dispute whether this Parliament.' The debate proceeded to a vote, and the outcome was recorded in a slightly cryptic note in the formal journal: 'This day it was resolved, upon the Question, That this Parliament is at present a Free Parliament.'[4]

It was an outcome that should have given Whitehall some pause. With the bishops unable to attend, the balance in the Lords was much tighter than before. More to the point, if one made the argument that Parliament was unfree now, because of the protests, then what about its actions during the Strafford trial? What about the presence of a Scottish army in northern England, until that summer? There was, surely, an argument that the king's party could make: that everything this Parliament had achieved had been, in some senses, under duress.[*] This was too much even for the moderate royalist Lords. The gains of 1641 must not be laid aside.

And yet, the vote had only been passed by four votes. Even without the bishops, the king's party were tantalisingly close.

As the twin cities awoke on the frosty morning of Wednesday 29 December, it was clear that something was about to snap. In the Commons, Speaker Lenthall arrived, as usual, at about 10 a.m., and there were prayers – but for the first time in weeks, the house was not quorate. It was virtually empty, and the reason was not hard to see.

---

*Sir John Bankes had even, during *Rex* vs *Hampden*, made a similar argument about Magna Carta. Because it was agreed during Civil War, when banners were displayed: 'This charter, as it was acknowledged by themselves, was granted at Running Mead, where the banners were displayed, when there was war or rebellion between the barons, commonalty, and the king. It was not assented unto, the king sitting in parliament: for parliaments are not called with arms, and in the field. It was, in truth, an inforced act from a distressed king. Shall this bind the crown?' (*State Trials*, III, pp. 1051–2).

Since the earliest hours crowds had been gathering outside, 'many of them being armed with halberds and other offensive weapons'.[5] Gradually, members picked their way through the throng, and debate began. The Lords in particular were on a tightrope. They wanted to end the tumults, but to do so in as peaceful a manner possible. They asked the judges to come up with a solution, and the suggestion came back to use the old medieval riot act. It was probably not enough, but neither were the peers happy for Parliament to place its own private force, under Essex, by the gates. Outside, the protests continued.

Whitehall meanwhile sat full of nervous energy. A meeting of the Privy Council that day – to discuss the price of wine – only attracted three attendees: Sir John Bankes, Lord Keeper Littleton, and John Bramston, the Lord Chief Justice of the King's Bench.[6] The chants from outside were loudly audible from within the walls and windows, helped by the echo created by the thin King Street, with its overhanging timber buildings: 'No bishops! No papist lords!' It was said of the protestors that 'their tongues were so lavish, that they talked treason so loud, that the king and queen did hear them'. Sometimes, 'they called out for Religion, sometimes for Justice'. Protestors were threatening Whitehall palace, giving out that 'they would have no more Porter's Lodge there, but would speak with the king when they pleased'.[7] For Charles this was understandably unnerving. The queen, though, seems to have been rather more stoic. According to one recollection, she was drawn to a window by the noise and, espying a tall man with close-cropped hair leading the crowd, exclaimed: 'What a handsome Round-head!' The man in question was 21-year-old Samuel Barnardiston, son of a Junto supporting MP.[8]

There was, too, an ever-increasing military presence to add more danger to the mix. The previous day, Charles had told the Lords of his intention to raise a force of 10,000 volunteers to subdue Ireland, and now some of these men were starting to gather at Whitehall, where the king feasted their captains. The lavish dinners were public enough for it to make the news reports – presumably as another deliberate show of strength by Charles.[9] There were concentrations of the Trained Bands under Crown control at the Abbey and Whitehall, while the Commons had ordered the local magistrates and bailiffs to be on watch in Westminster and its suburbs.[10] In the Lords, the Earl of Warwick offered to use two of his ships fitted out for the West Indies and currently in London dock, to transport 600 men for Ireland. The consequence of this would be the immediate appearance of troops near London, under Junto-supporting commanders.[11]

With armed forces in several locations, many simply milling around, it was inevitable that the tension would break somewhere. In the early evening, as the light gradually faded, a second feast was taking place within the walls of Whitehall for the Cavalier captains. At the same time, a group of protestors, returning to the City, passed by the protective rail outside the royal palace, next to a turning place for coaches by the Tilt Yard. Here, it seems, they decided to taunt the soldiers on guard there. They stopped and chanted: 'No bishops! No papist Lords! Pull down these papist Lords!' – taking off their hats and placing them on their long staves and waving them. Then, goading a particular group of Cavaliers behind the rail, someone yelled: 'There stands red coats, a knot of papists.'* The royalist troops growled in response that if the protestors had been soldiers rather than mere civilians, then they would have fought them with weapons. 'You near best do it, redcoats!' came the jeers from the protestors, some picking up clods of icy earth and gravel from the road and hurling it at the soldiers.

At last the guards cracked. Drawing their swords, they leapt over the rail and fell about the protestors, shouting that they were 'ram-headed rogues' (cuckolds).[12] A couple of officers were hurt in the melee, but somewhere between twenty and fifty of the protestors were badly wounded, with hands, arms, and the sides of faces cut. According to some reports, three or four were so severely hurt that they later died of their injuries, though it seems the officers tried to reduce casualties by slashing rather than thrusting with

*The reference to red coats may have been to the flamboyant clothing associated with Cavaliers.

their weapons.[13] In any case, within a few minutes the area had
been cleared, with nothing left there but the hats and cloaks of the
protestors, and smears of their blood.[14]

Around the same time, a messenger came to the door of Bishop
Matthew Wren at Ely Palace in Holborn. That morning, Wren had
sent a runner to enquire 'how all things went'. Soon afterwards, he
had received word that Archbishop Williams had called a number
of bishops to an urgent meeting. They had been 'in long and private
consultation' as to what to do. One of the things they decided upon
was to contact Wren.[15]

So, at 4 p.m., one James Samford, servant to the Bishop of Bath
and Wells, arrived with a message. It said that Williams and the other
bishops had composed a 'writing', to which they had all subscribed.
Samford had been ordered to bring it to Wren so he could add his
name to it. Picking up his little round spectacles, Wren took the
paper to a window where he could read it better, but it was four
in the afternoon, and 'it being in the twilight, he found that he
could not perfectly read it all'. He asked the messenger if the writing
could be left with him, allowing a more careful perusal, but Samford
replied: 'No, I am directed to bring it back again.' The matter was
urgent. So Wren looked at the ten or eleven names on the petition,
which he *could* read. 'I will trust to their experience and advice,' he
said, taking the paper into another room and returning with his
name duly added. But he had one more piece of guidance for the
messenger, so he later claimed. 'Make no use of this petition, till
they send, and have the hands of the Bishops of Winton and Sarum
[Winchester and Salisbury].' And send also to Fulham, to the Bishop
of London, and if possible to Bromley for the Bishop of Rochester.
This was extremely important. It needed the biggest names.

It was a suggestion with which Williams would undoubtedly
agree. But what Wren didn't know is that the archbishop already
had an even loftier name in mind.

––––––––

That night, there was more disorder in the City. A group of
apprentices had been arrested. At some point, a menacing crowd

of around 2,000 of their fellows gathered on Cheapside, crammed tight beneath the glass windows of the opulent shops there. Some kind of violent rescue seemed to be in the offing, but the MP John Venn heard of the disturbance and rushed to calm things down, telling the apprentices that he and the other Junto leaders would 'do any favour for you, and relieve you in your just grievances'. He would, he said, ensure the arrested lads were released as promptly as possible. This calmed tempers, and there were cries of 'Home! Home!' as the apprentices dispersed into the night.[16]

Not all of them, though. Some were unsatisfied, and made their way around the corner to the Wood Street Counter, another of London's dirty prisons, which they broke open hoping to find some of their fellows. None of the protestors were there, but others were gathering outside the Lord Mayor's house in Old Jewry, giving out that they would pull it down if he didn't release their comrades. When the sheriffs and their officers arrived, after hurrying to the scene, they managed briefly to arrest two members of the crowd, but as they were being dragged to Newgate prison, they were rescued on Cheapside.[17] Neither London's officers, nor the City's prisons, were proving equal to the task of keeping the population in check.

While this was happening, Archbishop Williams was at Whitehall. Here he brought his 'writing'. It was a petition, and it claimed, in a direct riposte to the Lords' order yesterday, that Parliament was unfree, since the bishops were unable to attend. Anything passed since the 27th, the day of the tumult in Westminster Hall, was declared invalid. The specific target here was the previous day's painfully narrow vote – against Digby – that the parliament was still a free one. There was a deeper, more troubling implication to it as well: that maybe a Parliament wasn't valid if the bishops weren't there. Maybe it could be dissolved, legitimately, by force.[18]

The king was preparing for bed, after a long cold day in which he had twice feasted his growing armed force and then seen them brawl with protestors in the icy roads outside Whitehall. When Williams arrived, a hasty audience was set up, with Nicholas present, and Charles was given the bishops' petition. In the candlelight, Charles took the paper without reading it and handed it immediately to Nicholas. Remarkably, if the Dutch ambassador had been accurately informed, Nicholas also failed to read the petition, waiting until the morning before passing it on to Lord Keeper Littleton. If this was an error on their part, then it would be a disastrous one. In Charles's case, such a momentary failure of due diligence was not entirely uncharacteristic. But Nicholas? Surely not.

The much more likely explanation is that Nicholas, and to be fair, probably Charles too, already knew about the contents of the petition. Digby may possibly have been the originator – but the plan went right to the top.[19] Charles, Digby and Nicholas were hoping this might be the pretext they needed to prorogue Parliament.

The next morning, Thursday 30th, Lord Keeper Littleton was called to Whitehall and instructed to present the bishops' petition to the Lords. He did as he was told, standing to read it to the assembled peers, but he did so without comment.[20]

Immediately, the petition was passed to the House of Commons. Carrying it were two more lawyers, one of whom was John Bankes.[21] They were to desire a conference with the lower house on how to proceed.

There is just a hint here, perhaps, that the court's leading lawyers, Littleton and Bankes, were starting to become disillusioned. The king was taking a more radical path, and the lawyers at Whitehall were losing faith, though it's not quite clear we can read too much into Bankes's choice as messenger. In any case, the bishops' petition immediately electrified the lower house. MPs reacted with a mixture of horror at what this might be a prelude to, and almost gleeful delight at the bishops' tactical howler.

D'Ewes, for one – usually a rather jittery character – was evidently cynical about the existence of a bigger conspiracy.[22] The fact, too, was that the bishops had a point. They had indeed been prevented from attending the house by the protests. But whether this meant Parliament was unfree, or could be legitimately dissolved, wasn't quite the issue. The issue was that it gave a plausible pretext. If the king could find the military strength to clear the houses, both the Commons and the Lords chambers could be shuttered within hours. Just for once, D'Ewes might actually have been too complacent. With the Cavaliers so visibly gathering just a few hundred yards away, it would take a brave MP to discount entirely any notions of an imminent royalist coup.

Whether by a gradual realisation, or whether through skilful manipulation by Pym, the mood of the house darkened. Pym proposed that the doors be locked. Others suggested clearing the adjacent rooms, and that no MP should go into the committee chamber. D'Ewes objected to the last part, as it placed restrictions on the freedom of MPs; so Speaker Lenthall suggested instead that no one in the committee chamber be permitted to speak to anybody out of the window, or to throw any papers to them. Then Pym made a proposal. His view was that the bishops' petition was the opening to some kind of armed move against the Commons, to be executed this very day. His motion was that the house immediately send to the City of London, tell them 'that there is a plot for the destroying of the house this day', and ask them to come down with the Trained Bands for assistance.[23]

For the Commons, on their own authority, to call out the Trained Bands without royal approval was a very dangerous step, and though Pym got some support, more MPs opposed. Some suggested adjourning the house to London's Guildhall, where they would de facto be protected by the City Trained Bands.[24] In the end, though, the Commons took a much more cautious path. They would go once more to the Lords and ask, yet again, that the peers join in petitioning the king for a guard commanded by Essex. In the meantime, they would impeach the twelve bishops, and request they be immediately 'sequestered', that is, arrested.* [25]

The Lords still held back: they did agree to the impeachment, but they would not yet join in the request for a guard under Essex. This was still a line that a majority of the peers wouldn't cross. All the Commons could do was to ask the local Westminster magistrates to provide a rather pathetic arsenal of twenty halberds, and order the MPs' own servants to come to Parliament with pistols.[26]

---

*Arrested on the charge of claiming a legislative veto (something, as it happened, their petition explicitly denies).

It had been a remarkable day, but the implications of those frantic hours were far from clear. Pym had tried to create a military force for the Commons, but he had failed. Parliament was vulnerable. If the king struck, then the gates were open.

Yet the impeachment of the twelve bishops was still a major victory for the Junto. It allowed them to achieve the long-held aim of destroying the episcopal vote in the Lords. There was little opposition in the Commons, though one member did say that he thought the bishops were better off in Bedlam than the Tower, since they were not traitors but merely 'stark mad'. The twelve bishops were remanded in custody – ten, including Williams, to the Tower; two of the more elderly to the care of Black Rod.[27]

What this meant was that the Junto legislative programme might suddenly be unblocked. Its three key proposals – the Impressment Bill, the Bishops' Exclusion Bill, and the Militia Bill – could all proceed. The Junto would control both houses, the county militia, and the new army for Ireland. To all intents and purposes they would control the English state. Charles's only hope now lay in either stalling Parliament until 12 January, by which time the loyalist members, in theory at least, would have returned, or in a much bolder, much riskier attack.

———

As Archbishop Williams reacquainted himself with the inner walls of the Tower, where he had spent a good part of the 1630s, the press enjoyed themselves at the fall of this puffed-up prelate. One picture mocked him up as a soldier carrying a musket (he was placed next to a pike-carrying Lunsford, who had a backdrop of burning houses), and another showed him as a decoy duck, leading his fellow bishops to their destruction.[28] One of the Tower's other inmates, William Laud, was said to have permitted himself a certain amusement at the humiliation of his erstwhile enemy.[29]

On the 30th, Robert Slingsby, a naval officer currently lodging in Covent Garden, penned a despatch to Admiral Pennington summing up the recent chaos. 'I cannot say we have had a merry Christmas,' he wrote, 'but the maddest one that I ever saw.' There had been tumults and skirmishes, with Sir Richard Wiseman leading the crowds against Archbishop Williams. 'I never saw the Court so full of gentlemen, everyone comes thither with his sword.' Those at Whitehall wore arms 'as in time of open hostility'. Both 'factions' – the Junto and the royalists – 'talk very big, and it is a wonder there is no more blood yet spilt'. There was 'no doubt but if the King do not comply with the Commons in all things they desire', then 'a sudden civil war must ensue'.[30]

The Junto was now close to full ascendency in both houses. At Whitehall, though, Charles's own military recruitment had picked up pace. Drummers had been sent through the streets of the capital to raise volunteers for the new expedition to Ireland.[31] Now, too, some 500 gentlemen of the Inns of Court came down to offer support to the king.[32] The Court of Guard was still busily being constructed, complete with a sentinel house, and a detachment of troops had been posted in Westminster Abbey. In London, the shops were shut in anticipation of violence.[33]

Yet there was one thing now missing. After the brawls of the 29th, the crowds – quite unexpectedly – stayed at home.

Were they tired? Had word got out of the king's sanguinary order to Gurney, directing the Trained Bands to 'slay and kill' anyone who refused to go home. Were they scared, 'the citizens being more tongue than soldier'?[34] Or did they feel that with the arrest of the twelve bishops they had now achieved their goals? Slingsby thought it was a combination. The protestors were 'satisfied with the impeachment of the twelve bishops', but he also noted how they were 'terrified with the multitude of gentry and soldiers which flock to the court', and – for the protestors – 'the rough entertainment [that] was like to be given to them if they came again'.[35] But whatever the reason, the route from Whitehall Palace to Westminster was clear. If Charles wanted to move, now was his chance.

Nothing happened. The 30th passed.

On the 31st, the low, sluggish winter sun rose over London and Westminster. The weather had taken a turn for the better, but the crowds were still missing.[36] Two days now they had stayed at home.

That morning, the House of Commons met, prayed, and got on with business. Sir Arthur Haselrig brought a report of a Catholic called Mr Robert Carson, who had given off that he hoped 'ere long to see half a dozen Parliament men hanged'.[37] Six heads, just like the Hercules Proclamation. At this point, there was still an expectation that the house would sit again tomorrow, despite it being New Year's Day. There was urgent business to be done. But there was a fear, too. What, realistically, was there to stop the king – or the more aggressive courtiers around him – from using his Cavaliers against Parliament?

That afternoon, the Junto MP Denzil Holles led a delegation to Whitehall to present a request to the king for a guard. Charles's response was predictably icy.[38] The Commons could be assured, he said, that he would protect them like he would his own children. But he would not agree to the guard. He would, though, consider the request if it came in writing, so Holles trudged back to the house. On informing them of the king's answer, he was ordered to prepare a written petition, which he duly did.[39]

Charles's demand was probably nothing more than a delaying tactic. The previous day, Edward Nicholas had written to the Lord Mayor telling him that the king desired a meeting of London's Common Council. On the afternoon of the 31st, this gathered in the Guildhall under Mayor Gurney and Recorder Gardiner. The great, airy medieval hall was much emptier now than a month ago, when Charles had feasted there with his nobles. Lord Newburgh, a relatively minor privy councillor, represented the king's interests. The topic was the tumults. It was not, Newburgh conveyed to the councilmen, the City's fault that such uproars had happened. Rather, they had come 'merely from the mean and unruly people of the suburbs'. The Common Council, for their part, thought some of London's officers could have been more active in keeping the peace and subduing the protests. They would redouble their efforts to keep the peace.[40]

The Common Council of 31 December came down in the name of order, and made soothing noises to the king and Nicholas. But there was something unusual about it. Contrary to normal practice, the newly elected councilmen – the victors of the elections of the 21st – had already taken their seats.[41] The royalists had the run of this particular meeting, for reasons that are not quite clear, but there was no certainty this would last. The balance in the City was already changing. Charles's time was running out.

Edward Nicholas remained optimistic. There had been, he wrote, 'great distempers here amongst us, by a rude multitude of loose people that have of late days flocked about the Parliament Houses'; however, 'by his Majesty's great care & wisdom they are now allayed, & so good guards set, that I hope we are freed from further fears of that nature'.[42] Yet the fact was that things were now careering towards a resolution. The Junto had control of Parliament; the king and his Cavaliers briefly had control of the streets. Neither would likely last.

The Junto needed to act within days to secure the government, meaning that Charles had to strike them before he lost the streets. It was now or never, for both sides.

16

Great and Treasonable Designs

Charles I was not a man to take rebellion lightly. Since 1640, the Junto men – MPs and peers – had challenged him, battered away his prerogatives, emasculated him in front of his people. No patriarch could suffer such insolence from his children. There came a point when the rod must be used.

In the last few days of December, London had come perilously close to anarchy. The protests had become brawls around Parliament and outside Westminster Abbey. There had been a bloody confrontation beside Whitehall Palace. As yet, people were not quite sure if anyone had actually died. On 3 January 1642, a young lawyer MP at Gray's Inn wrote to his father in Derbyshire: plenty of blood had been spilt, with 'very many wounded and hurt on both sides: some hands cut off, others arms, others sides of their faces cut off'. Yet, 'I do not hear of any that were slain,' he noted, 'unless Sir Richard Wiseman be since dead.'[1]

By then, however, the king was ready to launch his coup.

Before Charles struck, he had to win over as many allies as he could at Whitehall and beyond. There was the ghost here of the 'concessionary' strategy. On 30 December 1641, the Earl of Southampton, once a reformist, was sworn to the Bedchamber. There is also a strange payment made to the Puritan Lord Saye of a quite substantial sum, £1,200, for 'special and private service'. The reason for this is lost to posterity, though it may not be a coincidence that the day it was paid, Saye's son, Nathaniel Fiennes, stood up in the Commons to defend the Earl of Bristol.[2] Another intriguing action, on 28 December, was the granting of a key to Whitehall Palace to Lady Isabella Thynne, a vivacious eighteen-year-old who just happened to be the daughter of the Junto-supporting Earl of Holland.[3] The meetings between John Bankes and Saye and Mandeville had ended, but Charles was reaching out in other ways.

The biggest developments were on 1 January 1642. Now, Charles made a series of appointments to leading offices, all to moderates. People who had been aligned to the reformists but who had come over to the king's party. His net may even have been cast wider than this, for one rumour had him offering Pym the role of Chancellor of the Exchequer.[4] If this is true, then Pym promptly refused.

Charles did, though, succeed in bringing two impressive talents into his administration. The most notable success was when Lucius Cary, Lord Falkland, was persuaded to become the senior secretary of state, joining Edward Nicholas. The same day another king's party man, John Culpeper, was given the position of Chancellor of the Exchequer.

There had been another unsuccessful approach, too, this time to Edward Hyde. On the evening of New Year's Day, Hyde was summoned by Digby to come to Whitehall, where both Charles and Henrietta Maria were waiting for him in one of the palace's many rooms. They had an offer. It was that Oliver St John, the Junto-aligned Solicitor General, would be removed, and Hyde would take his place. It was a tempting proposal, but Hyde declined. Maybe he could see what was coming.[5]

––––––

Parliament had temporarily adjourned, ordering two of its committees to continue sitting. One was that for Irish Affairs, the other was a special committee ordered to wait upon, and respond to, any message from the king about a guard. This latter comprised a fairly radical band of Junto politicians: Holles, Pym, Erle, Strode, plus various others – mostly less prominent men.[6] It was ordered to sit at the Guildhall in the City of London, and when it met, according to at least one report, its members went there under armed guard.[7]

There is precious little evidence as to what it discussed, but there were rumours at the time. Ambassador Giustinian heard some of them.[8] What he heard was that they had decided to push forward with another impeachment – that of the queen.

If this talk reached Charles, it can only have concentrated his mind on the plan he was now finally putting into effect. It was meticulously plotted on 1 and 2 January, and it would be sprung first thing on the 3rd.

The king's close involvement is irrefutable, and he was almost certainly aided by Digby. The key document we have is a set of instructions, written in Charles's own hand, to the Attorney-General Edward Herbert.[9] It ordered that he accuse five members of the House of Commons of treason.

The five weren't named in this document, but they were to be John Pym, Denzil Holles, John Hampden, Arthur Haselrig, and William Strode. Attorney-General Herbert was also ordered to reserve the right to add more charges, and told that when the Lords appointed a committee to consider the matter, he must object to a list of peers, should they be named. These peers were core Junto men: Essex, Warwick, Holland, Saye, Mandeville, and Wharton.[10] Together they were the band of politicians that Charles planned to take down. It was a plan that, so he hoped, would finally crush the Junto.

Of the five MPs, the first name was an obvious one: Pym had been the visible leader of the Junto in the Commons and beyond. Holles, also, had a long history of opposition. He had been a ringleader back in 1629, when MPs held the Speaker down in his chair before Parliament could be dissolved. Elected to both the Short and Long Parliaments he, too, had been a central figure in the Junto.

Hampden was arguably a less active conspirator, but he was popular and his very name held charisma. After all, he was the martyr of Ship Money. The other two names were more obscure, but intriguing nonetheless. Strode was something of a firebrand, and one of the Junto's angrier supporters. He had played a part in some of the constitutional attacks on Charles's government. In recent memory it was Strode who had spoken so vehemently for the motion in October to take away Charles's power of appointments. And long before this, it had been Strode who'd first moved for a bill for regular parliaments – what would become the Triennial Act, a piece of legislation that Charles found especially galling. Haselrig, on the other hand, had introduced the Bill of Attainder against Strafford, and had more recently tried to introduce a bill giving Parliament control of the militia. The five were therefore the men behind some of the main constitutional attacks on Charles's rule: the resistance to Ship Money, the passing of the Triennial Act and the Strafford Attainder, plus now the attempt to remove the king's right to choose his government and control the militia.

The Junto peers for now could wait. Indeed they needed to. It is highly likely that Charles was planning to expand the attack to include at least some of the Junto lords, but to do so, he first needed that all-important evidence from the studies of Pym and Holles in particular.

There were seven broad accusations aimed at the five Commons men. The core was that they had 'traitorously endeavoured to subvert the fundamental laws and government of the kingdom of England' (a rather similar accusation to that levied against Strafford), that they had encouraged the Scots to invade, and that they had 'raised and countenanced tumults against the king and Parliament'. The last charge, meanwhile, was the most dramatic: that they had 'traitorously conspired to levy, and actually have levied war against the king'.[11]

These were not yet especially specific. Arguably not specific enough to constitute proper charges. But they might be provable – if only Charles could get his hands on the men's papers. This, not their persons, would be the first target.

————

On 2 January, the weather was tempestuous. As heavy rain lashed the windows of Whitehall Palace and as the impeachment plan was finalised, Charles – possibly persuaded by Digby – also decided to expand his initial list to include one peer.

The man Digby had in mind was someone who had been at the heart of things since the beginning, but who more recently had allowed his Chelsea residence to become a centre for Junto plotting. Someone, critically, who was still only a junior noble and was therefore an easier target, but whose papers were likely to have damning evidence of Junto collusion with each other and with the Scots. Someone who, perhaps by the entreaties of his loyalist father, might even turn king's evidence.

And so Charles asked for another sight of the brief order he had written to the Attorney-General. Taking out his pen, with two strokes he crossed out the word 'fyve', and replaced it with 'six'. He then looked down at the name 'Mandeville' on the list of peers to be barred from the expected Lords committee. With his pen again, he blotched it out so thoroughly that it was almost impossible to decipher. Instead, Mandeville's name would be added to the list of the accused. The hydra now had six heads.

The plan had been put together with considerable secrecy. It is entirely possible that the immediate aim was to busy Parliament. The impeachments, in this reading, were the latest strand to the 'disruption' strategy that Digby had been pursuing with the various attempts to get Parliament prorogued. That had backfired spectacularly with the bishops' petition, but a complex set of impeachments might still have the desired effect. Such a large-scale process was likely to dominate the Lords agenda way past the 12th, when the royalist MPs and peers were supposed to return. In whatever way the prosecutions ultimately panned out, the Junto's legislative programme would be dead.

There is a hint, just a hint, of a split in Whitehall over what was – by any measure – still a serious escalation by the king. Certain key moderates were definitely kept in the dark. Falkland and Culpeper, appointed just hours before, seem not to have been informed. Even Nicholas might have been unaware. He tended to add a short description for each document he kept, with a date, but neither of the two copies of the accusations of treason in the state papers – which contain many of his records – have his handwriting on them. Then, when the accusations were eventually brought before the House of Lords on the 3rd, the immediate response from the peers was annotated by Nicholas with a tone – almost – of surprise: '3 Jan 1641. Order of parliament *whereby it appears that* Mr Holles &c were accused of treason.'[12] Could this be the first he had heard of it?

––––––

On the 3rd, a Monday, the plan went into action. The initial focus would not be on arresting the six themselves, but on getting hold of their papers. It was a day that had to go right for the king.

Parliament was not due to convene until the afternoon, so this left the morning for the opening moves. Already, the accusations were being printed. Copies would be available on the bookstands within hours.

That morning, the Privy Council met. It was a notably full meeting, with twenty-three attendees. Had Charles made sure of this by summoning as many councillors as he could, to keep them busy? If they were in the council chamber at Whitehall, they wouldn't know about the raids taking place in the lodgings of the Junto MPs.

Remarkably, the main business of the morning was – of all things – the plight of the lamprey fishers of Hull. At some point before the spring of 1641, the lamprey fishers of the Thames had won a reduction in their customary payment to the king, from 20 shillings per 1,000 fish to the ancient rate of half that. Now their Hull counterparts wanted the same. Charles, sitting in council himself, was minded towards sympathy, and told the Treasury commissioners (including Bankes) to look into it.[13]

Not everyone attending, we may suppose, was particularly exercised by the fortunes of the Hull lamprey men. Essex, Holland, Saye, Leicester, Dorset, and Hamilton were all present. Thus a significant cohort of major political figures were at Whitehall, while the first part of the king's plan was being executed elsewhere. Of the names, none is more intriguing than that of Mandeville, attending for the first time in weeks. Was he summoned specifically to keep him out of the way?

Pym too was busy. He was about two miles away, at the Guildhall. A newsbook states quite clearly that one of Parliament's committees was meeting there on the morning of the 3rd, discussing the request for a guard and awaiting the king's response. Pym was reported as chairing the committee.[14]

What the Junto men couldn't yet know was that officers had already been sent 'from his Majesty' with warrants ordering them to raid the houses of some of the accused – specifically Pym and Holles – and to seize their papers. The officers were led by the Scot Sir William Fleming, a kinsman of Montrose. He was backed by William Killigrew, a longstanding and loyal English courtier. Tellingly, they had no order to take the men themselves. It was the papers that mattered.

As the committee closed its business at the Guildhall, and as Parliament drew in its members from across the two cities, ready to sit after lunch, the royal officers were hammering on the doors of the accused men's lodgings: gathering and rifling their papers and putting great locks on the wooden chests they used to store them. Later more muscle would come to take the chests safely to Whitehall, where willing eyes would be ready to scour them, looking for damning evidence. No doubt one eager reader would have been Edward Nicholas, for he had some form on this. In the 1630s he had been sent to search the dead dissident lawyer Edward Coke's papers; and he once found himself in the Tower of London, looking for seditious literature hidden in William Prynne's toilet. If anyone could ferret out the incriminating evidence, it was Nicholas.

The two houses assembled at just after 1 p.m. A number of the privy councillors who had been present that morning at Whitehall had now made their way to Westminster and ascended the stairs. In the Lords, Digby, who knew exactly what was about to happen, found himself sat next to Mandeville.

Immediately, Lord Keeper Littleton stood. He was, he announced, 'commanded by the king, to let their Lordships know, that His Majesty hath given Mr Attorney General command to acquaint their Lordships with some Particulars from him'.[15]

Eyes turned to Attorney-General Herbert, who was standing by the clerk's table.[16] In his hand was a paper.

The king, Herbert said, had ordered him to tell their lordships, 'that divers great and treasonable designs and practices' had come to light. Thus he had been commanded by the king, and in the king's name, to accuse six men – one member of the House of Lords, five of the Commons - 'of High Treason and other High Misdemeanours'. This he did by the delivery of articles in writing, 'which he had in his hand, which he received from his majesty'.

Herbert read the articles out in full. It will have taken about two minutes. Once the reading was complete, Herbert announced that he had more to say. First, on the king's behalf, he desired that a committee be appointed to examine witnesses to the matter, and that this committee be 'under a command of secrecy, as formerly'. Secondly, the king asked liberty – where new information came to light – 'to add and alter, if there shall be cause, according to justice'.[17] Thirdly, he asked that the Lords concur in securing the accused persons.

If Herbert expected support from the Lords, then he was quickly and starkly disabused. Instead, the peers seem to have been horrified.[18] Most remarkable of all, Digby suffered from a sudden lack of nerve. He had promised to stand and move for Mandeville's immediate arrest. But seeing the shock among his fellow Lords, he pretended to be 'most surprised and perplexed', and turned and whispered in Mandeville's ear that the king had been 'very mischievously advised' and that he – Digby – would hasten to Whitehall and find out who had done so.[19] Mandeville himself rose and declared that he was ready to obey, 'with a great deal of cheerfulness', whatever the house decided, asking 'as he had a public charge, so he might have a public clearing'.[20]

So it fell to the Lords to decide what to do. Their initial response was clear. They were polite, but they were firmly defiant. Rather than do as the Attorney-General asked, and create a secret committee to begin hearing witnesses, they decided to investigate the legality of the charge itself. They would appoint a committee, yes, but it wouldn't investigate the six men. Instead it would 'consider whether this Accusation of Mr Attorney ... be a regular proceeding, according to law'.[21]

It was a large committee, with a very strong Junto contingent. Critically it included all the men whom Charles had specifically asked to be barred from the proposed 'close committee': Essex, Warwick, Holland, Saye, Wharton and Brooke.[22] The issues were whether or not the Attorney-General could actually impeach a sitting peer in the Lords, and whether anyone might be imprisoned on a general charge, until specific accusations had been made.

Were the Lords simply playing for time? On the committee, for example, was the Earl of Bristol. The question of whether it was lawful for the Attorney-General to launch an impeachment in the Lords was one on which Bristol had some foreknowledge, given that in 1626 it had happened to him.[23] That said, his trial had stalled immediately, partly because Bristol himself commenced an impeachment against the Duke of Buckingham, so the precedent it set was questionable.

And the issue was not one of mere technicality, either. Although impeachment had only been rekindled as a parliamentary procedure as recently as the 1620s, there was already some developing sense of due process. Much later, this would be likened to the normal indictment process in the criminal courts, where first there was an accusation before a grand jury, and if this was found to be answerable, the accused would be tried before their peers in court. Impeachment was like a much more exalted version of this, where the Commons played the role of a grand jury, and the Lords heard the trial.[24] By putting the accusation straight before the Lords therefore, the Attorney-General was cutting out one layer of protection: a check and a balance. In the constitutionalist mindset of the age, this was a big question. A few days later, Nathaniel Fiennes would report to the Commons that he had consulted on this 'with very great lawyers' (he didn't say who). They concluded, he said, 'that no commoner can be accused by the attorney in the lords house till they be first accused in this house'. Process mattered.[25]

———

Word soon reached the House of Commons.

The five accused members of the Commons must by now have been passed information of the impeachment in the Lords. If they hadn't, then it will have become clear when Strode was sent to the upper house on Commons business. But, as yet, it seems, this knowledge had only partially seeped out. There is no mention of it in D'Ewes's diary until later – and this would surely have included such explosive revelations.

There was a clue, though, that something major had happened. Once Strode got back from the Lords, by which point some at least will have known what was suddenly at stake, the Commons – on Pym's motion – crossed a dangerous threshold. Having toyed before with the idea of summoning the London Trained Bands on their own authority, now they did so, directing the Lord Mayor, aldermen, sheriffs, and Common Council to put the City militia in readiness, 'for defence of the King's person and Commonwealth'. Two London MPs, Isaac Pennington and John Venn, would take the message to Mayor Gurney.[26]

But it was only somewhat later that the full scope of the king's attack became clear. Instead, when D'Ewes records the moment in which the impeachments were announced, he writes that 'the whole House *or at least the most of us* were much amazed', when Pym reported that his trunks, study, and chamber had been sealed up, as had those of Denzil Holles.[27]

The Commons, noted D'Ewes, resolved without division that it was a breach of privilege to impound the papers of any MPs, 'before their crime and offence was made known to this house'. If, therefore, anyone tried to seize the papers, trunks, or persons of an MP, then they were to be permitted to resist, and to call on local constables to help them. The two houses then went into conference, meeting in the Painted Chamber, with the Commons moving that 'the Violating the Privileges of Parliament is the Overthrow of Parliaments' and that the sealing of trunks was 'to the High Breach of Privilege of Parliament'. More than this, they specifically targeted the Cavaliers at Whitehall. 'The Parliament being the great Council of the Kingdom,' they complained, it 'ought to sit as a free Council; and no Force ought to be seated about them, without their own Consent.' However, 'notwithstanding, there is a Guard in a warlike Manner, placed at Whitehall, to the Breach of Privilege of Parliament'. Again, they would ask the Lords to join them in requesting a guard or, they suggested as an alternative, the Commons might adjourn 'to a Place of more Safety'.[28]

At last, the Lords agreed. After weeks of refusing, they would join the Commons in a petition to Charles for a guard. The document was ready immediately.

Finally, with the winter light almost gone, one of the king's serjeants-at-arms appeared in the Commons. He initially carried his mace, but the house insisted it was put aside as a show of deference, and the serjeant complied.[29] He asked them, quite simply and directly, to hand over the five accused members, 'I am commanded to arrest them, in his Majesty's name, of High Treason,' he announced.[30]

The Commons' response was immediate, and careful.[31] They promised to take the matter into 'serious consideration', and that the men – who were all present – would be ready 'to answer any legal charge laid against them' – although of course no charge had yet been presented to the Commons. A four-man delegation was to be sent to Charles, comprising two king's party men, Culpeper and Falkland, and two Junto supporters, Sir Philip Stapleton and Sir John Hotham. Then, one by one, the Speaker addressed the five accused members of the Commons: Pym, Hampden, Holles, Haselrig, and Strode. They must now attend, day by day, until there was a further order, Lenthall said.

The sudden appearance of the serjeant in the Commons seems to have given a certain pique, too, to the Lords. After all, it was they who had previously decided when and how those impeached should be arrested.[32] It was yet another provocation by the king. So the Lords responded by adding another voice of defiance. They ordered the locks on the trunks to be smashed, and the all-important papers to be returned. The peers, like the Commons, were taking a path of defiance.

———

As the four men – Stapleton, Hotham, Culpeper, and Falkland – entered the Palace of Whitehall, the new guardhouse will have been clearly visible, surrounded by Cavaliers all carrying swords. There, too, were loyalist youngsters from the Inns of Court, staring at the parliamentary delegation as they were ushered through the courtyards and into the royal presence. Here they presented the Commons' response to the impeachments.

Charles addressed the men, asking whether the house expected an answer? The delegation answered that their commission was only to deliver the message.[33] Charles was unimpressed, asking them directly what their view was 'as private persons'. The four, presumably here led by the more loyalist Falkland and Culpeper, gave Charles the truth: 'They conceived the House did expect an answer.' But, replied Charles, the house was already risen, so a reply would come in the morning. For now, they must inform the house that everything the serjeant-at-arms had done had been on explicit royal instructions.

The night outside was now black and freezing, the only light provided by the few flaming streetlights, the glimpse of candles in the frosty windows of the palace and of nearby houses, and the occasional link boy ushering people up and down King Street.

With the delegation gone, back out into the dark, Charles disappeared again into the depths of Whitehall.

PART FOUR

Hannibal Ad Portas

17

Neither Eyes to See, Nor Tongue to Speak

We have no way of knowing what happened at Whitehall on the night of 3 January 1642. What we can be reasonably sure of is that Charles sat in urgent discussion with the queen.

Henrietta Maria had almost certainly heard the rumours that she was about to be impeached. And these had been given a quantum of evidence that very afternoon. When William Strode had gone from the Commons to the Lords, before the charges had become widely known in the lower house, it had been to request that the peers join in an attack against the queen's Catholic entourage.[1] This could have been the first salvo in a much bigger strike against her and her court.

Since at least the late afternoon half-light, Charles's supporters had been engaged in further building up the military strength at or around Whitehall. Initially, Fleming and Killigrew had gone to the Inns of Court with a printed copy of the seven articles against the accused members, exhorting them 'to be in a readiness, upon all occasions, to come down to the Court if they should be required'.[2] Around the same time the Commons had ordered the pair to be apprehended for their role in sealing up the studies of Pym and Holles, but the men were still at large.

The immediate worry for the royal camp was that Mayor Gurney would obey the Commons' earlier order to call out the Trained Bands. If this force mustered under the Commons' direction, it would counter balance the Cavaliers. An urgent message was prepared for Gurney, written by Undersecretary Sidney Bere and hastily corrected by Nicholas, who was now very much involved. It noted the order from the Commons and told the mayor to 'take effectual care' that none of the bandsmen were raised without a special warrant direct from the king. Nicholas hoped this would reach Gurney before MPs Isaac Pennington and John Venn, the delegation from the Commons.[3]

The order also had a critical element. If, it demanded, the people were assembling 'in a tumultuous and disorderly manner', then the king's will was that the Trained Bands be quickly mustered, and well-armed. If protestors refused to return to their homes, or if they resisted arrest, then the captains, officers and soldiers of the Trained Bands were to be ordered 'by shooting with bullets or otherwise, to suppress those tumults, or destroy such of them as shall persist in their tumultuous ways and disorders'.[4]

It was the second 'shoot to kill' order issued by Nicholas in less than a week. This one was different, though, for whereas that of the 28th was broadly reactive – a response to crowds who had already come out for several days and presented a clear challenge to the Crown – the order of 3 January was pre-emptive. Nicholas was expecting trouble on the 4th.

That night Pym had been followed by two shadows, so the talk went. He'd kept a companion with him. When one of the shadows was seen making towards the MP, his fellow had rushed in to block the strange assailant. For a moment they'd scuffled, but then the shadow-man was gone.[5]

Deep in Whitehall, meanwhile, as the clocks marched on towards the darkest hours, Nicholas and Undersecretary Bere finished writing the order to Gurney and passed it to John Latch, a trusted messenger. Latch stuffed it in his pocket and hastened out of the palace, east and into the gloomy dark mass of the City. Latch was told that his business was directed by the king himself.[6] He had to get to Gurney before the night was too far gone.

But the clocks were wrong. Someone in the palace had made a mistake that morning when they set them, and their hands were running slow. The night was further advanced than Nicholas knew. When Latch arrived at the mayor's lodgings, he found Gurney had already gone to bed.

Gurney was raised. Thankfully for Latch, it was not too late. Pennington and Venn had already visited, but despite their persuasions Gurney had refused to act. He told Latch that in the morning he would open the orders from the king. This was enough.

There was disorder that night. At around 10 p.m., there was a noise at the Tower. The gates and drawbridges were opened and around thirty to forty men were seen entering. Rumour passed around by hushed night-time conversation that they were skilled artillery gunners. Within the stone walls, the usual guard had their weapons taken from them – to prevent them resisting a royalist takeover. Meanwhile, the men protecting the imprisoned bishops had been supplied with fresh blades.

By stealth, the king's supporters were taking control. At some point, too, presumably earlier that evening, a significant cache of weapons – halberds, bullets and powder – had been moved from the Tower and delivered to Whitehall, where it now sat ready in crates. One report said that Charles had already ordered enough ammunition and powder for 500 troops to be brought from the Tower to Whitehall.[7]

The introduction of the new gunners into the Tower was too noisy to go without being noticed. It caused immediate alarm. Woodturner Nehemiah Wallington recounted how, on hearing about the cannoneers, the City was put 'to much trouble and great fear'. Aldermen and the two sheriffs left their houses and mounted horses so they could ride the streets. The gates were manned and chains pulled up across the main thoroughfares. Messengers ran from house to house, banging on doors telling Londoners to stand upon their guard.[8] For a long, dangerous moment, it seemed like the City would suddenly erupt into violence.

And then, nothing. The alarm passed. People gradually started to go home. By the early hours, John Latch was still darting about the City on Nicholas's orders, but he 'found all places very well guarded and the tumultuous rout dispersed'.[9] The rest of the night passed quietly.

———

By the morning of the 4th, Whitehall was positively teeming with armed men. In the City, shops were kept closed and householders readied their weapons, placing halberds, swords, and pistols next to their doors.

In Parliament, MPs nervously assembled at St Stephen's Chapel. Early on, Falkland gave his account of the previous night's four-man delegation to the king. Then the house looked into what had happened at the Inns of Court during that day, specifically the circulation of the paper accusing the six Junto men: the five members of the Commons and Mandeville. Pym then brought in the articles accused against him and his fellows, and the house agreed to seek a conference with the Lords about what they termed a 'scandalous paper' – namely the published accusations of treason, which had come from the royal printer. The armed men at Whitehall were then declared a breach of parliamentary privilege, messengers were sent to the Inns of Court, and reports heard about the cannoneers in the Tower.[10]

Finally, just before the break at noon, there was a debate about sending a group of MPs, led by Nathaniel Fiennes, up to Whitehall to reconnoitre the gathering of Cavaliers, 'and to know by what authority they were assembled there'.[11] This was not agreed, but as MPs filed out for their lunch, Fiennes gathered up his coats and left the building. He would make the short journey to Whitehall anyway.

In the City, a parliamentary delegation had been sent to the Common Council. As it happened, the council had already taken matters in hand, establishing a 'Committee of Safety', with a robustly radical membership. The new committee immediately began drafting a petition to the king, and passed down an order to Mayor Gurney that he must without delay call out four companies of the City Trained Bands to protect London. The Common Council, now led by the Junto-supporting victors of the recent local elections, was taking control of the London militia. Meanwhile, orders went out from the mayor's office to curb tumultuous assemblies, including the throwing up of chains in the streets at night, readying buckets of water against fires, the closing of gates and landing places on the river, and armed double guards.[12] London was once more preparing itself for a major outbreak of violence.

What no one could know, though, was that at Whitehall, Charles was suffering a crisis of confidence. According to a lost but believable contemporary account, the king had made his plan the previous night, but in the morning of the 4th, became 'apprehensive of the hazard'.[13] So he went to the queen's apartment. Here, attending Henrietta Maria, was the courtier Lady Carlisle.

The royal couple retired into the queen's closet. Lucy Carlisle remained outside. Behind the door, Charles discoursed with the queen 'about the consequence of the design'. He 'urged many reasons against it, and expressed his resolution not to put it in execution'. The discussion could just about be heard through the thin partitions, but when the queen raised her voice in frustrated anger, her feelings were clear enough. '*Allez, poltroon!*' she is said to have shouted at her husband. '*Go! Pull these Rogues out by the Ears, or never see my face more!*'

We need to be careful with statements like this. How did this intimate information get out? Was not the manipulative shrewishness of the queen in this tale rather a misogynist trope? There can be very few reliable sources for this intimate gossip. There might be one, though, and that is Lucy Carlisle herself. Because the one thing we can say with pretty good assurance is that she did betray the king. At some point, Carlisle realised that Charles was toying with a violent attempt on Parliament, and she decided to warn the intended victims.

The evidence for this is plentiful indeed. The gossipy Philip Warwick, writing up his memoirs rather later, was explicit. Charles, he said, was 'betrayed by that busy stateswoman, the Countess of Carlisle'.[14] Hyde's memoirs would later give another name – William Morray – but that seems unlikely given his proven loyalty to Charles.[15] Indeed, in the manuscript for Hyde's later history, before it was edited for publication, he specifically notes how, at this point, Northumberland, Holland, Leicester, *and the Countess of Carlisle* all deserted Charles.[16] Not only was Lucy thus named, but so were a group of men she was intimately connected with: her brother, her suitor, and the husband of her sister Dorothy.

Others were more explicit than Hyde. The lawyer Bulstrode Whitelocke, in his memoirs, noted that the Five Members had 'received a secret notice from a great Court Lady, their friend (who over heard some discourse of this intended action, and thereof gave timely notice to these Gentlemen)'.[17] This can only be Lucy Carlisle, warning the members that Charles was planning to come and arrest them. Meanwhile, a paper recounting the accusations of treason against Mandeville, and later collated as part of a great collection of documents by the parliamentary clerk John Rushworth, reports how 'a certain Member of the House' announced at one point on the 4th that he had a 'private intimation from the Countess of Carlisle, sister to the Earl of Northumberland, that endeavours would be used this day to apprehend the Five Members'.[18] Finally, much later, one of the Five Members themselves, Sir Arthur Haselrig – in a speech to a later Parliament – specifically named Lady Carlisle as being the individual who had warned them.[19]

Another memoirist, the French courtier Madame de Motteville, blamed Carlisle and claimed the queen never forgave herself for letting the plan slip. Motteville's story is implausible in itself, but the claim of the queen's regret is hard to explain away.[20] It implies, rather strongly, that Henrietta Maria herself informed Lucy Carlisle of the plan. Which in turn doesn't quite tally with the 'poltroon' story, for in this Lucy *overheard* the queen from the shadows. But for Henrietta Maria to have had such cause for regret, she was more likely to have *told* her attendant.

But there is one more clue, and it comes, of all places, from Sir Simonds D'Ewes.

In D'Ewes diary entry for 4 January, he noted how Mandeville and the Five Members had received warning 'yesternight' of the king's 'intended design'.[21] The warning had come the night before – D'Ewes is specific about this. It is a statement supported, too, by the journal of Ralph Verney, MP for Aylesbury, who notes 'information' that the five accused 'should be taken away by force', and places this information first thing in the morning.[22] Thus it was likely received overnight.

D'Ewes's reference to *Mandeville* getting the information is particularly telling. For he – of course – did not sit in the Commons and was therefore never under direct threat that afternoon. Instead, it seems likely that he was the one who conveyed the warning to the Commons men. And where did he get that information? Surely, from his old friend Lucy Carlisle. The most plausible conclusion, then, is that the queen somehow spilled to her *the night before*, and Carlisle – almost immediately – passed the information on to Mandeville. Maybe he was at Leicester House, just a short coach ride in the dark, through London's frosty streets from Whitehall. Maybe Carlisle slipped away in the dead of a London night, fresh from attending on the queen, and told everything to her family friend, whom she believed might be in imminent danger. The next day she was back at court, and the king and queen were unaware they had been betrayed. It was then, maybe, that Carlisle heard the 'poltroon' story, something she later divulged. Perhaps.

———

The midday break had arrived, and as the Commons dispersed to find food and refreshment, Nathaniel Fiennes made the short walk up to Whitehall to take a nother view of the soldiers there. In the palace, Charles was once more feasting the 'Irish captains', the Cavaliers who had volunteered for the forthcoming reconquest.[23] Outside, men were milling about. Fiennes managed to speak to some of them, asking what their instructions were. They had been told, they said, that they were 'to obey William Fleming in all things that he should enjoin them'.[24] Fleming was clearly still evading arrest for his raids on Pym and Holles, despite Parliament's best efforts, for he was safely at Whitehall.

The Earl of Essex was there too, in his role as Lord Chamberlain. The House of Lords was not yet sitting and he had stayed at the palace to keep an eye on preparations, suspecting (or knowing) that something was about to happen. Around midday he had seen enough to be thoroughly jittery, and so sent word to the

Five Members, warning them that something very dangerous was coming, although he couldn't necessarily say what. He thought a design was at hand, that the king was preparing to come to the house and seize them. But Essex didn't know when or even whether it was likely to happen.[25]

With dinner now over, the Commons returned. They received Fiennes's report that the Cavaliers were preparing to follow Fleming, and sent a delegation for a conference with the Lords. During this meeting, the peers heard that the Commons were concerned about the guard at Whitehall, 'which were in a warlike manner'.[26] The previous night they had asked the Lords to join in an appeal to this king to have the guards dismissed. Now they were asking again.

Somewhere near the gates of Whitehall Palace, a Frenchman Hercules Langres had been told to watch. He was a gentleman in service to the queen, and he was also in contact with the French embassy.[27] Today he had been asked by the ambassador to keep his eye on Whitehall, and if any armed assault came to pass, he was to rush to Westminster and give warning as quickly as he could. La Ferté, it would appear, was worried about what such an attack might mean for the Junto, whom the French embassy had been busily cultivating.[28]

Also at Whitehall was William Lilly.[29] He was a yeoman's son from Leicestershire who had recently moved to London, where he was trying to make it as a professional astrologer. For reasons not precisely recorded, on 4 January 1642, he found himself dining at the palace. It was not a dinner invite from the higher echelons of the court apparently, for the meal was taken in a room that was rather conspicuously full of large wooden chests.

With dinner still being eaten – presumably sometime around 1 p.m. – Lilly was disturbed by a great noise outside the room. Suddenly entering was Sir Peter Wich, Comptroller of the Royal Household. As Lilly looked up in some startlement, Wich came into the room with a group of lackeys. Immediately, they started breaking open the wooden chests. In them, Lilly and his party could see, were the dull blades of numerous halberds. Weapons, Lilly surmised, that had come from the Tower.

This caused considerable fright among the dining party. They could tell what was about to happen. One of them pushed out of Whitehall to run to warn MPs that the king was preparing to come to the Commons.

———

Everyone at Whitehall, it appears, knew what was going on. The Great Court in the centre of the palace was full of armed men. Wich was organising the passing out of halberds. The king, though, was nowhere to be seen. He was still deep in the palace.[30] Then, just before 3 p.m., he appeared in a chamber adjoining the court. In the January chill, he called out to his assembled guards: 'Follow me, my most loyal liege-men and soldiers!'[31] Sir William Fleming rallied the men. Allowing Charles to pass through them to the palace gate, they clutched their weapons – swords, pistols, and halberds – and started pressing towards the exit, and towards King Street.

There had evidently been an element of impulse, for there was no royal coach ready. Instead, a private coach was commandeered – either one that was parked outside the palace or one that just happened to be passing. The startled coachman was ordered to drive. The destination was Parliament.

King Street was a narrow slimy mess of sludge and ice, a road battered by winter horse-hooves. So the coach went slowly. In it were the king, his nephew, the Elector Palatine, and the Earl of Roxburgh. They were probably purposeful choices: the elector was a potential pretender – so here he was in another conspicuous act of loyalty to his uncle. Roxburgh, meanwhile, had always been seen as a dangerous blade. His presence was menacing. Trailing the king's coach, too, was a band of some four to five hundred armed men on foot, each bragging and weaponed. It was a startling, terrifying sight on the streets of the capital.

The sluggish speed of the entourage only increased the drama, but it also meant that a runner could outpace them. Hercules Langres had been watching Whitehall for much of the day, so when he suddenly saw the king and his immediate attendants appear at the palace gate, followed by hundreds of armed men, he knew exactly what to do.

He left his post and hastened along the thin street. He rushed past timbered houses with their wooden doors and glass windows, and past cloaked men and basket-carrying skirted women. As he ran, they likely will have scarcely minded him – another Londoner rushing about in that busy, scurrying city. But then they would have seen the coach, and the huge gang of guards behind it. Some may even have caught a glimpse of the unmistakable, thin, goateed silhouette of the king, sitting back in his seat in the coach. Or the young elector, peering nervously out at the streets below. Or the glowering face of Roxburgh.

By now Langres had reached Parliament. Hastening up the stairs of Westminster Hall, he pushed through the usual milling crowds, and here he saw Nathaniel Fiennes.[32] Immediately, Fiennes realised what was happening, and he rushed into the corridors of Westminster to make his way to St Stephen's, to the House of Commons.

As Charles's party continued to make their ponderous approach, Fiennes got his word to Pym, Holles, Hampden, Haselrig, and Strode. They must withdraw. The king was coming. He had armed men with him.

The house responded. After urgent discussion, the accused members were allowed to withdraw if they wished. Some thought the house should order them out, 'to avoid all tumult', but in the end their evacuation was to be voluntary.[33] Pym, Holles, Hampden, and Haselrig understood. One by one they rose and withdrew from the chamber. In the passages outside they gathered together. They knew what to do. First, they went to the empty Court of King's Bench and laid low. Then, they disappeared deeper into the building, and made for the steps that led down to the river.

The only one who havered was Strode. He was still in his seat. He was not a married man, he said. Whatever happened next, he would stay and fight. But Walter Erle, his old friend, remonstrated with him. He pleaded with Strode to go. Fighting now would achieve nothing. Go with the others to the City where you will be safe. The fight could continue another day. Still Strode stood firm until Erle grabbed him by the cloak and pulled him out of the chamber and away to join his fellows.[34]

By now, the royal party had reached Parliament. First, several hundred men entered the Palace Yard, then strode up the steps into Westminster Hall. The usual crowds of people were suddenly brought to silence. Stall-keepers eyed the men nervously. Some of those in the hall urgently slipped out. Most of the soldiers – 'two or three hundred' according to one account – were told to remain there, but a party ascended the stone stairs out of the hall, thudding boots echoing through the corridors.[35] This brought them to a large lobby, where they stopped. Eighty men or so filled the room, all armed with swords and pistols. Before them was the closed door that led to the House of Commons.

In the chamber, the debate had suddenly silenced. The clerk, keeping the record, for the second time broke off mid-sentence and put down his quill pen. It was just after 3 p.m.

There was a rattling knock at the door. Someone from inside the chamber pushed it open, setting their eyes immediately on the armed men in the lobby.[36] A soldier ordered him to summon the Speaker. The king was at the door, and Lenthall was commanded to sit still, with the mace before him.[37]

It was now that King Charles entered the house. With him was just his nephew, the elector, but members could now see the armed band through the door. Some of the men had their hands on their pistols and swords. At the door, leaning on it, stood the grim-faced Roxburgh. Prominent among the men in the lobby was Captain David Hyde, one of the most notorious and violent of the Cavaliers. Charles ordered the men outside not to follow him in, 'upon their lives'.[38] For now, at least.

As Charles entered, there was a sudden, sharp shuffle as the members instinctively rose to their feet and removed their hats. Lenthall stood in front of his chair. Charles made his way towards the Speaker, his own hat off, bowing to each side of the house, while the MPs bowed back. He was now right in front of Simonds D'Ewes, and before Speaker Lenthall.[39]

'Master Speaker,' Charles began, almost excessively courteous. 'I must for a time make bold with your chair.'

Even D'Ewes had now laid down his pen. His attention was fixed. He would fill in his notes later. But the assistant clerk, John Rushworth kept writing.

Lenthall yielded. Charles stood before the chair, upon a step, not sitting down in it. Then he spoke.

'Gentlemen,' the king said. 'I am sorry for this occasion of coming unto you.' Yesterday he had sent his serjeant-at-arms to apprehend the members, 'whereunto I did expect Obedience, not a Message'. There was no privilege against an accusation of treason, he said, and 'so long as these Persons that I have accused (for no slight crime, but for treason) are here, I cannot expect that this House will be in the right way.' 'Therefore,' he said, 'I am come to tell you, that I must have them wheresoever I find them.'

Then he cast his eyes around the room. 'Is Master Pym here?' he asked, still looking.

The house was silent.

Charles looked around again. 'Is Master *Holles* here?' he asked. Silence once more.

Now Charles looked directly at Lenthall, who dropped immediately to his knee. Do you see any of the men? Charles demanded. Where are the men?

Lenthall was fastidiously polite. 'May it please your Majesty,' he replied. 'I have neither eyes to see nor tongue to speak in this place but as the House is pleased to direct me, whose servant I am here.' I humbly beg your majesty's pardon, he said, but 'I cannot now give any other answer than this to what your majesty is pleased to demand of me.'[40] I am the servant of the house, not the king, Lenthall was saying. A month ago, he had been desperate to retire. Now he was defying a king. From somewhere, Lenthall had found a startling reserve of fortitude.

Charles's temper was now rising. 'Well,' he snarled, 'since I see all the birds are flown, I do expect from you, that you shall send them unto me as soon as they return hither.' He cast his eyes around again: 'But I assure you on the word of a king,' he insisted, now suddenly defensive, 'I never did intend any force, but shall proceed against them in a legal and fair way, for I never meant any other.'[41]

Now Charles turned to leave. According to D'Ewes, who had a close view of the king's face, he was 'in a more discontented and angry passion than when he came in'.[42] As he left, MPs began to pick up courage. Gradually, a few voices became a chorus, shouting in unison: 'Privilege! Privilege! Privilege!'

Outside, the armed Cavaliers uttered threats and oaths. 'Zounds! They are gone, and now we are never the better for our coming!' one cursed. 'How strong is the House of Commons?' another asked, menacingly. 'A pox take the House of Commons, let them be hanged,' declared a third. 'When comes the word,' asked another.[43] Eyeing the door, yet another cocked his pistol. 'I warrant you, I am a good marksman, I will hit sure.'[44]

But Charles had decided against violence. As he left the Commons, his Cavaliers cried: 'Make a lane!' and soon he was out of the building and back outside in the cold.[45]

The Commons doors were shut immediately. Lenthall was unsure of what to do. Once some calm had returned, he asked the house whether he should make a report of the king's speech, but Sir John Hotham stood. We all heard it, he said. Instead, cries of 'Adjourn!' came from the benches.[46] It was decided they would, until tomorrow afternoon. It was now about half past three.

———

Charles was on his way back to Whitehall where, if a much later recollection can be believed, the queen was pacing around nervously awaiting news.[47] Eventually, the rumour became that when Charles returned, Henrietta Maria berated him for failing to pull the men out by the ears, giving him 'an unhandsome name, "poltroon" for that he did not take others out'.[48] But this cannot be reliable, for it is too similar to the (more plausible) reports of Charles arguing with the queen earlier in the day. That said, she likely wasn't especially pleased.

In any case, had the men been there, then Charles almost certainly would have tried to take them by force. It was only the fact they had been warned that stopped him doing so. It was a turn of events that could hardly be blamed on Charles himself. He was not the source of the leak. Ultimately, via Lady Carlisle, the Queen was.

Immediately, Charles sent out orders to the ports, telling officers to apprehend the men if they appeared.[49] But the Five Members were not planning to flee the country. Instead, they were making their way east, away from Parliament, along the river.

After a time, their rocking boat began to turn towards one of the City's many landing stairs, possibly the ancient Queenhithe, or Three Cranes, near the great mass of London Bridge. As soon as they alighted, they moved swiftly north. Crossing Watling Street and then Cheapside, they disappeared into the knotted mass of timber houses around the Guildhall. Their sanctuary was almost certainly Coleman Street – long a centre of City radicalism. The light was now fading fast.

18

To Your Tents, O Israel

Evening had once more cast its frosty shroud over London and Westminster. Only the glowering fires of wood and coal kept the nervous inhabitants in any comfort. Charles had returned to Whitehall where all he could do was warm himself and plan his next move. The Five Members had disappeared into the dusk. Shocked MPs were gradually returning to their lodgings after a horrifying day. D'Ewes, on getting back to his room, immediately began redrafting his will.[1]

The locksmith at Whitehall had been busy. New keys to the palace garden and lodgings were being issued for Sir John Culpeper and Lord Falkland, both new appointees to the government, and the Earl of Southampton. One, too, for the Elector Palatine, who at some point had lost his old set. Alas, the records do not allow us to say whether he lost them in the melee on the way to Parliament. But the knowledge that somewhere in the capital, there was a missing set of keys to the palace can hardly have helped the royal family feel secure.[2]

Charles was reeling from his failed attempt to seize the Five Members, so decided he needed to get his side of the story out as quickly as possible. In the Commons, the king had spied the clerk John Rushworth taking down his speech, and he was now summoned to Whitehall. Despite protests that it might land him in trouble with Parliament, Rushworth was persuaded to hand over his notes. The king then corrected them – 'all my birds are flown', for example, was edited to 'all *the* birds are flown' – and sent them for printing. They would be ready the next morning.[3]

Another who was busy was Henry Walker, the ironmonger turned pamphleteer and John Taylor's bête noir. He wanted to get out a short pamphlet relating the shocking events of the day, so he walked to the workshop of a printer called Thomas Paine.[4] Between them, the two worked through the night, to write and print the tract. It would be a hasty production, first recounting the articles of treason drawn up against the idiosyncratically spelled 'Lord Kimelton [Mandeville],* Mr John Pimme, Mr Densil Hollis, Sir Artgur Haslerick, Mr Hamden, Mr Stroud'. Then it would carry a brief account – just a couple of paragraphs – of the king 'going to the Parliament house on Tuesday 4 January 1641'. To this it would add a short petition to the king himself.

For this last part a suitable passage of Scripture would be needed, so Paine borrowed his wife's Bible. He took a passage from the Old Testament: 1 Kings, 12.15–16. It described the actions of the tyrant King Rehoboam, a man who listened to evil counsel but who 'harkened not unto his people', so with the rallying cry: 'To your tents, O Israel; Now see to thine own', those people were called to go back to their houses and to withdraw their support from the House of David.

It was a clear and pointed allusion. The tyrant Rehoboam, after all, was the son and successor to Solomon, a king on whom Charles's father, James I, had modelled himself. By the morning, enough copies were ready, and as the low sun rose, a bleary-eyed Walker gathered a stash of them in a bag. He headed back out again into the City streets. The tract's title was *VII Articles Drawen up Against Lord Kimelton...*, but it was the phrase 'To your tents, O Israel' by which it would be remembered.[5] It was only a small bundle of fragile paper, covered in blotchy ink, but it was about to play a role in bringing England to the precipice.

---

*Mandeville also bore the title of 'Lord Kimbolton'.

As morning dawned over a taut capital, Charles prepared for a second attempt on the Five Members. He knew they were no longer in Westminster. His intelligence told him they were somewhere in the depths of the City. It was to the City that he would go.

This time the king was more organised. He took a coach, and ordered Essex, Hamilton, Holland, and Newport to join him. The idea was either to reassure London that these men were safe, or to protect himself by taking cover under their public esteem. Unfortunately, the gesture immediately backfired, when the sight of Charles's coach heading eastwards with the four aristocrats led rumours to fly that he was taking the men to the Tower.[6] As word spread, Londoners began to come out of their houses and into the streets.

The king's actual destination was the Guildhall, perilously close, of course, to the probable hiding place of the Five Members at Coleman Street. Here, Charles entered and addressed the assembled Common Council. He knew the City was harbouring the Five, and said they should hand them over forthwith. He was met with a long silence, finally broken by shouts of 'Parliament! Privileges of Parliament!'

Others were more sympathetic. From the crowded room came some cries of 'God bless the King!' Charles invited those present to speak. 'It is the vote of this Court that your Majesty hear the advice of your Parliament,' came one bold response. To this, one royalist retorted: 'It is not the vote of this Court, it is your own vote.'

Charles now started to justify himself. 'Who is it,' he asked, 'that says I do not take the advice of my own Parliament? I *do* take their advice; but I must distinguish between the Parliament and some traitors in it.' Those, he finished, 'I would bring to a legal trial.'

It was no good. Another voice cried up, 'Privileges of Parliament!' Charles pressed his case again: 'I have and will observe the Privileges of Parliament, but no privileges can protect a traitor from a legal trial.'[7]

It was becoming less of a debate and more of a slanging match, and Charles was losing, so he made to withdraw. Once again the cries echoed out of 'Privileges of Parliament! Privileges of Parliament!' Passing out of the Guildhall, he could see that a huge crowd had gathered in the streets.

The coach picked its way gingerly through the mass of Londoners. Everywhere faces peered in at the king. Sometimes, members of the crowd got close enough to grab onto the wooden cabin as it jolted and jumped through the rough streets; some of them were holding papers – the text of Parliament's 'Protestation' in many cases: the Junto-boosting oath ordered in the lead-up to Strafford's death. After a journey that seemed to take an age, Charles arrived at the house of one of the sheriffs, George Garrett, next to the churchyard of St Mary Aldermary, a few hundred yards south of the Guildhall, where he would dine. Garrett was a Junto-sympathiser, but he was prepared to entertain the king.[8]

Dinner at Garrett's lasted until about 3 p.m., and then Charles began to make his way home. The route west towards his palace would take him through St Paul's, where Henry Walker was waiting. As the royal coach worked its way through the press of people, Walker was able to get close to it. Pushing against the window, he managed to throw a copy of his pamphlet into the jostling cabin. For a brief moment, the boundary between anointed king and one of his angry subjects had been breached. The significance of 'To Your Tents, O Israel', and the story of the tyrant Rehoboam, son of Solomon, can scarcely have been lost on Charles.[9]

Crowds continued to follow his coach, out of the broader space of St Paul's, down Ludgate Hill, past the Temple Bar, and along Fleet Street. It was said that when he returned through the gates at Whitehal, the relief on his face was all too plain.[10] Meanwhile, his allies in the City were faring little better. Mayor Gurney had accompanied Charles to the Temple Bar, after which he turned back towards the City. Near Ludgate, Gurney and the Recorder were surrounded by 'uncivil women' and 'rude citizens', who called them traitors to the City and dragged them from their horses, breaking some of their official regalia. A file of armed citizens had to be urgently called out to accompany the two men to their houses.

Back in Whitehall, Charles was offered a new plan by Digby and Lunsford. They would take a band of Cavaliers into the City and pull the Five Members out, with violence if necessary. Charles refused.[11] Instead, he put his signature to a warrant, for Edward Nicholas. The secretary was to draw up a proclamation, putting Charles's case against the Five Members (not, interestingly, Mandeville), who 'being struck with the conscience of their own guilt of so heinous crimes' had made their escape.[12] They were to be arrested and taken to the Tower immediately, and no one was to harbour them.

At the Guildhall, the Common Council had before it a petition, drafted by the newly created 'Committee of Safety' for London, which boldly criticised the king. His actions were causing uncertainty, danger, and exacerbating the slump in trade. It was time, the citizens implored, for the sovereign to listen to his parliament.[13]

In the Commons, meanwhile, MPs were in their seats just after dinner, and the doors were immediately ordered to be locked shut. Lookouts were posted outside to watch for anyone coming towards Westminster from Whitehall.[14] After prayers, the members fell to discussing the 'great breach of their privileges', in which the king had come there with (as D'Ewes put it) 'so great a number of officers of the late army and desperate ruffians armed some of them with halberds, and others with swords and pistols'.[15]

Some half a dozen or so MPs were prepared to defend Charles, the most eloquent of which was Sir Ralph Hopton, a future royalist general.[16] It was a thankless task, though, and instead of the indulgence Hopton craved for their king, the Commons began drawing up a declaration. It stated that because the king had come to the Commons 'attended with a great multitude of men, armed in a warlike manner', to the 'terror' of the house, they needed – for their own safety – to adjourn until next Tuesday, the 11th.[17] The critical thing about that date was that it was the day after the new common councilmen would officially take their seats, meaning the London militia would then be firmly in their hands.[18] Meanwhile, the Commons would name a committee, to meet at the Guildhall, to maintain its functions until then.[19] When the adjournment was put to a division, 86 opposed the move, but 170 supported, so it was easily passed. The king's party in the Commons was in disarray.

———

The next day, 6 January, London was still unbearably tense. At Whitehall, the Privy Council met for the first time since the morning of the 3rd. Only three days had passed, but the whole scene had changed. Now Charles chaired his council to try and decide what, if anything, he could do.[20]

It was a relatively full meeting, and one of those in attendance was John Bankes, making his first recorded public appearance since the last meeting on the 3rd. Surveying the wreckage of the last three days,the council focused its energies on Walker's *To Your Tents, O Israel*, and ordered a prompt investigation. It was, if anything, a testament to Charles's sheer tetchiness that he spent valuable council time going after an obscure and truculent journalist. But Walker's tract had struck a nerve: a royal warrant immediately went out against seditious books, and their authors. Many people, it said, had 'in a very licentious manner taken to themselves the liberty and boldness to print and publish great numbers of seditious and libellous books and pamphlets'. These were 'scandalous to our government' and aimed at 'the disturbance of the peace of our kingdom'. It was 'a crime not to be endured in a civil state'.[21] Soon, Walker and his printer – Thomas Paine – had been arrested and brought to prison.

As the heavy winter rains continued to batter the tiled roofs of Westminster and London, Charles was faltering. Yet the rumours were quite the opposite. Rather, people thought the king was planning a major attack on London. That day, he had a warrant written to Nicholas, endorsed with the 'sign manual' (the king's personal signature), which ordered the secretary to print the proclamation calling for the arrest of the Five Members.[22] Nicholas had fallen into a trough of depression about what he was being asked to do. In a letter that same day, the 6th, he described himself as 'tired and oppressed with an inundation of troublesome businesses'.[23] His undersecretary Bere could see the burden this was putting Nicholas under. Within a few days he would note that his master's wife, Jane, was also 'much afflicted', and she and probably Nicholas himself now wished he had never been made secretary.[24]

Charles's legal advisors were also wavering. Bankes attended the Privy Council when it sat, but is otherwise absent from the record. Even Attorney-General Herbert was now putting it about that he had urged the king against the prosecutions. The queen's attorney, Peter Ball, claimed to have met with Herbert, and told him point-blank that the impeachments were illegal. On this, Herbert admitted to being uncertain himself. Ball then asked why he did it, to which Herbert replied that he was visited 'sometimes' by courtiers, who pressurised him. Not liking this, he had gone to the queen, but she had simply told him to 'use his discretion'.[25] The implication was very strong, when this all came to light, that it was George Digby who was doing the pressing.

Most significant of all, though, were the actions of Lord Keeper Littleton, the senior law officer. He, 'and divers others' had protested that they knew nothing of the original impeachment. Then, when Nicholas and Charles produced the proclamation against the Five Members and passed it to Littleton for him to apply the Great Seal, he refused.[26] The proclamation was printed anyway, but it had been undermined before it was even issued. Proper procedure was everything in seventeenth-century England: it was held to be one of the ways the subject's liberty was protected; and a proclamation without the Seal was effectively worthless.[27] Littleton, according to some reports, offered his resignation, as well he might, but Charles didn't even feel able to accept it.[28] To a large extent, Whitehall had simply ceased to function. The Earl of Bristol, recently one of Charles's most effective advisors, had gone tellingly quiet. It was his unpredictable son, Digby, who was pushing the agenda.[29]

There was still the looming deadline set out in the Hercules Proclamation, ordering absent MPs to return to Parliament by 12 January. The theory was still that this would rebalance the forces in both houses, and bolster the king's party. The trouble was, the heavy rains and floods had prevented many from travelling, and those who were in London were staying away.[30]

The Cavaliers were there, though, waiting at Whitehall. And London feared what the king might do next. In the City, the wards were ordered to prepare their firefighting equipment. In the daytime, one of the king's serjeants-at-arms had been found searching for the Five Members and was 'much abused by the worse sort of people', if a royalist account is to be believed.[31] With such threats being talked up, the Commons committee didn't last long in the Guildhall. On the afternoon of the 6th, it took the decision to move again, even further within London's tangled knot of streets, to the Grocers' Hall, one of the grandest livery buildings in the capital.

With the onset of darkness, the terrors got worse. That night the watch at Ludgate received reports of 500 cavalrymen, raised for the Irish expedition, being moved from Barnet towards London. Another rumour had 1,500 Cavaliers gathering to launch a stealth attack on the City.

Then, in Covent Garden, a Cavalier's pistol suddenly went off.

Word spread rapidly, and people poured out of their houses. Citizens ran through the streets banging on wooden doors crying '*Arm! Arm!*' Orders came – from whom nobody was quite sure – to bring out the Trained Bands, and they were soon ready and fully weaponed. Ordinary folk – men, women, apprentices, servants – grabbed whatever they had: swords, halberds, clubs, anything. The gates were dragged shut and the portcullises pulled down. Women simmered scalding water in cauldrons, ready to pour from the City walls on anyone who dared attack.[32]

———

It was another false alarm. After a time, people returned to their beds. It was clear, though, that king and Parliament could no longer share the same place. Parliament had fled first, into London, but it was planning to come back on Tuesday 11th. When it did so, it was likely to be accompanied by a major show of strength, possibly involving military force. If the last few days had shown Charles anything, it was that he – and loyalists like Gurney – were fast losing control of the capital.

On the 7th, Charles sent a message to the City, justifying his fortifying Whitehall 'with men and ammunition', saying that his royal person had been put in danger 'by the disorderly and tumultuous conflux of people' and that 'seditious language' had been 'uttered even under his own windows'. Meanwhile, 'If any Citizens were wounded or ill treated', then 'his majesty is confidently assured that it happened by their own evil and corrupt demeanour.'³³ But now even Mayor Gurney was starting to waver. Charles ordered that a herald should stand in front of Whitehall Palace and announce that all six accused men – Mandeville included once more – were traitors. The mayor was told to do the same in London, but he refused. It could not be done, he said, for it was against the law. He was presumably referring to the fact the proclamation lacked the imprint of the Great Seal.³⁴

The next day, the 8th, the Privy Council met again. Charles was once more in the chair; Nicholas and Bankes were there, and this time there was a stronger contingent from the Junto. Their confidence was returning, while the king's shrank. The only recorded business was an order to try and get to the bottom of what had happened in London on the night of the 6th, when the Trained Bands had been called out without mayoral authority.

It was probably the realisation that this had happened, and could happen again, that pushed Charles to prepare his next step.

————

The 10th of January was a Monday. Plans were now in train to bring the Five Members back to Westminster in triumph. The City Trained Bands were put under the command of Philip Skippon, a Puritan hero of the Continental wars. Mariners and seamen, together with their captains and masters, offered to protect the river while the MPs returned. The City militia prepared itself to guard London, while their Southwark counterparts were ready to protect the South Bank. In the Grocers' Hall, the Five Members themselves now appeared, and it was John Hampden, the MP for Buckinghamshire, who stood up to announce that a mass of his fellow countymen were already en route to London with a petition in Parliament's support. Even the watermen offered their assistance; one can only guess how John Taylor will have reacted to this. The only force that was gently rebuffed was the offer of 10,000 apprentices to come out, armed, on the approaching day. With the City militia onside, there was little need to rely on an army of youngsters.[35]

For the king, this was all a humiliation too far. That day he suddenly began preparations to get out. Essex, Holland, and Lady Carlisle all tried to get those close to Charles to persuade him not to leave. If the king left the capital, what would his next move be? Surely to begin raising a force to take it back. Even the Dutch ambassador was asked to intervene, but he didn't dare.[36] There was a rumour too that Lord Mayor Gurney and other City royalists, realising that Charles's flight would destroy their own position in London, offered a guard of 10,000 men.[37] Even if this was true, Gurney was making promises he couldn't keep, for the new Common Councillors were busily consolidating their control of the London Trained Bands.

Charles realised that he no longer had military control of London. Lord Mayor Gurney could no longer protect him or his family. Even his Cavaliers were not likely to provide the safety he needed. With Henry Walker's seditious pamphlet *To Your Tents, O Israel* still in his mind, and fearful for his own safety and even more so that of the queen, he made his decision.[38] Later that day the royal family were hastily gathered beside one of Whitehall's riverside stairs. A barge was waiting for them, and as they carefully stepped down to the listing vessel they were met by a small team of servants. The royal party was rowed upriver, past the great Westminster Palace and the old parish churches at Chelsea and Battersea, past Putney and the Bishop of London's palace at Fulham, and out west aside frozen pastures and muddy plots. Their destination was Hampton Court.

No one was ready for them when they got there a few hours later. The huge brick mansion was airy and cold, and the fires had not been prepared. Such was the haste of their arrival that Charles,

Henrietta, and three of their children were forced to share a bed that night.

———

London feared trouble on the 11th. 'Every house abounds with ammunition,' said one report.[39] Among those staying safely at home was the woodturner Nehemiah Wallington, who worried that there would be 'some great slaughter at Westminster'.[40] As it happened, though, the day was a triumph for the Junto, for Parliament, and for the accused men.

On the river, packed barges and boats carrying streamers and military bands made their way from London to Westminster. Among them were the Five Members, soaking up London's joy at their deliverance. On land, the militia guarded the streets and crowds cheered, as Mandeville travelled to Parliament by coach.[41] Trained Bandsmen carried copies of the Protestation, stuck to the top of their pikes. Volleys of muskets were heard from the troops on the river. In Southwark, the local Trained Bands were out, and people stood on the South Bank watching the glorious river procession glide past. On land, many made their way to Westminster on foot, down King Street and past the great palace of Whitehall, now shorn of its royal guard and empty of the Stuart family. As one group passed, they peered into the palace, gloating at the few royal servants still there.

'What had become of the king, and his Cavaliers?' they asked.[42]

What indeed.

19

To Unsettle Them First

London was gone. It was no longer a city Charles could do business with. Its Westminster twin was little better. Charles had been forced out. It felt like exile.

But it wasn't. Not yet at least. In reality, Charles hoped, it was the beginning of a fightback.

London was not England. Most people were still loyal, so Charles persuaded himself. They hated King Pym and his Junto. They would rally. And Charles was a European sovereign, no less. If he could but ask, then he could get aid from abroad. His daughter was married to the Prince of Orange, and that had to count for something. And Charles's uncle was the King of Denmark. If only a messenger could get there, then an army could be landed to cow the rebellious English.

Since Charles's great defeat in the early months of the Long Parliament, culminating in the death of Strafford, he had adopted a series of strategies to win back control. He had tried, by fair means and foul, to gain control of Scotland. That had failed after the Incident. He had tried, with the help of Edward Nicholas and the queen, to build a royalist party in the Lords and Commons, and to win a majority of votes in Parliament. That had collapsed when he tried to arrest the Five Members by force.

The one thing he had not done yet was attempt a full-scale military assault. He had plotted coups and gathered troops to intimidate and secure enemies. But the only time he had come close to carrying this threat through, he had been thwarted. His birds had flown.

Now, though, this loomed much larger in his thinking. From here onwards, though he would jockey this way and that, his ultimate aim would be for a military solution. There would be optimists still who hoped for an accommodation, but their voices would struggle to be heard, and they would have to compete with the more militant advice of the queen.

In Parliament, there would be a different tone too. They wanted protection, not just of their persons, but of the constitutional and religious gains they had made. Some were willing to meet the king somewhere in between; others were considerably more bellicose. More than anything, it is clear that the trust was gone. It became all the more urgent to complete the Junto's constitutional revolution, and take control of the government.

———

Charles needed a port. He wanted to get the queen out of the country. She could take some of the jewels and use them to sweeten her already considerable powers of persuasion. Continental legions were sure to be forthcoming. And it was best to have her out of England anyway. The heat on Catholics would get worse before it got better, and rumours still spoke of an impeachment against her – a remarkable, fearsome prospect.

Edward Nicholas was summoned. The miserable, despondent secretary had been called to attend the king, and he had followed him to Hampton Court. He must write to the Earl of Newcastle and to a Captain named William Legg. Between them they were to take control of Hull on the Yorkshire coast, stocked as it was with arms and ammunition from the Scottish wars: some 900 barrels of powder, 50 cannons, and more than 7,000 firearms.[1] Not only this, Hull's fortifications overlooked the Humber estuary – one of the most promising locations for any large-scale troop embarkment. Hull must be taken for the king, but no one could know of the plan. Keep the order off the books, Nicholas was told, and he obeyed – though he let his secretarial senses get the better of him somewhat, and made a note of his authorisation not to keep a record.[2] Captain Legg prepared himself for the long journey north.

Another plan was now in action too. Portsmouth had already been put on standby. Even before Charles left Whitehall a ship had been despatched there to await instructions.[3] Now the king needed to clear a path to the south so he or the queen could get there. The first thing to do was to secure Surrey, and this meant taking hold of the county magazine at Kingston, a little town just a mile or so from Hampton Court. Watermen were paid to move saddles for horses from London upriver. Sir Thomas Lunsford and several hundred of the Cavaliers had taken up lodgings in the town, where they waited.[4]

Quickly things started to go wrong. The Hull plan was somehow leaked, and Parliament was already making their own moves to secure the town. The 11th was the first day back after the adjournment. Proceedings were interrupted by the thousands of Buckinghamshire gentlemen and freeholders, who gathered in the lobby to present their petition in support of the Junto.[5] By the evening, Westminster Hall was thronging with members of the City Trained Bands – around 2,400 soldiers, D'Ewes thought. Many carried copies of the Protestation on their pikes. At least one bandsman had pinned his copy to his chest.[6] As debate stuttered on against this hectic backdrop, the decision was made in the afternoon to appoint Sir John Hotham as governor of Hull.[7] The timing could have been a coincidence. But the speed with which they acted suggests that they knew the king's plan. Hotham was given specific instructions not to yield up the town without explicit orders from Parliament.

This wasn't quite enough, for Parliament knew their fates depended on taking physical control of the town. Thus, before Captain Legg had even left for the Great North Road, Hotham's son, also a John Hotham and also an MP, was ordered to make haste to Yorkshire and take Hull in the name of his father and in the name of Parliament. He was on the road before his royalist rival.

Portsmouth was another potential weak spot. Quickly, both houses agreed to send a message to Colonel Goring, telling him not to yield the town except 'by his Majesty's authority, signified by both Houses of Parliament'. It was a sly phrase for it allowed

Parliament to claim that it was they, not the king himself, who currently had custody of 'his Majesty's authority'.[8]

Then, on the 12th, chaos erupted at Kingston. Lunsford and his Cavaliers had been joined by a mounted Lord Digby, brandishing pistols, plus a large consignment of ammunition. The men were said to be riding about the town, firing their guns, carrying themselves 'in a disorderly manner, to the terror of the people', swearing 'bitter oaths that they should see bloody times 'ere long'.[9] Lunsford at one point called out to the town and issued a royal proclamation asking 'all of the King's party' to rally to him, thoughone report claimed he and his fellows were simply drunk.[10] Through out the day, the Commons received urgent despatches about the 'hurly-burly' in Kingston – a live incident until it fizzled out almost as quickly as it had begun.

The Tower was another flashpoint. The Commons wanted a bicameral appeal to Charles to replace the royalist lieutenant Sir John Byron with the more sympathetic Sir John Conyers.[11] Byron was asked to appear before Parliament, but he refused without a direct order from the king.[12] There were worrying reports that the fort was being prepared for a siege. Huge quantities of beer had been seen being rolled up the ramps in barrels, and some men had been spied delivering grenades which 'blew forth bullets'.[13]

———

The king had now moved once again. Word reached Parliament that he was abandoning Hampton Court for the stern grey castle of Windsor, further up the Thames and further away from London. His court was said to be 'in great distraction', but he did at least have the crown jewels with him, a rich source of wealth, and potential collateral for a foreign loan that Charles could use for who knows what.[14] Rumours said Charles might be heading for the south coast, or for his palace at Woodstock in Oxfordshire, or for York.[15] In reality he was already considering concessions. He took a small step back from his impeachment proceedings against the six Junto men. The current attack, he allowed, would be dropped.

But the prosecution would continue 'in an unquestionable way', he vowed, whatever that meant.[16]

For those who remembered, 12 January was the date by which the royalist MPs and peers needed to be in their seats. The harsh winter weather had slowed them down, of course, but once Charles had left Whitehall there was virtually no incentive left to return anyway. The opportunity for building a royalist party in both houses had passed. Parliament itself was reeling from the king's absence. To many, all the evidence pointed one way. The Kingston tumult, the attempt on Hull. Charles was trying to take control of as many military assets as he could. The French ambassador shared the general sense of fear. He thought that within two or three weeks most of the country would be in arms, and that had this all happened in any other country, the violence would already have begun.[17] Blood, it was said, would soon be as cheap as milk.[18] In Huntingdonshire, a magistrate named Ravenscroft (whom D'Ewes knew personally) had declared that it was now 'time to take the king's part or the Parliament's part'. If we take the King's, he said, 'we shall save our own lives and kill them and share in their lands'.[19] In London, people who met on the streets were asking each other if they would be for the king or for Parliament.[20] Such was the perpetual fear that two companies of militiamen, under Skippon, were tasked with providing a constant guard at Westminster.[21]

The shadow cast by the events of 4 January was very great. 'The minds of men throughout the kingdom' had come to see Parliament as the best guarantor of safety.[22] A sharp and militant declaration was prepared by the Commons, complaining of the 'papists, and other ill affected persons' who had been trying to create a 'division of the body of this commonwealth from the head thereof'. Some of these enemies had come to the Commons 'in a warlike manner to the very door', hoping 'to fall upon the said house & to have cut the throats of the members'. Their plan was, so the paper alleged, that 'this Parliament might have been dissolved in blood and confusion'. It was too much for the Lords, who refused to put their name to it.[23]

Despite all this, the Commons were still professing their allegiance. The idea of opposing the king himself remained largely unthinkable – it was still essential to frame it as opposition to certain evil influences around the monarch. On the 14th, MPs voted to declare their 'love and loyalty' to Charles, and the 'honour and safety' of the queen. More importantly, they discussed a clear disavowal of any desire – still widely speculated in rumours – that they wished to impeach her majesty.[24] Yet they were also now proceeding hastily with another new Militia Bill. The Christmas crisis had left the Junto in effective control of the Trained Bands in London, but now it was time to secure the forces everywhere else. Not only this, the Commons also began putting together a series of propositions for a settlement, the first of which, ardently supported by Pym, would be that the king should 'evacuate all the Privy Council, and would elect such as should be allowed by Parliament, as his majesty hath been graciously pleased to do in Scotland'.[25] Their terms for peace were decidedly revolutionary.

Faced with a resolute Parliament and wavering support, Charles now fell into a momentary crisis of confidence. Most worrying for him was the sheer sluggishness with which his nobles were rallying to him at Windsor. When one royalist MP reported to Parliament from there on the 14th, all he could say was that 'he never saw a thinner court', and he could see 'not 40 horse'.[26] The king was said to be 'so fleeting and so friendless', and 'so poor that he cannot feed them that follow him'.[27] All there was at Windsor, scoffed Pym, was a pack of 'giddy-headed young men'.[28] To Charles's utter embarrassment, many of those who had decided to attend on him were simply unpaid creditors wanting to call in some old debt or other.[29] By the end of January, Giustinian could inform Venice that Charles's hopes of winning back power by force were fading. He would simply have to negotiate.[30]

———

It was now 17 January, and although the torrential rains had abated, the roads around London were still soggy and flooded. Rivers had burst, fords were impassable, and bridges had been swept away.[31] Just two weeks had passed since Attorney-General Herbert introduced the impeachment charge in the Lords, but everything had changed.

The immediate fear of military conflict had now somewhat eased, particularly as the king's sudden weakness became apparent. An isolated king was much less dangerous than a strong one. The Buckinghamshire men, still in close contact with Parliament, had offered to march 'in array of war' to Hounslow Heath and suppress Lunsford's men at Kingston. But the Commons was content to thank them 'for their readiness to the good service of the state' and tell them to remain in their own county for now.[32] That said, the worry didn't dissipate entirely. The Marquess of Hertford had been sent to 'take care' of the Prince of Wales, 'lest he be conveyed out of the kingdom', and various caches of weapons around London – some held in bishops' houses, some at the royal arsenal at Vauxhall, were moved to secure locations.[33] Soon, though, a wagon-load of weapons belonging to Lord Digby – thirty-eight pistols, five muskets, and three small barrels of powder and bullets – would be seized in the tiny Wiltshire town of Mere.[34] Digby himself had now decided that an accommodation between king and Parliament was impossible, and on the 16th, he had fled the country for the Netherlands.

At Windsor, Charles was now seriously considering a retreat. He had summoned the Dutch ambassador, Heenvliet, and asked him to help facilitate peace: to act as an interlocutor with the Junto. In the meeting, Charles made it clear that he hated the Bishops' Exclusion Bill, now picking up some momentum again. It was nothing but an attack on royal power, Charles grumbled. But what, the exasperated ambassador pressed, should he pass back to the men at Westminster? What should be offered? Tell them you find me hard to satisfy, said Charles unhelpfully. He was hoping his stubbornness would wring concessions.[35]

Such a begrudging king was not much use to the ambassador, but Heenvliet did then have a much more promising audience with the queen, who seemed altogether more focused. The Commons' accusations against her were unfair, she said. The Irish rebellion was a detestable thing. Parliament could sit every three years if they wished. But they shouldn't meet perpetually. At present, her husband felt he was little better than a duke of Venice. Anyway, he had a new plan. The whole family would go down to Portsmouth, where the queen and princesses would remain. Charles would then travel north to Yorkshire.

But was this not a dangerous path, asked Heenvliet? No, replied the queen. Outside London the king was still loved. There was more gunpowder in Hull than the Tower of London, she thought. And of the Tower, Byron had been left orders to blow it up before he ever surrendered it to Parliament. As to the people, the king would soon produce a manifesto that would reassure them that he wanted peace. But ultimately Charles had to dig in – on the militia, especially.[36]

Even so, within three days, Charles had retreated. Now he wrote to Parliament through Littleton. The Lord Keeper had been shocked at Charles's recent actions, but he brought what he thought was a 'joyful message'. Charles suggested Parliament might put their wishes down on paper, then the two camps could negotiate.[37] Privately, the Portsmouth plan was off.

Not everything was going the Junto's way, though. News now arrived from Hull. The mayor had refused entry to the younger Hotham, as well as to the king's representatives, Legg and Newcastle. The town and its magazine were still very much in play. Trying to galvanise support, the Junto got the Commons to order that the Protestation be circulated to the country, for everyone to sign – not just officers. The idea, at least in part, was to show that England disapproved of the moves against the Five Members.[38] But then, on the 24th, came another blow for the Junto. The Commons, as ever more radical than the Lords, wanted to petition the king to appoint sympathetic commanders for the Trained Bands and forts. Still a majority of the Lords thought this remained a royal prerogative. After a brief moment of unity, the old split between Commons and Lords was threatening to re-emerge. It was looking like the autumn of 1641 again: the radicals in the Commons were attacking the royal prerogative and the Lords were resisting. Something would have to give.

––––––

The protests and mass political campaigns in London were now reaching a crescendo. On or around the 15th, Henry Walker and his publisher Thomas Paine were taken from their prison in Southwark across the river for trial at Newgate, but a crowd assembled at Blackfriars on the north bank, broke them free, and they disappeared.[39]

Another large gathering took place soon afterwards. When Sir Richard Wiseman had been wounded on 28 December by a hurled stone from Westminster Abbey, he was taken to a house on King Street. A couple of days later reports said he was recovering, but they were wrong. Instead, by 17 January at the latest, he was dead.[40] His funeral, on 19 January, was a dramatic affair. His hearse was pulled from King Street, through the West End, to the parish of St Stephen Coleman Street – the heart of radical London. He was accompanied by 200 apprentices carrying swords and black ribbons, plus 400 citizens also carrying swords. The occasion was commemorated with a single-page elegy, featuring an acrostic poem. It was a cheap, hasty piece, which not only erroneously declared him to be a member of the Commons but also misnamed him once as 'William Wiseman'. But it scarcely mattered. The Roundheads had their first martyr. Another printed eulogy came out at the same time, from the workshop of William Larner, the man who had published Katherine Chidley.[41]

On 20 January, a petition with 20,000 hands was delivered to Parliament by inhabitants of Essex, calling for the removal of the votes of the bishops and the popish lords.[42] Others followed, from Middlesex, Devon, and Hertfordshire.[43] And a group of City men also brought an appeal, lamenting the decay of trade and promising not to lend any more money until the country's many grievances were settled.[44] Seizing the moment, Pym pressed the urgent need for security against threats from Spain and Ireland, and from papists at home. He drew attention to the serious economic problems, and the fact these were causing growing disorder among the 'meaner sort of people'. He argued for a reduction in taxation and a freeing of the trade that brought 'life, strength, and beauty to the whole body of the commonwealth'. He also pointed to the continued power of the bishops 'and the corrupt part of the clergy'. It was the Commons that must take the lead, 'united in the public trust, which is derived from the commonwealth'.[45]

Despite Pym's attempts to galvanise support, there were still signs – against the odds – that the royalist party might be picking itself up again. None more ominous than when, on the 26th, the Duke of Richmond rose in the Lords. 'Let us put the question,' he suggested, 'whether we shall adjourn for six months.'[46] It was all too close to Digby's infamous suggestion, less than a month ago, that Parliament was unfree. According to the French ambassador, the debate in the House of Lords was absolutely furious, with swords nearly being drawn.[47] The duke was told to acknowledge his offence, but twenty-two peers protested that this was too mild a censure.[48] In the Commons, Richmond was declared an 'ill counsellor'.[49] He and the Earl of Bristol, the leaders of this brief royalist revival at Westminster, promptly left to join the king.[50]

Charles, meanwhile, remained isolated at Windsor, where he continued to resist Parliament's calls to be given command of the militia.[51] It was nothing short of a constitutional crisis. England's government had almost completely ground to a stop. With the 'barbarous and bloody' Irish rebellion still burning, and with no clear path out of the political labyrinth in England, traders were withdrawing their money and goods from circulation.[52] Employees were suddenly being laid off.

Finally, at the end of January, the storm broke.

––––––

On the 31st, crowds had started to gather once more outside Parliament.[53] That day, the Commons received a petition from 14,000 people in Suffolk demanding that the bishops and the Catholic lords lose their votes.[54] Then another petition came from 'divers artificers dwelling in and about London'.[55] This was much more socially radical, for it was from the capital's manual workers. There were between a dozen and twenty presenters who, D'Ewes noted, spoke 'boldly' at the bar of the house, desiring 'to know who were the obstructors of our happiness'.[56] They pressed for 'instant remedy because of their extreme wants'. Most remarkably of all, the artificers argued for a radical constitutional solution to the impasse.

If the Lords did not join with the Commons, then those peers who concurred with the votes of the lower house 'may be earnestly desired to join with you and to sit and vote as one entire body'.[57] It was a call for a single national assembly.

A conference was agreed between the houses, to meet in the Painted Chamber. Denzil Holles managed for the Commons. He read the artificers' petition aloud, and, in D'Ewes's words, 'did very boldly represent to the lords what dangers we were in if they did not speedily join with us for the securing of the commonwealth'. If they didn't, Holles argued that the Lords alone 'should be guilty of all the miseries that should happen thereby'.[58] It seemed for a moment as if the future of the upper house itself might be under threat.

That same afternoon, the Commons proposed an ordinance to name new militia commanders. The royalist Sir Ralph Hopton spoke ('very pertinently' said a wavering D'Ewes), arguing that this could not be done without an Act of Parliament – that is, without the royal assent. But the Commons voted it anyway. It was nearly 7 p.m. before the house rose. It was another major escalation. Ordinances were supposed to be for times in which the king was unavailable. Now Parliament were claiming they could also be used when the king was simply misinformed. It was a measure that would slice the king out of any remaining legislative role. Even the Junto's attempt to take control of the government hadn't gone this far.

The next morning, 1 February, there was a stunning scene outside Parliament. Once more the palace yards were full of Londoners, but this time the crowd was different, for it was dominated by women. Many brought children with them to emphasise the point. 'We had rather bring our children and leave them at the Lord's door than have them starve at home,' they said. They had a petition to present to Parliament.[59]

It was yet more pressure on the peers. The extent of the social crisis – the political uncertainty and the stuttering trade – was starting to look very serious indeed: like the very fabric of London was about to rupture. Charles, meanwhile, committed a serious blunder. Near the end of January, a thousand Londoners trudged out to present him with a petition. In a fit of panic, Charles ordered the local posse comitatus to be raised to protect him, but they refused to assemble.[60] So, smarting from his evident vulnerability, he summoned fourteen peers to make their way to Windsor. The trouble was, as their coaches picked their way through the rutted tracks of rural Middlesex, they were removing themselves from where they were most needed: in Parliament. By the 1st, when the question of the militia was reignited once more, and with the London women protesting at the door, the balance in the upper house had shifted decisively. That evening, the Lords agreed to join the Commons and desire parliamentary control of the militia and forts.[61]

Some remarkable speeches were now being made. That same day, Sir Henry Ludlow told the Commons that 'the king is derivative from the parliament and not the parliament from the king'.[62] There were angry royalists in the house too. Sir George Wentworth, brother of the late Earl of Strafford, was accused at one point of putting it about that: 'England was sick of peace and that it would never be well till it were new conquered.'[63]

The crowds remained, and some peers were surrounded as they left Parliament on the 1st: Lord Keeper Littleton was one who was given a thorough treatment by the assembled women and others.[64] The petitions continued, too. On the 2nd, one came from the porters of London – 'all with white towels over their shoulders' – containing 1,500 names. It complained of the decay of trade and ballooning unemployment.[65] There was, it claimed, an 'adverse, malignant, bloodsucking, rebellious, popish party' who had counselled that 'prerogative should trample upon all privileges of parliament'.[66] More petitions were on their way, from the Dorset gentry, from 16,000 clothiers from Suffolk, and from Surrey, signed by 10,000 knights, gentlemen, and others.[67] Most dramatic of all, on the 4th, the women's petition was brought to the house, supported by the radical Henry Marten. It focused – more so than the other petitions – on religion, but the key item was the usual: the removal of the parliamentary votes of bishops and popish lords. The women apologised for being so bold, but they noted the example of Queen Esther, who they said had petitioned for deliverance for the Church.

Esther was a Jewish queen of Persia, who had protected her religion from a foolish pagan king.[68]

Then, on 5 February, the Lords finally caved. As crowds still gathered outside, they passed a bill that had been sat on for what seemed like an eternity. They agreed that the bishops should be excluded from secular office. The fourteen royalist Lords whom Charles had summoned to Windsor had tipped the balance. At last, the Junto had managed to gut the Lords entirely of its episcopal choir. Presumably, it isn't a coincidence that immediately a message was sent to the City – including to the ministers of the Church – to ask them to do their best to prevent further tumults. The assemblies of the people, which had rocked Westminster for over two months now, could be stopped.[69]

It was a major blow for Charles, and the setbacks kept coming. News arrived that Hull had now opened its doors to the younger Hotham, with 700 men, meaning it was now held firmly by Parliament.[70] At the same time, the ambassador Heenvliet informed the king that the Prince of Orange, Charles's son-in-law, would not mediate for him.

Charles was stuck. All he could do now was offer concessions. On the 6th he told Parliament that he would accept their new militia commanders, so long as the actual appointment remained by his writ not theirs, and so long as he retained the right to refuse anyone he considered unfit. They should tell him, he demanded, how long they planned to exercise these new powers. Finally, too, he agreed to drop the proceedings against the six accused Junto men.[71]

It would not be enough. The second part of his offer was not fully trusted, and the first was so thoroughly hedged as to be meaningless. The next day, Charles sat down for another audience with Heenvliet. His despondency was now streaked with anger. 'How am I to take away the bishops having sworn at my coronation to maintain them?' he fumed. Every time he caved to his enemies they just demanded more. 'At the beginning I was told that all would go well if I would allow the execution of the Lord Lieutenant of Ireland,' he said. 'Then it was if I would grant a triennial Parliament,' he continued. 'Then it was if I would allow the present Parliament to remain sitting as long as it wished; now it is if I will place the ports, the Tower, and the militia in their hands; and scarcely has that request been presented, when they ask me to remove the bishops.' He had reached the limit of his patience. 'You see how far their intentions go,' he griped. He would accept the names of the new militia commanders when they came, he said, but 'they must tell me for how long a time this arrangement is to last, so that I may not strip myself entirely'. Charles knew full well that he was having all of his meaningful powers taken away from him.[72]

———

Now Charles's plan, by force of circumstances, shifted once more. The queen would leave the country at last and plead his case abroad. He, on the other hand, would make his way towards York. On the issue of the Tower, he capitulated: Byron would be replaced by Conyers. But it remained to be seen whether this conciliatory pose was in any sense meaningful. Indeed, the plan to seek help abroad was clearly aggressive.[73]

The royal couple were now at Greenwich. The day before Byron was removed, Henrietta Maria gave an audience to Giustinian, at which the ambassador was told, bluntly, that 'to settle affairs it was necessary to unsettle them first'. This was the only way of re-establishing her husband's authority.[74] It was an argument, as much as anything, for civil war.

There were two key pieces of legislation still in play. One was the long-expected Militia Bill, giving Parliament the right to choose the lords lieutenant in the counties. The other was the bill to exclude the bishops, which still required the king's assent. Inevitably the question was what should happen if Charles should refuse either, or both. One solution was proposed in the Commons by the 'fiery spirit' Henry Marten. In a speech described by D'Ewes as 'dangerous and ignorant', the Berkshire radical suggested that since the king had chosen the Lords, his vote could be considered to be included with that of the upper house. Thus, legislation (specifically in this case the Bishops' Exclusion Bill) could be passed by the two houses of Parliament without the king.[75] No king was necessary.

Soon the Commons were working through the practicalities of the Militia Bill, finalising the names of the new commanders. Each county was to have one lord lieutenant, nominated by the sitting MPs from that county, and then decided by the Commons as a whole. The list was discussed and confirmed on 10 and 11 February; it was still dominated by the nobility but the critical point was that these were to be nobles sympathetic to Parliament. One particularly eyebrow-raising appointment was of Lord Keeper Littleton to the lieutenancy of Radnorshire. For the king's senior lawyer to take a commission was a coup for the Junto indeed. But it was on Saturday 12 February, that the most surprising intervention took place.

The tiny town of Corfe Castle, below the old medieval fortress held by the Lord of the Isle of Purbeck, had traditionally sent two MPs to Parliament. The electorate of Corfe was around seventy householders, and the Lord of the Castle clearly enjoyed much influence.[76] In 1640, the unpopular secretary of state Francis Windebank had taken one of the seats (before he fled the country), with the other going to a local man. This was Giles Green, a friend of Sir John Bankes.*

Green was a merchant who had worked closely with Bankes in the 1630s.[77] He had already sat for Corfe Castle before that, and he had connections to the Dorchester Puritans, like the famous John White, who had helped found the colonial Massachusetts Bay Company. He was evidently a Junto man, but he remained on good terms with Bankes. Now, indeed, he was to prove immensely useful to the Lord Chief Justice. For, that Saturday, Green proposed a minor change to the military landscape of Dorset. Rather than the power of the lord lieutenant running across the whole county, Green suggested that the Isle of Purbeck should have its own separate commander.

Purbeck was a strange place, of course: not actually an island but separated from the mainland by the 'oozy, slubby' waters of Poole

---

*Green had been steward to Lady Hatton before Bankes bought the Purbeck estate, and he was sensibly kept on afterwards.

Harbour and a wide and bleak heathland. When Green moved that Sir John Bankes should lead the militia of Purbeck – the reasoning being that it was his hereditary right as Constable of Corfe – it led to a surprisingly long debate for such a local matter. 'Divers thereupon spake to it,' recorded D'Ewes, 'and some would have had it exempted; others spake to the contrary.' D'Ewes himself gave his thoughts. His view was that, since this was an issue of inheritance, it would be no disrespect to the actual lieutenant of the county (who was the Earl of Salisbury). Rather, since Bankes 'having deserved so well as he hath done of the public', he should have it. This itself was an interesting statement, given Bankes's role during the Personal Rule and given D'Ewes's detestation of, for example, Ship Money. Times had evidently changed.[78]

But why did Bankes want the position? He was a bookish lawyer, not a soldier, and by accepting it, he was giving his support to a dangerous, radical piece of legislation that took military power out of the hands of the monarch. Littleton had done so too, of course. But in some ways, this made Bankes's decision worse for the king. For if both the Lord Keeper and the senior active judge took commissions, then royalists would struggle to argue that what Parliament was doing was illegal. When he found out about Bankes's appointment, Charles was furious.

Bankes may well have been alienated from the king at this point. To many moderates it looked like Charles was fomenting conflict by absenting himself from Parliament. Bankes, Littleton, and others may have accepted – even supported – the Militia Ordinance because they thought it would prevent the king starting a war against Parliament.[79] On the other hand, what might also have tipped the balance for Bankes was that his wife was about twelve weeks pregnant. She had probably told him, in December, that her 'flowers' or 'terms' were late. Even a delay of a week or so was a hopeful sign of pregnancy. Mary was approaching her mid-forties, though, so this time it could just have been a sign of the 'cessation', something very rarely written about in the seventeenth century.[80]

But it wasn't. That winter, as John's world was convulsed by the political crisis, Mary was showing signs that she was carrying another child. By February, Mary was into her fourth month. It would be a tense pregnancy. Her previous one – at some time during the last year or so – had ended badly, probably in miscarriage. In the notebook in which the family added the names of their children, after Charles Bankes, born in September 1639, is a melancholy pencil note, recording 'A Little One, that shall be nameless.'[81] The preference would be for Mary to give birth at her usual home, at Stanwell in the Middlesex countryside. But what if war broke out? If so, it was imperative to make sure that she and the infant – plus the rest of the Bankes family – were safe. Corfe was the obvious place.

John and Mary Bankes could see what was coming.

20

Overthrow the Ship and Drown Them All

Charles was now at Canterbury with the queen.[1] At the ancient cathedral city, one of the oldest Christian sites in England, their plan was finally coming together. The king would grant concessions and go to Hull, where he would take control of the guns and powder there, and he would await relief from abroad. The queen would go to the Continent to procure that relief. One of the biggest questions was over what specific concession Charles should offer to buy time.

The choice came down to two of the bills being pushed by Parliament: the Militia Bill and the bill to exclude the bishops from secular roles, including their seats in the Lords. The king's inclination was to concede the Militia Bill, effectively granting Parliament control of the Trained Bands. But Sir John Culpeper, the Chancellor of the Exchequer, was convinced this would be a terrible mistake. Instead, Charles should allow the Bishops' Exclusion Bill. To Culpeper, this would likely settle the religious issue, and in order to persuade the king, he spoke to Henrietta Maria, who then worked on Charles. He could concede the bishops' exclusion, she said. But he must never yield control of the militia. This was key. Without a military, the monarchy was nothing.[2]

The Impressment Bill was now passed, to create a conscript army for Ireland. It gave the Junto the kind of force they wanted. Charles was also suggesting other concessions: stricter enforcement of the laws against Catholics, and more consultation with Parliament over religion. It led to an immediate positive response when, on 14 February, St Valentine's Day, both houses expressed their thanks.[3] That morning, they had carried up the formal impeachment of Attorney-General Edward Herbert for his articles against the Five Members and Mandeville. Oddly enough, this might have been something of an olive branch to Charles – Herbert was unlikely to suffer particularly grievously – and it would allow the king to blame the disastrous prosecutions of January on bad advice. All it needed was for Charles to abandon yet another of his servants.

Whatever the purpose, the outlook immediately darkened once more. Late that afternoon Pym had brought a packet of letters to the house, intercepted from George Digby.[4] The courtier was now holed up in Middelburg in the Netherlands, lodging in an inn called the Golden Fleece, adjoining the town's herb market. From here he had written to Edward Nicholas, to his own half-brother, Lewis Dyve, and to Henrietta Maria.[5]

A joint committee of MPs and peers was tasked with reading the letters, and the two to Nicholas and Dyve were cut open and read. The second was worrying indeed, for it contained the suggestion that the king should retire to a secure fort. Equally bad, it referred to the Parliamentarians as 'traitors'.[6] The committee was reluctant to open the third, addressed to the queen, but after consultation it was decided that the times necessitated the means. Just before 8 p.m., Pym brought the letter back to the Commons and read it out. In it, Digby promised loyalty. If Charles were to go to a place of safety, 'where he may avow and protect his servants from rage and fury', then Digby would return. If, on the other hand, 'his majesty shall think of ways of accommodation', then Digby was better off where he was.[7] The explosive element here was the strong implication that accommodation was just one option for Charles, and possibly not the preferred one. Within a week, Lord Digby would be impeached *in absentia* of high treason.[8]

Any glimmer of concession from Parliament was gone. The evidence was still the same. Whatever the king offered was worthless unless he also gave up all power to take it back by force. With remarkable speed, the bill for command of the militia was passed, sent to the Lords, and swiftly agreed by the peers. The Junto's grab of the defensive apparatus was nearly complete. All it needed was the royal assent – or something else.

———

For some time now, Parliament had been devoting a vast amount of time to the Irish expedition. It would cost £1 million, was one calculation, but once it was completed there would be 10 million acres ready for confiscation.[9] Parliament was putting together a plan for the expropriation of around a third of Irish land. They would have a bill ready soon, within weeks. It would be one of the last things Charles would give the royal assent to.

Charles was slowly moving further away, picking his path east by rickety coach, through the muddy and chalky highways towards the Kent coast.[10] From Canterbury he and Henrietta Maria made for Dover. On arrival, they were faced with frustration, not from their enemies at Westminster, but from the weather. The coastal winds were bad; the queen's departure would have to wait. So, too, would the militia, said Charles. On the 21st, he wrote to the Lords saying he would consider the bill they had sent once the queen was safely away. By the 23rd, the queen had finally sailed over the horizon, with her daughter Mary and in possession of the crown jewels, towards the Continent.[11] As soon as they were gone, and safe, the king's outlook changed.

Charles was also soon reunited with his eldest son, the Prince of Wales (the future Charles II). The king was ecstatic, and confirmed in his newfound vigour: 'Now I have gotten Charles, I care not what answer I send to them.'[12] More to the point, he had already promised the queen to be resolute. Having vacillated, Charles was increasingly determined. Now key members of his family were secure, he could pursue a much riskier path.

There was still the Militia Bill, and here Charles dug in. Yes, Parliament could have the officers it had appointed, but the commissions *must* still come from him. And he must be able to change the officers when he wished. It was little more than a denial, and when his response was read in the Commons on 28 February, it drew horror and calls for radical measures. There was an analogy, argued one MP, recorded in a diary just as 'Sir W' and never identified. It was the question of what would happen if 'the king should be desperate and would lay violent hands upon himself'. Or, what if the king were at sea, 'and a storm should rise and he would put himself to the helm and would steer such a course as would overthrow the ship and drown them all'.[13] A king who did this, who was mad enough to harm himself or to steer the country towards destruction. This king would be no king. His authority would have transferred somewhere else.

By now Charles was at Theobalds, north of London, and to that great mansion house – once beloved of his father – Parliament sent a delegation of six Lords and twelve Commons men to ask him to return.[14] It was a request that brought a sharp response: 'I wish it might be so safe and honourable that I had no cause to absent myself from Whitehall; ask yourselves whether I have not.'[15]

Then, on 3 March, Charles left Theobalds and began a new journey. He was going north, heading towards York. It would put a considerable distance between him and his Parliament. It would place him in the midst of a northern region that might retain strong allegiance to the Crown. It would also put him near Hull, nearer Newcastle, or even Chester (from whence he might either go to Ireland, or connect with the rebels there). Others thought he might be heading for Scotland.[16]

Certainly the response was swift, decisive, and utterly radical. On the 4th, a declaration of 'fears' was brought before the Commons by Pym. The tone was quite astonishingly accusatory: little less than a charge-sheet against the monarch. It recounted the reasons Parliament had to quake at the king's actions – going back to the wars against Scotland and the Tower Plot. Charles was accused of gathering armed men at Whitehall, 'which was to endeavour to divide your people by a civil war'. The attempted arrest of the Five Members exactly two months ago was 'a massacre intent upon the Parliament'.[17]

It was getting hard to see how things could de-escalate from here, and 5 March was a watershed moment for another reason. For, that day, Parliament decided to pass the Militia Bill, not for the royal assent, but as an ordinance. It would go into force immediately, whatever Charles said. The negative voice of the king would simply be ignored. It was needed, the text said, 'in this time of imminent danger'. It was the same two-word phrase that John Bankes had used to defend Ship Money, and he was specifically named in the ordinance as Lieutenant of the Isle of Purbeck and Constable of Corfe Castle.[18]

The Militia Ordinance, passed on 5 March against the wishes of the king, was radical, even revolutionary. Not just in what it decreed, but in the very method. It was revolutionary because it removed the king's veto. Not only that but it did so in order to take the king's soldiers away from him. Some of the theory behind it, though, was surprisingly old. When John Bankes had made the case for Ship Money, he had used the argument of necessity. In a time of 'imminent danger', it fell to the king to do what was necessary to preserve the safety of the realm.[19]

But what if the king himself was the danger? Or, more delicately, what if he was being manipulated and misled by those who had turned him into that danger? This was the conundrum the Militia Ordinance sought to answer. Now it must fall to Parliament, as representatives of the people, to act. Indeed, the very nature of the arguments now, and the situation England found itself in, exposed a fundamental divide. It was one that had been there all along. During the Ship Money case, Oliver St John had argued that in all except in the most extreme emergencies, it was for Parliament to decide what to do about it, not the king. It was only if Parliament was not sitting, and if some latter-day Hannibal was at the gates, that the king might act alone. The Militia Ordinance, in which St John had a major hand, was based on a similar premise: the fountain of authority was acting to preserve the kingdom. Only that fountain was Parliament alone, and Hannibal now was Charles. At its core, the question had become whether it was the king or Parliament who had the right to act in the public interest, and to decide what that public interest was.

———

That same afternoon, 5 March, a Cavalier colonel was in a Covent Garden tavern. There were plenty of places you might still find angry and drunk royalists in the capital. On this occasion, the Cavalier in question had a dangerous suggestion. He told his fellows that he hoped the king would soon raise his royal standard – the accepted symbol to raise forces to quell rebellion – and would defend his prerogative by force.[20] If Charles did, it would be a declaration of war.

For now, the king was simply trying to get north. He was a forlorn figure, travelling by coach with only a small entourage and about £600 in ready cash.[21] A few days after leaving Theobalds, he had only made it to the royal palace at Newmarket. At least it was somewhere that brought back fond memories. In happier times he had enjoyed hunting here, when he had been able to rule without Juntos or even parliaments. Now, though, he had also been caught up by some less welcome voices from the past. It was a delegation, led by the earls of Pembroke and Holland. They were both ex-courtiers but were here with a parliamentary declaration of 'fears and jealousies'. Charles was singularly unimpressed, for it was a belligerent, rebarbative document. It alleged a longstanding Catholic plot to overthrow the country, which had matured recently in the attempt on the Five Members and Mandeville. On 4 January, there had been an attack in 'so terrible and violent a manner as far exceeded all former breeches of Privileges of Parliament acted by your majesty or any of your predecessors'. Indeed, whatever Charles's intensions, there were 'divers' 'bloody and desperate persons' whose intentions were 'to have massacred and destroyed the members of that house'.

'That's false! 'Tis a lie!' was Charles's response at various points.[22] His formal riposte was angry and wounded, blaming Parliament for allowing 'tumults' and 'seditious pamphlets and sermons'. 'What would you have?' he asked. 'Have I violated your laws? Have I denied to pass one Bill for the ease and security of my subjects? I do not ask what *you* have done for *me*.' Pembroke queried if there might be some scope for compromise. Could the king not grant the militia for a time, perhaps? 'By God!' cried Charles, 'not for an hour.'[23]

In such an atmosphere of recrimination, any compromise was entirely elusive. Charles may by now have accepted the likelihood of war, and the constitutional positions of him and Parliament had drifted so far apart as to be effectively irreconcilable.[24] A newsletter of 12 March reported that 'the whole business of the kingdom [was] depending upon the act of Militia and upon the king's being so remote from Parliament'.[25] Physical remoteness combined with ideological. Pretty much the only thing the two camps could agree on was the subjugation of Ireland. Soon Charles would give his assent to the 'Adventurers' Bill', allowing for the eventual confiscation of Irish land to pay subscribers in England who had given money towards the war. In his initial response some weeks earlier, Charles had implied certain misgivings about the bill. Might it not make the Irish more desperate in their struggle? But he pointedly remarked that he didn't have time to think about this, and would just agree to it anyway.[26]

It would be this parliamentary act of brutality, ratified by Charles's petulance, which would eventually, several years later, underpin the Cromwellian conquest of Ireland. But by 1642, the violence had already begun. There were now several British expeditionary forces in play, totalling several thousand troops, including 1,500 under a young officer called George Monck.[27] Within a few days of the passing of the Adventurers' Act, an English commander, Sir Simon Harcourt, died during an attack on a fortification near Dublin. Harcourt was a loyal king's man, an associate of Laud and of Elizabeth of Bohemia, and a veteran of the wars against the Scots Covenanters. During the attack, in the words of one of his soldiers, Harcourt's troops 'slew man, woman, and child to the number of 300 or more'.[28] Another royal general, the Earl of Ormond, was given orders to burn any place that had harboured rebels and 'kill and destroy' anyone of military age.[29] Within months the violence of the English would be joined, too, by the Scots, who were just as bad.[30]

On 19 March, Charles arrived in York. It had been a difficult journey. At Cambridge, people told him he must return to his Parliament, and a feast put on by St John's College was marred by Charles's Cavalier followers indecorously stuffing their pockets with food for the journey. At York, he found many reluctant to come out to meet him, giving thin excuses. One said their horse was lame; some that they had other things to do.[31] He appeared, said one supporter, 'almost abandoned by all his subjects'.[32] Nonetheless, here, under the huge medieval minster, and hemmed in by the ancient walls, Charles set up his capital. He knew the city well, having decamped here in the summer of 1640 and stopped on his way to Scotland in the hot months of 1641. As with that last occasion, Charles based himself in the great mansion of Sir Arthur Ingram, a rich financier. The house, which adjoined the minster, was opulent and grand, yet Charles's own circumstances were now anything but. As safe as he was, he was now in urgent financial need.

Charles was still quibbling over a potential pardon for Mandeville and the Five Members. He wrote to Lord Keeper Littleton, still presiding over the Lords, saying that he would accept a bill clearing them, so long as the wording didn't reflect badly on himself. It was again a weak concession.[33] He was also receiving regular letters now from the queen. She had arrived in the Hague in February, and quickly put her energies towards raising support for her husband, and galvanising his resolve. 'Do not break your resolution,' she wrote in March, 'but follow it constantly and do not lose time.' He should summon the dissidents Essex and Holland to his side, and if they refused, he should take their offices from them. He should hold off on appointing a new Lord Treasurer, for that would be 'a bone that will make the dogs fight'. She remained dead-set against any further concessions. Rather, she wrote, Charles needed to strike for an eastern port, so as to allow the landing of troops. The queen knew the geography of the north-east well. 'Hull must absolutely be had,' she wrote, but if 'you cannot, you must go to Newcastle, and if you find that is not safe, go to Berwick, for it is necessary to have a seaport.' She implored him to stay the course, for in the past 'that want of perseverance in your designs has ruined you'.[34]

———

On 27 March, England celebrated Charles's Accession Day, with church bells rung and special sermons. One of those sermons would have particular resonance for Sir John Bankes. It was given by William Hall, the minister of St Bartholomew the Less in London, one of the closest churches to his residence at Holborn. Hall was the son of another preacher who in turn Bankes had once supported. When Hall came to publish his sermon, using a radical printer named Thomas Badger, he dedicated it to Bankes.[35]

Accession Day sermons were normally dedicated to the king, not to their judges, but Hall had a point to make. Certain men and women, he said, had made 'themselves the censurers of the magistracy', particularly 'disrelishing and taxing the actions of the sacred senate of our Commonwealth'. Parliament, in other words. Hall reminded his listeners, and readers, that some Roman emperors had tried to make 'them Gods who are but mortal men'. Modern divine-right kings were the same ilk, he implied. But in fact that earthly divinity, in so far as it existed, was shared between all rulers – kings and magistrates.

He spoke, too, of the origins of kings. Like the famous arguments of the philosopher Robert Filmer, he associated kingly power with that of fathers, but he jumped from this to argue that the power of rulers came from the people: 'Men learned to choose a ruler over them.' In the beginning, there had been no kings, but there had been fathers. These fathers, as society grew more complex, picked their rulers.

This led Hall to muse on the relationship between God and the constitution. 'Rulers then are all of Gods appointment,' he suggested. But there were different forms to that government, ultimately decided 'by the agreement of men'. There was no 'absolute necessity' that there be one ruler alone in all countries. Meanwhile, God might sometimes allow power to be put in the hands of tyrants: 'Tyrannical oppression' wasn't within God's ordinance, but those who committed it might take their power from him. On the other hand, 'unjust magistrates' (read, kings?) 'have more of Satan in them than of God'. Most pertinent of all, if 'earthly gods and rulers' impose 'impious or dishonest commands', these should be disobeyed. Hall ended by hoping that, 'God would unite the hearts more and more, of our king and Parliament.' But his conclusion carried a radical edge. The people should honour the king, Hall argued, but 'while we are faithful to him, we cannot, we must not be unfaithful to his counsellors', as Parliament's Protestation avowed. 'We owe them obedience,' Hall said, 'for this is due to the commands and laws of kings and rulers, *while they are consonant to those of God.*'

What Bankes himself thought of this is unrecorded, but it placed his name next to some remarkable arguments. The Junto, meanwhile, were making their own case in favour of the Militia Ordinance. They were claiming that it was they, not the king, who knew what was best for the public interest. This is because they were the representatives of the people. They also based their arguments on what they claimed was the nature of royal authority. The king, as was widely recognised, had two bodies: a body natural (his actual body) and a body politic. Parliament were suggesting that while the king's person had skulked up to York, his body politic had been left behind and was now in the custody of Parliament. Thus because the royal person had been 'possessed' by evil counsellors, he should effectively be treated like a child or someone who was mentally incapable of rule.

So, Charles called their bluff. He had to show that wherever his royal person currently was, there also resided his authority. The king may have had two bodies, but they were both currently in Yorkshire. His policy got off to a rather hapless start when Charles took the apparently innocuous step of summoning his royal wind instruments to his side. The players replied that they hadn't been paid for two years and so couldn't afford to come.[36] Yet Charles had other lines of attack. It was just over a month until St George's Day, and he decided that he wanted to have a feast with the Order of the Garter, an event he had prorogued the previous spring. So he wrote to all the members, including the earls of Essex and Holland, and demanded that they attend him on 18–20 April.[37] The Lords responded by ordering the earls to remain where they were. Essex and Holland stayed put.

But others were starting to drift north. The gentlemen-pensioners – loyal king's guards – were already on their way, and on 3 April a company of horse troopers left London and made for the Great North Road.[38] At last, almost three months after leaving Whitehall, the king was starting to gather real support. One day soon he might be in a position to move against his enemies.

Charles's first gambit would be – as the queen had urged him – to take control of Hull. She knew why he hadn't moved on it already. Charles wanted Parliament to declare war on him, so he could have the moral high ground. She thought this unwise, for by the time they did so he would already be out of money and forced to concede. There was a risk, too, that Parliament would moderate their demands, something she considered 'in effect, worse for you'.[39] Henrietta Maria was pushing a militant path on Charles. And that path led directly to Hull.

————

Buffeted by bitter north-easterly winds, Hull was a small port town, currently packed with powder and arms. It was held at that time by Sir John Hotham, who had taken command from his son, and had a garrison of some 700 men. The population, though, seem to have distrusted the soldiers, so Hotham was having to look nervously over his shoulder.[40] For Charles, it was a more than tempting target. Any worry about the escalation this would represent was sharply dismissed by the queen. Charles taking Hull would not be an act of violence, she wrote – that was on 'the rascal who refuses it to you'.[41] There was an added immediacy, too, for on 2 April, the Commons had voted that the arms at Hull be shipped down to London.[42] The king could delay no longer.

Initially, Charles sent members of his family. On 22 April, the Elector Palatine and the young James, Duke of York, were despatched ahead with a band of men. It was a market day, and they were able to enter the city unnoticed. Soon, though, they revealed themselves to Hotham, who received them warmly.[43] Naively, the men assumed this meant the town would submit and reported this back to Charles.[44] The next day the king left York, on the road to Hull, with around 300 cavalrymen. Soon, he was only a few miles away.

The first thing Charles did was warn Hotham, and demand he relinquish the town, and allow access. To give fair warning like this was punctilious – even chivalrous – of Charles. But it meant Hotham was fully prepared for what was coming.

The message came back from Hotham. He would not submit. Instead, the drawbridges to the town were hauled up and slammed shut. Hotham was prepared for a siege. Then, on 23 April, St George's Day, the king appeared. Looking down upon him from the town walls was Hotham. Charles demanded entrance. Hotham refused. He had given his word to Parliament that he would not yield the town.

It was a farce, with the two men shouting messages at each other. Members of Charles's party were furious, crying out to Hotham's garrison and telling them to chuck the MP over the walls. But Hotham's men stood firm. So Charles retired to a nearby house for an hour, before returning with one last plea.[45] Perhaps, he suggested, Hotham might allow him to enter with just twenty men. Hotham refused. He had managed to maintain the loyalty of his troops. He didn't want to push his luck with the townspeople too. All Charles could do was to have his heralds proclaim Hotham a traitor, and make a humiliated retreat.

Hotham's defiance on the walls of Hull was not only a personal mortification for the king. It was a moment of deep constitutional significance. Could the king be refused entry to an English town or fortress? Did he, in a real tangible sense, own the whole country? Or were there places that belonged to the people to which he could be denied access? What should happen when orders from king and Parliament contradicted each other? Which of the two should be obeyed? Charles, for his part, argued that what had happened would ultimately overthrow the notion of property itself: 'we would fain be answered what title any subject of our kingdom hath to his house or land that we have not to our town of Hull'.[46]

It also, clearly, had an even more foreboding significance. During the Ship Money trial, Edward Littleton had pointed out that war these days was less easy to define than it had been. A formal declaration was no longer really necessary. Now wars 'begin by the sword, not by the trumpet or herald'.[47] His point had been that the country could effectively be at war with the Channel pirates without a declaration. Now this took on a chilling resonance. As yet, no trumpet had blared out to announce the formal beginning of hostilities. Charles, so far, had not unfurled his royal standard to announce the quelling of a rebellion. But the king was being denied access to his own arms and forts. Was this not akin to rebellion and war? Charles certainly thought so. He wrote to Parliament, demanding that they disown Hotham's actions. They refused. To Charles, this confirmed that they were in active rebellion. 'Actual war is levied on us,' was his view of what had just happened.[48]

Within days, military preparations were being stepped up on both sides. On 5 May, Parliament finally put the Militia Ordinance into execution, calling out the Trained Bands across the country.[49] On the 10th, the London militia was paraded on Finsbury Fields, watched by Essex in a new gilt coach, numerous peers, plenty of gentry, and an 'infinite shoal of people'.[50] It was a dramatic and grandiose occasion, though if a royalist rhymester is to believed, the effect was somewhat tarnished when a Parliamentarian colonel panicked at the sound of musket fire and ('oh, the foul disaster of his arse!') did 'beshit his hose in every seam'.[51]

Meanwhile in Yorkshire the king was busily trying to win over the local gentry so they would rally to him. On 12 May, he summoned them to attend him at the county town. Here he told them of his predicament, complaining of what had happened at Hull. He wanted a guard to protect himself. The response was mixed: the Yorkshiremen were split down the middle. Exasperated, Charles simply issued an order. By the 20th, the Yorkshire gentry must appear in arms to provide him a personal guard.[52]

Both sides were mobilising, though for now their forces remained ostensibly defensive. Neither had yet committed to raise a large marching army. One thing, though, was definitely changing in the king's favour. For in May, there was an increased flow of supporters, leaving the capital or elsewhere, and travelling to York to join him. Charles himself helped to encourage this, deliberately forcing people to make their choice.

His boldest move of all was to summon to Yorkshire the remnants of his legal system. Despite the political crisis and the ever-encroaching sense of fear, the law courts had continued to sit. The assize judges had gone out on their winter circuit; local quarter sessions had continued to meet in county towns.

It was time, therefore, to remove its nerve centre from Westminster and towards the person of the king. So, on 15 May, Charles ordered that the central law courts be moved to York.[53]

He had also, earlier that month, finally summoned his senior active judge to his side. Sir John Bankes, at last, would have to make his choice.

21

Not Master of the People of England

The letter from Charles was dictated at York on 4 May. It arrived in London a few days later. Addressed 'To our trusty and right wellbeloved councillor Sir John Bankes', it bore the 'sign manual': the personal signature of the king. 'We have,' Charles wrote, 'some occasions of importance' in which 'we think good and are very desirous to receive your advice and assistance.' After all, the king had experience of Bankes's 'affection, wisdom and integrity'. To provide this counsel Bankes must come to York without delay.[1]

If he went, it would take him far away from Mary, who was now six months pregnant. Nonetheless, he made his decision. He sought contact with key members of the Parliamentarian leadership, and informed them that he had been summoned by the king, and that he planned to go to York. But he assured them that he would use his presence there to push for peace.[2]

On arrival at York, Bankes found a city brimming with courtiers and soldiers. The place had been transformed by the arrival of the royal court.[3] Bankes's journey was widely noted. Given his reluctance to leave London until now, and his acceptance of a commission under the radical Militia Ordinance, he had become a bellwether.[4] Quickly Bankes wrote to Northumberland in London. The king was concerned, he said, about 'intrusions upon his prerogative as cannot stand with monarchy', and that justice wasn't being done against those 'who scandalise the king's person and government by speeches, sermons, and pamphlets'. Charles was angry that eighteen months of the current Parliament hadn't brought a settlement of his revenue, and that the liturgy and discipline of the Church was being attacked. Charles also worried about the political loss of his bishops, which he considered to be a stalking horse for a constitutional revolution: 'a Presbyterian government as an introduction to a Commonwealth', i.e., a republic. In Bankes's view, Charles longstanding attachment to the episcopacy was really about protecting the monarchy; in his reading it was political rather than religious issues that were critical, while Charles's fear for his own person meant he was looking to protect himself with guards. Still, Bankes was breezily optimistic. 'I do not discern,' he told Northumberland, 'that the differences between his Majesty and the Houses are so great in substance.' If there was 'a willingness on all parts, they may be reconciled'.[5]

Northumberland wrote back, suggesting the negotiating position of Parliament – a way forward to an accommodation. Bankes was in a place where, wrote the earl, his 'wise and moderate counsels' might end 'unhappy differences'. Neither Parliament nor king 'are without fears and jealousies', Northumberland admitted. The king was rightly worried about having his 'authority and just rights invaded', just as Parliament feared 'losing that liberty which free born subjects ought to enjoy'. There were militants around the king, though, and there was a real fear that violent courses might be taken by either side. 'God forbid,' Northumberland continued, 'that either King or Parliament should by power and force go about to cure the present distempers, for that course can produce nothing but misery, if not ruin, both to King and People.'[6] Bankes must talk the king into peace, therefore. The alternative was unthinkable.

Bankes also wrote to the spidery Lord Saye. He and Bankes had shared involvement in the Treasury, and the viscount, though outwardly a radical Junto man, had kept himself secretly close to the king.[7] To Saye, Bankes reported that Charles was much offended by events at Hull. For this, the king 'desires satisfaction in point of honour' rather than 'revenue'. He reassured Saye that the decision of Charles to raise a guard – and to adjourn the law terms to York – had been taken before Bankes's arrival there (in a letter to another correspondent, he said he advised against them).[8] There was hope, too, for a reconciliation. If Parliament could put down their 'desires' about the Church and Commonwealth, then Charles could reply with his own expectations: 'For things to be brought into a right frame it must be effected by calm and moderate, not by violent ways.'[9]

Charles's preparations went on. On Friday 20 May, he ordered the publication of a collection of some of the supportive petitions he was now receiving from the country.[10] With the sun-set on the 21st, Bankes now sat down to write to Giles Green, his longstanding friend and ally, and MP for Corfe Castle. To Green, Bankes was more candid, and markedly less positive.

'It grieves my heart to see these distractions,' Bankes wrote. He had spoken his mind to the king, 'freely according to my conscience', but 'what hazards I have run of the king's indignation in a high measure, you will hear by other'. Charles was receiving contradictory counsel: 'All men give not the same advice,' he complained. 'I am here in a very hard condition, where I may be ruined both ways.' Worst of all, the king was 'extremely offended' with Bankes for his stance on the militia, saying he 'should have performed the part of an honest man in protesting against the illegality of the ordinance'. Charles had commanded him, upon his allegiance, to declare against the Militia Ordinance, but still Bankes was hesitant. It was too late now, anyway. He had given the king his view, but he didn't feel it was safe to give a legal opinion against the two houses. 'You know,' Bankes reminded Green, 'how cautious I have been in this particular.' He had tried not to offend either side. 'I have studied all means which way matters may be brought to a good conclusion between the king and the houses.' Force would be nothing but destructive, 'and if we should have civil wars, it would make us a miserable people'.[11]

There were real signs now of a threshold being crossed. Some people were becoming more outwardly radical. In the Commons, the MP Henry Ludlow shocked the chamber by declaring that Charles 'was not fit to govern nor wear a crown'.[12] Others were simply scared. 'We are like so many frighted people,' wrote Margaret Eure, a Yorkshire gentlewoman. 'For my part if I hear but a door creak, I take it to be a drum.'[13]

Parliament now believed Charles was raising a marching army, and on the 20th, it made the startling declaration that it thought the king, 'seduced by wicked counsel, intends to make war against the Parliament'.[14] Bankes's letters were widely talked about in London. Rumour had it that he had finally accepted the position of Lord Treasurer.[15] Bankes had written to Denzil Holles, one of the Five Members, who received his letter that day. Holles penned a response in the Commons chamber during a debate: 'I beseech your Lordship pardon this hasty scribble, written upon the clerk's desk.' With it, he enclosed the latest terms that Parliament wanted from the king. His view was that there was still considerable distance between the two sides, but if the king would 'forsake those counsels which carry him on to so high a dislike' of Parliament, then peace could still be found. Holles didn't say exactly who he meant.[16]

Another messenger had arrived in London on Saturday 21 May. This time he came from the king, and this time not publicly, but incognito. His name was Thomas Elliot, a groom of the Prince of Wales's bedchamber, and he was – in the euphemistic words of Edward Hyde – 'no polite man'.[17]

On arrival in the south, Elliot made straight for Westminster, and at around two or three in the afternoon, he presented himself at the office of Lord Keeper Littleton.

Since the turn of the year, Littleton had done much to offend the king. He had refused to put the Great Seal on the king's proclamation for the apprehension of the Five Members. He had voted in favour of the Bishops' Exclusion, and he had accepted that the Militia Bill was within the law.[18] And he had stayed resolutely at Westminster, with the Seal. If the king was to argue that his authority resided with his royal person, at York, then the absence of this key piece of state paraphernalia, and its keeper, was deeply inconvenient.

Some weeks earlier, the king had consulted with Hyde and Falkland about appointing a new Lord Keeper. John Selden, one of the greatest lawyers of the realm, had been suggested, but he was expected to refuse. The other option was John Bankes. The king, though, had serious misgivings. To Hyde and Falkland, who both respected Bankes very much, the problem was more that he was not quite resolute enough in these difficult times. He was, as Hyde recalled, too frightened, and 'not thought equal to that charge in a time of so much disorder, though otherwise he was a man of great abilities and unblemished integrity'.[19] So instead, the decision was taken to stick with who they already had.

When Elliot arrived in Westminster, Littleton had been suffering a sharpness of urine, which kept him indisposed, and led him to absent himself from the Lords. While laid up in his lodgings, he heard a knock at the door.

Elliot entered the chamber. Littleton was alone. The young man approached. He bore a letter from the king, he said, in the royal hand. It demanded that Littleton come to York and bring the Seal. If his health was so bad that he couldn't come quickly, he must give the Seal to Elliot, who would race back fast, and Littleton could follow.

Littleton was reluctant, but Elliot was insistent, menacing even. By Elliot's own account, he had to physically threaten the portly old judge. So Littleton yielded, and with the Seal now in his hands, Elliot saddled his horse and rode out to the north.

That Saturday evening, Littleton made it known that he was not to be disturbed, and he began his preparations. Then, in the early daylight of Sunday, he stepped into his coach and was away, out of London, and onto the great highway north.

It was only on Monday morning that the peers found their Speaker unexpectedly absent. The alarm was raised, and orders went out to apprehend him. A rider was despatched north as fast as possible, with orders to raise the posse comitatus if necessary. But it was already too late. The Lord Keeper was gone, as was the Great Seal. That evening London talked of little else.[20]

———

On that afternoon of 23 May, the day Littleton's flight became known about, a new committee was appointed in the Lords, to pen some new 'Propositions' to put to the king.[21] Of the peers involved, four were in contact with Bankes at York. It seemed at last that the peace initiative might be paying off.

The committee worked quickly, and by the morning of the 31st, was ready to report.[22] From the Commons, Holles was sent to hear them. He brought back fourteen proposals, which were read – one by one – and approved. Then a Commons committee, including Pym, Holles, Hampden, and St John, was appointed to see if any more could be added. They went off to another room in the palace, and were ready that evening. Four more demands had been added. Then, in the Commons the following morning, another was tacked on, so this was now a document of nineteen negotiating points.

The next morning, 1 June, the 'Nineteen Propositions' – the document that more than anything set out the Parliamentarian cause – was ready to be voted by the Lords. On the 2nd, a delegation began its journey up the Great North Road, to Charles, carrying the Junto's proposals for peace.

Their claims were for the thorough triumph of Parliament over the king. The government, the Privy Council, and the judges would now be chosen by the legislature. The Militia Ordinance would be accepted, in full, and fortresses put in Parliament's hands. There would be strong action against recusancy, with the children of Catholics educated as Protestants; the Church was to be reformed. No peers would be allowed to sit in the Lords without the consent of Parliament. All public matters must be debated in Parliament, and the Five Members and Lord Mandeville would be fully exonerated. If Charles accepted the Nineteen Propositions, he would be consenting to his almost complete annihilation as sovereign. He truly would be little more than a duke of Venice: a figurehead.

Conservatives continued to slip out of London and make for York, and both sides were now engaging in propaganda campaigns.

Parliament was printing its key declarations and Charles had his own printing press at York. He didn't shrink from a bit of public theatre, either. On 3 June he held a grand meeting on nearby Heworth Moor. Many thousands attended, covering the flat heathy landscape with horses, gentlemen in hats and coats, and a royal party complete with Charles's new armed guard. At one point, a young Yorkshire knight called Sir Thomas Fairfax rode up to the mounted king. He had a petition, setting out the Parliamentarian case. Charles refused to hear it, and Fairfax was jostled and abused by the Cavaliers. Still, he managed to lay the petition on the back of Charles's saddle.

As spring marched on towards summer, both sides were jockeying for position. Charles received discouraging word from Scotland, where his stock remained low, but much more positive news from Wales, where there was a rich vein of loyalty.[23]

Then, in early June, Charles seems to have resolved – finally – that he must formally declare war. In order to do so, he would raise his royal standard: the accepted signal that his people should flock to his banner and crush the rebellion. The decision was announced to a council of peers on the 7th, but the immediate reaction was very mixed, and Charles wavered.[24]

The mood in York among those who hoped for peace was evidently dark. Three lords shortly afterward left the city – apparently having entreated the king to abandon the plan. Two were leading moderates – Salisbury and Lord Clare (Denzil Holles's brother) – but the third was the Earl of Dorset, the loyalist whose guard had nearly fired on protesters in Parliament back in November.[25]

It was shortly after this – a day or two perhaps – that Bankes asked for another audience with the king.

———

All of York knew it was happening, and everyone heard of the outcome when Bankes left the royal presence. Charles had decided once more to pursue peace. Bankes had persuaded him to return to London.[26] The wounds of England might yet be healed. One might only imagine the joyous reception the king would receive as he travelled towards London. Some kind of constitutional monarchical settlement would be reached.

But nothing came. Charles changed his mind again. The king was vacillating wildly. For all the peacemakers like Bankes could do, Charles remained loyal to his queen. Back in March, she had heard rumours at the Hague that Charles would return to London. 'I believe nothing of it,' she wrote to him, 'and hope that you are more constant in your resolutions.'[27] Whatever Charles said to his peacemaker advisors, his loyalty was to her.

By now the queen was actually in a position to start sending her husband more than just encouraging letters: 100 barrels of powder, 6 cannons, and 200 pairs of pistols and carabines were ready to cross the North Sea.[28]

People were openly discussing the coming conflict. In Salisbury, on Friday 10 June, an apothecary called Thomas Stevens ended up in a row with one Henry Whatley, while they were both standing in the doorway of one Widow Howell. After speaking a while, 'they did talk of wars', and Whatley 'wished that there might be civil wars'. If there were, he said, salivating at the prospect of carrying on some obscure personal feud, 'the first that he would pitch upon should be John Braxton'. Whatley said that he would be a royalist: 'for the king'. Stevens was unimpressed, replying that for his part he would 'be also for the king', 'and', he emphasised, 'the Parliament'. To this Whatley scoffed: 'For the Parliament? I do not care a pin for the Parliament.' After all, 'they were a company of rebels'.[29]

Both sides were arming. On 10 June, Parliament launched a new appeal for money, claiming that 'enjoyments of the blessed fruits of this present Parliament' were likely to be ruined by 'wicked hands' unless they raised a force.[30] The next day Charles announced the so-called 'Commissions of Array'. These were somewhat archaic. Rendered into Latin, they ordered supporters to 'array' themselves in arms and rally to defend the king from rebels.

Then, suddenly, Charles was persuaded to issue a declaration promising that he really wanted peace. Forty-two names were included on the 'Protestation of Peace', including various leading nobles and Falkland, Culpeper, Nicholas, Littleton, and Bankes. It assured the public of the king's 'abhorring all designs of making war upon his Parliament'. They were, they professed, 'fully persuaded that his Majesty hath no such intention'.[31]

Charles was either hoping for peace and preparing for war – or he was simply being utterly deceptive. Such is the way with him that it is almost impossible to tell. In any case, with the ink barely dry on this declaration, Charles put the array into execution, raising troops in the counties to counter Parliament. Then, on 17 June, he at last got his North Sea port, for Newcastle had been taken in his name. It meant Charles could receive supplies from Henrietta Maria. He was getting stronger, more confident. One royalist, writing like a sports pundit predicting the outcome of a horse race, declared that the king was 'the favourite of the kingdom'.[32]

England was fraying. People were having to think about which side they would take. Printed declarations from both sides were circulated through the country. The minister of Ducklington in Oxfordshire kept a manuscript diary of all the texts he read – it is full of newsbooks, declarations, justifications, and propaganda from king and Parliament.[33] A choice was being thrust down people's throats. It was like they were caught between Scylla and Charybdis, one horrified Englishman wrote in July.[34]

Some tried to stay neutral; for others, the decision had long been obvious. The Five Members were as active as ever: far from being cowed, they had emerged as heroes of the cause – Mandeville too, though he had been hit by a personal tragedy that winter when his Puritan wife, Lady Anne, died. Edward Nicholas meanwhile had been at the king's side since January. He had followed him to York, and was thoroughly busy. 'I am tired with the care and pains of it,' he wrote of his employment from Theobalds, when his master was on his way north in March.[35]

He sounded like Speaker Lenthall had in December, but now the latter may even have been experiencing a new lease of life, as Nicholas would, too, in time. War was horrific, but for some it was galvanising. People could no longer hide from their own convictions.

Lady Carlisle, on the other hand, seems to shrink from the record in these months. With the royal court and the queen gone, she will have spent more of her time with her family, the Percys, either in London or at her sister Dorothy's country residence in Sussex. For now, she was keeping her head down.

Her old patron, Henrietta Maria, was still in the Hague, where her health was suffering grievously. The queen had constant toothache, so severe 'that I scarcely know what I am doing'. Her eyesight was beginning to fail. She was selling beloved jewels, including some of the king's pearl buttons – 'You cannot imagine how handsome the buttons were,' she wrote. She felt isolated, though some English courtiers like Digby were starting to visit her. She still pushed Charles to be firm. 'Remember your own maxims, that it is better to follow out a bad resolution than to change it so often,' she reminded him. 'Lose no time,' she wrote at the end of May, 'for that will ruin you.'[36]

John Bankes, meanwhile, spent much of June fretting about his decision to accept the Militia Ordinance. A series of letters had been written to Charles by Lord Willoughby of Parham, an aristocrat who was busily raising troops for Parliament in Lincolnshire. As his excuse, he cited the acceptance of commissions under the Militia Ordinance by Bankes and Littleton.[37] At a time when Bankes in particular was trying to act as a go-between, to encourage king and Parliament to come to a peaceful accommodation, this was damaging indeed, not least when Willoughby's letters were published, twice.[38]

Everywhere the rights and wrongs were debated in fields and alehouses and churchyards. 'I care not for the king, or his laws,' a Yorkshireman had announced in church that spring, on Charles's accession day, no less.[39] 'King Charles put on Pym's gown, and let Pym wear the Crown,' went one rhyme.[40] 'What speak you of the king? He is nothing but words,' said a Hertfordshire parishioner to a shocked clergyman.[41] A doctor was imprisoned and fined £100 for saying he would cut John Pym in pieces, despite offering the excuse that he had merely been drunk.[42] A short London pamphlet printed on 2 July lamented the divisions between 'Roundheads' and 'Cavaliers', and how 'discord hath made mens' tongues wrangle and jangle'.[43]

At least it was a world that still left room for controversialist writers like John Taylor, who remained his old self. Since January, the waterman's main focus had been a long-simmering dispute within his trade. On one occasion he launched an absolutely rancid attack on his enemies, jibing that his main antagonist in the company had the face of a baboon, and so did his mother. His old foe Henry Walker, meanwhile, was now of no little notoriety. In fact, he was on the run. It was only in the summer that he was apprehended (again) – at which point John Taylor popped up to note with malicious glee how his rival had begged for mercy in a most humiliating manner.[44]

––––––

It wasn't just the old scurrility that filled the presses now. There was a vibrant debate over the Militia Ordinance, the array, and the constitutional implications of Hotham's defiance on the walls of Hull. Charles himself had come to believe that without control of the militia, 'Kingly power is but a shadow.' Others that the royal prerogative itself was only ever derived from Parliament, so in an emergency Parliament could legitimately take control of armed force.[45] Most important of all, the Nineteen Propositions were energising arguments about power and the state. They were widely circulated. Ambassador Giustinian had them translated into Italian and sent to his masters in Venice.[46] Charles, meanwhile, began to organise a response. For this, he tasked Lord Falkland and John Culpeper, respectively the senior secretary of state and the Chancellor of the Exchequer.

Within weeks their text was ready. It attacked the Nineteen Propositions for their constitutional innovation, arguing that they were inherently subversive, not just of the king, but of the whole social order. They were grounded not in the ancient constitution, but in the Peasants' Revolt and other medieval rebellions. 'There being three kinds of government amongst men,' it declared: 'Absolute monarchy, Aristocracy and Democracy.' All these had good sides and bad, so the wisdom of our English ancestors had moulded a balance out of the three. What Parliament were suggesting would lean way too far towards democracy. The House of Commons in particular, was 'an excellent conserver of liberty, but never intended for any share in Government, or the choosing of them that should govern'. This was the critical matter. Falkland and Culpeper could accept the Commons protecting the privileges of the subject and defending English liberties. But they were not supposed to appoint executive officers. If all this were allowed, the king's *Answer to the XIX Propositions* famously claimed, then the common people – growing bored of manual labour – would rise, 'destroy all rights and properties, all distinctions of families and merits; and by this means this splendid and excellently distinguished form of Government' would 'end in a dark equal chaos of confusion, and the long line of our many noble ancestors in a Jack Cade or a Wat Tyler'. It was read in Parliament on 21 June, to considerable dismay at its 'high language'.[47]

Such was the complexity of the issues that there was a strong royalist critique of the *Answer to the XIX Propositions*. To Hyde, writing later, Falkland and Culpeper had committed a serious blunder by referring to the three estates as king, Lords, and Commons. Rather, the three estates were those who sat in Parliament: lords, bishops, and commons. The king should have been above them as arbitrator. Falkland and Culpeper had already relegated the monarchy to become just one part of a triumvirate.[48]

But the most explosive riposte came from the Parliamentarians, and particularly from a pamphleteer called Henry Parker. Hailing from a wealthy Sussex background, and a nephew of Lord Saye, Parker had already made his mark with a stirring attack on Ship Money in 1640. Now he turned his pen to Falkland and Culpeper. 'Power,' he argued, 'is originally inherent in the people.' All authority 'is but fiduciary'; a magistrate was 'more or less absolute, as he is more or less trusted'.[49] If the king had lost the trust of the people, then Parliament was now the custodian of legitimate authority. Parker was arguing, in essence, that because Parliament represented the people, *it* was the sovereign body, not the king.

———

By the end of June, there were still some faint voices of optimism. Dorset was one, against the odds: he thought, after everything, 'that an easy and safe way may be found to lead us all forth this dark and inextricable labyrinth'.[50] But the mood in the House of Commons was now unutterably grim.

On 1 July, Simonds D'Ewes was so horrified and despondent that he set down his pen: 'I, seeing all matters tending to speedy destruction and confusion, had no heart to take notes that afternoon.'[51] There had been some better news for Parliament when a naval squadron had managed to remove the Hull arsenal and carry it south to London, but Charles was now in the process of attempting to seize a large magazine in Leicestershire. And he received a stunning boost, too, when Lord Herbert, eldest son of the Earl of Worcester, appeared in York with nearly £100,000 in cash.[52] Enough to pay for an army.

The king also tried to take control of the navy. Charles had dismissed Northumberland as Lord High Admiral and sent the trusted Admiral Pennington from York all the way down to Kent to assume command. Parliament, though, wanted to appoint the Earl of Warwick. Pennington rode fast on his horse along the long chalky roads of Kent, but then stopped near his destination to await further instructions. In doing so he allowed Warwick to beat him to the Downs. Boarding the flagship, Warwick summoned the captains. Five tried to resist him and give their loyalty to Charles, but they found the crews on their own ships unwilling to support their act of resistance. So the navy was in Warwick's, and Parliament's, hands. It was a serious blow for Charles, and of course for Henrietta Maria – whose return to England might now need to be under the fire of enemy cannons.

To the Junto, the king's actions were little short of a declaration of war. On 4 July, a critical decision was reached. A new Committee of Safety would be appointed, which would act as an executive.[53] Having failed to cajole Charles into giving them a veto over the royal government, Parliament had now simply created its own. Then, on the 6th, Parliament voted to raise a marching army.

Now the royalists were reported to be gathering strength in the West Midlands, one of the strategic and economic heartlands of

England. The king himself granted commissions to raise cavalry, and on the 9th, appointed the Earl of Lindsey as general of his army. There was little pretence of peace left, and the Commons quickly put their vote for an army into execution. Ten thousand would be raised and there would be no further delay. The Junto peer Essex was made general. On 11 July, Parliament passed another declaration. It stated that the country was in a condition of war, and that the king had started it.

That same day, John Bankes wrote again to Saye. The tone was notably more recriminatory. The arguments over Hull could have been avoided, argued Bankes, if only you had listened. What *should* have happened, Bankes claimed, was that Parliament should have found a way to vindicate the king's honour, Hotham could then have been pardoned. Now the town was surrounded by cannons, Hotham had flooded the nearby fields of corn, grass and hay, and all that would follow was 'the effusion of Christian blood'.[54]

Back in May, Bankes continued, he had been told (he didn't say who by), that Parliament needed to ease off with the remonstrances and declarations, and simply 'make some short propositions unto his Majesty, who was then very well inclined to any honourable accommodation'. Instead, Parliament had persisted with their confrontational path, passing a vote saying the king intended to make war against Parliament. 'Then,' he wrote, 'comes the 19 Propositions.' His tone was one of exasperation. 'What answers could be expected?' Bankes demanded of Saye. The King, warned Bankes, 'is now in a condition not to have anything inforced from him'.[55]

Bankes was right. Since the beginning of June, the king's fortunes had dramatically improved. He had a port, he had soldiers, and he had money. He was offered major gifts of cash by the two universities: Oxford provided £10,000, Cambridge £6,000. For the first time in months, his military victory was possible. He had tried winning the votes in Parliament, he had tried conspiracy, and he had tried disruption. Each time he had been outmanoeuvred. Now, he was finally in the position to go all out with military force, an option he had toyed with numerous times. By July 1642, he had both the resources and the resolve.

There might just have been one last chance for peace. The Earl of Holland, an ambitious courtier, once a suitor to Lady Carlisle, and now one of the more moderate Parliamentarians, was sent with a petition to Yorkshire. He met the king at Beverley, where he reminded his sovereign of his father King James's motto: 'Blessed are the peacemakers.'[56] The petition offered a realistic basis for settlement: the king would stand down his forces, Hull would be restored to him, and a compromise would follow on the militia. But Charles was unmoved, indeed he was offended by the language of the petition, which he thought was reproachful and hurt his honour. An opportunity for accommodation swiftly passed.[57]

There had also been a major brawl in Manchester town centre between supporters of king and Parliament. At least one of those wounded later died – one report had said dozens were slain – and the scrap would have been even worse if the heavy incessant summer rain hadn't put out the musketeers' matches.[58] Everywhere there was bad blood. 'Many people grow bold, heady and audaciously violent,' it was said of North Wales, 'and spare not many of them to publish their minds in dangerous speeches.'[59] The talk was getting fiercer in Parliament too. 'Though the king be king of the people of England, yet he is not master of the people of England,' Henry Marten told the Commons.[60] The question now was simply *when* the country would finally cascade over the precipice.

———

By July, Mary Bankes was entering the final stages of her pregnancy. She was at the family retreat at Stanwell in Middlesex. Her husband, meanwhile, had been despatched from York with his fellow assize judges out on their circuits. Bankes's patch would be the Norfolk circuit, which covered East Anglia – a wealthy, Puritan stronghold. Aside from a short pass through Buckinghamshire, it would take him far distant from Mary.

Late in the month, Bankes had come south, apparently stopping briefly near London.[61] He surely took the opportunity to visit Mary, but soon he was riding out again. During the assizes, the king invited the counties to declare their grievances. In many cases, it was a request that backfired. A letter from the Grand Jury at Buckinghamshire, handed over to Bankes, declared that 'fear of civil war' was theirs. The reason was that the king was raising an army, which was 'a sight terrible to your people and not conducive to that amicable accommodation so much desired'.[62]

On 30 July, Bankes was at the assizes at Bury St Edmunds in Suffolk. Such was the divide in the county that two petitions were being prepared. One was remarkably forthright. It complained that 'the country is full of grief and fear for his majesty's long absence from his Parliament and refusal to be informed and advised by their counsel'. He had rejected their moves towards accommodation and their most recent plans to reform the Church. They were 'much affrighted' by the king's preparations for war and by his commissions of array. These, indeed, 'we humbly conceive [are] not agreeable to his majesty's frequent protestations of government by law and not by arbitrary power'. Indeed they were 'declared illegal by the Parliament, in whom the power of declaring the law doth reside'.[63]

The other petition was very different.[64] Its tone was considerably more deferential. It commended Charles for his 'great and general care for the safety and prosperity of us', and his 'religious vigilancy and endeavour for the suppressing of popery', as well for the 'equal prevention and stopping of the growth of anabaptism and other schisms'. It lauded his punishment of sedition, his support for the 'true Protestant religion', his ruling by law and not by arbitrary power, his maintenance of the privileges of Parliament 'as far as ever any of your royal predecessors have done'. It also commended Charles for punishing insurrections, riots, and unlawful assemblies, not to mention 'rogues, vagabonds, and disorderly persons'.

What Bankes didn't know, as he contemplated these two petitions, was that the very same day, Mary had given birth, to a healthy baby girl – named Arabella.[65]

In Warwickshire, that day, the 30th, there was a stand-off on Kineton Heath, beneath the crest of Edgehill. At about 10 o'clock in the morning, Lord Brooke, one of the staunchest Junto peers, was intercepted trying to transfer guns from Banbury to Warwick Castle, which he owned. His way was blocked by the royalist Earl of Northampton and a larger force. Eyeing his enemy across the heather, Brooke had his troops edge forward to just within musket shot. For a moment all was still.

A parley was agreed. The two commanders met while Brooke's soldiers visibly charged their weapons. Northampton demanded that Brooke hand over his ordnance, surrender Warwick Castle, and cease executing the Militia Ordinance. Brooke refused. Northampton suggested single combat. Brooke refused. Northampton suggested that twenty men be selected from both sides to fight it out. Brooke refused. As the day went on and the sun passed across the wide Warwickshire sky, local countryfolk brought bread and cheese and beer to reinforce Brooke's Parliamentarian troops. Others joined their ranks, and by 5 p.m., the two sides were much more evenly matched than they had been in the morning. A compromise was reached: Brooke would return to Banbury and give three days' notice to Northampton if he wished to move his guns again.[66]

It wasn't the only such moment. Within days, the Marquess of Hertford was trying to raise Somerset for the king, but was faced with a mass uprising among the local farmers, forcing him to retreat. All the while, the assizes were continuing to meet, providing an opportunity to air grievances and angry disagreement. On the western circuit, there were numerous complaints about the 'illegality' of the array.[67] In Warwickshire, one JP put in an indictment against Lord Brooke for executing the Militia Ordinance.[68] Different towns had different responses. When Richard Baxter was in Worcester, he heard cries of 'down with the Roundheads!'; when he was in Gloucester, he found a 'civil, courteous, and religious people, as different from Worcester as if they had lived under another government'.[69]

Parliament realised they would need money, so the vast sum of £100,000 was diverted from the Irish campaign to fund Essex's army.[70] They were also now discussing a manifesto that set out why they felt they had to take up arms. This was ready by 2 August. It bore Pym's influence, but there was also input from Northumberland, Holland, Pembroke, and Saye.[71] It was constitutionally radical, and politically uncompromising. A war was needed against those who had 'possessed' the king, it said. Giustinian thought that it was tantamount to a declaration of war.[72] The drafters, though, evidently believed that war had already begun. In the preamble to the declaration, it was alleged that there was 'a malignant party, prevailing with His Majesty, putting Him upon violent and perilous ways, and now in Arms against us'. They would not rest satisfied 'with having Hull, or taking away the Ordinance of the Militia'. Rather they wished 'to destroy the Parliament, and be masters of Our Religion and Liberties, To make Us slaves, and alter the Government of this Kingdom'. They would reduce this government 'to the condition of some other Countries, which are not governed by Parliaments, and so by Laws, but by the will of the Prince, or rather of those who are about him'. To stop this, Parliament resolved, therefore, to 'live and die' with Essex and the cause.[73]

Within days, word arrived of a major skirmish at Marshall's Elm in Somerset on 4 August, in which a Parliamentarian force had been ambushed, resulting in significant losses. More than two dozen had been killed, and three score taken prisoner.

That week, Charles was given another significant piece of positive news.[74] George Goring had been waiting out the political crisis in Portsmouth, where he remained military governor. He had always been loyal to Charles, but his revelations – now over a year ago – of the Tower Plot back in the spring of 1641, during Strafford's trial, had convinced some in the Junto that he was on their side. His cards had stayed hidden throughout the crisis. Now Goring the gambler had finally declared his hand. Portsmouth was delivered up to Charles. With this and Newcastle, the king was in a much stronger position than he had been two months ago, when he first decided to raise his standard as a formal declaration of war. Now, he could contemplate doing so again.

The crux came around the start of the second week of August, the very height of summer. On the 8th, Parliament agreed to a fiery declaration, calling out the Trained Bands and other troops to 'resist those who take up arms against Parliament'. Denouncing their enemies as 'traitors', it enjoined supporters to 'fight, kill and slay' anyone who opposed them by force.[75] At the same time, Charles was putting the finishing touches on a Proclamation that admitted out loud what everyone already knew – that England was in a state of civil war. Essex was proclaimed a traitor and his followers were given six days to lay down their arms. The Commons reacted with immediate horror, and through the 9th, members were told to declare that they would live and die with Essex. The few who showed reluctance were bullied into complying. One asked for more time and was told to declare his hand now. With the issue forced, the MP boldly refused. Speaker Lenthall then harangued him into changing his mind, at which point he was told that it was already too late. After this, no one dared raise objections.[76]

War, to all intents and purposes, had already arrived. On 12 August, Charles finally issued the proclamation that had been in preparation for some time. It signified the final step in the long descent. Loyal subjects were to rally to him on the 22nd of the month, when he would put up his royal standard in Nottingham. It was a town, some will have noted, only slightly closer to York than it was to London; and it was well placed to serve as a base for a royal march across the Midlands, gathering support – especially in the west.

Nobody could see the future. Some of the alehouse talk came remarkably close though. In Norwich, a group of tradesmen were found uttering 'very foul and scandalous words against the Parliament'. They had cried: 'A health to our gracious king, and confusion bring to factious Pym!', and predicted that: 'If the king should go to the Parliament,' then it 'would take way his Prerogative and commit him to prison, and take off his head'.[77]

By the third week of August, Charles was at Coventry. Here he was refused entry, unless he agreed to leave his Cavaliers outside with guns trained on them, so they didn't feel the urge to pillage.

This time, Charles was prepared for battle. His cannons opened fire on the walls of the old medieval city. According to Giustinian, still writing his despatches back to Venice from London, the king, 'filled with resentment', attempted 'to force a way in with a bomb'.[78] As yet the royalists only did limited damage, and when the king ordered the attack, his Cavaliers were severely bloodied and repulsed.

It was 22 August, and Charles now began a swift journey north, riding on horseback for speed, towards Nottingham. He arrived there in the afternoon. Within hours the royal standard, the symbol of open war, was ready.

Epilogue

The Highest Room

On 12 August, less than a fortnight before Charles raised his standard at Nottingham Castle, he publicly admitted that his own Personal Rule had been a mistake. He acknowledged 'the inconveniences and mischiefs which had grown by the long intermission of Parliaments, and by departing too much from the known rule of the law to an arbitrary power'.[1] But, he said, his enemies were now the ones abandoning the law. They were legislating without the royal veto – raising troops no less – and had denied the king access to his fortresses. They had even declared those who supported him to be traitors.

It is a remarkable statement of the royalist cause, and it reserved special ire for the six men Charles had tried to prosecute in January: Mandeville, and the Five Members. Reading it from his tiny Oxfordshire parish, the rector of Ducklington, Thomas Wyatt, noted the king's declaration, describing it as 'a very large and most excellent thing, reciting all wrongs offered to him'. It offered pardons 'to all his loving subjects', but not to a select group: 'Lord Kimbolton [Mandeville], Mr Holles, Mr Pym, Mr Hampden, Sir Arthur Haselrig, Mr Strode', and a small number of hardline radicals.* [2]

*These were Henry Marten, Sir Henry Ludlow, Isaac Pennington, Captain John Venn.

Charles had had the chance to arrest the Five Members. But they had been warned to absent themselves from the Commons that day, definitely by Lady Carlisle, and likely via Mandeville himself. It is one of those times where history could have turned out very differently. What if Lucy Carlisle hadn't warned them? Perhaps if Charles and the queen had been less dismissive of her brother Northumberland? Or what if Lenthall hadn't defied the king in the chamber? Perhaps if Edward Nicholas had been more sympathetic to the Speaker's request to be allowed to resign just a month previous. The crisis of 1641–2 is full of split-second moments like this, where several different paths were spread out ahead.

Yet there were deeper structural reasons too. The civil war was too momentous to have started on a mere coincidence. For, when the first blood was shed that winter – of Sir Richard Wiseman, the angry baronet, and of the protestors on their way past Whitehall, who clashed with the loyalist Cavaliers – it was during riotous crowd protests. These – the voice of the streets of London, the politics that took place 'out of doors' – formed the decisive backdrop against which the crisis played out. When Charles came to issue his declaration of 12 August, he castigated the Junto for, among many other crimes, bringing out the London crowd: 'Now their resort was to the people, whom upon several occasions they had trained down to Westminster in great multitudes with swords and clubs.'[3]

The civil war that followed was over many things. Religion lay very close to its heart. It was a fight over different visions of the Church: Puritans versus anti-Puritans, though within these two broad camps, there were many complexities. The royalists had support from moderates, Laudians and Catholics. The Parliamentarians would split between Presbyterians and Independents – but they also had some moderate Episcopalians and plenty of Separatists. When the actual fighting started, though, it wasn't so much about religion – directly at least – it was about who had control over the state: about the Militia Ordinance, Hull, and the demands in the Nineteen Propositions for parliamentary control of the government.

It was also about trust, and because it was about trust, it was about the right to hold onto power; and no single moment defined and exemplified that lack of trust more than when Charles took an armed force to Parliament to arrest the Five Members. Looking back, the astrologer William Lilly was convinced that this was the spark to what followed. 'This rash action of the King's lost him his Crown,' he wrote, for it 'left scarce any possibility of reconcilement; he not being willing to trust them, nor they to trust him.'[4]

There's a poem in John Bankes's personal archive, headed 'Up, Up, Wrong'd Charles'. It appears in a later collection entitled *On the Queen's Departure*, but the Bankes manuscript, which is not in his hand, dates it to '12 January 1641' (it uses old style dating, so it means 1642), immediately after Charles fled Whitehall following his attempt on the Five Members. It laments the plight of the king, and how, in a celestial universe, 'the inferior orbs aspire and do disdain/ to meet at all, unless they may obtain/ the highest room'. It would bring chaos, and 'cursed anarchy', 'sedition', 'murther', and 'rapine'. 'Take heed bold stars,' it warns, 'you'll set the world on fire.'[5] The audacity of these upstart orbs, the poet was saying, would burn the country. The world was turning upside down. It was 'a sad presage of danger to the land,' rhymed another royalist poem, 'when Lower strive to get th'upper hand'.[6]

In 1643, as the country realised this would not be a short war, one of the most entertaining royalist newsbooks began to appear. From their tentative beginnings in the workshop of John Thomas, the diurnals were now starting to flourish, and both sides were using the periodical press to get their side of the story across. The new royalist weekly was called *Mercurius Rusticus*, and was published in Oxford, which had by then become the king's capital. The name an attempt to co-opt the rural soul of England, against the strange City of London and its weird religious groups and upstart Parliamentarians. Its author was Bruno Ryves, a man well known to John and Mary Bankes, for until June 1642, he had been their minister at Stanwell.[7]

In one particularly notable passage, *Rusticus* reflects on the strange 'principles' that had come from 'these cobblers and tailors' who made up the ranks of the London sects and who supported Parliament. They argued that kings were a burden and a plague, that relations between master and servant had no basis in the New Testament. They said that noble titles were 'but ethnical and heathenish not to be retained amongst Christians'. Some had been heard attacking the idea that 'one man should have a Thousand pounds a year, and another not one pound, perhaps not so much, but must live by the sweat of his brows, and must labour before he eat'. Such inequality, so they said, 'hath no ground, neither in Nature or in Scripture'. Some argued that 'the common people' had hitherto been 'slaves to the nobility and gentry', but God had 'opened their eyes and discovered unto them their Christian liberty'. Now, therefore, the 'Nobility and Gentry should serve their Servants, or at least work for their own maintenance.'[8]

How much of this Ryves had actually heard is uncertain, but to him the Puritanism of the sects was inherently linked to social radicalism: a genuine economic egalitarianism that drew its inspiration from Scripture. In the beginning there had been no kings. There had also been no private property. The political challenge launched by Parliament against the king's regal power, and in favour of a much less hierarchical approach to religion, had the potential to open the door to a more thorough social revolution. So the royalist side thought, at least.

The Parliamentarians didn't consider themselves radicals. The vast majority would have baulked at the idea of tearing down the fabric of society. They tended to be Puritans, and were for the most part much more tolerant of the Independents and Separatists, though there was always a spread of opinions (and they would split irrevocably within a few years). Key to their beliefs, in the end, was the idea that royal power should be closely limited; that Parliament's issuing of the Militia Ordinance was constitutional; and that sovereignty, ultimately, lay with the legislature and the people it represented. To the royalists this was a challenge to the social order. Tear down bishops, or overturn the ancient constitution in favour of greater parliamentary control of the government, and social revolution would inevitably follow. They were wrong in this, and the social revolution would have to wait, but advocates of drastic change and renewal did appear within the Parliamentarian army. And in 1649, Charles would be put on trial and executed, and the monarchy abolished. We shouldn't underplay the sheer radicalism of this event. It was shocking, profound, and changed the country forever.

The royalists had always had a point about that. The Parliamentarian cause was more revolutionary than its adherents cared to admit. Indeed, in order to achieve their constitutional challenge to Charles in 1641 and 1642, the Junto – both Commons men like Pym, and leading peers like Essex, Warwick, and Northumberland – had played a dangerously demotic game. They had relied on their allies among the people of London. Charles didn't flee Parliament because they'd raised an army against him; but because they'd raised the streets. If it was one incident more than any that scared him away, it was Henry Walker's throwing his pamphlet, *To Your Tents, O Israel*, into the royal coach. This was a people's revolution as well as a noble revolt.

A few days after Charles set up his standard, there was a meeting of the Privy Council in Nottingham. Charles didn't attend; only seven people did, among them Edward Nicholas and John Bankes.[9] Very soon, Charles would move west towards the Welsh Marches, where he would raise a new army, ready to launch an attack on London. Nicholas would dutifully follow the king. Bankes, on the other hand, would peel off and head south.

One of the most pressing things John Bankes did, as a new winter approached, was to make his will. It is a document that shows how far he had come. His wealth was vast, and he ensured it was shared. He left a large endowment for his hometown of Keswick, to set up a house in which the poor could be provided with work. His legacy lives on in the town. His birthplace is currently occupied by a Wetherspoon's pub, which is only slightly inaccurately named 'The Chief Justice of the Common Pleas'. He is also commemorated by a plaque that lauds his 'love for his native place and his wise and generous sympathy for the poor and needy'. Intriguingly the only politician he left money to, aside from relatives, was Giles

Green – his Dorset neighbour and MP for Corfe Castle and, by this point, very much a Parliamentarian. Green was given a silver plate worth £10, and asked to be a trustee of part of the estate. The will is a fascinating document, but there is little sense in it of the coming violence. The only possible hint is in the preamble. Testators often wrote their wills when they believed they were close to death, noting that they were sick in body but sound in mind. Bankes did something different, stating that he was 'in perfect health and understanding' but was 'weighing the frailty and uncertainty of this mortal life'. At no year in recent English history can life have felt more frail and uncertain than 1642.[10]

On the day before Bankes completed his will, just south of Worcester one of the king's nephews encountered a force of Parliamentarian horse troopers. He was Prince Rupert, a man who had only recently come to England from the Continent, where he had grown up in an environment of war and plunder. Alerted to a Parliamentarian force approaching Worcester, then held for the king, Rupert had his men form up and ordered them to fire and charge. The Parliamentarians were routed, despite a heroic rear-guard action on Powick Bridge, an ancient stone crossing on the River Teme. Dozens were killed, mostly on the Parliamentarian side, though the royalists quickly abandoned Worcester anyway.

It was time for hiding away, or for taking sides. Usually events caught up with everyone, though. On 25 August, the Earl of Dorset's beloved Knole was attacked and plundered by Parliamentarian troops. John Taylor, meanwhile, found himself arrested for making snide comments about the Five Members. Luckily, there were no willing witnesses so he was released, after which he immediately headed to the tavern.[11] George Goring had long picked his side, and he would become a leading royalist commander, despite his wound in his leg. His 'crew' became, possibly unfairly, one of the most notorious royalist regiments for violence and destruction.[12] Edward Nicholas was another steadfast loyalist. He remained an advisor to Charles through the war, until the king's surrender in 1646.[13] Given six months to settle his affairs, Nicholas soon realised he would not be pardoned by the victorious Parliamentarians, so he fled the country. Through the republican years he was on the Continent, where he fell out with the queen but continued to serve the Stuart Pretender, who in 1660 would become Charles II. At the Restoration, Nicholas was rewarded, and returned to the English government. He was vigorous against the Regicides – those who put their names to Charles's death warrant – and he personally signed the order to have Oliver Cromwell's body exhumed and hanged in 1661. He had enemies, though, including the king's mistress, Barbara Villiers, and Henrietta Maria (now queen mother) herself, and in 1662, he surrendered his office. Retiring to Surrey, he spent his later years writing a history of the Long Parliament and an autobiography. He died there in 1669, survived by his wife, Jane – who lived until 1688, by which time another revolution was engulfing the Stuart kingdoms.

William Lenthall, meanwhile, had been pushed in the other direction. To Simonds D'Ewes, who remained in Parliament even though he was dismayed by the hardliners there, Lenthall was too much in a thrall to the 'fiery spirits'. Either way, the quiet Speaker from sleepy Oxfordshire would not be allowed to rest yet. He died after the Restoration, thoroughly defeated, at Burford in 1662, requesting that his only epitaph be the Latin, *Vermis Sum*: 'I am a worm.'[14] D'Ewes was long dead by then too.

Lucy Hay, Lady Carlisle, for her part, found the world a very different place in 1642 than it had been. Now there was no glittering royal court in which to make her way. Instead, she maintained her contacts with the nobles and politicians around her brother Northumberland. Her world was that of the Earl of Essex, Mandeville, and Denzil Holles. She remained close to her brother-in-law Leicester though, who was struggling to pick his own path. 'I am suspected and distrusted of either side,' he wrote to Lucy in August 1642.[15] Eventually, he would become an advocate of peace and settlement, then a rather reluctant royalist, while she would go on to spy for the king.[16] After Charles's execution in 1649, Carlisle was imprisoned in the Tower for over a year. In the 1650s, she was still considered the epitome of wit and eloquence, though as one rather qualified admirer quipped, her sparkly letters were marred by the fact 'she uses that word, *faithful*, she that never knew how to be so in her life'.[17] Lucy survived the Republic, dying in Hertfordshire in November 1660. She had been planning to make a journey to visit Henrietta Maria.

Mandeville, on the other hand, would rise to a leading position in the Parliamentarian army.[18] When his moderate father died late in 1642, he ascended to the title of Earl of Manchester, and became the commander of the fearsome 'Eastern Association' – the best section of the whole force. It was from the association that the New Model Army would, in 1645, draw much of its strength, though by then it was stripped of its old leadership. Manchester was out, after falling out very publicly with the association's best cavalry officer, Oliver Cromwell. Manchester fell into the background when Charles I was tried and executed. But when the monarchy was restored in 1660, Manchester supported Charles II, and found himself basking in royal favour, carrying the sword of state at the king's coronation in 1661. He died in 1671, a popular and a moderate man, among whose honours later in life were that he became a fellow of the Royal Society.

Of the Five Members, two were dead by the end of 1643: John Pym from cancer – having just triumphantly persuaded the Scots to enter the war on the side of Parliament. The alliance probably saved the cause, for by then the likes of Rupert and Goring were winning the war for Charles. John Hampden was a casualty of this, dying from wounds taken at the battle of Chalgrove Field in Oxfordshire on 18 June. It was one of Rupert's greatest victories, though he also benefited from the stout leadership of Henry Lunsford, Thomas's brother, who commanded the royalist infantry. Strode died, too, before the war was out – of a fever at Tottenham in 1645. Haselrig and Holles survived. Sir Arthur Haselrig ended up as a true republican – and a thorn in the side of both Oliver Cromwell and the restored monarchy. He hadn't supported the regicide, but Charles II hated him anyway, and he was one of the few of those who had not signed the late king's death warrant who were nonetheless exempted from pardon. His life was spared, but he was sent to the Tower where he died on 7 January 1661.

Denzil Holles, meanwhile, lived to a ripe old age. The veteran of the tumults of 1629, the bête noir of Charles in 1642, who brought the 'artificers' petition' to Parliament that January to threaten the Lords, ended up staking his reputation on opposition to the New Model Army in 1647. He feared the religious Independents more than anything, but he was no match for this new force in English politics, coming from the radical soldiery. In the end, they had him impeached – just as Charles I had – and rather than face trial he fled the country, consoling himself by writing a rebarbative memoir. He refused a role in the royalist government in exile, and eventually Cromwell allowed him back home, and so Holles retired to Dorset. From here, on the eve of the Restoration, he was elected as an MP once more. Under Charles II, he became a rather grumpy old man, a sometime diplomat, privy councillor, and general annoyance to everyone.[19] When he died in 1680, he was something of a bothersome ally to the more sophisticated opposition leader, the Earl of Shaftesbury – another Dorset landowner.

Quite a lot of seventeenth-century roads lead back to Dorset; and as war spread in late 1642, this was the path for Mary and John Bankes. Mary had been reposing at Stanwell as she recovered from her pregnancy. But once little Arabella had survived those dangerous first weeks, Mary prepared to move.

Soon, John and Mary would see each other again. As they each, in turn, crossed the heathlands around Wareham, they spied the stone keep of Corfe peeking over the horizon, in its little gap between the Purbeck Hills. 'An Englishman's house is his castle,' its previous owner Edward Coke had loved to say. Now the time for castles and fortifications was on England again.

Neither Corfe nor John Bankes would survive the war. The castle was repeatedly besieged by the Parliamentarians, until it was captured in 1646, by which time it was one of the last royalist strongholds anywhere in England. Before then, Mary had another baby there: William, born on 10 June 1644, just weeks before King Charles suffered a terrible defeat at Marston Moor in Yorkshire.[20] Both William and Arabella survived their wartime childhood, though William died in his twenties. Arabella lived until she was eighty-one, dying in a fashionable part of Westminster in 1724.[21]

Mary Bankes played a heroic role in keeping Corfe secure, though by the time it fell she had left for Oxford. It was at Oxford, too, that Sir John died, in 1644, aged in his mid-fifties. Buried in Christ Church Cathedral, he had seen a life of service to king and country. It had brought him high office, respect, wealth, and eventually ruin. Initially one of those in whom Parliament retained some trust, by 1644, they had decided he was thoroughly delinquent. In July that year, he had finally been accused by the Commons of high treason.

In later centuries, partly due to his wife's heroism and to the efforts of John and Mary's minister at Stanwell, Bruno Ryves, the Bankeses became legendary royalists. The family estates survived, and moved their centre to a new country house at Kingston Lacy, which was grandly rebuilt in the 1660s – inspired by Edward Hyde's new mansion in London. At Kingston Lacy today, visitors can marvel at the much later bronze statues of John, Mary, and King Charles. They are by the famous French-Italian sculptor Baron Carlo Marochetti (1805–67), whose work also adorns the Houses of Parliament in the form of a famous equestrian bronze of Richard I. Marochetti's work at Kingston Lacy is a tableau of loyalty, with John and Mary flanking the seated king: John is in his robes as Lord Chief Justice of the Common Pleas; Mary holds the keys to Corfe. There's a piquancy to John's statue, though – surely unintentional. For he is wearing his serjeant's coif – undoffed in the presence of the king, as was his right as a learned advisor. It is true to Bankes's role. (Marochetti, meanwhile, has a somewhat troubled relationship with headwear – another of his works, a statue of the Duke of Wellington in Glasgow, finds itself regularly adorned with a traffic cone.)

What Kingston Lacy's bronzes also can't quite convey is how moderate, and how complex, Sir John's royalism was. He opposed Charles's authoritarianism in the 1620s, then did much to make it work in the 1630s. By 1641 he was linked to the Earl of Bedford – arguably the last hope for peace – and in early 1642, he was one of those whose acceptance of the Militia Ordinance gave the

Parliamentarians confidence in the justice of their cause. Even when he went to York in May, he was an advocate for peace, writing detailed letters to some of the leading Junto figures, and to his Parliamentarian ally Giles Green. It was only in the summer, when peace became impossible, that he finally became a true royalist.

Bankes was always, as the Earl of Strafford had said, 'betwixt the sow's ear and the silken purse'. It may partly have been a comment on his rural background (and growing wealth), but it summed up the life of a moderate too. Yet even moderates eventually had to make a choice. Everyone found themselves between two opposite sides: between Scylla and Charybdis, between Westminster and Whitehall, London and York, the Junto and the Cavaliers. No one could stay out of this conflict, however much they might try; else they would – in Sir John's words written to his Dorset neighbour, friend, and Parliamentarian rival – 'be ruined both ways'.

Acknowledgements

Books are remarkable things. In the end, it's one person's name on the cover, but really they could never be brought into being without scores of people supporting that singular author. This book is no different. It is a work of many hands.

My brilliant agent Charlotte Merritt, at Andrew Nurnberg Associates, has been a critical friend to the project all the way through: Charlotte is always acute in her judgements and usually – quite frankly – right. The book probably wouldn't exist without her, and even if it did, it would have been a lot worse. In the US, Robin Straus has also been a splendid advocate for the work too, while at Bloomsbury, I've benefited from the incredible insight of my editor Jasmine Horsey, plus the support of other members of their team, particularly Francisco Vilhena, Gurdip Ahluwalia and Jonny Coward. At Knopf, Todd Portnowitz has been a thoughtful and supportive editor, and Margot Lee has done great work with the publicity. The book was proofread meticulously by Katie Johnson.

I've had many fascinating discussions about the Civil War and the crisis of 1641-2 with fellow historians. Among those who stand out are John Adamson, Waseem Ahmed, Andy Hopper, Paul Lay, Miranda Malins, Fiona McCall, Michael Molcher, Ismini Pells, John Rees and Rebecca Rideal. Academic colleagues at Oxford have been inspirational as ever, especially the historians at our Department for Continuing Education, particularly Tom

Buchanan, Janet Dickinson, Heather Falvey, Elizabeth Gemmill, Yasmin Khan, Stephen Mileson and Mark Smith. The president and fellows at Kellogg College have been terrifically supportive too: of so many, Jonathan Michie has always shown a great interest in my writing, and Tara Stubbs has been a brilliant colleague over the years. Of my old tutors, Martin Ingram's meticulous empiricism, and the late Clive Holmes's incredible sense for the drama of history, have both had a lasting impact on my writing, or at least I hope they have. I would also like to extend heartfelt thanks to all the wonderful library and archive staff who have helped me in the course of writing this book, particularly those at the Weston Library in the Bodleian, the National Archives at Kew, and the Dorset History Centre in Dorchester.

It was my parents who first gave me a love of the past, and it was they who first took me to Corfe, when I was very little. It's still my favourite castle, and readers will not be surprised to learn I've seen a lot. My grandma and my late grandad have always supported my writing over the years too. Similarly crucial has been the support of old friends. They are too many to mention, but the book wouldn't be the same without Phil Abraham, Noel Hunwick, Matthew Holdcroft, Adrian Fradd, Liz and Vach Kashyap (and Cate, James and Charlie), Katy Pullen, Paz Tayal and Mayank Kanga (and Anya, Ravi, and Anushka), and Rachel Antony-Roberts. Writing this book has also coincided with my daughter Alice growing older starting school, something which has been made much more fun thanks to the nursery and school parents. Alice herself has been a source of joy and inspiration. History is still, I think, her favourite subject. She knows all about the Great Fire of London, though I once made the mistake taking this as an opportunity to explain to her the difference between the City and the rest of the capital. Now she tells her friends who live in Westminster that they don't live in 'real London'. The fault is mine.

And most of all, my wife Sophie has always been my biggest champion. We've been together much longer than the Long Parliament was, and thankfully without interruptions by angry kings, Puritan generals, or outbreaks of plague. Back when we were undergraduates, she was more into political history than me: she was fascinated by Machiavellian schemers and the intricacies of Parliament and Whitehall. This book sees me at last coming around to her point of view. It is dedicated to her with the utmost love and gratitude.

Further Reading

The first specific modern narrative of these tumultuous events was John Forster's *The Arrest of the Five Members by Charles I*, published in 1860. A friend of Charles Dickens, Forster was an accomplished literary critic and writer, and his study is an invaluable starting point. That said, it does exhibit an occasionally somewhat uncritical approach to its sources, and it is not to be trusted in the detail. Also, its title references an event that didn't actually happen. Much more reliable, and still well worth a read, is the tenth volume of the great Victorian historian Samuel Rawson Gardiner's *History of England from the Accession of James I to the Outbreak of the Civil War, 1603–1642* (1883–1908). Later general histories have revised Gardiner, but the essentials of his narrative still hold up remarkably well. As always, C.V. Wedgewood is a fine and evocative storyteller. Our narrative here sits across two of her Civil War trilogy: *The King's Peace* (1955) and *The King's War* (1958). Meanwhile one of the best 'revisionist' histories is that of Conrad Russell: *The Fall of the British Monarchies* (1995). More recently, John Adamson's *Noble Revolt* (2007) is a brilliantly written, almost cinematic, account of the years 1640 to 1642. It is essential reading, not least for his placing of the Junto lords at the centre of the story.

Probably the best introduction to the causes of the English Civil War is Anne Hughes, *The Causes of the English Civil War* (1991). There are also fine narratives in Austin Woolrych's *Britain in*

Revolution (2002) and Michael Braddick, *God's Fury, England's Fire* (2008). Clive Holmes's *Why Was Charles I Executed?* (2006) has a splendid chapter on the Long Parliament. On more specific topics, Richard Cust's *Charles I: A Political Life* (2005) is the best biography of the king. The social breakdown in 1640–42 is covered in forensic detail by David Cressy: *England on Edge* (2006). London's role in the revolution is brilliantly studied in Valerie Pearl's *London and the Outbreak of the Puritan Revolution* (1961), while the popular politics of the time is the subject of Keith Lindley's *Popular Politics and Religion in Civil War London* (1997). There are plenty more works worth reading, and some of these can be found in the endnotes.

Notes

Bodleian	The Bodleian Library, Oxford
BL	The British Library, London
CSPV	A.B. Hinds (ed.), *Calendar of State Papers relating to English Affairs in the Archives of Venice* (vols. 25-26, London, 1924-5).
Clarendon, History	E. Hyde, *The History of the Rebellion and Civil Wars in England begun in the Year 1641* (5 vols., Oxford, 1992).
CJ	*Journal of the House of Commons*, v. 2: 1640–1643. https://www.british-history.ac.uk/series/house-commons-journals
Constitutional Documents	S.R. Gardiner (ed.), *The Constitutional Documents of the Puritan Revolution, 1625–1660* (3rd ed., Oxford, 1906).
D'Ewes, *Journal*	W. Coates (ed.), *The Journal of Sir Simonds D'Ewes, from the First Recess of the Long Parliament to the Withdrawal of King Charles from London* (London, 1942).
DHC	The Dorset History Centre, Dorchester
HMC	*Historical Manuscripts Commission Reports*

History of Parliament, 1603–1629	A.D. Thrush and J. Ferris (eds.), *The History of Parliament, 1604–1629: the House of Commons* (Cambridge, 2010).
House of Commons, 1640–1660	S. Roberts (ed.), *The History of Parliament: the House of Commons, 1640–1660* (9 vols., Woodbridge, 2023).
LJ	*Journal of the House of Lords*, v. 4: 1629-1642, v. 5: 1642-1643. https://www.british-history.ac.uk/series/house-lords-journals
ODNB	*Oxford Dictionary of National Biography*, online, edited by Lawrence Goldman, www.oxforddnb.com (Oxford, 2005–13),
PJ	W. Coates, A. Young, and V. Snow (eds.), *The Private journals of the Long Parliament 3 January to 1 March 1642* (London, 1982).
Rushworth	J. Rushworth (ed.), *Historical Collections of Private Passages of State* (8 vols., London, 1721): https://www.british-history.ac.uk/series/rushworth-private-passages-state
TNA	The National Archives, Kew.

INTRODUCTION

1 On these theories, see: M. Judson, *The Crisis of the Constitution; An Essay in Constitutional and Political Thought in England, 1603–45* (new ed., New York, 1988); J. P. Sommerville, *Royalists and Patriots: Politics and Ideology in England, 1603–1640* (2nd ed., Abingdon, 1999); J. Sanderson, *'But the People's Creatures': the Philosophical Basis of the English Civil War* (Manchester, 1989).

2 C. Carlton, *Going to the Wars: the Experience of the British Civil Wars, 1638–1651* (London, 1992).

3 J. Morrill, 'The Religious Context of the English Civil War', *Transactions of the Royal Historical Society*, 34 (1984), p. 178.

I THE SOLDIER, THE POET, THE KING, AND THE TRAITOR

1 *An Exact Collection of all Remonstrances, Declarations, Votes, Orders, Ordinances, Proclamations, Petitions, Messages, Answers, and other Remarkable Passages betweene the Kings most Excellent Majesty, and his High Court of Parliament* (London, 1643), pp. 215–35; C. Russell, 'The First Army Plot of 1641', *Transactions of the Royal Historical Society*, 38 (1988), pp. 85–106; J. Adamson, *The Noble Revolt: the Overthrow of Charles I* (London, 2007), pp. 278–312.

2 For the economic and demographic history of England in this period, see: K. Wrightson, *Earthly Necessities: Economic Lives in Early Modern Britain, 1470–1750* (London, 2000).

3 There are several biographies of Charles. The best starting point for understanding Charles's political beliefs is R. Cust, *Charles I: A Political Life* (London, 2014); C. Carlton, *Charles I: the Personal Monarch* (2nd ed., London, 1995), is still very useful, but marred by its sometimes questionable use of psychoanalysis. Two accessible popular biographies, both of which are broadly sympathetic to Charles, are: L. De Lisle, *White King: Charles I, Traitor, Murderer, Martyr* (London, 2018), and M. Turnbull, *Charles I's Private Life* (Barnsley, 2023). Also sympathetic is M. Kishlansky, *Charles I: An Abbreviated Life* (London, 2014). One of the best ways to get a sense of the debate around Charles is to read the debates that followed: M. Kishlansky, 'Charles I: A Case of Mistaken Identity', *Past and Present*, 189 (2005), pp. 41–80; see: C. Holmes, 'Charles I: A Case of Mistaken Identity', *Past and Present*, 205 (2009), pp. 175–88; R. Cust, 'Charles I: A Case of Mistaken Identity', *Past and Present*, 205 (2009), pp. 201–12.

4 Cust, *Charles I: A Political Life*, p. 2.

5 Strong, *Henry, Prince of Wales and England's Lost Renaissance* (London, 1986), p. 12.

6 Carlton, *Charles I*, p. 10.

7 De Lisle, *White King*, p. 8.

8 Cust, *Charles I: A Political Life*, pp. 15–16.

9 For a summary of the Church under Charles's father, see: T. Harris, *Rebellion: Britain's First Stuart Kings, 1567–1642* (Oxford, 2014), pp. 93–115, 208–12. Other contributions to the debate about the early Stuart Church include: J. Davies, *The Caroline Captivity of the Church: Charles I and the Remoulding of Anglicanism, 1625–1641* (Oxford, 1992); K. Fincham (ed.), *The Early Stuart Church, 1603–1642* (Basingstoke,

1993); P. Lake, *On Laudianism: Piety, Polemic and Politics during the Personal Rule of Charles I* (Cambridge, 2023); still very useful is: P. Collinson, *The Birthpangs of Protestant England: Religious and Cultural Change in the Sixteenth and Seventeenth Centuries* (Basingstoke, 1988).

10 Cust, *Charles I: A Political Life*, pp. 95–6.

11 Cust, *Charles I: A Political Life*, p. 1.

12 Judson, *Crisis of the Constitution*, p. 175. There are many narrative histories of the early Stuart period. S. Gardiner, *The History of England from the Accession of James I to the Outbreak of the Civil War, 1603–1642*, 10 vols (London, 1895–9) is still invaluable. For a more recent synthesis, see: Harris, *Rebellion*.

13 Cust, *Charles I: A Political Life*, p. 36.

14 R. Cust, *The Forced Loan and English Politics, 1626–28* (Oxford, 1987).

15 P. Christianson, 'Politics, Patronage, and Conceptions of Governance in Early Stuart England: the Duke of Buckingham and His Supporters in the Parliament of 1628', *Huntington Library Quarterly*, 60 (1999), p. 299.

16 Sommerville, *Royalists and Patriots*, p. 37.

17 Cust, *Charles I: A Political Life*, pp. 70–71.

18 *Constitutional Documents*, pp. 66–70.

19 Sommerville, *Royalists and Patriots*, p. xii (quoting the philosopher Robert Filmer).

20 W. Jones, *Politics and the Bench: the Judges and the Origins of the English Civil War* (London, 1971), p. 87n.

21 Cust, *Charles I: A Political Life*, p. 133.

22 C. Russell, 'Sir John Eliot (1592–1832), politician', *ODNB*; J. Morrill, 'Denzil Holles, first Baron Holles (1598–1680), politician', *ODNB*; C. Firth and L. Reeve, 'William Strode (1594–1645), politician', *ODNB*.

23 The biggest study of the 'Personal Rule' is K. Sharpe, *The Personal Rule of Charles I* (London, 1992); for a more critical perspective, see: Gardiner, *History*, VII–VIII; also E. Cope, *Politics without Parliaments, 1629–40* (London, 1987); and for more succinct recent summaries, see: C. Holmes, *Why Was Charles I Executed?* (London, 2006), pp. 1–34; Harris, *Rebellion*, pp. 279–344. Bodleian, MS Bankes, 9/28, 57/11.

24 R. Cust, *Charles I and the Aristocracy* (Cambridge, 2013), pp. 88–9.

25 For an introduction to the background to the Scottish revolution, see: Harris, *Rebellion*, pp. 168–85, 360–72; D. Stephenson, *The*

Scottish Revolution, 1637–44: the Triumph of the Covenanters (Edinburgh, 1973).

26 Carlton, *Charles I*, p. 206.

27 Cust, *Charles I: A Political Life*, p. 245.

28 Cust, *Charles I and the Aristocracy*, pp. 178–9.

29 Cust, *Charles I: A Political Life*, p. 255.

30 Cust, *Charles I: A Political Life*, p. 258.

31 D. Cressy, *England on Edge: Crisis and Revolution, 1640–1642* (Oxford, 2006), pp. 110–26; J. Walter, ' "This Infamous, Scandalous, Headless Insurrection": the Attack on William Laud and Lambeth Palace, May 1640, Revisited', *English Historical Review*, forthcoming.

32 T. Clayton, 'Sir John Suckling (bap. 1609, d. 1641?), poet', *ODNB*.

33 Adamson, *Noble Revolt*, pp. 53–88.

2 JUSTICE AND EXECUTION

1 *House of Commons, 1640–1660*, I, pp. 31–81.

2 *House of Commons, 1640–1660*, I, p. 47.

3 V. Wedgwood, *Thomas Wentworth, first Earl of Strafford, 1593–1641: A Revaluation* (London, 1961); J. Merritt (ed.), *The Political World of Thomas Wentworth, Earl of Strafford, 1621–1641* (Cambridge, 1996).

4 A. Milton, 'Thomas Wentworth and the Political Thought of the Personal Rule', in Merritt, *Political World*, p. 146.

5 Adamson, *Noble Revolt*, p. 18.

6 Adamson, *Noble Revolt*, pp. 100-1.

7 C. Russell, 'The Theory of Treason in the Trial of Strafford', *English Historical Review*, 80 (1965), pp. 30–50.

8 Adamson, *Noble Revolt*, pp. 167–70.

9 Edward Herbert, quoted in Adamson, *Noble Revolt*, pp. 193–4; *Constitutional Documents*, pp. 144–55.

10 C. Russell, 'John Pym (1585–1643), politician', *ODNB*; S. Roberts, 'Pym, John', *House of Commons, 1640–1660*, VII, pp. 949–1001.

11 C. Russell, 'The Parliamentary Career of John Pym, 1621-9', in P. Clark, A. Smith and N. Tyacke (eds), *The English Commonwealth, 1547–1640: Essays in Politics and Society presented to Joel Hurstfield* (Leicester, 1979), pp. 147–65.

12 P. Lake, 'Antipopery: the Structure of a Prejudice', in R. Cust and A. Hughes (eds), *Conflict in Early Stuart England: Studies in Religion and Politics, 1603-1642* (London, 1989), pp. 72–106.

13 Bodleian, MS Clarendon 19, no. 1427, f. 34r.

14 Adamson, *Noble Revolt*, pp. 210–11.

15 Adamson, *Noble Revolt*, p. 212.

16 Adamson, *Noble Revolt*, p. 213.

17 Russell, 'First Army Plot', pp. 100–1.

18 Adamson, *Noble Revolt*, pp. 220-26.

19 Russell, 'Theory of Treason', p. 34.

20 J. Timmis, *Thine is the Kingdom: the Trial for Treason of Thomas Wentworth, Earl of Strafford, First Minister to King Charles I and Last Hope of the English Crown* (Tuscaloosa, 1974); Adamson, *Noble Revolt*, pp. 215–305; Russell, 'Theory of Treason'.

21 Adamson, *Noble Revolt*, pp. 248–54.

22 Adamson, *Noble Revolt*, pp. 220–26.

23 Adamson, *Noble Revolt*, p. 278.

24 Adamson, *Noble Revolt*, pp. 281–2.

25 Adamson, *Noble Revolt*, pp. 283–4.

26 A. Fletcher, *The Outbreak of the English Civil War* (London, 1981), p. 15.

27 *LJ*, 6 May 1641.

28 B. Manning, *The English People and the English Revolution* (London, 1976), pp. 20–32; K. Lindley, *Popular Politics and Religion in Civil War London* (Aldershot, 1997), pp. 19–26.

29 Adamson, *Noble Revolt*, pp. 275, 299.

30 L. De Lisle, *Henrietta Maria: Conspirator, Warrior, Phoenix Queen* (London, 2022), p. 200.

31 *LJ*, 8 May 1641.

32 *LJ*, 7 May 1641.

3 THE SOW'S EAR AND THE SILKEN PURSE

1 H. Brierley (ed.), *The Registers of Crosthwaite, Cumberland*, 4 vols (Penrith, 1928–31), I, p. 97. On Bankes's life, see: C. Brooks, 'Sir John Bankes (1589–1644), judge', *ODNB*; P. Hunneyball, 'John Bankes (1589–1644)', *History of Parliament, 1603–1629*.

2 A. Winchester, *Harvest of the Hills: Rural Life in Northern England and the Scottish Borders* (Edinburgh, 2000), p. 133.

3 A. Appleby, *Famine in Tudor and Stuart England* (Liverpool, 1978).

4 TNA, ADM 74/2/2-65, Castlerigg and Derwentwater Manor, 1584–1731.

5 Cumbria Archives (Carlisle), PROB/1616/WINVX9, Will and Inventory of John Bankes of Keswick, 1616.

6   TNA, STAC 8/52/19, *Bankes* vs *Uyrall*, 1607.

7   D. Lloyd, *Memoires of the lives, actions, sufferings & deaths of those noble, reverend and excellent personages that suffered by death, sequestration, decimation, or otherwise, for the Protestant religion and the great principle thereof, allegiance to their soveraigne, in our late intestine wars, from the year 1637 to the year 1660* (London, 1668), p. 586.

8   A. Appleby, 'Agrarian Capitalism or Seigneurial Reaction? The Northwest of England, 1500–1700', *American History Review*, 80 (1975), pp. 574–94.

9   TNA, ADM 76/83, No. 96: Defendants' counsel was 'Mr Banks of Grays Inn'; Bankes kept a copy of this proclamation in his official papers: Bodleian, MS Bankes, 25/8.

10 DHC, D-BKL/H/A/78. B. Donagan; 'Lady Mary Bankes [née Hawtrey] (d. 1661), royalist landowner', *ODNB*.

11 Hunneyball, 'Sir John Bankes'.

12 Jones, *Politics and the Bench*, p. 92.

13 The legal papers for the transfer are in DHC, D-BKL/A/A/29-35. It is usually, incorrectly, stated that the Bankeses bought the Purbeck Estates in 1634, but the purchase was largely complete by 1631.

14 W. Knowler (ed.), *The Earl of Strafforde's Letters and Dispatches*, 2 vols (London, 1739), I, p. 294.

15 DHC, D-BKL/H/A/9.

16 D. Underdown (ed.), *William Whiteway of Dorchester: His diary, 1618–1635*, Dorset Record Society (Dorchester, 1991), p. 131.

17 Bodleian, MS Bankes, 9/28; 57/11.

18 R. Sibbes, *The Soules Conflict with itselfe, and Victorie over it selfe by Faith* (London, 1635); R. Powell, *Depopulation Arraigned, Convicted and Condemned, by the Lawes of God and Man: A Treatise Necessary in these Times* (London, 1636).

19 DHC, B-BKL/H/A/9.

20 DHC, B-BKL/H/A/35.

21 D. Reeve, 'The Decline of Holt Forest, Chase and Park, Wimborne Minster, Dorset, in the 17th century', *Proceedings of the Dorset Natural History and Archaeological Society*, 129 (2008), pp. 9–10.

22 TNA, E 178/5262.

23 DHC, B-BKL/E/A/3/8.

24 R. Hoyle, 'Introduction: Custom, Improvement and Anti-Improvement', in R. Hoyle (ed.), *Custom, Improvement and the*

Landscape in Early Modern Britain (Farnham, 2011), pp. 11–48; P. Slack, *The Invention of Improvement: Information and Material Progress in Seventeenth Century England* (Oxford, 2014).

25 Published in: M. Forrest, J. Halling Barnard, R. Mitchell and M. Papworth (eds), *Treswell's Survey of Purbeck, 1585–6*, Dorset Record Society (Dorchester, 2017).

26 J. Larkin (ed.), *Stuart Royal Proclamations, Volume 2: 1625–1646* (Oxford, 1983), II pp. 464–6.

27 Bodleian, MS Bankes, 63/34.

28 Bodleian, MS Bankes, 41/53.

29 Bodleian, MS Bankes, 43/35.

30 W. Lamont, *Marginal Prynne, 1600–1669* (London, 1963), pp. 11–48. For a revisionist account of Prynne's first trial, see: M. Kishlansky, 'The Whipper Whipped: the Sedition of William Prynne', *Historical Journal*, 56 (2013), pp. 603–27.

31 TNA, SP 16/354/180.

32 TNA, PC 2/48, p. 40; DHC, D-BKL/H/A/26.

33 Bodleian, MS Bankes, 58/1–2.

34 Carlton, *Charles I*, p. x.

35 Sommerville, *Royalists and Patriots*; A. Cromartie, *The Constitutionalist Revolution: A Essay on the History of England, 1450–1642* (Cambridge, 2006); J. Kenyon (ed.), *The Stuart Constitution: Documents and Commentary, 1603–1688* (Cambridge, 1966).

36 D. Keir, 'The Case of Ship-Money', *Law Quarterly Review*, 52 (1936), pp. 547–74; Sharpe, *Personal Rule*, pp. 545–95, 717–23; H. Langelüddecke, '"I finde all men & my officers all soe unwilling": the Collection of Ship Money, 1635–1640', *Journal of British Studies*, 46 (2007), pp. 509–42; D. Chan Smith, 'Hannibal *Ad Portas*: Necessity, Public Law and the Common Law Emergency in the *Case of Ship Money*', in P. Halliday, E. Hubbard and S. Sowerby (eds), *Revolutionising Politics: Culture and Conflict in England, 1620–60* (Manchester, 2021), pp. 31–54; C. St John Smith, 'The Judiciary and the Political Use and Abuse of the Law by the Caroline Regime' (University of Oxford, DPhil, 2016), pp. 216–25; the original arguments can be found in: 'Proceedings in the Case of Ship-Money', in T. Howell (ed.), *A Complete Collection of State Trials*, 33 vols (London, 1809–26), [hereafter *State Trials*], III.

37 Cust, *Charles I: A Political Life*, p. 129.

38 Cust, *Charles I: A Political Life*, p. 193.

39 Bodleian, MS Bankes, 63/27–28.

40 Russell, 'Theory of Treason', p. 36n.

41 A. Gill, 'Ship Money during the Personal Rule of Charles I: Politics, Ideology and the Law, 1634–1640', (PhD thesis, University of Sheffield, 1990), p. 456.

42 *State Trials*, III, p. 1015; J. Collins, 'The Long Parliament and the Law of Necessity in Seventeenth Century England', *Past and Present*, 247 (2020), pp. 16–19.

43 *State Trials*, III, p. 1018. Emphasis added (might).

44 *State Trials*, III, p. 1017.

45 *State Trials*, III, p. 1021.

46 *State Trials*, III, p. 1064.

47 [H. Parker], *The Case of Shipmony briefly Discoursed, according to the Grounds of Law, Policie, and Conscience* (London, 1640), p. 2.

48 Q. Skinner, 'Classical Liberty and the Coming of the English Civil War', in M. Van Gelderen and Q. Skinner (eds), *Republicanism: A Shared European Heritage*, 2 vols (Cambridge, 2002), II, pp. 9–28, esp. pp. 15–16.

49 Gill, 'Ship Money', p. 457.

50 Mary Bankes's family accounts are in DHC, D-BKL/H/B/1. For the couple's children, see: DHC, D-BKL/H/A/78.

51 Bodleian, MS Bankes, 18/3, 58/1–2.

52 Bodleian, MS Bankes, 52/17.

53 Bodleian, MS Bankes, 18/8.

54 DHC, D-BKL/H/A/38. This intriguing document has not attracted much attention. It can be fairly confidently dated to 1640 because it uses a specific date to give an example of a writ of summons, 13 April. This was the date of the meeting of the Short Parliament. It is tempting, given the way it places the right to call Parliaments front and centre, to wonder if it was a direct response to the Petition of Twelve Peers.

55 Rushworth, IV, pp. 1–45, 68–99.

56 St John Smith, 'Judiciary', p. 7.

57 Brooks, 'Sir John Bankes'.

58 Cressy, *England on Edge*, pp. 380–1.

59 C. Kyle and C. Thompson, 'Ralph Hawtrey', *History of Parliament, 1604–1629*; F. Sheppard (ed.), *Survey of London, Vol. 36: Covent Garden* (London, 1970), pp. 25–34.

60 J. Baker, *The Order of Serjeants-at-Law: A Chronicle of Creations, with related texts and a historical introduction*, Selden Society, 26 (London, 1984), p. 440.

61 DHC, D-BKL/H/A/63.

62 St John Smith, 'Judiciary', p. 22.

63 Rushworth, IV, pp. 134-65 (misdated as 25 January).

64 Bankes retained a copy of this decision in his personal papers: DHC, D-BKL/H/A/46; *LJ*, 26 February 1641; *LJ*, 27 February 1641.

65 J. Cockburn, *A History of the English Assizes, 1558–1714* (Cambridge, 1972), p. 272.

66 Adamson, *Noble Revolt*, p. 298.

67 Adamson, *Noble Revolt*, p. 262.

68 B. Quintrell, 'John Williams (1582-1650), archbishop of York', *ODNB*.

69 C. Russell, *The Fall of the British Monarchies, 1637–42* (Oxford, 1991), p. 279; Adamson, *Noble Revolt*, p. 299.

70 *An Exact Collection*, p. 233.

4 THESE PREPOSTEROUS TIMES

1 Cressy, *England on Edge*, p. 41.

2 Adamson, *Noble Revolt*, p. 313.

3 W. Stacy, 'Impeachment, Attainder, and the "Revival" of Parliamentary Judicature under the Early Stuarts', *Parliamentary History*, 11 (1991), pp. 40–56.

4 M. Braddick, 'Lionel Cranfield, first Earl of Middlesex (1575–1645), merchant, financier, and government minister', *ODNB*; M. Peltonen, 'Francis Bacon, Viscount St Alban (1561–1626), Lord Chancellor, politician, and philosopher', *ODNB*.

5 A point made by Adamson, *Noble Revolt*, p. 266.

6 Russell, *Fall*, p. 177; M. Jansson, *Proceedings in the Opening Session of the Long Parliament*, 7 vols (Woodbridge, 2000), VI, p. 7.

7 Adamson, *Noble Revolt*, pp. 415–16.

8 C. Hibbard, 'Henrietta Maria (1609–1669), queen of England, Scotland, and Ireland, consort of Charles I', *ODNB*; A. Plowden, *Henrietta Maria: Charles I's Indomitable Queen* (Stroud, 2001).

9 De Lisle, *Henrietta Maria*, p. 51.

10 Carlton, *Charles I*, pp. 86–7.

11 Sharpe, *Personal Rule*, pp. 46–7.

12 Fletcher, *Outbreak*, p. 111.

13 CSPV, 24 May 1641; 28 June 1641 [both dates N.S.].

14 Cressy, *England on Edge*, p. 370.

15 TNA, ASSI 45/1/3/66.

16 Cressy, *England on Edge*, p. 163.

17 J. Spencer, *A Short Treatise Concerning the Lawfullnesse of Every Mans exercising his gift as God shall call him thereunto* (London, 1641).

18 Cressy, *England on Edge*, p. 197.

19 *Brothers of the Separation, or a True Relacion of a Company of Brownists* (London, 1641), a4r. The pamphlet is attacking Rogers for these alleged words, but the allegation rings entirely true.

20 Russell, *Fall*, pp. 341–2.

21 Fletcher, *Outbreak*, p. 112.

22 J. Harris, *The Puritanes Impuritie, or The Anatomie of a Puritane or Seperatist* (London, 1641), p. 1.

23 R. Carter, *The Schismatick Stigmatized, wherein all Make-bates are Branded* (London, 1641), a2v.

24 CSPV, 19 July 1641 [N.S.].

25 K. Thomas, 'Women and the Civil War Sects', *Past and Present*, 13 (1958), p. 47.

26 CSPV, 2 August 1641 [N.S.].

27 *A Discoverie of Six Women Preachers* (London, 1641).

28 Cressy, *England on Edge*, pp. 244–5.

29 *A Description of the Sect called the Familie of Love* (London, 1641).

30 Cressy, *England on Edge*, p. 243.

31 Holmes, *Why Was Charles I Executed?*, p. 57.

32 [E. Waller], *A Speech Made by Master Waller Esquire in the Honourable House of Commons Concerning Episcopacy* (London, 1641).

33 Cressy, *England on Edge*, p. 185.

34 Cressy, *England on Edge*, p. 336.

35 Cressy, *England on Edge*, p. 185.

36 See: S. Hindle, *The State and Social Change in Early Modern England, c. 1550–1640* (Basingstoke, 2000).

37 J. Taylor, *A Reply as True as Steele, to a Rusty, Rayling, Ridiculous, Lying Libell* (London, 1641).

38 William Grant, *The Vindication of the Vicar of Istleworth, in the County of Middlesex. From a scandalous pamphlet* (London, 1641), pp. 17, 19; cf. *The Petition of the Inhabitants of Istlevvorth ... against William Grant* (London, 1641).

39 Bodleian, MS Top Oxon, c. 378, p. 321.

40 Cressy, *England on Edge*, p. 300.

5 THE UNQUESTIONABLE RIGHT OF KINGS IN ENGLAND

1 Bodleian, MS Top Oxon, c. 378, pp. 320–1.

2 Cressy, *England on Edge*, p. 64.

3 P. Slack, *The Impact of Plague in Tudor and Stuart England* (Oxford, 1985), p. 22.

4 *Certain Orders Thought Meet to Be Put in Execution against the Infection of the Plague* (London, 1641); J. Merritt, *Westminster: A Royal City in a Time of Revolution, 1640–1660* (Manchester, 2013), pp. 34–5.

5 Plowden, *Henrietta Maria*, p. 200.

6 Cressy, *England on Edge*, p. 333.

7 For Taylor's life, see Bernard Capp's brilliant study: B. Capp, *The World of John Taylor the Water-Poet, 1578–1653* (Oxford, 1994).

8 J. Taylor, *A Juniper Lecture. With the Description of all Sorts of Women, Good and Bad* (London, 1639).

9 J. Taylor, *Divers Crab-Tree Lectures* (London, 1639); *The Womens Sharpe Revenge. Or an Answer to Sir Seldome Sober that Writ Those Railing Pamphlets called the Juniper and Crabtree Lectures* (London, 1639).

10 J. Taylor, *A Swarme of Sectaries and Schismaticks* (London, 1641).

11 H. Walker, *An Answer to a Foolish Pamphlet entitled A Swarme of Sectaries* (London, 1641).

12 Taylor, *Reply as True as Steele*.

13 H. Walker, *Taylors Physicke has Purged the Divel* (London, 1641).

14 G. Richardson, *The Irish Footman's Poetry* (London, 1641).

15 Cressy, *England on Edge*, p. 268.

16 Cressy, *England on Edge*, p. 219; Edward Dering: the precise quotation is from the winter, but it mirrors the sentiment in his speeches throughout much of 1641.

17 House of Lords, Main Papers: HL/PO/JO/10/1/73, 24 November 1641, Information of Robert Stevens.

18 [G. Digby], *The Third Speech of the Lord George Digby to the House of Commons concerning Bishops and the Citie Petition of the 9th of Febr. 1640* (London, 1641), p. 5.

19 Adamson, *Noble Revolt*, p. 323.

20 Adamson, *Noble Revolt*, p. 416.

21 D. Smith, *Constitutional Royalism and the Search for Settlement, c. 1640–1649* (Cambridge, 1994), pp. 1–106.

22 CSPV, 3 July 1641 [N.S.].

23 Edward Nicholas is one of many seventeenth-century figures crying out for a good full biography. For now, there is: S. Baron, 'Sir Edward Nicholas (1593–1669), government official', *ODNB*; and: D. Nicholas, *Mr Secretary Nicholas (1593–1669): His Life and Letters* (London, 1955).

24 Nicholas, *Mr Secretary Nicholas*, p. 37.

25 Nicholas, *Mr Secretary Nicholas*, p. 66.

26 For example, Nicholas, *Mr Secretary Nicholas*, pp. 69–70.

27 Nicholas, *Mr Secretary Nicholas*, p. 40; Baron, 'Sir Edward Nicholas'.

28 Nicholas, *Mr Secretary Nicholas*, p. 116.

29 Nicholas, *Mr Secretary Nicholas*, p. 119.

30 TNA, SP 16/482/96.

31 Nicholas, *Mr Secretary Nicholas*, pp. 132–3.

32 Adamson, *Noble Revolt*, p. 337.

33 Adamson, *Noble Revolt*, p. 343.

34 Clarendon, *History*, I, p. 394.

35 Russell, 'First Army Plot', p. 87.

36 Adamson, *Noble Revolt*, p. 313.

37 Russell, *Fall*, p. 319.

38 Gardiner, *History*, IX, pp. 397–400.

39 *Constitutional Documents*, pp. 163–6.

40 The text of the oath does not actually survive, though Giustinian seems to have seen a draft. See Adamson, *Noble Revolt*, p. 336. For the Ten Propositions, see: *Constitutional Documents*, pp. 163–6.

41 Adamson, *Noble Revolt*, pp. 341–2.

42 Adamson, *Noble Revolt*, p. 339.

43 Lindley, *Popular Politics*, p. 93; Adamson, *Noble Revolt*, pp. 344–5.

44 Adamson, *Noble Revolt*, p. 344; Russell, *Fall*, pp. 366–7.

45 Adamson, *Noble Revolt*, p. 343.

46 TNA, PC 2/53, p. 177.

47 J. Evelyn, *The Diary of John Evelyn, FRS to which is subjoined the private correspondence between King Charles I and Sir Edward Nicholas, and between Sir Edward Hyde (afterwards earl of Clarendon) and Sir Richard Browne*, 4 vols (London, 1882), IV, 53; Cockburn, *History of the English Assizes.*

48 J. Taylor, *John Taylors Last Voyage and Adventure* (London, 1641).

6 RED CRIMSON SINS

1 *A Relation of the Kings Entertainment into Scotland on Saterday the 14 of August* (London, 1641).

2 Adamson, *Noble Revolt*, p. 346.

3 Cust, *Charles I: A Political Life*, p. 303.

4 Evelyn, *Diary*, IV, p. 64; Adamson, *Noble Revolt*, p. 396; Russell, *Fall*, pp. 303–29; A. MacDonald (ed.), *Letters to King James the Sixth from the Queen, Prince Henry, Prince Charles* (Edinburgh, 1835), p. lxxxi.

5 Adamson, *Noble Revolt*, p. 397.

6 CSPV, 18 October 1641 [N.S.].

7 *HMC Fourth Report*, Appendix, p. 295.

8 Evelyn, *Diary*, IV, p. 49.

9 Evelyn, *Diary*, IV, pp. 50–1.

10 Evelyn, *Diary*, IV, p. 96.

11 Nicholas, *Mr Secretary Nicholas*, p. 137; Evelyn, *Diary*, IV, p. 51.

12 Russell, *Fall*, p. 321.

13 Evelyn, *Diary*, IV, p. 57.

14 Bodleian MS, Bankes 43/1.

15 Evelyn, *Diary*, IV, pp. 53–4.

16 Manning, *English People*, pp. 140–7; J. Walter, *Understanding Popular Violence in the English Revolution: the Colchester Plunderers* (Cambridge, 1999), pp. 100–5.

17 House of Lords, Main Papers, HL/PO/JO/10/1/69, 5 August 1641, Petition of Sir Robert Heath, kt.

18 Evelyn, *Diary*, IV, p. 60.

19 Bodleian, MS Tanner, 66, f. 178.

20 Russell, *Fall*, p. 367.

21 J. Bettey (ed.), *Calendar of the Correspondence of the Smyth Family of Ashton Court, 1548–1642* Bristol Record Society, 35 (Bristol, 1982), p. 172.

22 Adamson, *Noble Revolt*, pp. 354–61.

23 Evelyn, *Diary*, IV, pp. 65–7.

24 Evelyn, *Diary*, IV, pp. 67–9.

25 Adamson, *Noble Revolt*, p. 389.

26 Russell, *Fall*, p. 403.

27 TNA, SP 16/484/68.

28 Holmes, *Why Was Charles I Executed?*, pp. 51–2.

29 Cressy, *England on Edge*, p. 259.

30 Russell, *Fall*, pp. 402–3.

31 Holmes, *Why Was Charles I Executed?*, p. 52.

32 Cressy, *England on Edge*, p. 262; J. Spraggon, *Puritan Iconoclasm during the English Civil War* (Woodbridge, 2003), pp. 100, 138–44.

33 Cressy, *England on Edge*, p. 55; W. Dugdale, *The History of St Pauls* (London, 1658), a3v. The phrase itself is Dugdale's, but he is ventriloquising Hatton.

34 TNA, SP 16/484/63.

35 CSPV, 4 October 1641 [N.S.].

36 Bodleian, MS Rawlinson, D 843, f. 48r. Another copy survives in the hand of the Earl of Salisbury in the Hatfield MSS. Adamson suggests that Salisbury, generally a Junto supporter, was sympathetic to the text and may even have written it. I'm less convinced. The reference to the country being saved by the 'gentry' doesn't quite suggest a noble author, and the sheer vehemence of the denunciations of people Salisbury would have to work with gives pause for thought. Another interpretation, of course, is that he copied it because he thought it was dangerous: Adamson, *Noble Revolt*, p. 361.

37 Cressy, *England on Edge*, p. 60.

38 Cressy, *England on Edge*, pp. 65–6.

39 CSPV, 6 September 1641 [N.S.].

40 Evelyn, *Diary*, IV, p. 60.

41 Evelyn, *Diary*, IV, pp. 71–2.

42 Carlton, *Charles I*, p. 32.

43 Cust, *Charles I: A Political Life*, p. 356.

44 Evelyn, *Diary*, IV, pp. 73–4.

45 Adamson, *Noble Revolt*, p. 371; Cust, *Charles I: A Political Life*, p. 280.

46 Evelyn, *Diary*, IV, p. 74.

47 Adamson, *Noble Revolt*, p. 369.

48 Evelyn, *Diary*, IV, p. 77.

49 Evelyn, *Diary*, IV, pp. 75–77.

50 Evelyn, *Diary*, IV, pp. 78, 82.

51 Evelyn, *Diary*, IV, p. 82.

52 Evelyn, *Diary*, IV, p. 84.

53 Evelyn, *Diary*, IV, p. 89.

54 A point made in Russell, *Fall*, pp. 325–7.

55 The duel incident isn't always directly connected by historians to the plot (see Russell, *Fall*, p. 321), but at least one observer at the time considered it 'but an untimely birth of this Plot': J. S., *The Truth of the Proceedings in Scotland, containing the Discovery of the Late Conspiracie* (London, 1641), p. 2. Adamson takes this line and to my mind is convincing: Adamson, *Noble Revolt*, pp. 398–9.

56 Adamson, *Noble Revolt*, pp. 409–10.

57 S., *The Truth of the Proceedings in Scotland*, p. 8.

58 Adamson, *Noble Revolt*, p. 409 and fn.

59 S., *The Truth of the Proceedings in Scotland*, p. 2.

60 Russell, *Fall*, p. 328.

61 Clarendon, *History*, I, p. 410.

62 Fletcher, *Outbreak*, p. 130.

63 Evelyn, *Diary*, IV, p. 91.

64 Evelyn, *Diary*, IV, p. 92.

65 Clarendon, *History*, I, p. 395.

66 CSPV, 1 November 1641 [N.S.].

67 Evelyn, *Diary*, IV, p. 92.

68 Adamson, *Noble Revolt*, p. 408; *The Discovery of a Late and Bloody Conspiracie at Edenburgh in Scotland* (London, 1641).

69 Adamson, *Noble Revolt*, p. 408; Fletcher, *Outbreak*, p. 133.

70 K. Chidley, *The Justification of the Independant Churches of Christ being an answer to Mr Edwards his booke* (London, 1641); I. Gentles, 'Katherine Chidley (fl. 1616–1653), religious controversialist and Leveller', *ODNB*; P. Baker, 'Thomas Edwards (c. 1599–1648), Church of England clergyman and religious controversialist', *ODNB*.

71 *A Nest of Serpents discovered; or, A Knot of old Heretiques revived, called the Adamites* (London, 1641).

72 Evelyn, *Diary*, IV, p. 82.

7 A VAST RECEPTACLE OF A DISORDERED MULTITUDE

1 *Die Martis 5 October 1641. It is this day ordered …* (London, 1641).

2 TNA, ASSI 45/1/3/68.

3 Fletcher, *Outbreak*, p. 127.

4 *A Discovery of Many Great and Bloudy Roberies, committed of late by Dissolute and Evill Affected Troopers* (London, 1641).

5 Nicholas, *Mr Secretary Nicholas*, p. 122.

6 TNA, PC 2/53, pp. 189–92.

7 Based on the diagram in Adamson, *Noble Revolt*, p. xx; and: https://www.historyofparliamentonline.org/files/images/places/westminster-plan.jpg.

8 Cust, *Charles I and the Aristocracy*, p. 3.

9 Nicholas, *Mr Secretary Nicholas*, pp. 64, 118.

10 P. Griffiths, *Lost Londons: Change, Crime and Control in the Capital City, 1550–1660* (Cambridge, 2008), p. 303.

11 D. Lupton, *London and the Country Carbonadoed and Quartered into Several Characters* (London, 1632), p. 1.

12 Griffiths, *Lost Londons*, p. 1.

13 Griffiths, *Lost Londons*, pp. 36, 48.

14 Griffiths, *Lost Londons*, p. 41.

15 E. Hubbard, *City Women: Money, Sex & the Social Order in Early Modern London* (Oxford, 2012), p. 20.

16 Hubbard, *City Women*, p. 19.

17 A. Sharp, 'John Lilburne (1615?–1657), Leveller', *ODNB*; P.R.S. Baker, 'William Larner (d. 1672?), printer and Leveller', *ODNB*.

18 Hubbard, *City Women*, p. 37.

19 Hubbard, *City Women*, p. 182.

20 Lupton, *London and the Countrey Carbonadoed*, pp. 92–3.

21 Hubbard, *City Women*, p. 168.

22 L. Gowing, *Domestic Dangers: Women, Words and Sex in Early Modern London* (Oxford, 1996), pp. 59–110.

23 Hubbard, *City Women*, p. 178.

24 Griffiths, *Lost Londons*, p. 99.

25 I owe this to Prof. Steven Gunn and his work on Tudor accidental deaths.

26 Hubbard, *City Women*, p. 182.

27 Griffiths, *Lost Londons*, p. 343.

28 Griffiths, *Lost Londons*, pp. 332–60.

29 Griffiths, *Lost Londons*, p. 337.

30 Hubbard, *City Women*, p. 148.

31 Bridewell Hospital Archives, BCB 8, f. 348v.

32 Bridewell Hospital Archives, BCB 8, f. 338r.

33 Bridewell Hospital Archives, BCB 8, f. 318v.

34 Hubbard, *City Women*, p. 207.

35 M. Hailwood, *Alehouses and Good Fellowship in Early Modern England* (Woodbridge, 2016), pp. 2–3.

36 Hubbard, *City Women*, p. 156.

37 Griffiths, *Lost Londons*, pp. 84, 153.

38 Griffiths, *Lost Londons*, p. 85.

39 Griffiths, *Lost Londons*, p. 78.

40 Griffiths, *Lost Londons*, p. 221.

41 Griffiths, *Lost Londons*, p. 255.

42 Griffiths, *Lost Londons*, p. 238.

43 Griffiths, *Lost Londons*, pp. 89–90.

44 Bridewell Hospital Archives, BCB 8, f. 322r.

45 Gowing, *Domestic Dangers*, pp. 66–7.

46 Bridewell Hospital Archives, BCB 8, f. 338r.

47 Griffiths, *Lost Londons*, p. 103.

48 Griffiths, *Lost Londons*, pp. 207, 391.

49 Nicholas, *Mr Secretary Nicholas*, p. 116.

50 Griffiths, *Lost Londons*, p. 190.

51 Griffiths, *Lost Londons*, p. 43.

52 Sharpe, *Personal Rule*, pp. 404–6.

53 Hubbard, *City Women*, p. 206; *An Excellent New Ditty: Or, which Proveth that Women the Best Warriers Be* (London, 1635).

54 F. Heal, 'The Crown, the Gentry and London: the Enforcement of Proclamation', in C. Cross, D. Loades and J. Scarisbrick (eds), *Law and Government under the Tudors: essays presented to Sir Geoffrey Elton, Regius Professor of Modern History in the University of Cambridge, on the Occasion of His Retirement* (Cambridge, 1988), pp. 211–26.

55 T. Barnes, 'The Prerogative and Environmental Control of London Building in the Early 17th Century: the Lost Opportunity', *California Law Review*, 58 (1970), pp. 1332–63. House of Lords, Main Papers, HL/PO/JO/10/1/50, 5 February, Petition of Ralph Macro.

8 WHAT IS BEGUN WITH THE TONGUE AND THE PEN

1 M. Maslen (ed.), *Woodstock Chamberlain's Accounts, 1609–50* Oxfordshire Record Society, 58 (Stroud, 1993), p. 197.

2 Maslen, *Woodstock Chamberlain's Accounts*, pp. 196–7.

3 CSPV, 4 October 1641 [N.S.].

4 D'Ewes, *Journal*, p. 11.

5 S. McGee, *An Industrious Mind: the Worlds of Sir Simonds D'Ewes* (Stanford, 2015).

6 McGee, *Industrious Mind*, p. 19.

7 McGee, *Industrious Mind*, p. 20.

8 McGee, *Industrious Mind*, p. 29.

9 McGee, *Industrious Mind*, p. 43.

10 J. Bruce, 'The Long Parliament and Sir Simonds D'Ewes', *Edinburgh Review*, 84 (1846), p. 81.

11 BL, Sloane MS 1467, f. 101r.

12 Fletcher, *Outbreak*, p. 112.

13 *LJ*, 20 October 1641.

14 *CJ*, 21 October 1641 and 23 October 1641.

15 Fletcher, *Outbreak*, p. 133.

16 D'Ewes, *Journal*, p. 25; the division is not reported in the *Commons Journal* because the Commons was sitting as a Committee of the Whole House.

17 D'Ewes, *Journal*, pp. 29–30.

18 D'Ewes, *Journal*, p. 37.

19 *A Damnable Treason by a Contagious Plaster of a Plague Sore, wrapt up in a letter sent and sent to Mr Pym* (London, 1641).

20 *LJ*, 26 October 1641.

21 D'Ewes, *Journal*, pp. 44–7.

22 Adamson, *Noble Revolt*, p. 419.

23 Evelyn, *Diary*, IV, p. 101.

24 L. Glow, 'The Manipulation of Committees in the Long Parliament, 1641–1642', *Journal of British Studies*, 5 (1965), p. 39.

25 D'Ewes, *Journal*, p. 51.

26 Bridewell Hospital Archives, BCB 8, f. 354r.

27 *LJ*, 23 October 1641.

28 Merritt, *Westminster*, p. 37.

29 CSPV, 8 November 1641 [N.S.].

30 Evelyn, *Diary*, IV, p. 103.

31 Evelyn, *Diary*, IV, p. 103.

9 THE WIZARD'S DAUGHTER

1 Lady Carlisle awaits her biographer. There is some useful material in: L. Betcherman, *Court Lady and Country Wife: Two Noble Sisters in Seventeenth-Century England* (New York, 2005); also R. Schreiber, 'Lucy Hay [née Percy], countess of Carlisle (1599–1660), courtier', *ODNB*; I have made much use of the excellent 2015 MA thesis by Ingrid Lemstra: I. Lemstra, 'Lucy Percy Hay (1599–1660), Countess of Carlisle: Wanton Seductress or Influential Broker', Leiden University MA thesis (2015). Lucy Hay is also one of the key characters in N. Akkerman, *Invisible Agents: Women and Espionage in Seventeenth-Century Britain* (Oxford, 2018). See also the same author's superb essay: 'A Triptych of Dorothy Percy Sidney (1598–1659), Countess of Leicester, Lucy Percy Hay (1599–1660), Countess of Carlisle and Dorothy Sidney Spencer (1617–1684), Countess of Sunderland' in M. Hannay, M. Lamb, and M. Brennan (eds.), *The Ashgate Research Companion to the Sidneys, Volume 1: Lives* (London, 2016), pp. 133–50.
2 Lemstra, 'Lucy Percy Hay', p. 7.
3 Carlton, *Charles I*, p. 29.
4 Bodleian, MS Clarendon 18, no. 200.
5 Betcherman, *Court Lady*, p. 186.
6 TNA, SP 16/275/23.
7 Nicholas, *Mr Secretary Nicholas*, p. 97.
8 Lemstra, 'Lucy Percy Hay', p. 55; Betcherman, *Court Lady*, p. 144.
9 Betcherman, *Court Lady*, pp. 132, 163.
10 Betcherman, *Court Lady*, p. 157.
11 Betcherman, *Court Lady*, p. 212.
12 *HMC De Lisle and Dudley*, VI, p. 337.
13 Adamson, *Noble Revolt*, pp. 133–4, 153.
14 House of Lords, Main Papers, HL/PO/JO/10/1/46, 2 January 1641, list delivered by the Lieutenant of the Tower.
15 P. Warwick, *Memoirs of the Reign of Charles I* (London, 1702), p. 225.
16 Evelyn, *Diary*, IV, p. 75.
17 Evelyn, *Diary*, IV, p. 77.
18 Clarendon, *History*, I, pp. 388–9.
19 Evelyn, *Diary*, IV, p. 118.
20 For a succinct summary see: Harris, *Rebellion*, pp. 142–68, 347–60; J. Ohlmeyer, '"Civilizing of those Rude Partes": Colonization within Britain and Ireland, 1580s–1640s', in N. Canny (ed.), *The*

Oxford History of the British Empire, Volume I: The Origins of Empire (Oxford, 1998), pp. 124–47; N. Canny, *Making Ireland British, 1580–1650* (2001); M. Perceval-Maxwell, *The Outbreak of the Irish Rebellion of 1641* (London, 1994).

21 TNA, SP 16/485/56.

22 Adamson, *Noble Revolt*, p. 378. To Adamson, the involvement of Charles and Henrietta Maria in the Irish army scheme 'can neither be definitively confirmed nor entirely ruled out'.

23 Adamson, *Noble Revolt*, pp. 421–2; Clarendon, *History*, I, p. 397.

24 Clarendon, *History*, I, p. 398.

25 Perceval-Maxwell, *Outbreak*, p. 229; E. Darcy, *The Irish Rebellion of 1641 and the Wars of the Three Kingdoms* (Woodbridge, 2013), pp. 68–70.

26 On Irish refugees, see: B. Marsh, ' "Lodging the Irish": An Examination of Parochial Charity Dispensed in Nottinghamshire to Refugees from Ireland, 1641–1651', *Midland History*, 42 (2017), pp. 194–216.

27 N. Wallington, *Historical Notices of Events Occurring Chiefly in the Reign of Charles I*, 2 vols (London, 1870), II, pp. 41–2.

28 D'Ewes, *Journal*, p. 68; McGee, *Industrious Mind*, p. 17.

10 TO SPEAK PLAIN ENGLISH

1 J. Bossy, *The English Catholic Community, 1570–1850* (London, 1975), p. 188.

2 Merritt, *Westminster*, pp. 24–8. The story about James being put in the stocks was offered in mitigation by a fellow Catholic, though as Merritt points out it is plausible.

3 Merritt, *Westminster*, p. 36.

4 De Lisle, *Henrietta Maria*, pp. 204–6; Merritt, *Westminster*, p. 29.

5 De Lisle, *Henrietta Maria*, p. 204.

6 Cust, *Charles I: A Political Life*, p. 312; D'Ewes, *Journal*, pp. 58–9; *LJ*, 30 October 1641.

7 Plowden, *Henrietta Maria*, p. 202.

8 Clarendon, *History*, I, p. 399.

9 D'Ewes, *Journal*, pp. 78–9.

10 House of Lords, Main Papers, HL/PO/JO/10/1/73, 1 November 1641, Certificate of the Justices of Westminster; 4 November 1641, Certificates of the Constables of St Olave's Southwark, St Thomas's Southwark, St Saviour's Southwark, and St George's Southwark.

11 D'Ewes, *Journal*, p. 92.

12 D'Ewes, *Journal*, p. 103; Bodleian, MS Rawlinson, D 932, ff. 14b–15a.

13 D'Ewes, *Journal*, p. 95, Gardiner, *History*, X, p. 55.

14 D'Ewes, *Journal*, pp. 97–8; Gardiner, *History*, X, pp. 58–9; *CJ*, 6 November 1641.

15 D'Ewes, *Journal*, p. 105.

16 D'Ewes, *Journal*, p. 111.

17 Adamson, *Noble Revolt*, p. 434.

18 Gardiner, *Constitutional Documents*, pp. 202–32.

19 Cust, *Forced Loan*, pp. 62-7.

20 Evelyn, *Diary*, IV, p. 117.

21 D'Ewes, *Journal*, p. 130.

22 Evelyn, *Diary*, IV, p. 121.

23 Evelyn, *Diary*, IV, pp. 115–16.

24 Evelyn, *Diary*, IV, pp. 124–5.

25 Evelyn, *Diary*, IV, pp. 100, 109, 117, 120, 125.

26 Adamson, *Noble Revolt*, p. 429.

27 Cressy, *England on Edge*, pp. 47–9.

28 House of Lords, Main Papers, HL/PO/JO/10/1/73, 14–15 November, Informations.

29 House of Lords, Main Papers, HL/PO/JO/10/1/73 13 November, Returns by the Justices of Middlesex and Westminster.

30 *LJ*, 15 November 1641.

31 House of Lords, Main Papers, HL/PO/JO/10/1/73, 15 November 1641, Examination of Father Browne.

32 D'Ewes, *Journal*, p. 144.

33 Evelyn, *Diary*, IV, p. 126.

34 Russell, *Fall*, pp. 422–3; D'Ewes, *Journal*, pp. 144–5; *LJ*, 15 November 1641.

35 TNA, SP 16/485/90; Fletcher, *Outbreak*, p. 139, accepts that the Junto were genuinely fearful.

36 *Five Most Noble Speeches Spoken to his Majestie returning out of Scotland into England* (London, 1641).

37 *Five Most Noble Speeches*, a2v.

38 *Five Most Noble Speeches*, a3v.

39 Evelyn, *Diary*, IV, p. 127.

40 Evelyn, *Diary*, IV, p. 132.

41 Russell, *Fall*, p. 418.
42 CSPV, 22 November 1641 [N.S.].
43 Evelyn, *Diary*, IV, p. 131.
44 TNA, SP 16/484/68.
45 Evelyn, *Diary*, IV, p. 131.
46 D'Ewes, *Journal*, p. 177.
47 Clarendon, *History*, I, p. 419.
48 D'Ewes, *Journal*, p. 183.
49 Russell, *Fall*, pp. 427–8.
50 Bodleian, MS Rawlinson, D 932, ff. 48–9; R. Verney, *Verney Papers. Notes of Proceedings in the Long Parliament, temp. Charles I*, ed. J. Bruce (London, 1845), pp. 121–5.
51 Bodleian, MS Rawlinson, D 932, f. 49r. My emphasis.
52 Bodleian, MS Rawlinson, D 932, f. 49r.
53 Verney, *Papers*, pp. 122–3.
54 Verney, *Papers*, p. 124.
55 Clarendon, *History*, I, p. 419.
56 Evelyn, *Diary*, IV, p. 133.
57 Evelyn, *Diary*, IV, p. 133.
58 Gardiner, *History*, X, pp. 76–7.
59 D'Ewes, *Journal*, p. 187n.
60 Adamson, *Noble Revolt*, p. 435.
61 *CJ*, 22 November 1641.
62 Clarendon, *History*, I, p. 420.
63 *The Heads of Several Proceedings in this Present Parliament* (London, 22–29 November 1641), p. 3.
64 D'Ewes, *Journal*, p. 196 and note.
65 D'Ewes, *Journal*, pp. 214-6; Manning, *English People*, pp. 63–4. A key piece of evidence for this is in an unnamed and undated report in the Clarendon papers: Bodleian, MS Clarendon, 20, no. 1542. It dates the events to the 'the day on which Mr Palmer was sent unto the Tower'. This would be 25 November, but as this was the day of the king's procession it seems highly unlikely that a large mobilisation of Londoners would be possible without causing a significant incident, so I have followed Gardiner and Lindley in dating this to the 24th, the day that the house debated Palmer's case for some six hours: Gardiner, *History*, X, pp. 86–7; Lindley, *Popular Politics*, p. 95. Russell places the evidence in the context of a later protest on the

29th (on which, see below), but while this may have been the reason for gathering the evidence, the protest itself was evidently earlier, given the clear reference to Palmer: Russell, *Fall*, p. 433.

66 Bodleian, MS Nalson, 13/33.

11 LONDON'S JOY

1 J. Bond, *The Parliaments and Londons Preparation for His Majesties Return* (London, 1641), a3v.

2 Evelyn, *Diary*, IV, p. 127.

3 S. Keenan, *The Progresses, Processions, and Royal Entries of King Charles I* (Oxford, 2020), p. 184.

4 Keenan, *Progresses*, pp. 184–5.

5 J. Taylor, *Englands Comfort, and Londons Joy* (London, 1641).

6 *King Charles his Entertainment and Londons Loyaltie* (London, 1641), p. 5.

7 Keenan, *Progresses*, p. 185.

8 Rushworth, IV, pp. 421–36.

9 Russell, *Fall*, p. 429.

10 Rushworth, IV, pp. 421–36.

11 *Ovatio Carolina, the Triumph of King Charles* (London, 1641), p. 11.

12 *Ovatio Carolina*, p. 11.

13 *Heads of Several Proceedings* (22–29 November 1641), p. 5.

14 Adamson, *Noble Revolt*, p. 439.

15 *Ovatio Carolina*, p. 13.

16 *Ovatio Carolina*, pp. 13–16.

17 Keenan, *Progresses*, p. 188.

18 *Ovatio Carolina*, p. 17.

19 Taylor, *Englands Comfort*, p. 4; Adamson, *Noble Revolt*, p. 439.

20 *Ovatio Carolina*, pp. 18–19.

21 L. Price, *Great Britaines Time of Triumph* (London, 1641), title page.

22 Adamson, *Noble Revolt*, p. 445.

23 Adamson, *Noble Revolt*, p. 442.

24 Adamson, *Noble Revolt*, pp. 443–4.

25 Rushworth, IV, pp. 421–36.

26 Price, *Great Britaines Time of Triumph*, a3v.

27 Taylor, *Englands Comfort*, p. 5.

28 M. Butler, 'Politics and the Masque: *The Triumph of Peace*', *The Seventeenth Century*, 2 (1987), pp. 117–41.

29 Keenan, *Progresses*, p. 187.

30 D'Ewes, *Journal*, pp. 196–9.

31 D'Ewes, *Journal*, p. 197; *CJ*, 25 November 1641.

32 Taylor, *Englands Comfort*.

33 *The Brothers of the Blade; Answerable to the Sisters of the Scaberd* (London, 1641).

34 The following section is based on J. Raymond, *The Invention of the Newspaper: English Newsbooks, 1641–1649* (Oxford, 1996), pp. 20–5, 80–126.

35 Fletcher, *Outbreak*, p. xxviii.

36 Russell, *Fall*, pp. 433–4.

37 *HMC Buccleuch*, I, pp. 286–7.

38 *Heads of Severall Proceedings* (22–29 November), p. 6.

39 Adamson, *Noble Revolt*, p. 447.

40 CSPV, 13 December 1641 [N.S.].

41 Russell, *Fall*, p. 405.

42 *Five Most Noble Speeches*, a3r.

43 *King Charles His Entertainment*, p. 6.

44 Taylor, *Englands Comfort*, p. 8.

12 INDISCREET RASHNESS

1 N. Millstone, 'Evil Counsel: *The Propositions to Bridle the Impertinency of Parliament* and the Critique of Caroline Government in the late 1620s', *Journal of British Studies*, 50 (2011), pp. 813–39.

2 TNA, SP 16/151/24; Jones, *Politics and the Bench*, p. 88.

3 On Dorset, see: D. Smith, 'The Political Career of Edward Sackville, fourth Earl of Dorset (1590–1652)', University of Cambridge PhD thesis (1990); D. Smith, 'The 4th Earl of Dorset and the Politics of the Sixteen–twenties', *Historical Research*, 65 (1992), pp. 37–53; D. Smith, 'The Fourth Earl of Dorset and the Personal Rule of Charles I', *Journal of British Studies*, 30 (1991), pp. 257–87; D. Smith, '"The More Posed and Wise Advice": the Fourth Earl of Dorset and the English Civil Wars', *Historical Journal*, 34 (1991), pp. 797–829.

4 Smith, 'Political Career', pp. 279–84.

5 Clarendon, *History*, I, p. 75.

6 Cust, *Charles I and the Aristocracy*, p. 122.

7 Griffiths, *Lost Londons*, p. 83.

8 Gardiner, *History*, X, p. 86.

9 Clarendon, *History*, I, p. 451.

10 Russell, *Fall*, p. 425.

11 D'Ewes, *Journal*, p. 208; Russell, *Fall*, p. 436.

12 D'Ewes, *Journal*, p. 209.

13 *HMC Buccleuch*, I, p. 287.

14 D'Ewes, *Journal*, p. 213 and n.

15 Bodleian, MS Rawlinson, D 932, f. 56.

16 D'Ewes, *Journal*, p. 211n, quoting the manuscript notes of the House of Lords.

17 Bodleian, MS Rawlinson, D 932, f. 56; *Heads of Several Proceedings* (29 November–6 December 1641), pp. 1–2; Lindley, *Popular Politics*, pp. 96–7; Manning puts part of this disturbance on the 28th (Sunday) (Manning, *English People*, p. 65), but his sources do not state this explicitly. The summoning of the four protestors to the Lords can only have taken place the next day, Monday, as reported in the *Heads*, so unless they were in Westminster Hall on Sunday but only brought before the peers on Monday, the disturbance being described must be that of the 29th.

18 *HMC Buccleuch*, I, p. 287.

19 Clarendon, *History*, I, p. 451.

20 Lindley, *Popular Politics*, pp. 96–7; Manning, *English People*, p. 66; Bodleian, MS Rawlinson, D 932, f. 56r.

21 D'Ewes, *Journal*, p. 211.

22 Clarendon, *History*, I, p. 450.

23 Bodleian, MS Rawlinson, D 932, f. 56r.

24 D'Ewes, *Journal*, p. 212; Bodleian, MS Rawlinson, D 932, f. 56v.

25 D'Ewes, *Journal*, pp. 212–13n.

26 W. Chernaik, 'William Chillingworth (1602–1644), theologian', *ODNB*.

27 *Heads of Several Proceedings* (29 November–6 December 1641); Manning, *English People*, p. 73.

28 D'Ewes, *Journal*, p. 214.

29 D'Ewes, *Journal*, pp. 217–19; Bodleian, MS Clarendon, 20, no. 1544.

30 *HMC Buccleuch*, I, pp. 286–7; TNA, SP 16/486/28; SP 16/486/63.

31 D'Ewes, *Journal*, p. 207.

32 Adamson, *Noble Revolt*, pp. 449–50.

33 TNA, SP 16/486/36.
34 V. Wedgwood, *The King's War, 1641–1647* (London, 1958), p. 35.
35 Gardiner, *History*, X, pp. 88–9; Rushworth, IV, pp. 436–71.
36 *His Majesties Speech to Both Houses of Parliament: December the Second* (London, 1641).
37 D'Ewes, *Journal*, pp. 223–6.
38 D'Ewes, *Journal*, pp. 225–6.
39 D'Ewes, *Journal*, p. 226.
40 D'Ewes, *Journal*, p. 227; Gardiner, *History*, X, p. 92.
41 D'Ewes, *Journal*, p. 228.
42 Verney, *Papers*, p. 131.
43 *CJ*, 3 December 1641.
44 D'Ewes, *Journal*, p. 230.
45 D'Ewes, *Journal*, pp. 229–31.
46 *Ovatio Carolina*, pp. 23–9.
47 *Ovatio Carolina*, pp. 23–32.
48 D'Ewes, *Journal*, p. 58.
49 Paraphrased by D'Ewes, *Journal*, p. 173.
50 TNA, SP 16/486/21–22.
51 TNA, SP 16/486/21–22.

13 DANGEROUS EXPECTATION

1 Lindley, *Popular Politics*, p. 99.
2 Lindley, *Popular Politics*, pp. 99–100.
3 *HMC Second Report*, p. 48; *HMC Buccleuch*, I, p. 288.
4 TNA, SP 16/486/63.
5 TNA, SP 16/486/29.
6 *HMC Buccleuch*, I, p. 288.
7 Gardiner, *History*, X, p. 95.
8 TNA, SP 16/485/49.
9 TNA, SP 16/486/11.
10 Manning, *English People*, p. 85.
11 Adamson, *Noble Revolt*, pp. 457–8, 480.
12 Cust, *Charles I: A Political Life*, p. 124.
13 Gardiner, *History*, X, p. 98n.
14 L. Schwoerer, ' "The Fittest Subject for a King's Quarrell": an Essay on the Militia Controversy, 1641–2', *Journal of British Studies*, 11 (1971), pp. 45–76; Adamson, *Noble Revolt*, p. 460.

15 D'Ewes, *Journal*, p. 245.

16 D'Ewes, *Journal*, pp. 246–7.

17 TNA, SP 16/486/28.

18 D'Ewes, *Journal*, p. 261.

19 Bodleian, MS Rawlinson, D 932, f. 68v; D'Ewes, *Journal*, p. 263; A warrant to the JPs to bring out 'one hundred able and sufficient men … well armed & arrayed' is in the House of Lords, Main Papers, HL/PO/JO/10/1/74, 10 December 1641.

20 D'Ewes, *Journal*, p. 265.

21 Gardiner, *History*, X, p. 97; *His Majesties Speciall Command under the Great Seale of England* (London, 1641).

22 Merritt, *Westminster*, p. 38.

23 *The Citizens of London's Humble Petition* (London, 1641).

24 TNA, SP 16/486/45.

25 Manning, *English People*, p. 75.

26 Lindley, *Popular Politics*, p. 101.

27 Manning, *English People*, p. 80.

28 Larkin, *Stuart Royal Proclamations*, pp. 752–4; TNA, SP 16/486/72.

29 TNA, PC 2/53, pp. 200–1.

30 DHC, D-BKL/H/A/8.

31 Gardiner, *History*, X, p. 99.

32 Adamson, *Noble Revolt*, p. 464; *By the King. A Proclamation for the Attendance of the Members in Both Houses in Parliament* (London, 1641); also in Larkin, *Stuart Royal Proclamations*, II, pp. 754–5.

33 Noted in Bodleian, MS Rawlinson, D 932, f. 77v on 14 December 1641.

34 D. Cressy, *Dangerous Talk: Scandalous, Seditious, and Treasonable Speech in Pre-Modern England* (Oxford, 2010), p. 11.

35 Adamson, *Noble Revolt*, p. 465.

36 CSPV, 27 December 1641 [N.S.].

37 TNA, SP 16/486/64.

38 D'Ewes, *Journal*, p. 287.

39 TNA, SP 16/486/62.

40 TNA, SP 16/486/83.

41 *His Majesties Speciall Command.*

42 TNA, SP 16/486/61; *His Majesties Speciall Command*; *Diurnall Occurrences, or, the Heads of Severall Proceedings in both Houses of Parliament* (London, 13–20 December 1641).

43 D'Ewes, *Journal*, pp. 283–4.

44 *Diurnall Occurrences* (13–20 December 1641); Rushworth, IV, pp. 436–71.

45 D'Ewes, *Journal*, p. 286.

46 TNA, SP 16/486/61.

47 *Diurnall Occurrences* (13–20 December 1641).

48 D'Ewes, *Journal*, p. 290 and n.

49 D'Ewes, *Journal*, pp. 294–5.

50 CSPV, 27 December 1641 [N.S.].

51 TNA, SP 16/486/62.

52 TNA, SP 16/486/69.

53 TNA, SP 16/486/62.

54 TNA, SP 16/486/64.

55 Cressy, *England on Edge*, p. 49.

56 *HMC Buccleuch*, I, p. 289.

57 *Diurnall Occurrences* (13–20 December 1641).

58 *LJ*, 17 December 1641.

59 *The Discovery of a Swarme of Seperatists, A Leathersellers Sermon* (London, 1641).

60 *The Discovery of a Swarme of Seperatists.*

61 V. Pearl, *London and the Outbreak of the Puritan Revolution* (London, 1961), pp. 132–40.

62 M. Wren, 'The Disputed Elections in London in 1641', *English Historical Review*, 64 (1949), pp. 34–52.

63 Manning, *English People*, p. 75.

64 *CJ*, 21 December 1641.

14 THE JAWS OF DESTRUCTION

1 *HMC Eighth Report*, p. 212.

2 TNA, C3/418/251-2; C8/65/116.

3 Bodleian, MS Rawlinson, C 827, unfol., 2 Feb., 13 Car.

4 Bodleian, MS Bankes, 7/6; MS Rawlinson, C 827, unfol., 1 June, 14 Car; 6 June, 14 Car.

5 Bodleian, MS Rawlinson, C 827, unfol., 6 June, 14 Car; Rawlinson D 720, f. 50r.

6 House of Lords, Main Paper, HL/PO/JO/10/1/46, 7 January 1641, Petition of Dame Susanna Wiseman; his fine had already been mitigated by that point: TNA, SP 16/461/16.

7 *HMC Buccleuch*, III, p. 405.

8 House of Lords, Main Papers, HL/PO/JO/10/1/68, 4 August 1641, Deposition of Henry Winter; HL/PO/JO/10/1/69, 5 August, Deposition of Ralph Patterel.

9 Bodleian, MS Bankes, 18/21.

10 Bodleian, MS Rawlinson, C 827, unfol., 9 Feb., 13 Car.

11 P. Gregg, *Free-Born John: A Biography of John Lilburne* (London, 1961), p. 400.

12 J. Lilburne, *The Christian Mans Triall* (2nd ed., London, 1641); on Lilburne, see: M. Braddick, *The Common Freedom of the People: John Lilburne and the English Revolution* (Oxford, 2018).

13 M. Stoyle, 'The Cannibal Cavalier: Sir Thomas Lunsford and the Fashioning of the Royalist Archetype', *Historical Journal*, 59 (2016), p. 298.

14 Gardiner, *History*, X, p. 110.

15 Clarendon, *History*, I, p. 447.

16 *Diurnall Occurrences* (20–27 December 1641) puts this report on the previous day, but this is impossible to reconcile with D'Ewes's journal: D'Ewes, *Journal*, p. 330.

17 D'Ewes, *Journal*, pp. 330–31.

18 TNA, SP 16/486/84.

19 TNA, SP 16/369/58.

20 TNA, SP 16/461/95.

21 Cressy, *England on Edge*, p. 388.

22 Stoyle, 'Cannibal Cavalier', p. 302.

23 Adamson, *Noble Revolt*, pp. 486–7.

24 Clarendon, *History*, I, p. 478; I. Roy, 'Sir Lewis Dyve (1599–1669), royalist army officer', *ODNB*.

25 *Diurnall Occurrences* (20–27 December 1641); Gardiner, *History*, X, pp. 108–9. Austin Woolrych attributes this to Edward Hyde, saying he had 'skilfully drafted' it for Charles. A. Woolrych, *Britain in Revolution, 1625–1660* (Oxford, 2002), p. 209. Hyde had indeed written a riposte, which was then published after consultation with the Privy Council: TNA, PC 2/53, p. 209; E. Hyde, *The Life of Edward Earl of Clarendon*, 2 vols (Oxford, 1857), I, pp. 79–81, but Hyde is clearly talking about *His Majesties Declaration, to all His Loving Subjects: Published with the Advice of His Privie Councell* (London, 1642). Hyde discusses the king's initial response in his *History* but doesn't claim authorship: Clarendon, *History*, I, p. 437,

although neither does he here claim he wrote the later *Declaration* (which we know he did): I, p. 493. Both texts can be found together in J. Nalson (ed.), *An Impartial Collection of the Great Affairs of State*, 2 vols (London, 1682–3), II, pp. 744–50. There are a couple of clues which might suggest Woolrych wasn't far off the mark: first, Hyde spoke about both Falkland and Digby seeing his papers at a time when the king hadn't yet put out any response, and he also remembered insisting that his work only be published after being seen by the Privy Council. We know from the council register that his full manuscript was discussed on 6 January, but there is also a copy of the 23 December response in the State Papers, to which a memorandum is attached with the king's command to deliver it to 'Your Lordships': 'which his Majesty thought fit their Lordships should be acquainted withal before it came to them by a second hand'. The 'Lordships' are presumably the Lords of the Privy Council: TNA, SP 16/486/3i. In sum, it is quite possible that the king's response was partly based on Hyde's work, perhaps via Digby or (more likely) Falkland.

26 Lindley, *Popular Politics*, p. 104.
27 D'Ewes, *Journal*, p. 336; House of Lords, Main Papers, HL/PO/JO/10/1/75, 23 December 1641, Petition.
28 D'Ewes, *Journal*, p. 337. Gardiner, *History*, X, p. 110.
29 D'Ewes, *Journal*, pp. 337–8; The editorial comments made in Nalson, *Impartial Collection*, II, p. 775, snobbishly attacking the role of 'every little blue-apron boy behind the Compter' are, of course, of later provenance, but they probably reflect conservative opinion in 1641 as well.
30 D'Ewes, *Journal*, pp. 339–40.
31 J. Rees, *The Leveller Revolution: Radical Political Organisation in England, 1640–1650* (London, 2016), p. 17.
32 Rees, *Leveller Revolution*, p. 17.
33 *Diurnall Occurences* (20–27 December 1641).
34 D'Ewes, *Journal*, p. 346.
35 Gardiner, *History*, X, p. 111.
36 *LJ*, 24 December 1641.
37 *CJ*, 24 December 1641.
38 D'Ewes, *Journal*, p. 347.
39 Rees, *Leveller Revolution*, p. 17.

40 Manning, *English People*, p. 89.

41 Wallington, *Historical Notices*, I, pp. 276–7.

42 Lindley, *Popular Politics*, p. 106; Manning, *English People*, p. 89.

43 TNA, PC 2/53, p. 203.

44 *Diurnall Occurrences* (27 December 1641–3 January 1642).

45 *Diurnall Occurrences* (27 December 1641–3 January 1642). There is a bit of uncertainty about how many official proclamations were made, but only one is recorded on the docket book, so it seems only one was formally issued, Bodleian, MS Eng. Hist., c. 230, f. 24r; Larkin, *Stuart Royal Proclamations*, II, pp. 756–7.

46 J. Bramston, *The Autobiography of Sir John Bramston, K.B.* (London, 1845), p. 82; Lindley, *Popular Politics*, p. 106.

47 D'Ewes, *Journal*, p. 352.

48 D'Ewes, *Journal*, p. 352.

49 Lindley, *Popular Politics*, p. 107; Manning, *English People*, p. 90.

50 Manning, *English People*, p. 91; Rees, *Leveller Revolution*, p. 18.

51 Manning, *English People*, pp. 90–1; Cressy, *England on Edge*, pp. 389–90; Merritt, *Westminster*, p. 40.

52 Manning, *English People*, p. 91.

53 House of Lords, Main Papers, HL/PO/JO/10/1/114, 15 January 1642, Petition of Peter Scott; Lindley, *Popular Politics*, pp. 107–8.

54 Manning, *English People*, p. 91.

55 Adamson, *Noble Revolt*, pp. 478–9.

56 Adamson, *Noble Revolt*, p. 477.

57 Manning, *English People*, pp. 92–3.

58 Gardiner, *History*, X, p. 118.

59 Manning, *English People*, p. 92.

60 *HMC Hastings*, 2, 1930, p. 83.

61 Bodleian, MS Tanner, 66, f. 220.

62 Manning, *English People*, p. 90.

63 *The Scots Loyaltie to the Protestants of England and Ireland* (London, 1642).

64 *Diurnall Occurences in Parliament* (27 December–2 January [sic]), p. 2.

65 Lindley, *Popular Politics*, p. 108.

66 Manning, *English People*, p. 93.

67 Lindley, *Popular Politics*, p. 109.

68 Bodleian, MS Tanner, 66, f. 220.

69 Manning, *English People*, p. 93; Wren notes specifically that the confrontation at the abbey took place in the evening: 'And (indeed) that evening they assaulted the Abbey Church': Bodleian, MS Tanner, 66, f. 220.

70 Manning, *English People*, p. 93; Lindley, *Popular Politics*, pp. 109–10.

71 Merritt, *Westminster*, p. 40, suggests these apprentices had been apprehended the previous day, although it seems more likely they were arrested on the 28th.

72 *PJ*, pp. 91-2 (D'Ewes); p. 97 (Moore).

73 D'Ewes, *Journal*, p. 358fn.; *A Bloody Masacre Plotted by the Papists intended first against the City of London, and consequently against the whole land* (London, 1641), p. 6; *PJ*, pp. 91–2 (D'Ewes); p. 97 (Moore).

74 Merritt, *Westminster*, pp. 40–1.

75 *HMC Cowper*, II, pp. 302, 303; Rushworth, IV, pp. 473–94; Lindley, *Popular Politics*, p. 111.

76 TNA, LC5/135 unfol., 28 Dec 1641, order.

77 Manning, *English People*, p. 94; Adamson, *Noble Revolt*, pp. 480–1.

78 Stoyle, 'Cannibal Cavalier', p. 308.

79 Lindley, *Popular Politics*, p. 110.

80 *By the King. His Majestie taking into His Princely Consideration the Manifold Inconveniences and Mischiefs* (London, 1641).

81 Bodleian, MS Johnson, c. 1, Gaol Delivery, 1641–2, ff. 17r, 30v, 34r; Lindley, *Popular Politics*, pp. 110–11.

82 TNA, SP 16/486/99.

15 THE MADDEST ONE THAT I EVER SAW

1 There are copies in the Bankes papers in the Bodleian, and Nicholas's collection in the BL: Bodleian, MS Bankes, 55/14–15; BL Egerton MS, 2541, ff. 266–71; discussed in C. Russell, 'Charles I's Financial Estimates for 1642', in C. Russell, *Unrevolutionary England, 1603–1642* (London, 1990), pp. 165–76. Russell's forensic examination of these and other accounts is essential reading to grasp the financial position of the Crown in the winter of 1641/2, but he seems not to have been aware of the duplicates in the Bankes papers. Both Nicholas's and Bankes's copies are annotated in their own hands.

2 Adamson, *Noble Revolt*, p. 457. Adamson sees Digby and Bristol as representing the last gasp of the 'Bedfordian' settlement. On the

other hand, relations between the father-son pair and the Junto were exceedingly strained, which helps explain why Digby threw his weight behind the Lunsford scheme.

3 Adamson, *Noble Revolt*, p. 482.

4 Gardiner, *History*, X, p. 119n; *LJ*, 28 December 1641.

5 *Diurnall Occurrences* (27 December 1641–3 January 1642), a3r.

6 TNA, PC 2/53, pp. 203–4.

7 W. Dugdale, *A Short View of the Late Troubles in England, briefly setting forth their Rise, Growth, and Tragical Conclusion* (Oxford, 1681), p. 81.

8 J. Hart, 'Sir Samuel Barnardiston (1620–1707) first baronet', *ODNB*.

9 *Diurnall Occurrences* (27 December 1641– 3 January 1642), a3v.

10 Merritt, *Westminster*, p. 42.

11 Adamson, *Noble Revolt*, p. 481.

12 Lindley, *Popular Politics*, pp. 111–12.

13 *PJ*, p. 131 (Gawdy). Russell, *Fall*, p. 445, incorrectly dates this fracas to the 31st.

14 Merritt, *Westminster*, p. 41.

15 Bodleian, MS Tanner, 66, f. 220.

16 Lindley, *Popular Politics*, pp. 112–13; *A True Relation of the Most Wise and Worthy Speech made by Captain Venn* (London, 1641).

17 Lindley, *Popular Politics*, p. 113.

18 The text of the petition is in: *LJ*, 30 December 1641.

19 Gardiner, *History*, X, pp. 122–3.

20 Adamson, *Noble Revolt*, p. 483.

21 Adamson, *Noble Revolt*, p. 484.

22 D'Ewes, *Journal*, pp. 365–6.

23 D'Ewes, *Journal*, pp. 365–6.

24 D'Ewes, *Journal*, p. 366.

25 *LJ*, 30 December 1641.

26 D'Ewes, *Journal*, p. 369; *CJ*, 30 December 1641.

27 Gardiner, *History*, X, p. 125.

28 *Come freind, Array your Selfe, and Never Looke* (London, 1642); *The Decoy Duck: Together with the Discovery of the Knot in the Dragons Tayle* (London, 1642).

29 Gardiner, *History*, X, p. 125.

30 TNA, SP 16/486/110.

31 Gardiner, *History*, X, p. 125.

32 TNA, SP 16/486/110.

33 *Diurnall Occurrences* (27 December 1641–3 January 1642); Lindley, *Popular Politics*, p. 114.
34 The words are those of the astrologer William Lilly: Manning, *English People*, p. 101.
35 TNA, SP 16/488/29.
36 TNA, SP 16/486/102; CSPV, 11 January 1642 [N.S.].
37 D'Ewes, *Journal*, p. 371.
38 *CJ*, 31 December 1641.
39 D'Ewes, *Journal*, p. 373.
40 *A Common Councell Held at Guild-Hall in the City of London the 31 of December 1641* (London, 1642); Lindley, *Popular Politics*, p. 116.
41 Pearl, *London*, pp. 139–41.
42 TNA, SP 80/10 f. 157.

16 GREAT AND TREASONABLE DESIGNS

1 *HMC Cowper*, II, p. 302; Thomas Coke to Sir John Coke at Melborne.
2 Russell, *Fall*, p. 447n; Adamson, *Noble Revolt*, p. 485.
3 TNA, LC 5/135; on Thynne, see: Akkerman, *Invisible Agents*, pp. 43–5.
4 Gardiner, *History*, X, p. 127n. The source for this, a letter by Edward Dering, is not especially reliable, and the rumour is not to my knowledge recorded elsewhere.
5 Adamson, *Noble Revolt*, p. 486.
6 *CJ*, 31 December 1641.
7 Lindley, *Popular Politics*, p. 118; D'Ewes, *Journal*, p. 373.
8 CSPV, 17 January 1642 [N.S.].
9 Printed in Adamson, *Noble Revolt*, plate section.
10 Adamson, *Noble Revolt*, pp. 488–92.
11 *Constitutional Documents*, pp. 236–7.
12 TNA, SP 16/488/8.
13 TNA, PC 2/53, pp. 207–08.
14 *The Passages in Parliament* (3–10 January 1642), a1v.
15 *LJ*, 3 January 1642.
16 *LJ*, 3 January 1642.
17 *LJ*, 3 January 1642.
18 Clarendon, *History*, I, p. 482.
19 Clarendon, *History*, I, p. 484.
20 *LJ*, 3 January 1642.
21 *LJ*, 3 January 1642.

22 Gardiner, *History*, X, p. 131; *LJ*, 3 January 1642.

23 A point made in a pamphlet from five years later: *An Apologie of John Earl of Bristol* (Caen, 1647); Gardiner, *History*, X, p. 133 and n.

24 e.g. Hansard, House of Lords, 21 February 1805: https://hansard.par liament.uk/Lords/1805-02-21/debates/5538f80b-0aff-479e-a33a-af516 9f5137b/LordsChamber.

25 *PJ*, p. 59 (Moore).

26 D'Ewes, *Journal*, p. 376. For the role of Pennington and Venn, see: TNA, SP 16/488/13; *CJ*, 3 January 1642.

27 Whitelocke says that the trunks of all five were sealed up, but from D'Ewes it appears that – as yet – only those of Pym and Holles were: B. Whitelocke, *Memorials of the English Affairs* (London, 1732), p. 52; D'Ewes, *Journal*, p. 377. That it was just Pym and Holles is supported independently by Verney, *Papers*, p. 138. Gardiner follows Forster in saying that the trunks of Pym, Holles, and Hampden had been sealed up, but this seems to be based on a misreading of D'Ewes: J. Forster, *The Arrest of the Five Members, by Charles the First* (London, 1860), pp. 119–20; Gardiner, *History*, X, p. 132.

28 *CJ*, 3 January 1642.

29 Adamson, *Noble Revolt*, p. 493.

30 TNA, SP 16/488/9; *PJ*, p. 5 (Hill and Peyton). *CJ*, 3 January 1642.

31 *CJ*, 3 January 1642.

32 Gardiner, *History*, X, pp. 132–3.

33 *CJ*, 4 January 1642.

17 NEITHER EYES TO SEE NOR TONGUE TO SPEAK

1   D'Ewes, *Journal*, pp. 374–5; *LJ*, 3 January 1642.

2   *CJ*, 4 January 1642; D'Ewes, *Diary*, p. 378.

3   TNA, SP 16/488/7; Forster, *Arrest*, p. 155.

4   TNA, SP 16/488/7.

5   Wallington, *Historical Notices*, I, pp. 279–80.

6   TNA, SP 16/488/13.

7   Wallington, *Historical Notices*, I, p. 279.

8   Wallington, *Historical Notices*, I, p. 280.

9   TNA, SP 16/488/13.

10 *CJ*, 4 January 1642; D'Ewes, *Journal*, pp. 379–81.

11 D'Ewes, *Journal*, p. 380.

12 Lindley, *Popular Politics*, pp. 119–20.

13 L. Echard, *The History of England from the First Entrance of Julius Caesar and the Romans to the Conclusion of the Reign of James the Second* (London, 1720), p. 520.

14 Warwick, *Memoirs*, p. 225.

15 Clarendon, *History*, I, p. 484.

16 Clarendon, *History*, I, p. 479n.

17 Whitelocke, *Memorials*, p. 53.

18 Rushworth, IV, pp. 473–94.

19 T. Burton, *The Diary of Thomas Burton, Esq.*, ed. H. Colburn, 4 vols (London, 1828), III, pp. 85–118 [7 February 1659].

20 Recounted in Forster, *Arrest*, pp. 138-9; A. Strickland and E. Strickland, *Lives of the Queens of England from the Norman Conquest*, 8 vols (Cambridge, 1854), V, 286.

21 D'Ewes, *Journal*, p. 384.

22 Verney, *Papers*, p. 138.

23 *The Passages in Parliament* (3–10 January 1642).

24 Adamson, *Noble Revolt*, p. 495.

25 Adamson, *Noble Revolt*, p. 495.

26 D'Ewes, *Journal*, p. 380; *LJ*, 4 January 1642.

27 D'Ewes, *Journal*, p. 383n.

28 TNA, PRO 31/3/73, f. 10.

29 W. Lilly, 'Observations on the Life and Death of King Charles', in F. Maseres (ed.), *Select Tracts relating to the Civil Wars in England* (London, 1815), pp. 171–2.

30 Adamson, *Noble Revolt*, p. 496.

31 Adamson, *Noble Revolt*, p. 496.

32 D'Ewes, *Journal*, p. 384.

33 Verney, *Papers*, p. 138.

34 D'Ewes, *Journal*, p. 384.

35 Verney, *Papers*, p. 138.

36 Whitelocke, *Memorials*, pp. 52–3.

37 Verney, *Papers*, p. 138.

38 TNA, SP 16/488/30; Verney, *Papers*, p. 139.

39 D'Ewes, *Journal*, p. 381.

40 Gardiner, *History*, X, p. 140.

41 Rushworth, IV, 473–94; and Whitelocke, *Memorials*, pp. 52–3.

42 D'Ewes, *Journal*, p. 382.

43 *PJ*, pp. 49–50 (Moore); D'Ewes, *Journal*, p. 383.

44 Gardiner, *History*, X, p. 141.

45 *PJ*, p. 23 (D'Ewes).

46 D'Ewes, *Journal*, p. 382.

47 Forster, *Arrest*, pp. 138–9.

48 Burton, *Diary*, III, pp. 85–118.

49 https://www.sothebys.com/en/buy/auction/2022/history-in-man uscript-letters-and-documents-from-a-distinguished-collection/ king-charles-i-document-signed-ordering-the-arrest

18 TO YOUR TENTS, O ISRAEL

1 Gardiner, *History*, X, p. 141.

2 TNA, LC 5/135.

3 TNA, SP 16/488/15; Rushworth, IV, pp. 473–94.

4 D. Como, *Radical Parliamentarians and the English Civil War* (Oxford, 2018), pp. 112–14.

5 *VII. articles drawen up against Lord Kimelton. M. Iohn Pimme. M. Densil Hollis. S. Artgur Haslerick. M. Hamden. M. Stroud.* (London, 1642).

6 Gardiner, *History*, X, p. 142.

7 Gardiner, *History*, X, p. 142.

8 Pearl, *London*, p. 299; For the location of Garrett's house, see: *The Kings Majesties demand of the House of Commons concerning those Members who were accused of High Treason* (London, 1642).

9 *A Letter from Mercurius Civicus to Mercurius Rusticus: or, Londons confession but not repentence* (London, 1643).

10 TNA, SP 16/488/27.

11 Gardiner, *History*, X, p. 143.

12 Larkin, *Stuart Royal Proclamations*, II, pp. 757–8; TNA, SP 16/488/18.

13 TNA, SP 16/488/20.

14 *CJ*, 5 January 1642.

15 D'Ewes, *Journal*, p. 384.

16 D'Ewes, *Journal*, p. 385.

17 *CJ*, 5 January 1642.

18 Adamson, *Noble Revolt*, p. 498.

19 D'Ewes, *Journal*, p. 385; *CJ*, 5 January 1642.

20 TNA, PC 3/53, p. 209.

21 House of Lords, Main Papers, HL/PO/JO/10/1/114, 6 January 1642, Copy of the King's Warrant.

22 TNA, SP 16/488/24.

23 TNA, SP 16/488/26.

24 TNA, SP 16/488/54.

25 *PJ*, pp. 221–2 (Moore).

26 Bodleian, MS Tanner, 66, f. 234; TNA, SP 16/488/54.

27 Judson, *Crisis of the Constitution*, pp. 37–8.

28 Brooks, 'Littleton'.

29 Cust, *Charles I: A Political Life*, p. 323.

30 TNA, SP 16/488/29.

31 TNA, SP 16/488/28.

32 Lindley, *Popular Politics*, pp. 123–4.

33 House of Lords, Main Papers, HL/PO/JO/10/1/114, 7 January 1642, Copy of the King's Answer.

34 Gardiner, *History*, X, p. 147.

35 Gardiner, *History*, X, pp. 148–9.

36 Gardiner, *History*, X, pp. 149–50.

37 Pearl, *London*, p. 145.

38 Cust, *Charles I: A Political Life*, pp. 326–7.

39 Bodleian, MS Tanner, 66, f. 234v.

40 Lindley, *Popular Politics*, p. 125.

41 Gardiner, *History*, X, pp. 150–1.

42 Lindley, *Popular Politics*, p. 126.

19 TO UNSETTLE THEM FIRST

1   Cressy, *England on Edge*, pp. 402–3; Gardiner, *History*, X, pp. 152–3.

2   TNA, SP 16/488/50.

3   TNA, SP 16/488/51. Turnbull, *Charles I's Private Life*, p. 114; Glamorgan Archives DTD/8-11.

4   *A True relation of the Late Hurliburly at Kingston upon Thames* (London, 1642).

5   *PJ*, pp. 34–5 (D'Ewes); the petition is printed in *PJ*, p. 542.

6   *PJ*, p. 39 (D'Ewes).

7   *PJ*, pp. 35–7 (D'Ewes), also *CJ*, 11 January 1642; Gardiner, *History*, X, p. 153.

8   *LJ*, 12 January 1642.

9   *CJ*, 12 January 1642; *A True relation of the Late Hurliburly*, p. 1.

10 TNA, SP 16/488/56.

11 *CJ*, 13 January 1642.

12 Gardiner, *History*, X, p. 155.

13 *PJ*, pp. 48–9 (Moore).

14 *PJ*, p. 43 (D'Ewes); Gardiner, *History*, X, p. 156.

15 Fletcher, *Outbreak*, p. 187.

16 Gardiner, *History*, X, p. 155.

17 TNA, PRO 31/3/73 f. 13v.

18 Fletcher, *Outbreak*, p. 204.

19 *PJ*, p. 264 (Gawdy).

20 *HMC Second Report*, p. 47.

21 Fletcher, *Outbreak*, p. 233; Gardiner, *History*, X, p. 154.

22 Clarendon, *History*, I, p. 522.

23 *LJ*, 14 January 1642.

24 *PJ*, p. 65 (D'Ewes).

25 *PJ*, p. 99 (Moore).

26 *PJ*, p. 75 (Gawdy); cf. p. 71 (Moore).

27 Cressy, *England on Edge*, p. 396.

28 Fletcher, *Outbreak*, p. 235.

29 Russell, *Fall*, p. 458.

30 CSPV, 31 January [N.S.].

31 Russell, *Fall*, p. 467.

32 *PJ*, p. 103 (Peyton).

33 *LJ*, 14 January, 17 January 1642.

34 House of Lords, Main Papers, HL/PO/JO/10/1/114, 22 January 1642, The Gentleman Usher's Note.

35 Gardiner, *History*, X, p. 158.

36 Gardiner, *History*, X, p. 158; Adamson, *Noble Revolt*, p. 517.

37 *PJ*, pp. 124–5 (Moore).

38 CJ, 20 January 1642; on the Protestation, see: D. Cressy, 'The Protestation Protested, 1641 and 1642', *Historical Journal*, 45 (2002), pp. 251–79; J. Walter, *Covenanting Citizens: the Protestation Oath and Popular Culture in the English Revolution* (Oxford, 2017).

39 Como, *Radical Parliamentarians*, p. 114.

40 *PJ*, p. 97 (Moore).

41 Rees, *Leveller Revolution*, p. 19; Merritt, *Westminster*, pp. 40–41; *Londons Teares, upon the Never Too Much to be Lamented Death of our Late Worthie Member of the House of Commons, Sir Richard Wiseman* (London, 1642); *The Apprentices Lamentation, together vvith a Doleful Elegie upon the Manner of the Death of that Worthy, and valorous*

Knight, Sr Richard Wiseman (London, 1642); *The Scots Loyaltie to the Protestants of England and Ireland* (London, 1641).

42 *PJ*, p. 126 (Gawdy).

43 *PJ*, pp. 144–5 (D'Ewes) and fn.

44 *PJ*, pp. 161–2 (D'Ewes).

45 *LJ*, 26 January 1642.

46 Gardiner, *History*, X, p. 160.

47 Russell, *Fall*, p. 470.

48 Gardiner, *History*, X, p. 160.

49 *PJ*, p. 200 (Gawdy); *CJ*, 27 January 1642.

50 Cust, *Charles I: A Political Life*, p. 330.

51 *PJ*, p. 218 (D'Ewes).

52 House of Lords, Main Papers, HL/PO/JO/10/1/114, 29 January 1642, Resolution of the Lords and Commons.

53 Gardiner, *History*, X, p. 162; Lindley, *Popular Politics*, pp. 130–37.

54 *PJ*, pp. 227–8 (D'Ewes).

55 *PJ*, p. 228 (D'Ewes).

56 *PJ*, p. 231 (Moore); p. 228 (D'Ewes); *To the House of Commons. The Petition of Many Thousand Poore People in and about the Citie of London* (London, 1642).

57 *PJ*, p. 231 (Moore).

58 *PJ*, p. 229 (D'Ewes).

59 *PJ*, pp. 240–1 (D'Ewes).

60 TNA, SP 16/489/3; Cust, *Charles I and the Aristocracy*, p. 273.

61 *PJ*, p. 251 (Peyton).

62 *PJ*, p. 249 (Gawdy).

63 *PJ*, p. 282 (D'Ewes).

64 Lindley, *Popular Politics*, p. 135.

65 *PJ*, p. 259 (Moore); p. 264 (Gawdy).

66 *PJ*, pp. 259–60 (Moore). *To the Honourable the Knights, Citizens and Burgesses in the Commons House of Parliament now Assembled: the Humble Petition of 15000 Poore Labouring Men, Known by the Name of Porters, and the Lowest Members of the Citie of London* (London, 1642).

67 *PJ*, pp. 269–73 (Moore).

68 *PJ*, p. 277 (Gawdy); *To the Right Honorable, the High Court of Parliament; the Humble Petition of Many Hundreds of Distressed Women, Trades-mens Wives, and Widdowes* (London, 1642). Both

diarists Gawdy and Moor give the number of signatories as 1,500 even though the printed petition claims a larger figure of 15,000.

69 *PJ*, p. 287 (Moore); p. 288 (Gawdy).

70 *PJ*, p. 322 (Gawdy).

71 Gardiner, *History*, X, p. 164.

72 Gardiner, *History*, X, pp. 164–5.

73 A point made by Cust, *Charles I: A Political Life*, p. 332.

74 Fletcher, *Outbreak*, p. 229.

75 *PJ*, p. 313 (D'Ewes).

76 *House of Commons, 1640–1660, Vol. 2: Constituencies*, pp. 158–60.

77 P. Little, 'Giles Grene (c. 1596–1656), of Afflington, Isle of Purbeck, Dorset', *House of Commons 1640–1660*, V, pp. 408–24.

78 *PJ*, p. 356 (D'Ewes); p. 361 (Moore); p. 364 (Gawdy).

79 This is the suggestion made by Russell, *Fall*, p. 472.

80 P. Crawford, 'Attitudes to Menstruation in Seventeenth-Century England', *Past and Present*, 91 (1981), pp. 47–73.

81 DHC, D-BKL/H/A/78, unfol., circa 1642, top of page.

20 OVERTHROW THE SHIP AND DROWN THEM ALL

1 Gardiner, *History*, X, pp. 165–6.

2 Cust, *Charles I: A Political Life*, pp. 333-4.

3 *CJ*, 14 February 1642; *LJ*, 14 February 1642.

4 *PJ*, p. 375 (Moore).

5 *PJ*, p. 367 (D'Ewes).

6 Rushworth, IV, p. 555.

7 *PJ*, p. 378–80 (Moore).

8 Gardiner, *History*, X, p. 167.

9 *PJ*, p. 399 (Gawdy); Gardiner, *History*, X, p. 173.

10 On 19 February, it was reported in the Commons that the roads around London were 'so foul' as to be largely impassable by coach: *PJ*, p. 423 (Moore).

11 Gardiner, *History*, X, p. 168.

12 Gardiner, *History*, X, p. 171.

13 *PJ*, p. 482 (Moore).

14 *CJ*, 1 March 1642.

15 Gardiner, *History*, X, p. 171; Russell, *Fall*, p. 479.

16 *HMC Second Report*, p. 47.

17 *PJ*, p. 509 (Hill).

18 *An ordinance of the Lords and Commons in Parliament. For the safety and defence of the Kingdom of England, and Dominion of Wales* (London, 1642).

19 C. Brooks, *Law, Politics and Society in Early Modern England* (Cambridge, 2008), pp. 237–40; Collins, 'Long Parliament', pp. 25–8.

20 Fletcher, *Outbreak*, p. 281.

21 Gardiner, *History*, X, p. 207.

22 Rushworth, IV, pp. 516–52.

23 Rushworth, IV, pp. 516–52.

24 Cust, *Charles I: A Political Life*, p. 337.

25 Bodleian, MS Tanner, 66, f. 291r.

26 Gardiner, *History*, X, p. 173.

27 Gardiner, *History*, X, p. 173.

28 Gardiner, *History*, X, p. 174.

29 Gardiner, *History*, X, p. 174.

30 Gardiner, *History*, X, p. 175.

31 Cressy, *England on Edge*, pp. 401–2; Edward Walker, *Iter Carolinum* (London, 1660), pp. 1–3.

32 Cust, *Charles I: A Political Life*, p. 337.

33 Bodleian, MS Clarendon 20, no. 1575.

34 M. Green (ed.), *Letters of Queen Henrietta Maria: including her Private Correspondence with Charles the First* (London, 1857), pp. 52, 55.

35 *A Sermon Preached At St Bartholomevvs the Lesse in London* (London, 1642); on Thomas Badger, see: Como, *Radical Parliamentarians*, p. 189. For a useful analysis of this sermon, see: E. Kiryanova, 'Images of Kingship: Charles I, Accession Sermons, and the Theory of Divine Right', *History*, 100 (2015), pp. 31–3.

36 Russell, *Fall*, p. 496.

37 Cust, *Charles I and the Aristocracy*, p. 277.

38 Gardiner, *History*, X, pp. 184–5.

39 Green, *Letters of Queen Henrietta Maria*, p. 61.

40 Bodleian, MS Tanner 66, f. 256r.

41 Green, *Letters of Queen Henrietta Maria*, p. 59.

42 Gardiner, *History*, X, p. 184.

43 CSPV, 9 May 1642 [N.S.].

44 Gardiner, *History*, X, p. 192.

45 Cust, *Charles I: A Political Life*, p. 340.

46 *LJ*, 7 May 1642.
47 M. Mendle, 'The Ship Money Case, the Case of Shipmony, and the Development of Henry Parker's Parliamentary Absolutism', *Historical Journal*, 32 (1989), p. 524.
48 Rushworth, IV, pp. 564–80.
49 Cust, *Charles I: A Political Life*, p. 341.
50 Fletcher, *Outbreak*, p. 334.
51 TNA, SP 16/490/51.
52 Gardiner, *History*, X, p. 195.
53 Gardiner, *History*, X, p. 196.

21 NOT MASTER OF THE PEOPLE OF ENGLAND

1 DHC, D-BKL/H/A/67.
2 Bankes's role as peacemaker is discussed in: Fletcher, *Outbreak*, pp. 278–9; Russell, *Fall*, pp. 513–14; and Cust, *Charles I and the Aristocracy*, pp. 283–7.
3 W. Thurlow, 'Charles I at York', *History Today*, 27 (1977), p. 497.
4 For example, Bodleian, MS Top Oxon, c. 378, p. 333; B. Schofield (ed.), *The Knyvett Letters, 1620–1644*, Norfolk Record Society (London, 1949), pp. 101–2.
5 *HMC Eighth Report*, p. 211.
6 G. Bankes, *The Story of Corfe Castle, and of Many who Have Lived There* (London, 1853), pp. 122–3.
7 TNA, PRO 30/24/7/465.
8 Bankes, *Story of Corfe Castle*, pp. 134–5.
9 *HMC Eighth Report*, p. 211.
10 Fletcher, *Outbreak*, p. 284.
11 Bankes, *Story of Corfe Castle*, pp. 134–6.
12 Fletcher, *Outbreak*, p. 235.
13 Gardiner, *History*, X, p. 213.
14 Russell, *Fall*, p. 507.
15 *HMC Cowper*, II, pp. 316–17.
16 Bankes, *Story of Corfe Castle*, pp. 124–6.
17 Clarendon, *History*, II, pp. 116–18.
18 Brooks, 'Littleton'; Russell, *Fall*, p. 471.
19 Clarendon, *History*, II, p. 114.
20 *HMC Buccleuch*, I, p. 301.

21 C. Tyler, 'Drafting the Nineteen Propositions, January–July 1642', *Parliamentary History*, 31 (2012), p. 275.

22 *CJ*, 31 May 1642.

23 Gardiner, *History*, X, pp. 200, 203.

24 *His Majesties Resolution Concerning the Setting Up of His Standard* (London, 1642). Discussed in Fletcher, *Outbreak*, p. 279; also see Cust, *Charles I and the Aristocracy*, pp. 282–3.

25 Fletcher, *Outbreak*, p. 279.

26 *His Majesties Resolution Concerning the Setting Up of His Standard.*

27 Green, *Letters of Queen Henrietta Maria*, p. 55.

28 Green, *Letters of Queen Henrietta Maria*, p. 77.

29 Bodleian, MS Tanner, 63, ff. 66–7.

30 *CJ*, 10 June 1642.

31 *His Majesties declaration to all his loving subjects* (London, 1642).

32 Gardiner, *History*, X, p. 206.

33 Bodleian, MS Top Oxon, c. 378, pp. 329–53.

34 Cressy, *England on Edge*, p. 416.

35 TNA, SP 16/489/63.

36 Green, *Letters of Queen Henrietta Maria*, pp. 63–5, 80, 99.

37 *HMC Eighth Report*, p. 212.

38 *Ten Matters Worthy of Note* (London, 1642); *Six Matters worthy of Note* (London, 1642).

39 West Yorkshire Archives, WR Sessions, Indictment Book, 1637–42, f. 213r.

40 Bodleian, MS Top Oxon, c. 378, p. 332.

41 Cressy, *England on Edge*, p. 412.

42 Cressy, *England on Edge*, pp. 406–7.

43 *A Remonstrance of Londons Occurrences* (London, 1642).

44 Capp, *World of John Taylor*, pp. 145–7.

45 Schwoerer, 'Fittest Subject', pp. 45, 67–8.

46 CSPV, 13 June 1642 [N.S.].

47 Tyler, 'Drafting the Nineteen Propositions', p. 285.

48 Hyde, *Life*, I, pp. 130–1.

49 H. Parker, *Observations Upon Some of His Majesties Answers and Expresses* (London, 1642), pp. 1, 20.

50 Fletcher, *Outbreak*, p. 280.

51 McGee, *Industrious Mind*, p. 368.

52 Gardiner, *History*, X, p. 207.

53 Gardiner, *History*, X, p. 209

54 *HMC Eighth Report*, p. 212.

55 *HMC Eighth Report*, p. 212.

56 *Advertisements from Yorke and Beverley, July the 20th* (London, 1642).

57 Cust, *Charles I and the Aristocracy*, pp. 293–5.

58 Cressy, *England on Edge*, p. 419.

59 Fletcher, *Outbreak*, p. 378.

60 Russell, *Fall*, p. 518.

61 Bodleian: MS Tanner 63, f. 111r; Bankes, MS 55/30; MS Tanner, 63, f. 110.

62 Fletcher, *Outbreak*, pp. 268–70.

63 Bodleian, MS Bankes, 52/30; 56/4.

64 Bankes seems to have received his copy a few days later.

65 DHC, D-BKL/H/A/78.

66 Fletcher, *Outbreak*, pp. 372–3.

67 Fletcher, *Outbreak*, p. 362.

68 Fletcher, *Outbreak*, p. 366.

69 Fletcher, *Outbreak*, pp. 396, 399.

70 Gardiner, *History*, X, p. 215.

71 Gardiner, *History*, X, p. 215; discussed more extensively in Russell, *Fall*, p. 519; Q. Skinner, 'Rethinking Political Liberty', *History Workshop Journal*, 61 (2006), pp. 167–8; *A Declaration of the Lords and Commons assembled in Parliament* (London, 1642).

72 CSPV, 15 August 1642 [N.S.].

73 *A Declaration of the Lords and Commons assembled in Parliament.*

74 Gardiner, *History*, X, pp. 216–17.

75 *LJ*, 8 August 1642; *A Declaration of the Lords and Commons Assembled in Parliament for the Raising of all Power and Force* (London, 1642).

76 Gardiner, *History*, X, p. 217.

77 *HMC Portland*, I, p. 53.

78 CSPV, 5 September 1642 [N.S.].

EPILOGUE

1 *His Majesties Declaration to All His Loving Subjects of August 12 1642* (York, 1642); discussed in Cust, *Charles I: A Political Life*, pp. 325–6.

2 Bodleian, MS Top Oxon, c. 378, p. 345.

3 *His Majesties Declaration to All His Loving Subjects*, p. 29.

4 Lilly, 'Observations', p. 171.

5 DHC, B-BKL/H/A/80; A. Brome (ed.), *Rump, or, An Exact Collection of the Choycest Poems and Sonds Relating to the Late Times* (London, 1662), pp. 67–8.

6 *HMC Fifth Report*, p. 414.

7 J. Raymond, 'Bruno Ryves (c. 1596–1677), dean of Windsor and journalist', *ODNB*.

8 *Mercurius Rusticus, or, The Countries Complaint of the Murthers, Robberies, Plunderings, and other Outrages Committed by the Rebells on His Majesties Faithful Subjects*, III (Oxford, June 1643), pp. 21–2.

9 TNA, PC 2/53, p. 213.

10 TNA, PROB 11/197/137.

11 Capp, *World of John Taylor*, p. 150.

12 F. Memegalos, *George Goring (1608–1657): Caroline Courtier and Royalist General* (Aldershot, 2007).

13 S. Baron, 'Sir Edward Nicholas (1593–1669).

14 S. Roberts, 'William Lenthall (1591–1662), lawyer and speaker of the House of Commons', *ODNB*.

15 Schreiber, 'Lucy Hay'; Blencowe, *Sydney Papers*, pp. xxi–xxii.

16 Akkerman, *Invisible Agents*, pp. 45–62.

17 Schreiber, 'Lucy Hay'.

18 I. Gentles, 'Edward Montagu, second Earl of Manchester (1602–1671), politician and parliamentarian army officer', *ODNB*.

19 P. Crawford, *Denzil Holles, 1598–1680: A Study of His Political Career* (London, 1979).

20 DHC, D-BKL/H/A/78.

21 DHC, D-BKL/B/A/1/29.

Index

Image Credits

King Charles I portrait by Anthony van Dyck: Classic Paintings/ Alamy Stock Photo; Henrietta Maria portrait by Anthony van Dyck: © National Maritime Museum, Greenwich, London; London view from Southwark: Ian Dagnall/Alamy Stock Photo; map of Westminster: history_docu_photo/Alamy Stock Photo; the House of Commons, by Wenceslaus Hollar: Classic Image/Alamy Stock Photo; Whitehall Palace: FalkensteinPhoto/Alamy Stock Photo; portrait of John Bankes: © Kingston Lacy, The Bankes Collection (National Trust); view of Keswick: Joana Kruse/Alamy Stock Photo; Corfe Castle: © Look and Learn / Bridgeman Images; portrait of John Pym: The Picture Art Collection/Alamy Stock Photo; portrait of Denzil Holles: ART Collection/Alamy Stock Photo; Lord Mandeville: © National Portrait Gallery, London; Edward Nicholas: Art Collection 2/Alamy Stock Photo; portrait of William Lenthall: GL Archive/Alamy Stock Photo; John Hampden statue: Maurice Savage/Alamy Stock Photo; Thomas Wentworth: © National Portrait Gallery, London; portrait of Lucy Hay, Countess of Carlisle: ARTGEN/Alamy Stock Photo; John Taylor on the water: Reading Room 2020/Alamy Stock Photo; To Your Tents, O Israel: courtesy of the author; 'A Reply as true as Steele': from the British Library Archive/Bridgeman Images; 'Taylors Physicke has purged the Divel': from the British Library Archive/Bridgeman Images; 'Come Friend Array Your Selfe', an engraving of Bishop Williams and Thomas Lunsford: from the

British Library Archive/Bridgeman Images; Justification of the Independent Churches of Christ: courtesy of the author; Edward Nicholas order for the Trained Bands to suppress protests: The National Archives, ref. SP16/486/99; *The Attempted Arrest of the 'Five Members' by Charles I in 1642*, by Charles West Cope: The Picture Art Collection/Alamy Stock Photo; *The Flight of the Five Members*, by Lucas John Seymour: Artepics/Alamy Stock Photo; Charles demanding entrance at the Beverley Gate, Hull: Chronicle/Alamy Stock Photo; Lady Bankes statue: © National Trust; A True and Exact Relation of the Manner of his Majesty's Setting up of his Standard at Nottingham: Bridgeman Images; Bankes's 'Family Bible': © National Trust.

A Note on the Author

Born in Leeds in 1982, Jonathan Healey is a historian of the sixteenth and seventeenth centuries. He writes history from the bottom up, focusing on ordinary people – their lives, loves, culture and politics. He is Associate Professor in Social History at the University of Oxford. His previous book, *The Blazing World: A New History of Revolutionary England,* was picked as a Book of the Year by the *Telegraph*, the *Economist* and the *New Yorker*. He is a former winner of the BBC New Generation Thinkers competition.

A Note on the Type

The text of this book is set Adobe Garamond. It is one of several versions of Garamond based on the designs of Claude Garamond. It is thought that Garamond based his font on Bembo, cut in 1495 by Francesco Griffo in collaboration with the Italian printer Aldus Manutius. Garamond types were first used in books printed in Paris around 1532. Many of the present-day versions of this type are based on the *Typi Academiae* of Jean Jannon cut in Sedan in 1615

Claude Garamond was born in Paris in 1480. He learned how to cut type from his father and by the age of fifteen he was able to fashion steel punches the size of a pica with great precision. At the age of sixty he was commissioned by King Francis I to design a Greek alphabet, and for this he was given the honourable title of royal type founder. He died in 1561

Turnmill brook

From Hampstead

From Pottenhanourt

Tiborpne Brook

THE RIVER